Fearful Joy

Fearful Joy

Papers from the
Thomas Gray
Bicentenary Conference
at Carleton University

Edited by
JAMES DOWNEY
and
BEN JONES

McGill-Queen's University Press   Montreal, London 1974

© 1974 McGill-Queen's University Press
ISBN 0-7735-0132-0
Library of Congress Catalog Card No. 73-79499
Legal deposit first quarter 1974

Design: Peter Dorn, MGDC

Printed in Canada by The Bryant Press Limited, Toronto
Illustrations between pages 140 and 141 printed by
The Meriden Gravure Company, Connecticut, U.S.A.

While some on earnest business bent
Their murmuring labours ply
'Gainst graver hours, that bring constraint
To sweeten liberty:
Some bold adventurers disdain
The limits of their little reign,
And unknown regions dare descry:
Still as they run they look behind,
They hear a voice in every wind,
And snatch a fearful joy.

'Ode on a Distant Prospect of Eton College', ll. 31-40.

Contents

———◆◆◆———

vi

Illustrations

Frontispiece

Thomas Gray, 1747, from the painting by John Giles Eccardt. National Portrait Gallery, London.

Plates between pages 142 and 143

Preface

———— ◆•◆ ————

'The value of centenaries and similar observances', Northrop Frye has said, 'is that they call attention, not simply to great men, but to what we do with our great men. The anniversary punctuates, so to speak, the scholarly and critical absorption of its subject into society.' Frye had Blake in mind when he wrote these words, and applied to Blake they are entirely correct: scholarly and critical acclaim preceded the more general and popular celebration he now enjoys. With Gray, however, popular and critical acclaim were coincident (an occurrence that is more often the exception than the rule in the history of English poetry). His absorption into society as a poet was effected almost immediately upon the publication in 1751 of the 'Elegy'. Not at any time in the past two hundred years has that poem wanted for readers: it is, simply, one of the best-loved and best-known poems in our literature. Nor has it been neglected by scholars. In the twentieth century it has been the subject not only of intensive study, but also of spirited if civil controversy.

But what of the rest of Gray? What of his other poems, especially the two Pindaric Odes he himself thought so highly of? What of his correspondence (by no means ignored by scholarship, but far from exhausted as a source of information about his own life and perceptions and those of his age)? What of his diversely curious mind, moving easily and without apology about and between what our more fragmented age has sometimes called 'two cultures'; could there not be in Gray's habits of thought an aid to a slightly clearer understanding of the world of eighteenth-century learning and scholarship – of its 'humanism'? What of his illustrators, commentators, and critics (in his own time and after); what had they found in Gray to excite their imaginations and claim their allegiance, or, as in the notable case of Dr. Johnson, provoke their ire; what, especially, of Blake – so temperamentally different as man and artist from

Gray – what had he seen in Gray's poems to inspire him to illustrate them so copiously and beautifully? What, finally, of Gray the man: was his 'vale of life' so 'cool' and 'sequestered' as it had often appeared; or was it that his kind of passion had frequently been ignored because it proved embarrassing to most Gray scholars of the past; if so, were we now ready to examine it forthrightly? These were the matters we felt a scholarly conference on Thomas Gray ought to reflect upon. And reflect it did, honestly, perceptively, knowledgeably, upon these matters – and others.

We were not at all sure what Gray, who, as Kenneth MacLean remarks, was a child of slow time, would have thought of the idea of busy scholars taking time off from a host of professional duties to fly to Ottawa from as far away as Aberystwyth to the east and Los Angeles to the west to deliver a dozen or so learned lectures on him in three days – he who never gave a lecture in all his years at Cambridge. But whatever his initial reaction might have been, we feel sure that several features of the Conference would have pleased him. He would have been pleased, in the first place, by the emphasis the participants gave to the great Odes, which Gray felt – though his contemporaries and posterity have not agreed with him in this – were his crowning achievement. There is, in these two poems, as Arthur Johnston shows, a special kind of 'daring' which deserves to be recognized. He would have taken pleasure, too, from the fact that the other half of his literary genius – his correspondence – was given the attention it deserves as an index to his thoughts and feelings. Gray talked little about poetry in his letters, but the acute and discriminating perceptions which made possible his own poems are, as Ian Jack and George Whalley demonstrate, much in evidence.

An intensely private and diffident man all his life, Gray would have been embarrassed to have heard his personal life and feelings discussed. Yet surely he would have gained a measure of satisfaction from the very sensitive and sympathetic manner in which it was done. Rarely has a conference got off to a better start than did this one with Jean Hagstrum's perceptive and moving interpretation of Gray the man – his fears, his hopes, his friendships, loves, passions – the qualities and experiences which shaped his poetic imagination. Finally, he would have been pleased, perhaps, that although many papers connected him with 'Neoclassical' and 'Romantic' poets there was no attempt to treat him retrospectively or proleptically, or as anything other than a poet who belonged to a definite and identifiable cultural period. For a long time scholars of this period have argued that mid-eighteenth-century writers had a present as well as a past and future. One encouraging aspect of the Gray conference was that this fact was not argued: it was assumed. And the ghost of Matthew Arnold ('Gray, a born poet, fell upon an age of prose') not only failed to haunt; it nearly failed to appear.

Gray and Johnson; Gray and Smart; Gray and Blake; Gray and Wordsworth; Gray and Coleridge; Gray and Keats: Gray is well and truly connected in this volume, and in the process almost every important feature of his life and work is touched upon. If there is a lacuna in this collection it is that Gray's humour (his natural bent, according to Walpole) is not sufficiently stressed. But perhaps it is as well to leave something for tercentenary celebrations.

Only two of the papers in this book were not given at the Conference. Clarence Tracy's 'Melancholy Marked Him For Her Own' was read to a meeting of the Royal Society of Canada held at Carleton two weeks after the Conference. It was felt that, because of the proximity in time and place of its presentation, this paper ought to be included in this collection. Curiously, it is the only essay which deals primarily with the 'Elegy', and for that reason is all the more welcome. James Steele's paper, 'Gray and the Season for Triumph', grew directly out of its author's involvement in the Conference, and is an attempt to examine Gray's work from a Marxist viewpoint.

Carleton University   J.D.
Ottawa, Canada   B.J.

Acknowledgements

The 'Thomas Gray and the Humanist Tradition' conference was held at Carleton University from 18-20 May 1971. It was sponsored jointly by the host University and the Canada Council. The success of the Conference was made possible in the first place by their generous support.

The editors wish to thank the other members of the Conference Committee – Alistair Tilson, Robin MacDonald, and George McKnight – for their invaluable help and suggestions, and Cynthia Mitchell for her able assistance in handling Conference arrangements.

A particular debt of gratitude is due to Mr. A. D. Dunton, then President of Carleton University, who gave the Conference both official and – when it was necessary, and with the help of Mrs. Dunton – personal support.

The staffs of the Carleton University Library and the Information Office – and, in particular, Miss Hilda Gifford, Mrs. Jean Carter, and Mr. Don Pattison – were extremely helpful in acquiring books and prints, setting up displays, and designing and producing Conference materials. The National Library of Canada allowed us to hold an afternoon session in its main auditorium and provided another room for an exhibition of eighteenth-century illustrations of Gray and early editions of his poems. Bernard Quaritch, Ltd., London, were kind enough to lend us more than twenty hand-coloured printed proofs of Blake's illustrations of Gray. The British High Commissioner to Canada, Sir Peter Hayman, and Lady Hayman graciously entertained Conference members at Earnscliffe. To all these people we should like to express our thanks.

We are grateful also to those scholars who, although not represented in this volume, participated in the Conference as chairmen of the sessions: A. M. Beattie, R. M. Wiles, John Stedmond, George Johnston, William Powell Jones, Trevor Tolley, and Bernard Wand. The enter-

Acknowledgements

taining oratory of Albert Trueman and Charles Haines, and the advice and generosity of Gordon Wood, contributed to the success of the Conference banquet and thus to the success of the Conference.

Mary Wilson assisted in the editing of the papers and the preparation of the manuscript: her work deserves especial acknowledgement.

The title, 'Fearful Joy', was suggested by Charles Beer of McGill-Queen's University Press. We are grateful to him for this suggestion and for his careful shepherding of the manuscript.

For permission to reproduce some of William Blake's and Richard Bentley's illustrations to the poems of Gray, acknowledgement is gratefully made to Mr. Paul Mellon, Sir Geoffrey Keynes, Mr. Lessing J. Rosenwald and the Library of Congress, and the Beinecke Rare Book and Manuscript Library, Yale University. The portrait of Gray by John Giles Eccardt is reproduced by courtesy of the National Portrait Gallery, London.

Finally, we should like to thank the people who attended the Conference. Rarely has a more congenial and interesting group gathered together for a conference of any sort.

Abbreviations

————◆◆————

Poems | The Poems of Thomas Gray, William Collins, Oliver Goldsmith, ed. Roger Lonsdale (London, 1969)

Corres. | The Correspondence of Thomas Gray, ed. Paget Toynbee and Leonard Whibley, 3 vols. (Oxford, 1971)

Mason | Mason, William. The Poems of Mr. Gray. To which are Prefixed Memoirs of His Life and Writings, 2nd ed. (London, 1775)

Lives | Johnson, Samuel. Lives of the Poets, ed. G. B. Hill, 3 vols. (Oxford, 1905)

Boswell's Life | Boswell, James. Boswell's Life of Johnson, ed. G. B. Hill, rev. L. F. Powell, 6 vols. (Oxford, 1934-50)

Gray | Ketton-Cremer, R. W. Thomas Gray: a Biography (Cambridge, 1955)

For Thomas Gray
died 1771

———◆◆———

English as Shakespeare, as firm a name;
two hundred years flown, living he did not
wander far or for good from those other
halls, today housing thoughts of him.
Languid spread of pelouses, cloud-wiped,
rustle, trail,
air's strong shiver, sour-fresh cut of water,
Cambridge, under load of everlasting
youth, willow-weary from learning's alertness,
10   battling time with ring of chisel and mended
regulations. To less sound than Beethoven,
Wordsworth, Scott, quiet life quietly honoured
in lecture, conference of scholars,
pilgrimage between rose-trees of the now
garden churchyard.
Quiet man even among a people
not wholly brash: proud,
finicking, ironic,
luminous-eyed, neat in velvet, brocade,
20   later in life, plump: famous with Forster
on little output, like him seen sometimes
in the streets, drawing eyes
of the knowledgeable to sight
immortality among them.

Cloistered to learning, he lived the scholar's peace
without taut stretch of professional bow.

None had to make from his shaft, in an age
of sniping. Humour dissolved
malicious barb of eyed and feared acclaim.
30   Time for the best, to be known for knowing
the best; rumoured omniscience haloed
him. From seclusion a royalty of taste
in one who had suffered and spoken
humanity's pain,
had best in his era dignified death.
Two poets:
one of skied, and inward personal, ode,
and elegy – lyrist of arrowy stress,
the filtered phrase: and other unacknowledged
40   poet of field and wood, flower, temperatures
and weathers; whose eye incised appearance
and behaviour with ageless, lucid
words. Another man who used
to notice such things.

        He observed
        the elm putting out
        the lime and hornbeam green
        the almond in bloom
        the swallows flying
50   jasmine and acacia spread.

        He noted gloomy weather
        cold and sunshine
        the fine day, hard rain
        at night, the small rain
        white flying clouds
        the thunder.

    And in that final summer,
    of earlier east winds,
    after the hawthorn and chestnut flowering,

60   after the white umbrella discs of elder,
            in late July among continuing roses
            going off,
            the white stock, pinks and lavender,
            tawny wheat against
            the saddening green
            and swallows flying
            six days of ending
            in the fine and warm weather.

Auden has said poetry makes nothing happen,
70 meaning, in that place, does not explode in event.
But it's there. We keep it.
It transmits.
In youth a stir, a straining of trees in wind like
blown hair,
stress in calm, hint of disintegration in the globe
of summer,
cry of surprise's power to match young need for life's
seeming kaleidoscope.
Later it shows a trodden way to gleams of cloud-racked
80 truth through veers and shifts into the meshed dark
of bordering woods, or where the eye is blind with flash
of sun through leaves.
This thing, living. It passing, you passing, not coinciding.
Poetry tries to join,
catch from the slipping pageant something to hold and save;
swings us up free, inbreathing a soared order
on chaos of custom's order,
uncages the self
for it can say better, be better, than the man,
90 better too while he writes, clear of earth ego's press,
than we who read, giving us
eyes, hovered,
whole if a moment in glide
of sky's one.

Gray sleeps in that landscape quietly
as his unknown dead,
not mute:
survives in a personal aura
whose lasting allure

100   evades analysis' net:
in his poetry transcends
some limits of self;
speaks to the living still
of the human state nakedly seen,
Ἄνθρωπος· ἱκανὴ πρόφασις εἰς τὸ δυστυχεῖν,
bequeathes us sympathy, courage, control,
the dignity of man.

There is the young journey to the high mountains
slicing sky, tempting ascent; the scaling

110   of some peaks, crossing the Alps, but generally
through the passes. The journey into the
Italy of beauty's awakening
leads on by plains to the churchyard.
Cambridge, London, Stoke, travels to the North:
after the dream of the long highway becomes
memory of dream, our lives fall into
patterns of event which hold in place
the fractured self, helping to keep an
inner poise between past and future

120   over that human point of contact with
the streamed continuum we call the present.
What do we send out on the endless band
from the hidden life; how far can it extend?
Three generations' reach and then
oblivion, or history
if some memorial however frail;
for scholarship cannot create a man
again, the essence gone.
We can at best be grateful for the use

130   of powers for others-self, self-others,
       inextricable knot of aims; for work
       which lives in the world's terms, to gladden.
       In other terms, other answers.

ALASTAIR MACDONALD

July 1971

Notes

lines 2–4   But what – I dream! Two hundred years are flown
         Since first thy story ran through Oxford halls,
           And the grave Glanvil did the tale inscribe
         That thou wert wander'd from the studious walls
           To learn strange arts, and join a gipsy-tribe;
           And thou from earth art gone
         Long since, and in some quiet churchyard laid –
           Some country-nook, where o'er thy unknown grave
           Tall grasses and white flowering nettles wave,
         Under a dark, red-fruited yew-tree's shade.
           MATTHEW ARNOLD, *The Scholar-Gipsy*, ll. 131-40.

11–12   Beethoven, Wordsworth, b. 1770; Scott, b. 1771.

20   E. M. Forster, d. 1970.

43–44   Thomas Hardy, poem, 'Afterwards'.

45–56   'Found' section, made from Gray's own phrases in letters and diaries.

69   W. H. Auden, 'In Memory of W. B. Yeats'.

105   'I am a man, sufficient excuse for being unhappy'. Menander, Fragment. Gray's motto for 'Ode on a Distant Prospect of Eton College'.

114   Gray was never abroad again after returning from the Continent in 1741. From Cambridge his movements took the shape of regular sojourns in London and Stoke Poges, occasional travels to the north and to other parts of England and Wales, and one journey to Scotland.

JEAN H. HAGSTRUM { *Gray's Sensibility*

'Ah, tell them they are men!' is Gray's sigh as he sees 'the little victims' at play on the fields of Eton, 'regardless of their doom'. 'Teach me to . . . know myself a Man' is Gray's prayer for himself at the end of the 'Ode to Adversity'. Before being anything else Gray desired to be a loving, forgiving, generous, self-scanning human being, and deeper than his humanism is his humanity.

To be a man, however, is, with fatal inevitability, to be melancholy. To lose youthful innocence means to be ambushed by a 'murth'rous band' of misfortune and passion. Being a man brings eschatology into the living present, for man is doomed well before the Last Judgement, and he goes through the Great Tribulation on this side the Jordan River. To be a man is to be condemned to pain, the pain of the passions – tender, hideous, social, private, running the entire Burkean range from the pathetic to the sublime or even the gamut of the century itself, from the social tear of Shaftesbury to Dr. Johnson's solemn and austere realism. The doom is as universal as it is inescapable:

> To each his sufferings: all are men,
> Condemned alike to groan;
> The tender for another's pain,
> The unfeeling for his own.
>
> ('Eton', ll. 91-94)

Amazingly, this pessimistic definition of man was written when Gray was between twenty-five and twenty-six years of age, a few months before he confided to West (who was soon to die) that he suffered from white melancholy (with its attendant insipidity and ennui). He could describe that condition as 'a good easy sort of a state' only because the black melancholy came intermittently. The dark, hideous mood, which he 'now

6

and then felt', came often enough for him to cry out, 'from this the Lord deliver us!' (*Corres.*, I, 209).

Viewing Gray's life in perspective whole, we must conclude that he did not suffer from two illnesses, leucocholy (chronic and white) and melancholy (black and occasional), but from only one, of which the white was the temporary remission of the black. If we apply Freud's distinction[1] to Gray, we must say that his was melancholia, not grief; for it was a fixed condition, 'deep' in the fullest modern sense, a 'doom' because it was so persistent and because it arose inexorably and mysteriously from the deep well of the unconscious. It was also a doom because it tortured him into a state of dejection that inhibited his activity and poisoned his quiet. Fixed and permanent, though with blessed remissions, Gray's passions were also hot and searing – a fact that his proverbial silence and sadness, as of a man in grief, his compulsive neatness, his finicky meticulousness, and his quirkish fears (like the fear of fire) should not be allowed to obscure. We must not assume that because the outer man was retiring, the inner man was not intense or that his emotional life was tepid or starved. Judging from the emotion expressed in the poetry and in the greatest of the sad letters, there was that within which passed show. The true man was Gray Agonistes, and the true poetry was carved in a language where emotions press powerfully against cool lapidary statement. The young poet writes compulsively of the 'pangs of Passion', of 'fury Passions' called 'the vultures of the mind'. These include 'pining Love', 'Jealousy with rankling tooth', 'Envy wan', and 'grim-visaged comfortless Despair'. They can be regarded as primarily private, but they have social consequences that make the human environment painful, as Infamy grins and Shame skulks ('Eton', ll. 61-80).

Black melancholy was so 'frightful' – the word is Gray's (*Corres.*, I, 209) – that it might have had two issues, 'moody Madness laughing wild/ Amid severest woe' or self-inflicted death ('Eton', ll. 79-80). Gray might have stood in the line of Romantic suicides. In the 'Elegy' he is half in love with easeful death. Of the Welsh poet, who plunges from a high mountain to endless night, shouting, 'To triumph, and to die, are mine', Gray said, 'I felt myself the Bard'.[2] Writing to West, whose death was imminent, he confessed, 'I converse, as usual, with none but the dead: They are my old friends, and almost make me long to be with them' (*Corres.*, I, 202).

Gray might have joined his beloved dead by an unnatural act had it not been for his intellectual and artistic interests – the notebook jottings as well as the letters, the bibliographical lists as well as the poetic lines. It is precisely because *sensibility* is a term broad enough to include all these interests and dispositions that I have preferred it as a title to *melancholy*, even though melancholy is the more basic and potent word. But melancholy is too private and too isolated a condition adequately to describe the Gray of the humanist tradition, and we must use the broader and milder term sensibility, however much it may suggest fashionable posturing and the drenched handkerchief.

But is sensibility, after all, so tame a word? In *Sense and Sensibility* Jane Austen uses it to describe a disruptive passion that could easily have led to death,[3] and in *Northanger Abbey* she associates it with the 'luxury of a raised, restless, and frightened imagination'.[4] In the *Mysteries of Udolpho* Mrs. Radcliffe has the father warn the heroine of the very real dangers of heightened sensibility.[5] In *Rambler* 28 Johnson mentions sensibility along with 'perturbation'.

Sensibility, then, can refer to powerful feeling, to melancholy, both the white and the black. But it does connect the individual to the world of travel, books, pictures, and poems. It is in fact a link between these realms of taste and the deep passions. Sensibility unites, as melancholy alone does not, the Gray of private suffering and the Gray who loved the pictorial and the picturesque, valleys and mountains, and landscapes that he called 'the *savage*, the *rude*, and the *tremendous*' (*Corres.*, II, 586).

The relation between Gray's influential public taste and his individual feelings can be viewed in two ways. (1) The poetic, scholarly, and intellectual interests are suffused with Gray's own sensibilities. Mountains he finds ecstatic because he himself knows or desires ecstasy. (We assume throughout that Gray used language sincerely and precisely.) (2) Gray's intellectual interests are socially and personally accepted substitutes for the more dangerous personal passions, which may not be fully understood and are neither mastered nor suppressed. To the first of these alternatives – that his researches, say, into newer sources of sensibility are directly caused by his emotional condition and reflect it – Gray seems to give some support: 'It is indeed for want of spirits, as you suspect, that my studies lie among the Cathedrals, and the Tombs, and the Ruins. To think ... has been the chief amusement of my days; and when I would not, or cannot think, I dream' (*Corres.*, II, 565, 566). If he dreams and thinks of medieval remains, well and good. He is illustrating a venerable belief, as old as it is simple, that the artistic and intellectual preoccupations are sincere and reveal the man – a belief affirmed by Burke, Johnson, Tolstoy, I. A. Richards, Fielding, and Aristotle, to name a few.[6] Gray's mountains are pregnant with religion and poetry because Gray's own soul is.

If, however, the man of taste dreams of other things as he studies his ruins, he invokes the second view – that the changing objects of his shifting sensibility are *indirectly* related to the man and that they are the calm and manageable substitutes for potentially disruptive passions. That belief may be less persuasive, and Freud may offend where Fielding pleases. Still a direct line or nerve from Gray's heart to his writing hand or walking feet may in fact be too strait and narrow a way to permit us to see all that needs to be seen. And it is at least an attractive hypothesis that travel may be a psychologically necessary substitute for travail and that some of Gray's poetry is as much a covering cloak as a revelation.

Ian Jack has persuasively argued that sensibility struggles with stoicism as the 'Elegy' takes its final shape, and that sensibility prevails.[7] But stoicism keeps returning – necessarily, one feels – as though disciplined virtue had to be applied like a cold compress to the burning brow of sensibility. Consider one of the most revelatory letters in all of Gray, a letter to the young Bonstetten that includes a passage about Plato (*Corres.*, III, 1117-19). Charles Victor de Bonstetten had come to Gray already in love with dark forests, mountain ascents, the cry of eagles in lonely places, and the horror of birds of prey screeching in the fastnesses. His taste did not need to be formed, and in their many *soirées* together the middle-aged poet may have been pleased to see in the young Swiss the triumph of his own newer sensibilities. But at the same time there is a return to Gray of the stoicism of the forties, and the circumstances appear to be dramatic. The fifty-three-year-old poet has been overmastered by a passion that is driving him past the line of decorum to the brink of madness. At that point the poet decides that the young man's morals need forming, and the ideal man of the *Republic* is introduced in the middle of a letter that begins and ends in passion. The first paragraph discloses a man on the rack, even his frail body sympathizing with the unquiet of his mind: 'I am grown old in the compass of less than three weeks. . . . I did not conceive till now . . . what it was to lose you [he has learned that Bonstetten must leave England], nor felt the solitude and insipidity of my own condition, before I possess'd the happiness of your friendship.' The last paragraph of the letter is similarly a cry of the heart: Gray wants the young man, about to be exposed to Continental and urban gaieties, to 'shew me your heart simply and without the shadow of disguise, and leave me to weep over it'. Between these tortured paragraphs Gray transcribes from his own notebook Plato's description in the *Republic* of a 'Genius truly inclined to Philosophy' and sets up as a model to the young man a mind gentle, vivacious, magnanimous and a character that loves truth, probity, and justice. Undoubtedly, of the several virtues Plato recommends it is moderation and temperance that Gray wishes most to enforce on the young friend who had so discomposed his spirits – that quality in the soul of a good man that keeps him but 'little inclined to sensual pleasures'. Gray is in such anguish that it is difficult to regard the teaching of sensual discipline as merely disinterested instruction. A week later in a letter to Bonstetten in which he quotes Nicholls, whose mind Gray had years before similarly attempted to form, the poet reveals the source of his suffering about Bonstetten: it is that the boy will be exposed to 'every danger and seduction', subject to the 'allurements of painted Women . . . or the vulgar caresses of prostitute beauty, the property of all', the body and mind turned over to 'folly, idleness, disease, and vain remorse' (*Corres.*, III, 1128). In brief, Gray is jealous, sexually jealous. I realize I have risked placing his sermon on stoic virtue under a cloud. But it is a risk one must take. Let the candid reader confront the disciplined ideal of the *Republic* in the midst of these torturing passions and then try to escape the implications of that juxtaposition, which incidentally is Gray's, not mine.

The earlier letter to Bonstetten contains this sentence: 'If you have ever met with the portrait sketch'd out by Plato, you will know it again: for my part (to my sorrow) I have had that happiness: I see the principal features, and I foresee the dangers with a trembling anxiety.' One pauses at the word *trembling*. Is not Gray confronting his own condition and applying Plato as much to it as to Bonstetten's? Both men need stoical ice. The phrase 'tremling anxiety' in the letter takes us back to the 'trembling hope' of the 'Elegy':

> *No farther seek his merits to disclose,*
> *Or draw his frailties from their dread abode,*
> *(There they alike in trembling hope repose)*
> *The bosom of his Father and his God.*

(11. 125-28)

In both the late letter and the earlier poem 'frailties' and 'trembling' are associated. Is it possible that before the Epitaph had achieved its Parian perfection the same fires had burned in the poet's heart that were to burn again toward the end of his life, almost causing its extinction?

Hope 'trembles' in the 'Elegy' because of guilt and the prospect of

Judgement. Anxiety 'trembles' in the late letter because of amorous jealousy. Sensibility may have trembled all through Gray's life as a result of intense friendships, which can be regarded as the matrix for the triumphs alike of his taste and poetic genius. Poetic expression is of course complexly caused, and causative emotions become inextricably involved in language, image, landscape, topos, icon, and traditions of seeing, knowing, believing, and speaking. But, still, the deepest source of true artistic passion is human passion. Even though the manner is cool, and the passions are capitalized and personified conventionally, Gray the passionate friend guides the hand of Gray the young poet in the early odes.

If it is true that friendship formed the *Gestalt* of Gray as man and poet from the very beginning of his career, many traditional views will have to be revised. Bonstetten himself was surely wrong when he said that Gray had never loved (*Gray*, p. 253), and Roger Martin, that fine scholar, when he calls Bonstetten Gray's 'premier amour'.[8] We cannot possibly find Lord David Cecil's terminology and tone adequate when he calls Gray a 'confirmed celibate' worried that Bonstetten will go off to revolting sexuality.[9] And Ketton-Cremer may be missing the central drama in Gray's life when he says that the young Swiss aroused in him such emotions as he 'had never experienced before, emotions obsessive and overwhelming' (*Gray*, p. 251). The probabilities, from what we know about the friendship with West and what we do not know about the friendship with Walpole, are that Gray's emotions were even then overwhelming and obsessive. The hectic months with Bonstetten constitute the last in a series of attachments that make conventional views of Gray flat and unconvincing. To view the essential and memorable Gray as a shy fastidious bachelor, his heart, however, not totally invulnerable, there being one woman in his life, a woman whose charms may have endangered his quiet briefly, and there being also that awful late flare-up of incomprehensible emotions never before experienced – all this is to carry respectability and reticence too far. It was hardly thus that Gray knew himself a man.

As we have said, Bonstetten's comment that Gray had never loved is totally wrong, unless perchance he means that as an adult Gray had never loved a woman. So understood, the young and somewhat preposterous visitor to Cambridge provides us an insight among others that cannot be ignored. Bonstetten reports that Gray teased out of the young man a full account of his life but that the older man in his turn was totally reticent about his past, between which and the present there yawned 'un abîme

11

infranchissable'. Whenever Bonstetten touched on Gray's past, dark clouds arose to cover it. Bonstetten, who perceived that melancholy lay at the heart of Gray's character, said of it: 'cette mélancholie n'est qu'un besoin non-satisfait de la sensibilité' (*Gray*, p. 253). Bonstetten's is perhaps the most penetrating brief comment on Gray ever made: *sensibilité* is love, and love never fully satisfied cast a pall over the man's spirits.

The clouds that the young man could not dispel from Gray's past we cannot dispel either. But, with the benefit of modern insights into the psyche, we can look a little farther than some critics have. Gray's father was a cruel man, perhaps an alcoholic, who kicked, punched, and cursed his wife.[10] The legacy of the father was one of angry quarrels, vile scenes of verbal and physical violence. On a sensitive boy the effects must have been devastating. As Brydges said in 1834, 'the misfortunes of his infancy dwelt like a nightmare on his heart'.[11] Certainly one important wound was inflicted by the lack of a father who could have provided a model for the boy's own future manhood. From such circumstances one expects that the mother will be excessively loved, and Mason said that Gray 'seldom mentioned his Mother without a sigh' (*Corres.*, III, 926, n.3). Early, Gray feared the loss of her as a trauma in which he could not see 'the least Shadow of comfort' (*Corres.*, I, 67). Later, in 1766, he confesses he had kept the loss of his mother green for over thirteen years – 'every day I live it sinks deeper into my heart' (*Corres.*, III, 926). Upon his death he joined his mother in the tomb at Stoke Poges, and the anticipation of that final resting place must have been a kind of comforting ritual, since he urged on his younger friend Nicholls precisely the same kind of burial.[12]

Those are egregiously wrong who think that Miss Speed was the only woman in Gray's life – on two counts: his mother occupied that position and Miss Speed he never really treated as a woman. In very strange language to address to a friend, Gray announced what he chose to regard as a discovery made late in life – 'a thing very little known, wch is, that in one's whole life one can never have any more than a single Mother. you may think this is obvious, & (what you call) a trite observation. you are a green Gossling!'[13] Certainly so powerful a maternal orientation as that neither Miss Speed nor any woman could reverse. We owe much to Miss Speed, but no love poetry, not even poetry of feeling. To her wit and sprightliness we are indebted for comparable qualities in Gray – notably that exquisite *vers de société*, 'A Long Story'. And when the lady finally did marry, Gray writes one of his dryest, wryest, and sharpest vignettes: 'she is a prodigious fine Lady, & a Catholic . . . not fatter than she was: she had a cage of foreign birds & a piping Bullfinch at her elbow, two little Dogs on her cushion in her lap, a Cockatoo on her shoulder, & a slight suspicion of Rouge on her cheeks' (*Corres.*, III, 923). Really wonderful stuff, but like the charming verses, it is born of total emotional security. Gray was never in the remotest danger. He was fully free to be Robin Goodfellow.

Gray early describes himself as a 'solitary fly' whose 'joys no glittering female meets' ('Ode on the Spring', ll. 44, 45). That fly possessed a sting, not only for women but for marriage. Very young, the poet was somewhat curious about union between the sexes. Middle-aged petulance, bordering on cruelty, replaced that curiosity. When Mason thought of getting married, Gray asked him about his intended: 'Has she a nose?' (*Corres.*, II, 821). Was he perchance wondering if the female was like one of Hogarth's syphilitics, *sans* that protuberance?

A pattern appears to be emerging: the late-life passion for a young man; an excessive love of his mother; fear of the father; a witty passionless heterosexual friendship; and cold-hearted impoliteness in contemplating the marriage of one of his friends. These details, tending as they do to organize themselves into a *Gestalt*, constitute an illuminating biographical supplement to the psychology of Gray as he expressed it in a Latin poem, addressed to West and begun in Florence shortly before, after, or during the breach with Walpole.[14] That didactic poem discusses the senses, and its most interesting and substantial verse paragraph is devoted to the sense of touch. To that sense – quite remarkably – is given the priority usually accorded the sight: it plays the leading role in our sensuous life, coming first and leading the lesser crowd. As first born, it has the rights of primogeniture and asserts a wider sway than the others, not being subject to normal restrictions. Living in the warp and woof of the skin, it is widely diffused through the whole body. Its life begins prenatally in the womb, and birth is a trauma. For then come pain, trembling, savage fury. Touch in Gray's Latin verse is a stunning parallel to the torturing passions of the early odes, those passions that define manhood as a doom. It is an equally stunning description of pregenital, pancorporal sexuality, the physical love of boyhood, the kind preferred by those who shun normal adult responsibilities and attach themselves to an earlier, a more manageable, and what is regarded as a more pleasurable stage.

The poem on touch may have been written between the shipwrecked friendship with Walpole and the deeply renewed friendship with West. The surviving evidence permits no one to call these and other friendships of Gray overtly homosexual. But no one who wishes to master the master-traits of the poet's life and literary expression – or indeed who wishes to be an honest biographer – can ignore their human intensity. The friend-ships, together with the beautiful and subtle letters they produced and the poems they ultimately induced, form an unassailable integrity.

The relations with Walpole began in the prelapsarian Eton, upon which the somewhat older poet looked back in the mood of Adam after the Expulsion. The friendship continued at Cambridge with banter, verbal love-play, high spirits, and wit. It was smashed on the Continent, for reasons one can imagine but cannot be certain about. It was at length restored to a relationship of dignity that reopened cautiously and coolly and that ended in respect and even affability – always, however, a sober-ing contrast to the fevers, palpitations, and racy informalities of the true and early friendship. It was that earlier phase – late Eton, Cambridge, and early Continent – that bore literary and intellectual fruit. The lan-guage of Gray's letters to Walpole is a marvel of flexible, colloquial writing, moving from the rhythms of excited and fluttery love-speech to *double-entendre* and parody, mocking Restoration literary poses and even heroic and biblical style. The whole spirit of the young man was involved in this friendship, which provided bright relief from the drunken, illiterate, dull, loutish circles at Cambridge. Walpole's an-nounced visit to the University produced 'great extasie' in Gray, 'Con-vulsions of Joy', in fact (*Corres.*, I, 13). Gray longed for the minister's son and showed a fretful jealousy toward Ashton. There is a bit of flutter about what to do with the letters – should Gray keep them (absolutely private of course) or should he burn them? Let Walpole decide. One let-ter takes notice of a love affair that Walpole appears to have half con-fided to Gray: 'I confess', Gray replied, 'I am amazed: of all likely things this is the last I should have believed would come to pass.' He refers to this affair as 'the new study you have taken a liking to' and calls it 'the most excellent of all sciences'. Then comes a most revealing passage, full of psychological implications and with who knows how much intended or unintended double meaning:

> would you believe it, 'tis the very thing I would wish to apply to myself? ay! as simple as I stand here: but then the Apparatus neces-sary to it costs so much; nay, part of it is wholly out of one's power to procure; and then who should pare one, & burnish one? for they would have more trouble & fuss with me, than Cinderaxa's sisters had with their feet, to make 'em fit for the little glass Slipper: oh

yes! to be sure one must be lick'd; now to lick oneself I take to be altogether impracticable, & to ask another to lick one, would not be quite so civil; Bear I was born, & bear, I believe, I'm like to remain: consequently a little ungainly in my fondnesses, but I'll be bold to say, you shan't in a hurry meet with a more loving poor animal, than

your faithful Creature

Bruin.

(*Corres.*, I, 79-80)

Why did the boys fall into parody? Were they simply high-spirited about language, determined to show their virtuosity – much to the delectation of posterity? Or did a high-flown, mock-heroic style permit confidences without embarrassment and a role-playing which in the raw would have been painful? Adopting the manner of *The Turkish Spy*, Gray sighs: 'When the Dew of the morning is upon me, thy Image is before mine eyes.' Again, 'thou art sweet in my thoughts as the Pine-apple of Damascus to the tast.' Again, 'Be thou unto me, as Mohammed to Ajesha' – that is, as the Prophet was to his wife (*Corres.*, I, 14, 15).

The intense friendship with West that immediately followed the rupture with Walpole did not lead to the kind of verbal love-play that recalls and mocks the Song of Songs. In the period of Walpole's dominance the letters to and from West were strained or perfunctory. Relaxing somewhat during the Grand Tour, they became, after the breach with Walpole, profound and moving, touching on the great issues of life, death, and mental health, to say nothing of the technical poetic interests shared by two young writers. Suffused with melancholy sentiment and even thoughts of suicide, they almost seem inexorably to move to the climax that so disrupted the whole inner being of Gray, casting a shadow before it happened, the death of West.

Vastly more influential than any literary model or cultural trend, more intimately related to his mind and heart than the trial and sentencing of the rebel Scottish lords in London, the friendship with West was the soil from which the 'Elegy' grew, a traditional view that needs reviving.[15] But in an even longer perspective – for poetic causes are not necessarily immediate, since human beings never really forget deep experiences but use them even after the lapse of time and memory – we ought to regard both the friendships, with West and Walpole, as the matrix of the poem. Both engaged the deepest recesses of Gray's heart. Both had their joys, but these, to use Gray's poetic phrases, were 'imperfect Joys', 'fearful joy'.[16] Both moved from calm to turmoil and then from agitation to a profound desire for peace and even death. Both the young friends had 'died', Walpole as a friend and West as a creature of dust. Both deaths blighted hopes that had been green and tender, both left love unfulfilled. Doubtless both relations were streaked with guilt and potential danger. And of both it can be said that high though the youths had mounted in delight, in their dejection they did sink as low – with fears, fancies, dim sadness, and blind thoughts:

> We Poets in our youth begin in gladness;
> But thereof come in the end despondency and madness.[17]

If the youthful friendships of Gray are the ultimate causes of the 'Elegy', we must surely find unpersuasive Ketton-Cremer's view that the poet at the climax of the final version of the poem is the 'complete anti-thesis' of the author, a vision 'conjured up by the swain' in language that is theatrical (Gray, p. 101). In fact, both the later Christian and sentimental ending and the earlier stoical conclusion are exquisitely sober renditions of Gray's own experience in passionate friendship – experience refined, to be sure, by thought, literary example, austere taste, and the passage of time. Even the rejected lines of the original ending, which everyone praises as more controlled and 'classical' than the later, are suffused with recollections of suffering and loss. The cry for calm is in low accents, rising from the ground, but it is piercing. The poet really longs for a death-in-life, the 'cool and silent' death of 'ev'ry fierce tumultuous Passion', of 'anxious Cares & endless Wishes'. When applied to the losses Gray suffered in his early friendships, the language is hauntingly precise. And so is the language of the Epitaph. The Swain's sight of the poet is Gray's vision of himself. Even minor details are parallel. The Swain saw the poet stretch his listless length under a beech at noontide poring upon the brook that babbled by. Gray in his letters confesses that he could 'grow to the Trunk' of a tree (also a beech) contemplating a natural scene (Corres., I, 47, 48). From his Spring-like relations with Walpole and from his friendship with West, so autumnal, so red-leafed for men so young, imagine what exact analogues Gray might have drawn to these phrases in the 'Elegy': 'wayward fancies', 'forlorn', 'crazed with care', 'crossed in hopeless love'. Far from being overly dramatic, such language must be regarded as a sober and understated description of the poet's own friendships in their moments of greatest intensity. And the following famous sentences, which have been smoothed into proverbs, imply possessiveness and exclusiveness both towards the beloved partner and towards the emotions aroused: 'He gained from Heaven ('twas all he *wished*) a friend. . . . And Melancholy marked him *for her own.*'[18]

Unlike the wound of Philoctetes, Gray's was a guilty one – or so he regarded it – and it did not permit him often to draw his bow. But when he did, the strength of his arm and the accuracy of his aim are owing to his suffering. He arouses an echo in every bosom because in his best serious poetry he knew himself a man. At the heart of his humanity was his sensibility; at the heart of his sensibility was his melancholy; at the heart of his melancholy – to continue opening this Chinese nest of boxes – lay his friendships, enlivening at first but finally inhibited; and at the heart of each hopeless love frustrating its fulfilment was . . . . But who can go deeper? Who can say what he saw within as he dreamed of some kind of union in mind and body that the evidence suggests his nature deeply craved? Did he see his mother? Or his mother and his father (unreal and idealized) together and in love? Or did he see other successful lovers in the serene and perfect joy he never knew? Traveling in Italy, Gray was wont to set down subjects for paintings that he had never seen executed.[19] Perhaps in dreaming about some of these un-realized subjects he revealed his own deepest self. One of them that he himself would have liked to do had he been an artist Blake realized triumphantly in illustrating Milton, the two angels Ithuriel and Zephon lighting their own way into the bower of bliss in which Adam and Eve lay.[20] Where in such a picture would Gray's artistic triumph have lain? In rendering the accomplished bliss of our first parents? Or, if he painted, as he wrote, from his own experience, might it not have been in portray-ing the two angels viewing but never achieving bliss?

Gray petitioned the great stoical and Christian goddess Adversity to teach him 'Exact my own defects to scan' ('Adversity', l. 47). Perhaps some-what too boldly we have snatched Gray's private and privileged self-examination from his hands and looked unceremoniously at his suffering heart. We may indeed have violated his own injunction, not to 'draw his frailties from their dread abode'. We can only hope that forgiveness is owing affectionate curiosity, a deep sympathy for the man's torturing passions, a modern's tolerance of what once was called aberration, enor-mous respect for his personal and artistic controls, and gratitude for the thin but golden poetic achievements.

The order and beauty of the early odes and the 'Elegy' bear to the early friendships the very relation that the created universe bears to chaos. Gray's chaos may have been without form but it was not void, for on it the poet could breathe the creating word. The good estate of Gray's poetry was blessed with rich black soil, his sensibility – in the fullest sense of that weighty eighteenth-century term. Gray did not achieve the ideal of Dr. Johnson – 'the solitude of adversity without its melancholy, its instructions without its censures, and its sensibility without its perturbations'.[21] In fact, Gray's adversity is compounded of melancholy, censure, and perturbation. The compensation was that he achieved 'Thoughts that breathe and words that burn' ('Progress of Poetry', 1. 110). And the procedure we have followed, of trying to imagine the passion that lay behind the word, will, it is hoped, serve the humanistic tradition better than the censoring scissors of William Mason, who sacrificed the humanity of the poet to a false ideal of chilling and inhuman respectability, from which too much of the race and vigour of the poet's life was omitted.[22]

Northwestern University

Notes

1. 'Mourning and Melancholia' (1917), in *Sigmund Freud: Collected Papers*, 5 vols. (New York, 1959), IV, 152-70.

2. 'The Bard', 1. 142. Gray's identification with the Bard is quoted in *Gray*, p. 134.

3. Marianne Dashwood says of her recent almost fatal seizure of sensibility: 'Had I died, – it would have been self-destruction' (chap. 46).

4. End of chap. 7.

5. See first ed. (1794), 4 vols. (I, 13-14). The father worries about Emily's 'susceptibility' which is 'too exquisite to admit of lasting peace'.

6. For a fuller discussion of sincerity, see Jean H. Hagstrum, *Samuel Johnson's Literary Criticism* (Chicago, 1967), pp. 45-46.

7. 'Gray's *Elegy* Reconsidered', in *From Sensibility to Romanticism*, ed. F. W. Hilles and H. Bloom (New York, 1965), esp. pp. 145-46.

8. *Essai sur Thomas Gray* (London, Paris, 1934), p. 119. Despite my slight disagreement on this point, I admire Martin's study greatly; it is still the profoundest analysis of Gray's character and poetry.

9. *Two Quiet Lives* (London, 1948), pp. 184-85. Although less penetrating than Martin, Cecil does acknowledge that Gray was passionate.

10. See *Corres.*, Appendix A.

11. See the *Autobiography, Times, Opinions and Contemporaries of Sir Egerton Brydges*, 2 vols. (London, 1834), II, 395. Brydges knew Bonstetten, to whom apparently he had talked about Gray.

12. See *Correspondence of Gray and Nicholls*, ed. John Mitford (London, 1843), p. 15, where a letter by T. J. Mathias on the death of Norton Nicholls is quoted.

13. *Corres.*, III, 926. William Powell Jones has written, 'Gray never loved any woman except his mother. . . . He was intimate only with men'. (*Thomas Gray, Scholar* [Cambridge, Mass., 1937], p. 27.)

14. *De Principiis Cogitandi*, Liber Primus, ll. 64-84. For a discussion of date, see *Poems*, pp. 321-22.

15. I now abjure the view which I derived from Frank Ellis and expressed in *The Sister Arts* (Chicago, 1958), p. 295 and n.12, that the Epitaph is intended primarily for the dead peasant-poet. I believe it refers primarily and most profoundly to Gray himself.

16. 'Eton', l. 40; 'Sonnet on the Death of Mr. Richard West', l. 8.

17. 'Resolution and Independence', ll. 48-49. See also ll. 24-28.

18. Emphasis added. I have reversed the order of lines 120 and 124 of the "Elegy".

19. Duncan C. Tovey, ed., *Letters of Gray*, 3 vols. (London, 1900-1912), III, 64n.3, where Mason is quoted.

20. I owe this example to Roger Martin, *Essai*, pp. 364-65; he quotes it from Mason.

21. *Rambler*, no. 28, par. 9.

22. On Mason's excisions, see *Corres.*, I, xiii-xvi and editors' notes to several letters from one to 52, and also Roger Martin, *Chronologie de la Vie et de l'Oeuvre de Thomas Gray* (London, Paris, 1931), pp. 16-17.

His letters were the best I ever saw.

HORACE WALPOLE

Learning is a peculiar compound of memory, imagination, scientific habit, accurate observation, all concentrated, through a prolonged period, on the analysis of the remains of literature. The result of this sustained mental endeavour is not a book, but a man.

MARK PATTISON.[1]

Listen to the voices of three scholars talking about their lives:

In the fifty second year of my age, after the completion of a toilsome and successful work, I now propose to employ some moments of my leisure in reviewing the simple transactions of a private and litterary life. . . . A sincere and simple narrative of my own life . . . will expose me, and perhaps with justice to the imputation of vanity. Yet I may judge from the experience both of past, and of the present, times, that the public is always curious to *know* the men who have left behind them any image of their minds . . . . The author of an important and successful work may hope without presumption that he is not totally indifferent to his numerous readers: . . . and I must be conscious that no one is so well qualified as myself to describe the series of my thoughts and actions.

Here is the second voice:

As life may not be granted me to write out all I can remember, I shall begin with my coming up to Oxford in the year 1832, leaving my boyish years for a later book of reminiscences. For I have really no history but a mental history. When I read other persons' autobiographies I feel that they were justified in writing them by the variety of experiences they have gone through, and the number of interesting persons they have known. . . . I have seen no one, known none of the celebrities of my own time intimately, or at all, and have only an inaccurate memory for what I hear. All my energy was directed upon one end – to improve myself, to form my own mind, to sound things thoroughly, to free myself from the bondage of unreason, and the traditional prejudices which, when I began first to think, constituted the whole of my intellectual fabric. . . . If there is anything of interest in my story, it is as a story of mental development.

And here is the third voice:

It is indeed for want of spirits, as you suspect, that my studies lie among the Cathedrals, and the Tombs, and the Ruins. To think, though to little purpose, has been the chief amusement of my days; and when I would not, or cannot think, I dream. At present I find myself able to write a Catalogue, or to read the Peerage book, or Miller's Gardening Dictionary, and am thankful that there are such employments and such authors in the world. Some people, who hold me cheap for this, are doing perhaps what is not half so well worth while. As to posterity, I may ask, (with some body whom I have forgot) what has it ever done to oblige me?[2]

Although Gibbon is aware that he may be accused of vanity in writing his *Memoirs*, his tone is completely assured, as becomes 'the historian of the Roman empire'. While Mark Pattison apologizes for his bad memory, and for the fact that he has known no celebrities, he has no doubt that the history of his own mental development is worth writing, no sense that his adventures in the realm of ideas may have been unimportant. Thomas Gray (you will notice) is much more diffident than either of these men, acknowledging that his life of thought may have been passed 'to little purpose': it is characteristic of him to call thinking merely his 'chief amusement'.[3] At the moment of writing he does not even feel capable of useful thought, and is reduced to compiling a catalogue – a very common occupation of his, as anyone who has examined his Common-Place Books will be constrained to agree. Yet no less revealing is the flash of defiance directed at those who 'hold [him] cheap', those who sometimes asked (as we may be sure) what important and 'toilsome' work he would leave behind him as his monument. Gray had reason for his defiance. Gibbon is remembered today, and will probably always be remembered, as the greatest of English historians: but *The Decline and Fall* is more celebrated as a title than as a book, and the number of people who now read it through must be relatively small. Mark Pattison is remembered only by readers of *Middlemarch*, and by scholars interested in the Victorian period – and what they read is his *Memoirs*, rather than his scholarly works. Of the three men it is Gray who left behind him the 'image of [his] mind' which has proved most enduring. If he had done nothing but write the 'Elegy', he would have assured his immortality. Gray was not the sort of man to produce a volume of *Memoirs*, but he did write letters, letters which are among the most interesting in the language, and it is with these letters, their style and tone and the light that they throw on the strangely inconclusive shape of his career, that I am concerned in this essay.

'You well know how rapidly and carelessly I always write my Letters', Horace Walpole once wrote to Gray (*Corres.*, I, 373), and it was a foible common to almost every letter-writer of that age to insist that he wrote carelessly and without premeditation. In Gray's early letters to Walpole, however, we are less likely to be struck by artlessness than by artifice. A sophisticated young Etonian, writing to the son of the Prime Minister, Gray is very much on his mettle, and he is clearly determined not to be a bore as he addresses an epistle to Downing Street or St James's Square. And so we have a letter with the superscription:

> With care   To mie Nufs att London   Present
>   Carridge pade   These
>
> (*Corres.*, I, 5-6)

The style of this letter reminds one of another Etonian making fun of a supposedly uneducated writer, Henry Fielding in *Shamela*. A week or two later Gray is writing in the style of *The Turkish Spy*, and a little later (again) he reminds us of 'The Humble Petition of Frances Harris':

> May it please your We-ship
> In consideration of the time your Petitioner has past in your honours Service, as also on account of the great Services your petitioner's relations have had the honour to perform for your Honour's Ancestors; since it is well known that your petit^{rs} Grandmother's Aunt's Cousin-german had ye honour to pull out your honour's great Uncle's Wive's brother's hollow tooth; as also, to go further backwards, your Pet^{rs} relation was Physician to King Cadwallader .... (*Corres.*, I, 24)

Walpole knew a good letter when he saw one, and we have reason to be thankful that he could not bring himself to destroy 'those early blossoms of his friend's wit, genius and humour'.[4] It seems unlikely that Gray thought less highly of Walpole's letters, but unfortunately only one of his early letters to Gray survives, and in it we find Walpole playfully imitating the 'method' of Addison's *Remarks on Several Parts of Italy* (*Corres.*, I, 29-33).

The habit of epistolary playfulness remained with Gray. In a letter to West, written in 1737 and only recently added to the collected *Correspondence*, he apologizes for sending so little news in the style of a small tradesman apologizing 'for the backwardness of my payments' and adds dummy enclosures from Walpole and Ashton at the end – Walpole's communication being a row of asterisks, and Ashton's a blank side of paper, discovered when one obeys the injunction to 'Turn over' (*Corres.*, III, 1315-19). Another letter to West, dating from December 1738, is obviously inspired by *The Battle of the Books*. A year later, in Florence, Gray framed the greater part of a letter to Wharton in the form of a parody of 'Proposals for printing by Subscription, in THIS LARGE LETTER The Travels of T: G: Gent.' (*Corres.*, I, 138-43). Such stylistic flourishes were usually a sign of good spirits, and it is interesting to find that the much later letter in which Gray sent Walpole a copy of the 'Elegy' concludes as follows:

> You will, I hope, look upon it in the light of a *thing with an end to it*; a merit that most of my writings have wanted, and are like to want, but which this epistle I am determined shall not want, when it tells you that I am ever
>
>
>
> Yours,
>
> T. Gray.
>
>
>
> Not that I have done yet; but who could avoid the temptation of finishing so roundly and so cleverly in the manner of good queen Anne's days? . . . . (*Corres.*, I, 327)

In 1755 we find William Mason joining in the game, and beginning a letter in this way: 'Amongst the variety of rational entertainments that Travel affords to a thinking mind, I have always rankd with the principal that fund wch it presents of new Ideas, peculiarly proper to be thrown upon paper in order to form that wch we call a free Epistolary correspondence' (*Corres.*, I, 422). That might almost be Smollett, writing seriously in his *Travels*, and it is something of a relief to find Mason commenting near the end of the letter, 'how strangly is my stile changd since the beginning!', and to be reassured that the greater part of what he has written is a parody of the style of the second-rate travel-books of the day. Mason was simply playing the epistolary game, as Gray did again, years later, in his first letter to Norton Nicholls:

Sr
I received your letter at Southampton, & as I would wish to treat
every body according to their own rule & measure of good-breed-
ing, have against my inclination waited till now, before I answer'd
it, purely out of fear & respect, & an ingenuous diffidence of my own
abilities. if you will not take this as an excuse, accept it at least as a
well-turn'd period, wch is always my principal concern. (*Corres.*, II,
851-52)

The letter ends with a claim that Gray had 'prepared a finer period than
the other to finish with, but d-mn it! I have somehow mislaid it among
my papers. you shall certainly have it next summer.' A later letter to
Nicholls includes 'the beginning of a letter' by an unknown writer which
Gray pretends to have found and which he is sending on because it may
prove useful on 'some great occasion':

Dear Sr
After so long silence the hopes of pardon & prospect of forgiveness might seem entirely extinct or at least very remote, was I not
truly sensible of your goodness & candour, wch is the only Asylum
that my negligence can fly to: since every apology would prove insufficient to counterballance it, or alleviate my fault. how then shall
my deficiency presume to make so bold an attempt, or be able to
suffer the hardships of so rough a campaign? &c.: &c: &c. (*Corres.*,
III, 1067-68)

We are reminded of the tradition of parody which helped Jane Austen
to become a novelist.

As one would expect, the most self-conscious of Gray's letters are the
earliest. Soon he learned to write in an informal manner which recalls
Hazlitt's classic distinction between a familiar and a vulgar style: 'It
is not easy to write a familiar style. Many people mistake a familiar for
a vulgar style, and suppose that to write without affectation is to write at
random. On the contrary, there is nothing that requires more precision,
and, if I may say so, purity of expression, than the style I am speaking
of. . . . It is not to take the first word that offers, but the best word in
common use; it is not to throw words together in any combinations we
please, but to follow and avail ourselves of the true idiom of the language.'[5] No wonder Hazlitt admired Gray's letters, in which 'the true
idiom of the language' is exemplified in a rich variety of ways: in conciseness, for example, as when Gray expresses his fear of fire in the

following words, in a letter from London: ' 'tis strange, that we all of us (here in Town) lay ourselves down every night on our Funeral Pile ready made, & compose ourselves to rest; while every drunken Footman, & drowsy Old-Woman, has a candle ready to light it before the morning' (*Corres.*, II, 654). For an example of conciseness which is as true to the idiom of English life as it is to the idiom of the English language it would be hard to beat the opening of one of the early letters to Walpole: 'It rains, 'tis Sunday, this is the country' (*Corres.*, I, 49).

Walpole told Cole that 'Gray never wrote anything easily but things of humour: humour was his natural and original turn',[6] and wit and humour are particularly evident in the letters to Walpole, not least when Gray was sending him his first impressions of Cambridge, 'a great old Town, shaped like a Spider, with a nasty lump in the middle of it, & half a dozen scambling long legs' (*Corres.*, I, 3). He describes Peterhouse as 'a thing like two Presbyterian Meeting-houses with the backside of a little Church between them' (*Corres.*, I, 23-24), the Masters of the Colleges as 'twelve grey-hair'd Gentlefolks, who are all mad with Pride', the Fellows as 'sleepy, drunken, dull, illiterate Things', and the Sizars as 'Graziers Eldest Sons, who come to get good Learning, that they may all be Archbishops of Canterbury' (*Corres.*, I, 3). In a later letter he tells Walpole, who has been looking for an amanuensis, that 'we have a Man here that writes a good Hand; but he has two little Failings, that hinder my recommending him to you. he is lousy, & he is mad: he sets out this Week for Bedlam; but if you insist upon it, I don't doubt he will pay his Respects to you' (*Corres.*, I, 349). It is to Walpole (again) that Gray writes that 'the worst thing, that can befall a Rascall (& especially a Parson) is to attain the height of his wishes' (*Corres.*, II, 829). But wit is likely to appear anywhere in these letters, as when Gray tells West (adapting a saying of another celebrated letter-writer, Mme de Sévigné) that 'Mont Cenis, I confess, carries the permission mountains have of being frightful rather too far',[7] or sends Wharton a pessimistic forecast of his own future existence in Cambridge:

Time will settle my Conscience, Time will reconcile me to this languid Companion [the Spirit of Lazyness]: we shall smoke, we shall tipple, we shall doze together. we shall have our little Jokes, like other People, and our long Stories; Brandy will finish what Port begun; & a Month after the Time you will see in some Corner of a London Even:ng Post, Yesterday, died the Revnd Mr John Grey, Senior-Fellow of Clare-Hall, a facetious Companion, & well-respected by all that knew him. (*Corres.*, I, 318)

It was to another friend, Richard Stonhewer, that Gray wrote that 'The mode of free-thinking is like that of Ruffs and Farthingales, and has given place to the mode of not thinking at all' (*Corres.*, II, 583).

'I have often said,' Walpole once wrote to Lady Ossory, 'this world is a comedy to those that think, a tragedy to those that feel.'[8] One of 'those that feel' was Richard West, whom we find addressing Gray in the following words, on the 5th of June 1740:

> Dear Gray! consider me in the condition of one that has lived these two years without any person that he can speak freely to. I know it is very seldom that people trouble themselves with the sentiments of those they converse with; so they can chat about trifles, they never care whether your heart aches or no. Are you one of these? I think not. But what right have I to ask you this question? Have we known one another enough, that I should expect or demand sincerity from you? Yes, Gray, I hope we have; and I have not quite such a mean opinion of myself, as to think I do not deserve it. (*Corres.*, I, 165)

Gray replied: 'You do yourself and me justice, in imagining that you merit, and that I am capable of sincerity. I have not a thought, or even a weakness, I desire to conceal from you; and consequently on my side deserve to be treated with the same openness of heart.... as mutual wants are the ties of general society, so are mutual weaknesses of private friendships' (*Corres.*, I, 167-68). Soon we find Gray telling West that re-union with him is 'the principal pleasure I have to hope for in my own country', and sending him a 'picture' of himself, as changed by two years of travel: 'On the good side you may add a sensibility for what others feel, and indulgence for their faults or weaknesses, a love of truth, and detestation of every thing else' (*Corres.*, I, 181). At the risk of over-simplifying, we might say that in the early letters Walpole appealed to the Augustan side of Gray, West to the Sentimental.[9]

It was to West, on whose sympathy he could rely, that Gray wrote this famous passage:

> I own I have not, as yet, any where met with those grand and simple works of Art, that are to amaze one, and whose sight one is to be the better for: But those of Nature have astonished me beyond expression. In our little journey up to the Grande Chartreuse, I do not remember to have gone ten paces without an exclamation, that there was no restraining: Not a precipice, not a torrent, not a cliff,

but is pregnant with religion and poetry. There are certain scenes
that would awe an atheist into belief, without the help of other
argument. (*Corres.*, I, 128)

It was to West that Gray described a view near Tivoli, 'the most noble
sight in the world':

The weight of that quantity of waters, and the force they fall with,
have worn the rocks they throw themselves among into a thousand
irregular craggs, and to a vast depth. In this channel it goes boiling
along with a mighty noise till it comes to another steep, where you
see it a second time come roaring down (but first you must walk two
miles farther) a greater height than before, but not with that
quantity of waters; for by this time it has divided itself, being
crossed and opposed by the rocks, into four several streams, each of
which, in emulation of the great one, will tumble down too; and it
does tumble down, but not from an equally elevated place; so that
you have at one view all these cascades intermixed with groves of
olive and little woods, the mountains rising behind them, and on
the top of one . . . is seated the town itself. (*Corres.*, I, 156)

Gray's journey to Scotland, twenty-five years later, occasioned some
equally fine descriptive passages, as did his tour of the Lakes in 1769.
Here is his description of the Lodore waterfall:

the crags, named *Lodoor-banks* now begin to impend terribly over
your way; & more terribly, when you hear, that three years since an
immense mass of rock tumbled at once from the brow, & bar'd
all access to the dale (for this is the only road) till they could work
their way thro' it . . . down the side of the mountain & far into
the lake lie dispersed the huge fragments of this ruin in all shapes
& in all directions. something farther we turn'd aside into a cop-
pice, ascending a little in front of *Lodoor* water-fall. the height
appears to be about 200 feet, the quantity of water not great, tho'
(these three days excepted) it had rain'd daily in the hills for near
two months before: but then the stream was nobly broken, leaping
from rock to rock, & foaming with fury. on one side a towering
crag, that spired up to equal, if not overtop, the neighbouring cliffs
(this lay all in shade & darkness) on the other hand a rounder
broader projecting hill shag'd with wood & illumined by the sun,
wch glanced sideways on the upper part of the cataract. the force of
the water wearing a deep channel in the ground hurries away to
join the lake. (*Corres.*, III, 1080)

It is difficult to read such a passage without remembering the letters of another traveller in the Lake district, almost half a century later. We know that Keats attended the lecture in which Hazlitt described Gray's letters as 'inimitably fine',[10] and we may conjecture that if Keats had not read the letters before that day in 1818, he almost certainly got hold of them soon afterwards, for when he wrote his own descriptions of northern scenery a month or two later he seems to have been stimulated by the example of Gray.

One has only to mention the letters of Keats, however, to become aware of certain limitations in the letters of Gray. Above all, they contain disappointingly little on the subject of poetry. The death of West seems to have stimulated Gray to write some of his best poetry – as the death of Arthur Henry Hallam was to stimulate Tennyson a century later – but it also removed the friend with whom he found it most natural to discuss poetry in his letters. It is true that he sometimes wrote about poetry in his correspondence with Mason; but it is usually Mason's own poetry, and while we admire the friendly meticulousness with which Gray comments on *Caractacus* it is impossible not to wish that he had had more distinguished verse on which to exercise his powers as a critic. Of his own poetry he says hardly anything. As we read the letters of Keats we are privileged to overhear a poet discussing his own poetry and the poetry of others, and speculating about the imagination and the validity of its vision of life: above all, we have the experience of watching a great poet growing to maturity under our eyes. When he finishes a letter, Keats is often further along the road to great poetry than when he began. When Gray discusses poetry in his letters, on the other hand, he discusses it much as any intelligent critic or scholar might do. This difference is partly due to the difference between two ages, the Age of Johnson and the Age of Coleridge: by the time of Keats there had developed a much greater interest in the nature of the imaginative process itself. But it is also due to a fundamental difference between the lives of the two men, and the place that poetry occupied in their lives.

Referring to the passage in a letter of Walpole's describing the road near the Grande Chartreuse, in which he wrote that he and Gray 'wished to be poets', Ketton-Cremer comments: 'Walpole could write that . . . without a suspicion that the greatest poet of their generation had been jogging on mule-back at his side' (*Gray*, p. 35). I have always felt uneasy about that remark. Perhaps the author of the 'Elegy' should be described as a great poet, yet I do not think that Gray himself would have liked to be described as 'the greatest poet of [his] generation', and I am not sure that the diffidence I am imputing to him would have been unreasonable. It is not merely that Keats wrote more great poetry in twenty-five years than Gray wrote in fifty-four. It is rather that Keats devoted his life to poetry, as Wordsworth devoted his. Remembering Keats, one of his fellow-students was later to comment: 'Poetry was ... the zenith of all his Aspirations – The only thing worthy the attention of superior minds – So he thought – All other pursuits were mean & tame.' Gray might have agreed with Keats that 'The greatest men in the world were the Poets', but it could hardly have been said of him, as it was of Keats, that 'to rank among them was the chief object of his ambition'.[11] Gray did not devote his life to poetry: he devoted it to learning. Although Gray's letters exhibit imagination as well as sensibility, to describe them without qualification as the letters of a poet would be misleading – whereas it would be unthinkable to describe the letters of Keats in any other way.

When poems occur in the letters of Keats they come (in his own phrase) 'as naturally as the Leaves to a tree'.[12] It would be an exaggeration to say that when poems occur in the letters of Gray it is as if another man had taken the pen – as if a second, secret Gray had taken over for a few moments, before the return of the witty, self-depreciatory scholar, with his notes about his classical reading, his observations on natural history, and his gossip about poor mad Kit Smart and the more ordinary Fellows of the Colleges. It would be an exaggeration, but an exaggeration of a real impression of which the reader is aware. There is a striking contrast between the way in which Keats introduces the 'Ode to Psyche', for example – with the observation that it has been 'done leisurely', unlike his other poems, and the comment: 'I think it reads the more richly for it and will I hope encourage me to write other thing[s] in even a more peacable and healthy spirit'[13] – and the way in which Gray sends Walpole a copy of his first considerable English poem, the 'Ode on the Spring', with the brief remark: 'I annex (as you desired) another Ode. all it pretends to with you is, that it is mine, & that you never saw it before, & that it is not so long as t'other' (*Corres.*, I, 250). Even more striking is the comment with which Gray sent Bedingfield a copy of 'The Bard', one day in 1756: 'I accept too with pleasure the marks of approbation you bestow on my two fragments, but here I have still greater scruples. I will not enter into a discussion of them; but only tell you, that *admiration* is a word, that has no place between two people, that ever mean to come together. besides (believe me) there is but one thing in life, that deserves it, & that is not Poetry' (*Corres.*, II, 475).

Gray was not driven to the writing of poetry by a powerful creative genius, the stirring of great imaginative powers which demanded an outlet. Whereas Keats published *Endymion* in the full consciousness of its being 'a feverish attempt, rather than a deed accomplished',[14] Gray had to be driven to publication, even in the case of the 'Elegy'. He told Walpole that 'the *still small voice* of Poetry was not made to be heard in a crowd' (*Corres.*, I, 296). The best description of Gray as a poet was in fact written in the age of Keats, with no specific reference to Gray. 'A poet is a nightingale', Shelley wrote in 'A Defence of Poetry', 'who sits in darkness and sings to cheer its own solitude with sweet sounds.'[15]

If this comparison with another poet has helped to place Gray, a comparison with another scholar may provide a useful cross-bearing. At first glance, Gray and Gibbon have something in common. Each was a delicate child, the only survivor of a numerous family of children, and each was sent to one of the great public schools and to one of the universities. Each had to wait until early middle life before he received a modest inheritance which rendered him independent, and was preserved equally (as Gibbon believed essential for a scholar) from the privations of a garret or the luxuries of a palace. Each travelled abroad – and each was entertained in Florence by Sir Horace Mann. Each began to keep a common-place book 'according to the precept and model of Mr. Locke',[16] and each soon abandoned Locke's method. Each died in his fifties, unmarried, a scholar and man of letters with a European reputation. But these superficial similarities conceal deep differences. While Gray was deeply attached to his mother, who survived until he was a man of 36, Gibbon owed a great deal to an aunt, but scarcely knew his mother, who died while he was still a boy. While Gray escaped from a home made miserable by a violent and neurotic father, to spend the nine happiest years of his life at Eton, ill-health allowed Gibbon little more than two years at Westminster, the rest of his education being sporadic and irregular. While Gray was as satirical about Cambridge as Gibbon was to be about Oxford, he continued at his university for the remainder of his life, whereas Gibbon left his after fifteen months. There is nothing in Gray's life to correspond to Gibbon's immature conversion to Catholicism, or his subsequent and formative period at Lausanne. Gibbon's later travels were very different from Gray's tour with Horace Walpole, while 'the sublime beauties of Nature'[17] were of much less significance to Gibbon than to Gray. But the two most important differences are the fact that Gibbon did not sentimentalize his boyhood, and the fact that Gray did not complete any 'toilsome and successful work' of scholarship.

In his account of his own early life in his *Memoirs*, Gibbon wrote as follows:

> At the conclusion of this first period of my life, I am tempted to enter a protest against the trite and lavish praise of the happiness of our boyish years, which is echoed with so much affectation in the World. That happiness I have never known; that time I have never regretted. ... My name, it is most true, could never be enrolled among the sprightly race, the idle progeny of Eton or Westminster, who delight to cleave the water with pliant arm, to urge the flying ball, and to chace the speed of the rolling circle. But I would ask the warmest and most active Hero of the play field, whether he can seriously compare his childish with his manly enjoyments; whether he does not feel, as the most precious attribute of his existence, the vigorous maturity of sensual and spiritual powers, which Nature has reserved for the age of puberty.[18]

Here Gibbon acknowledges that he is using 'images extricated from metre'[19] as he records his disagreement with the view of boyhood expressed in Gray's 'Ode on a Distant Prospect of Eton College'. Gibbon's confident reference to 'the vigorous maturity of sensual and spiritual powers, which Nature has reserved for the age of puberty' could never have been written by Gray. In the *Lives of the Poets* Johnson wrote that he contemplated Gray's poetry 'with less pleasure than his life', yet it is difficult to feel that Gray's adult life, for all his learning, was a very emphatic success. Gray would not (I think) have argued that he had been particularly unlucky, and yet the sense of the transitoriness of human life which is at the heart of his best poetry is closely associated with a sense of imperfect self-fulfilment. One cannot imagine Gray writing, with Gibbon: 'When I contemplate the common lot of mortality, I must acknowledge that I have drawn a high prize in the lottery of life.'[20]

The greatest difference between the adult lives of the two men was that the learning of the one bore fruit in the greatest historical work in the English language, while the learning of the other – which was even wider in its scope[21] – did not result in a single published book, or edition, or pamphlet, or review. During his lifetime, if an Irishism is permitted, the learning of Gray was an iceberg of which ten-tenths remained below the surface. When he looked back on his own life, Gibbon delighted in tracing its various stages: he says of his period in Lausanne, for example, that 'Such as I am in Genius or learning or in manners, I owe my creation to Lausanne: it was in that school, that the statue was discovered in the block of marble'.[22] The centre of the pattern was the composition of *The Decline and Fall,* 'the daily task, the active pursuit which gave a value to every book, and an object to every enquiry'.[23] It is fitting that he should have recorded the conception of his great work in his journal, and that this description of the moment 'in the Church of the Zoccolanti or Franciscan fryars, while they were singing Vespers in the Temple of Jupiter on the ruins of the Capitol' should be balanced by the memorable sentences in which he recorded the evening when he 'wrote the last lines of the last page in a summer-house' in his garden at Lausanne.[24] Such a moment of triumphant achievement had never been known to Gray, who had the greatest difficulty in completing a short poem, and who never even managed to write an inaugural lecture. It is impossible to imagine a greater contrast to Gibbon, working at the *Decline and Fall,* than Gray in the library of the British Museum, 'who only read to know, if there were any thing worth writing, & that not without some difficulty' (*Corres.,* II, 630). It is hardly surprising to find Gibbon citing Gray in a footnote to his *Memoirs* as an example of the scandalous 'indolence' of English professors: 'Gray Prof. of modern history at Cambridge, £400 a year (Mem., p. 333), in three years never once read [a lecture] — his remorse – Mason's excuses, p. 395-399 – Never admonished by any superiors.'[25]

'The miseries of a vacant life', Gibbon observes with some complacency, 'were never known to a man, whose hours were insufficient for the inexhaustible pleasures of study.'[26] The same could never be said of Gray, who is bored, or in flight from boredom, or pretending to be bored, from the first of his letters to his last. In one of his earliest letters he tells Walpole that 'in Cambridge there is nothing so troublesome, as that one has nothing to trouble one. every thing is so tediously regular, so samish, that I expire for want of a little variety'.[27] A few days later he tells Walpole that he has 'kept [himself] alive all this long Christmas by the help of your letters', and soon he is explaining to West that 'almost all the employment of my hours may be best explained by Negatives'. Of course there was an element of affectation and irony in all this. Often when he wrote in this strain Gray was reading (as he once admitted to learning Italian) 'like any dragon'. Yet there is the ring of truth in the passage in which he told West that 'Low spirits are my true and faithful companions; they get up with me, go to bed with me, make journeys and returns as I do . . . but most commonly we sit alone together, and are the prettiest insipid company in the world'. He is afraid that he has fallen under the spell of Laziness, 'the Spirit of the Place' (Cambridge). He is bored when he visits Stoke, as he is bored in Cambridge. He has no doubt about the remedy: 'to be employed is to be happy. This principle of mine' – he goes on – 'and I am convinced of its truth, has, as usual, no influence on my practice. I am alone and *ennuyé* to the last degree, yet do nothing.' As he freely acknowledges to Mason, one reason for his writing letters was to escape from boredom: 'I write to you *pour me de-sennuyer*, tho' I have little enough to say.' In 1760 he repeats that 'to find oneself business (I am persuaded) is the great art of life'. This gives particular interest to a passage in a letter to Walpole, written in 1768: 'To what you say to me so civilly, that I ought to write more, I reply . . . I will write, because I like it; and because I like myself better when I do so. If I do not write much, it is because I cannot.'

Here Gray seems to be thinking of poetry, and Mason relates that Gray often told him that 'Reading was much more agreeable to him than writing' (Mason, p. 171). Even so, we are bound to wonder why a man of such learning was so singularly unproductive. It is true that Gray was not obliged to write. If Samuel Johnson had enjoyed a private income, or had been admitted to the privilege of living in a College, we might well have had 'The Vanity of Human Wishes' but would certainly have been without the *Dictionary* and probably without the *Lives of the Poets*. It is also true that Gray lacked the confident temper that led Gibbon to undertake *The Decline and Fall*. But I think that there was another reason for his failure to publish, and that a hint of it may be found in a letter in which he is commiserating with Walpole on a fit of the gout. Attributing his own comparative freedom from the disease to exercise, Gray wrote: 'Man is a creature made to be jumbled, & no matter whether he goes on his head or heels, move or be moved he must.'[28]

Granted that it took the genius of Johnson and Gibbon to make from the circumstances of their (very different) lives a 'series of . . . thoughts and actions'[29] that culminated in the composition of their voluminous works, it is noticeable that Gray's adult life was singularly deficient in sources of stimulation. His early experiences – Eton and the friends that he made there, the tour with Walpole, the death of West – all seem to have contributed to his first period of fertility as a poet. Later it is clear that he enjoyed his visits to London. In 1746, for example, he wrote to Wharton: 'I have been in Town . . . flaunting about at publick Places of all kinds with my two Italianized Friends. the World itself has some Attraction in it to a Solitary of six Years standing; & agreeable well-meaning People of Sense . . . are my peculiar Magnet. it is no Wonder then, if I felt some Reluctance at parting with them so soon; or if my Spirits, when I return'd back to my Cell, should sink for a time' (*Corres.*, I, 255).

Retiring as he was, and often awkward in society, Gray found stimulus in conversation, and there is a certain wistfulness in a sentence in a letter to Walpole where he alludes to a passage in Cicero's *Tusculan Disputations* and describes a happy time when 'the better sort ... did not ... run away from society for fear of its temptations: they passed their days in the midst of it: conversation was their business: they cultivated the arts of persuasian, on purpose to show men it was their interest, as well as their duty, not to be foolish, and false, and unjust' (*Corres.*, I, 263). Against this we may set a remark of Gibbon's about his experience as a Member of Parliament: 'After my foreign education, with my reserved temper, I should long have continued a stranger in my native country had I not been shaken in this various scene of new faces and new friends: had not experience forced me to feel the characters of our leading men, the state of parties, the forms of office and the operation of our civil and military system.'[30] A man with at least as great an interest as Gibbon or Matthew Arnold in discovering 'the best that had been said and thought in the world', Gray was confined, for the greater part of his life, to mid-eighteenth-century Cambridge, 'a place, where no events grow, tho' we preserve those of former days by way of *Hortus Siccus* in our libraries' (*Corres.*, II, 805). It is noticeable that he was always stimulated by travel, and it is tempting to speculate that he might have written more if only he had more frequently been 'jumbled' – to use his own word – or 'shaken' – to use Gibbon's, who remarks that he 'never found [his own] mind more vigorous, or [his] composition more happy, than in the winter hurry of society and parliament'.[31] Gray's 'Leucocholy' was the spiritual equivalent of Walpole's gout.

Whereas Gibbon and Mark Pattison wrote *Memoirs*, Gray wrote none, and it is hard to imagine him even contemplating such an undertaking. His life must have seemed a very inconclusive affair, as he reflected on it while he lay in Pembroke during the days of his final illness. He remembered Eton (we may be certain), and his travels with Walpole, and the quarrel that had so long been made up, and the returned letter that gave him his first hint of the death of West. He must have been glad to have written a poem that was already recognized as a masterpiece. But his life cannot have presented any clear pattern to him, as Gibbon's did to the triumphant historian of the Roman empire. As we look back on Gray's life, however, two centuries later, I think that it presents a very definite pattern. At the centre we see the 'Elegy', which is at once the classic statement in English of 'that natural desire we have of being remembered' (Mason, p. 203n.) and a surer claim to remembrance than any volume of autobiography; and behind it, more prominently perhaps than the remaining poems, an incomparable collection of letters which forms as appropriate a record of Gray's life as the *Memoirs* do of Gibbon's, a record more diffident, more inconclusive, and (dare one say it?) more sensitive: a collection of letters so remarkable that all that Mason had to do, to inaugurate a new chapter in the history of biography, was to limit his role to that of 'a compiler . . . rather than a biographer' (Mason, pp. 400-01), simply providing passages of introductory and connecting matter. It is ironical that a poet who wrote so little poetry, and had such difficulty in ever producing anything that had an end to it, should be the author of the best-remembered poem of the eighteenth century. It is ironical that a scholar who lacked the power of conceiving a large-scale work, and who was to be accused by Arnold of 'never speaking out', should have left us the best and fullest first-hand account we have of the life of a scholar during the most distinguished period in the history of our prose.

Pembroke College, Cambridge

Notes

1. Walpole's 'Memoir of Gray', in *Corres.*, III, 1287; Mark Pattison, *Isaac Casaubon 1559-1614*, 2nd ed. (London, 1892), p. 435.
2. Edward Gibbon, *Memoirs of My Life*, ed. Georges A. Bonnard (London, 1966), pp. 1-2; Mark Pattison, *Memoirs* (London, 1885), pp. 1-2; *Corres.*, II, 565–66.
3. Cf. note 21, below.
4. Note written by Walpole to accompany his collection of Gray's early letters: printed in *The Correspondence of Gray, Walpole, West and Ashton*, ed. Paget Toynbee, 2 vols. (Oxford, 1915), I, XXXIII.
5. *Table-Talk*, Essay xxiv: *The Complete Works*, ed. P. P. Howe (London, 1930-34), VIII, 242.
6. *Correspondence of Horace Walpole*, ed. W. S. Lewis and others (New Haven, 1937–), I, 367.
7. *Corres.*, I, 129 and note.
8. Walpole, *Correspondence*, XXXII, 315. Walpole included the remark among his 'Detached Thoughts' (*Works*, IV, 369).

9. Walpole himself was by no means without 'sentiment', though perhaps it became more obvious after his boyhood. He noted his own 'sensibility' in the description of himself in his *Memoirs*, and Cole once told him that 'It is a misfortune to have so much sensibility in one's nature as you are endued with'. (*Horace Walpole*, by W. S. Lewis, [London, 1961], pp. 78, 46.)

10. *Lectures on the English Poets*, 1818, Lecture VI, in *The Complete Works*, v. 118. Cf. *The Letters of John Keats*, ed. H. E. Rollins (London, 1958), I, 237.

11. Henry Stephens to G. F. Mathew, in *The Keats Circle*, ed. H. E. Rollins, 2nd ed., 2 vols. (Cambridge, Mass, 1965), II, 208.

12. *The Letters of John Keats*, I, 238.

13. Ibid., I, 106.

14. The Preface to *Endymion*.

15. *The Complete Works of Percy Bysshe Shelley*, ed. R. Ingpen and W. E. Peck (London, 1965), VII, 116.

16. Gibbon, *Memoirs*, p. 79.

17. Ibid., pp. 79-80.

18. Ibid., pp. 43-44.

19. Ibid., p. 252.

20. Ibid., p. 186.

21. There is no need to quote Temple's assessment of Gray as 'Perhaps . . . the most learned man in Europe', readily accessible in Johnson's *Lives*. A. E. Housman, on being paid a similar compliment, replied: 'It is not true, and if it were, - - - - would not know it.' (*A. E. Housman*, by A. S. F. Gow, [Cambridge 1936], p. 39.) With reference to Gray's description of thinking as 'the chief amusement of my days', quoted above on p. 21, it is interesting to recall Temple's observation that Gray 'could not bear to be considered . . . merely as a man of letters; . . . his desire was to be looked upon as a private independent gentleman, who read for his amusement'.

22. *Memoirs*, p. 86. Curiously enough, the image may well have been suggested to Gibbon by one of the 'maxims' which Gray seems to have intended to use in his poem on 'The Alliance of Education and Government': 'The different steps and degrees of education may be compared to the artificer's operations upon marble; it is one thing to dig it out of the quarry, and another to square it; to give it gloss and lustre, call forth every beautiful spot and vein, shape it into a column, or animate it into a statue' (Mason, p. 201n.).

23. *Memoirs*, p. 164.

24. Ibid., pp. 136, 180.

25. Ibid., p. 256.

26. Ibid., p. 140.

27. *Corres.*, I, 16 followed by quotations from I. 19, 39, 61, 66, 317; II, 520, 567, 666; and III, 1018.

28. Ibid., III, 1148. In fact Gray was to die of gout.

29. *Memoirs*, p. 2.

30. Ibid., p. 117.

31. Ibid., p. 159.

CLARENCE TRACY *Melancholy Marked*
*Him For Her Own**

Several years ago, when I was working for a few weeks in Cambridge, I had the pleasure of visiting in Pembroke College an acquaintance who was a senior fellow of that society. We had our coffee on his terrace so that I could admire the splendid quad, which was then gay with spring flowers, and when we had finished it my host said brightly: 'Would you like to see our storeroom?' Obviously being expected to say 'yes', I did so with as much enthusiasm as I could, but when we reached it, it did not look promising: concrete walls, naked lights, and steel files smelling of unsettled accounts and dead records. My host, apparently unaware of my feelings, reached down an oblong steel box and extracted from it a large bound volume that looked like a ledger, opened it, and put it into my hands. But when I saw the opened page, as Browning said, 'suddenly the worst turned the best to the brave'. For what I was holding was a manuscript of Gray's 'Elegy Written in a Country Churchyard', one of the three manuscripts of that poem that survive in the poet's hand. I recalled then that Gray had spent many years in Pembroke, walking the studious cloister's pale. My host also showed me some of Gray's voluminous and painstaking notes on his reading, which are treasured in the storeroom, as well as the college Buttery Books, which delighted me with their daily record of the charges Gray and his friends had run up for extra pints of beer. These made him a more agreeable figure than I had expected. But the most thrilling part of this experience was the sensation of holding in my hands an actual manuscript of one of the most famous and most beloved poems in our language.[1]

Gray had not expected the 'Elegy' to become famous; indeed he had not planned to publish it, and he affected to be indifferent to its fame.

* We are grateful to the Royal Society of Canada for permission to publish this paper which was first printed in the *Transactions of the Royal Society of Canada*, vol. IX (1971), 313-25.—Eds.

If he was surprised, he had every reason to be. For a popular poet, he was the oddest choice imaginable. Shy, bookish, and celibate, he lived a secluded life in Cambridge, mixing with only a small circle of friends, and avoiding the undergraduates and most of the fellows, whom he likened to the wild asses of the desert. Mason once remarked that his 'life was spent in that kind of learned leisure, which has only self-improvement and self-gratification for its object' (Mason, p. 335). He was, in fact, an academic introvert unconcerned about the world outside university walls, a man for whom the proper turn of an alcaic stanza was the most important thing in the world. His early poems were mainly in Latin, which it is said he wrote better than any English poet before him except Milton, and those in English were intricate structures of words, perfect in their china-shepherdess fashion, but not everybody's meat. Even the 'Elegy' is often Latinate in diction, and its word order must cause difficulties for readers not brought up on Virgil and Horace. But, in spite of these drawbacks, it at once hit the fancy of the poetry-reading public. The record of edition after edition in the twenty years following its publication in 1751 is alone evidence of its wide circulation, but there is more telling proof in the number of familiar quotations that it has given us. 'The paths of glory lead but to the grave', 'Full many a gem of purest ray serene', 'Some village-Hampden that with dauntless breast/The little tyrant of his fields withstood', 'Some mute inglorious Milton', 'Far from the madding crowd's ignoble strife' – these are merely a few of the lines that all remember. For once Gray had got on everybody's wave-length. As Johnson explained: 'The Church-yard abounds with images which find a mirror in every mind, and with sentiments to which every bosom returns an echo. . . . Had Gray written often thus, it had been vain to blame and useless to praise him' (*Lives*, III, 441-42). Posterity has endorsed the verdict.

How had Gray managed for once to catch the ear of the common reader, and what, in fact, did the 'Elegy' mean to him? A little investigation of its history, as of that of all enduring works of art, shows that it has not meant the same thing to different generations of readers. In Gray's time the sententious moralizing in the opening part made it popular, for moralizing was in fashion; the Miltonic diction, though a stumbling block for many of us, was also in vogue in an age in which Milton was idolized; and the macabre tone produced by the graveyard scenery and the moping owl was not uncongenial to readers who chose ruins and urns for their garden ornaments. The theme, of course, was commonplace, but that was no disadvantage in a time when the highest reach of poetry was to say 'What oft was thought but ne'er so well expressed'. So it is not hard to explain why the eighteenth century took the poem to its heart.

The nineteenth, while rejecting most great eighteenth-century poetry, made an exception in favour of the 'Elegy', which continued to be read and quoted. Before long it got into school readers, where it remained well into the twentieth century, and generations of children committed it to memory. But the nineteenth-century reader saw meanings in it that had not been apparent before. He saw in it a 'preromantic' poem – one that glorified the common man, the hardy peasant who, in spite of his short and simple annals, made up the backbone of the English character. A change was consequently made in the accentuation of a familiar line; where the eighteenth-century reader had declaimed 'The paths of glory lead but to the *grave*' his successor now read 'The paths of *glory* lead but to the grave'. For the former, the subject of the poem was the inevitability of death; for the latter it was a stern warning to the ruling classes. The great and the proud need to be brought down to earth and told of their fate. Their trophies and their monumental brasses will not put off for them the inevitable hour. So the poem was still beloved, but for a different reason, for a real or imagined anticipation of themes now familiar in Burns and Wordsworth. Arnold, the greatest of Victorian critics, completed the image of preromanticism by declaring that Gray, though the most minor of the great English poets, was greater than all other eighteenth-century poets, because he had almost spoken out, had almost opened his soul and delivered himself of things too deep for tears. The poem, in the course of a century, had thus almost completely changed its meaning.

Today neither of those meanings seems altogether wrong, and neither of them altogether right. Both have been largely abandoned while critics quarrel, pointing their fingers at obscurities and incoherences in Gray's text and inventing explanations for them. Some wonder what connection the second part of the poem, in which the poet seems to be writing about himself, has with the first. Others speculate that what fertilized Gray's imagination was the death either of his friend, Richard West, or of his beloved aunt, or of his uncle, or of the Jacobite lords who were executed on Tower Hill in August 1746, and that the real subject of the poem is one of those griefs. Still others invent ingenious explications of Gray's rhetorical ironies. One feels that earlier readers would have to blush, were they still on earth, for having loved the poem without noticing these problems. But our puzzlement over them is evidence not of superior critical perspicacity so much as of our having somewhere lost the clue. Allusions must be explained to us that eighteenth-century readers caught easily, and we are thrown off balance by transitions that came naturally to them. Moreover, earlier readers responded to the poem with their imaginations and hearts whereas we respond with our heads and our blue pencils.

At least our stance should give us objectivity and enable us to investigate unemotionally – if that is a good thing – what the poem does say. Let us begin with the obvious question: does it in fact glorify the peasantry at the expense of the gentry? Right away one balks at the improbability that Gray would have sided with the underdog, for his letters and the records of his life show little trace of a social conscience. He lived for years on public patronage, and his friend Mason made it a virtue in him that he never dirtied his mind with any intention of earning his living. Looking at the poem closely, however, one finds that although the initial subject is assuredly the common grave that awaits us all, he has subtly weighted the dice in favour of the peasantry. If he had wished to make only a general statement about death, he need not have dichotomized the race as he did into rich and poor. He provoked comparisons merely by setting up that polarity. Then almost everything that he wrote about the great is pejorative. The 'boast of heraldry' and 'the pomp of power', 'the shrine of Luxury and Pride' heaped 'With incense kindled at the Muse's flame' – those phrases may not have had the chilling sound in the eighteenth century that they have for us, but certainly they do not make me wish to take my place with the great as they freeze behind their black purgatorial rails. On the other hand, the poor, for all their grinding poverty, have compensations. Their 'cool sequestered vale of life' does not sound unattractive, and their 'sober wishes' are a welcome contrast to the vanity, cruelty, and hypocrisy of the rich. In fact, Gray used warmer colours for the poor. The three early stanzas in which he referred to their domestic affections and to the delightful music of the 'incense-breathing morn' in which they rise to go about their chores have no counterpart in his account of the rich. I do not know why he cancelled the exquisitely lovely later stanza in which he developed this theme further –

> There scatter'd oft, the earliest of the Year,
> By Hands unseen, are show'rs of Violets found;
> The Red-breast loves to build and warble there,
> And little Footsteps lightly print the Ground

– unless he felt that he had already overstressed it. Moreover even the longing for immortality in the poor is sincere and appealing, whereas in the rich it is only vanity and pride of life. Even in death the poor are not entirely still: the turf that covers them 'heaves ... in many a mouldering heap', and 'Ev'n from the tomb the voice of nature cries,/Ev'n in our ashes live their wonted fires.' By contrast, the rich are silent and stiff.

But the Victorians saw this bias in Gray too clearly, and we must guard ourselves against a similar overemphasis. The peasantry was only a secondary theme for Gray. All the glory he gave to the peasant amounts to no more than this: the narrowness of his lot in life prevents him from doing much harm. The mute inglorious Miltons of the village are frustrated, to be sure, but the potential Cromwells are also kept from being guilty of their country's blood and wading through slaughter to a throne. Better to spend one's life dully in the common round of rural duties, Gray implied, than run the risk of turning into a bloodthirsty tyrant. His view of human nature was as bleak as that; man is altogether inclined towards evil, and the more freedom of action you give him the more evil he is likely to do. Glorification of the peasantry? I hardly think so. Affirmation of the doctrine of total depravity, more likely.

In fact, the theme of the 'Elegy' is not so much love of the peasantry as estrangement from the gentry. He had felt this estrangement first, perhaps, at the time of his quarrel with Walpole, and though he forgave Walpole and forgot his grievances, he never ceased to be conscious that he did not belong to the great world. He was poor; he was an uncourtly scholar living a lonely life in a dull provincial town. He dwelt indeed in a sequestered vale, and his wishes had had to be sober even if he never suffered from real poverty. Others of his class, the poorer gentry, had climbed into affluence and power by hanging on to the coattails of the richer, but not Gray. He had chosen the low road, and wanted to defend that choice in this poem.

Gray's image of himself is made clear in the Epitaph which he appended to the later versions. Here are his words:

> *Here rests his head upon the lap of earth*
> *A youth to fortune and to fame unknown.*
> *Fair Science frowned not on his humble birth,*
> *And Melancholy marked him for her own.*
>
> *Large was his bounty and his soul sincere,*
> *Heaven did a recompence as largely send:*
> *He gave to Misery all he had, a tear,*
> *He gained from Heaven ('twas all he wished) a friend.*

No farther seek his merits to disclose,
Or draw his frailties from their dread abode,
(There they alike in trembling hope repose)
The bosom of his Father and his God.

(ll. 117-28)

Notice how it all began on that note of estrangement that I have mentioned: 'A youth to fortune and to fame unknown'. Fame, of course, later overtook him, but it never broke down the barriers between him and the brilliant world. Science (i.e. knowledge or education), he went on to say, was not denied him, in spite of his humble birth, and so his bounty (i.e. his blessings) was large. In addition to an education, he was given a friend – just one, but ' 'twas all he wished'. His soul, he told us, was sincere, and he had pity (if nothing more) for the poor. Most important of all, he was melancholy. I shall return to his melancholy presently, but before leaving it now, I must mention that Gray was melancholiac all his life and was perpetually talking about it. 'Low spirits are my true and faithful companions', he wrote to West in 1737; 'they get up with me, go to bed with me, make journeys and returns as I do; nay, and pay visits, and will even affect to be jocose, and force a feeble laugh with me; but most commonly we sit alone together, and are the prettiest insipid company in the world' (*Corres.*, I, 66). He was fond of calling it a 'white melancholy', and he listed it among the blessings that Heaven had bestowed upon him, not looking upon it as an affliction.[2] Clearly, he was on easy terms with it.

Many readers of the 'Elegy', as I mentioned earlier, are puzzled over how such a personal passage got tacked on to a poem the first part of which is an impersonal study of life and death. In the early draft of the poem, the Epitaph and the six highly personal stanzas preceding it were wanting; instead the poem concluded on an only mildly personal note in four stanzas that he later cancelled. That version was more coherent than the later one and more consistent in tone and theme; but it was less striking, and Gray evidently felt that he had not said in it all he had meant to say. In his revision, however, he created difficulties. In the first 92 lines he had mentioned himself only once, right at the start:

And leaves the world to darkness and to me.

(l. 4)

But his transition to the new personal conclusion begins:

For thee who, mindful of the unhonoured dead,
Dost in these lines their artless tale relate . . . .

(ll. 93-94)

Why did he now refer to himself in the second person singular, when his previous reference had been put into the first? Some critics are so bothered at the awkwardness of it that they look aside to see at whom else Gray might have been pointing. But nobody else is there. Further, who is the 'hoary-headed swain' who immediately afterwards appears out of nowhere to answer the enquiries of a 'kindred spirit' about Gray's career? Of a sudden there is a plethora of dramatis personae, all vaguely differentiated.[3] But most puzzling of all is the biographical sketch given of Gray by the swain:

> *Oft have we seen him at the peep of dawn*
> *Brushing with hasty steps the dews away*
> *To meet the sun upon the upland lawn.*
>
> *There at the foot of yonder nodding beech*
> *That wreathes its old fantastic roots so high,*
> *His listless length at noontide would he stretch,*
> *And pore upon the brook that babbles by.*
>
> *Hard by yon wood, now smiling as in scorn,*
> *Muttering his wayward fancies he would rove,*
> *Now drooping, woeful wan, like one forlorn,*
> *Or crazed with care, or crossed in hopeless love.*
>
> (ll. 98-108)

Identification with the peasantry here, if you will, but counterfeit; those are not peasant manners, nor were they Gray's. Some of it is not even very good poetry. It helps very little to explain that the lines are in the pastoral tradition and that they were required to ease the difficult transition from the opening part of the poem to the Epitaph.

The clue to this problem lies in a poem with which Gray was familiar, and which was much imitated in his time: 'Lycidas'. Milton mourned in it the death of a young man named Edward King, who had been up at Cambridge when he was, and with whom he had shared a way of life. Milton chose to express himself allegorically in the pastoral manner:

> *Together both, ere the high Lawns appear'd*
> *Under the opening eye-lids of the morn,*
> *We drove a field, and both together heard*
> *What time the Gray-fly winds her sultry horn,*
> *Batt'ning our flocks with the fresh dews of night,*
> *Oft till the Star that rose, at Ev'ning, bright*
> *Toward Heav'ns descent had slop'd his westering wheel.*[4]

There is the source of Gray's 'upland lawn' and 'peep of dawn', as well as of the pastoral convention and the general feel of the opening part of the speech of Gray's swain. Milton had even led into the passage in the same way Gray led into his: he had called on the muses to begin a lament for Lycidas, and had gone on:

> *So may som gentle Muse*
> *With lucky words favour my destin'd Urn,*
> *And as he passes turn,*
> *And bid fair peace be to my sable shrowd.*

> (ll. 19-22)

(That is, may some poet, when I am dead, do me the same favour and speak an epitaph over my corpse.) Gray imitated those lines exactly:

> *For thee* ...
> *If chance* [i.e. by chance] ...
> *Some kindred spirit shall inquire thy fate,*
> *Haply some hoary-headed swain may say* ....

> (ll. 93-97)

And so on to the Epitaph. Pointing out this source may not improve our opinion of Gray's lines, but it makes them easier to follow, and it explains why eighteenth-century readers, who generally knew their Milton better than readers today, were not troubled by the incoherences that trouble us. The pattern Gray was following had been imprinted on their minds by Milton.

But after this opening, Gray went off on a different tack from Milton. In 'Lycidas', when the sun set, there was flute music, folk song, and the dancing of satyrs and fauns. The students, in other words, were hotting it up! The scholarly life depicted by Milton had a good deal more vitality than that depicted by Gray, who shut his doors and windows more firmly than Milton ever did to exclude the sounds of academic revelry. The contrast is even greater with a third Cambridge scholar, A. E. Housman, who behind a front of academic reclusion, created an alter ego for himself in a country lout, to whom he gave a rich fantasy life of drunken brawls and fornications. But the student in Gray's poem, who is Gray himself, spent his whole day walking in the woods, muttering to himself and avoiding all human contact. One cannot for a moment imagine him, like the Shropshire lad, leaving his necktie 'God knows where'. His behaviour, indeed, is the very paradigm of that of the melancholiac.

Before one can understand what melancholy meant for Gray and what he was attempting to express in this part of the 'Elegy', one must investigate what Milton meant by it and what Miltonic associations the word had for Gray and other eighteenth-century readers of poetry. The place to go, of course, is Milton's 'Il Penseroso'. In reading it one must be careful not to strip off the allegory altogether in an attempt to read that rich and complex poem as if it were a prescription for a specific pattern of behaviour. But undoubtedly among other things it records a day in the life of a man living the contemplative life. It begins, like the 'Elegy', in the evening, with the melancholy man wandering alone through the woods, until he is driven indoors by the weather. The remainder of his night he devotes to reading books – Greek tragedy, Chaucer, the romances, even the magical works of Hermes Trismegistus. At dawn he goes outside again, and Milton's lines describing his actions recall the ones I have already quoted from 'Lycidas':

> *And when the Sun begins to fling*
> *His flaring beams, me Goddes bring*
> *To arched walks of twilight groves,*
> *And shadows brown that Sylvan loves*
> *Of Pine, or monumental Oake,*
> *Where the rude Ax with heaved stroke,*
> *Was never heard the Nymphs to daunt,*
> *Or fright them from their hallow'd haunt.*
> *There in close covert by som Brook,*
> *Where no profaner eye may look,*
> *Hide me from Day's garish eie,*
> *While the Bee with Honied thie,*
> *That at her flowry work doth sing,*
> *And the Waters murmuring*
> *With such consort as they keep,*
> *Entice the dewy-feather'd Sleep . . . .*

(ll. 131-46)

Those lines could no doubt be read in more ways than one, but their most profound meaning emerges when they are read, like the similar ones in 'Lycidas', as an allegory of the contemplative life. The allegory and the parallel with 'Lycidas' are made even more striking when Milton goes on:

> *But let my due feet never fail,*
> *To walk the studious Cloysters pale . . . .*

(ll. 155-56)

Milton was describing the life of a devotee totally absorbed in the task of gaining wisdom and heavenly insight into the mysteries of things through knowledge and self-discipline. It was the road of the mystic, leading to illumination:

> *And may at last my weary age*
> *Find out the peacefull hermitage,*
> *The Hairy Gown and Mossy Cell,*
> *Where I may sit and rightly spell*
> *Of every Star that Heav'n doth shew,*
> *And every Herb that sips the dew;*
> *Till old experience do attain*
> *To something like Prophetic strain.*

(ll. 167-74)

The ultimate reward is true poetic power, which, to Milton's romantic way of thinking, is mysterious and bardic. Certainly for Milton melancholy was not an affliction but a creative power – the means to truth and poetic inspiration. No wonder that in his opening lines he had said that divinest Melancholy wore black only to avoid blinding the weak eyes of mortals!

Gray's lines gain point when they are read against the background not only of 'Lycidas' but also of 'Il Penseroso'. I have already noted that when Gray wrote *'Melancholy marked him for her own'*, he did not brand melancholy as an affliction, but rather associated it with *Fair Science* as a part of his large bounty. It was Contemplation also that brought the kindred spirit to the spot, and the suggestion of the contemplative life in Milton's sense of the term is not lost on the reader of the 'Elegy'. Moreover, the second stanza in the speech of the hoary-headed swain is obviously derived from the lines in 'Il Penseroso' that I have just quoted:

> *'There at the foot of yonder nodding beech*
> *'That wreathes its old fantastic roots so high,*
> *'His listless length at noontide would he stretch,*
> *'And pore upon the brook that babbles by.'*

It is reasonable to believe, from these parallels with Milton, that Gray was meaning to allude through them to his own studious way of life and to justify in some measure his choice of academic seclusion, far from the madding crowds of London, as a means of achieving wisdom and inspiration. One recalls his obsessive and far ranging reading: classical literature and archaeology, Gothic architecture, Norse, Erse, Welsh, and Gaelic literature, music, and botany. One recalls his celibacy. And one recalls that in later years in his own poetry he strove after something of that prophetic strain that Milton had alluded to. In his last poem, moreover, his 'Ode for Music', written in 1769 to celebrate the installation of his patron, the Duke of Grafton, as Chancellor of the University, he called up Milton himself, who 'struck the deep-toned shell' and said:

'Ye brown o'er-arching groves,
'That Contemplation loves,
'Where willowy Camus lingers with delight!
'Oft at the blush of dawn
'I trod your level lawn,
'Oft wooed the gleam of Cynthia silver-bright
'In cloisters dim, far from the haunts of Folly,
'With Freedom by my side, and soft-eyed Melancholy.'

(ll. 27-34)

There in eight lines is the personal message of the 'Elegy' over again. It was Gray's constant theme.

Gray was often accused by his contemporaries of being obscure in his allusions, and although much less obscurity was found in the 'Elegy' than in other works, it may well be that he escaped censure in it because readers found so many other things to interest them. The allusions that I have been drawing out of the 'Elegy' are indeed obscure – private meanings that he had no right to expect the generality of his readers to understand. Even his friends, who knew what melancholy meant for him, must have felt that his presentation of the idea was pallid when they compared it with Milton's rapturous one. The explanation given by Matthew Arnold of Gray's failure to speak out on the grounds that he was living in an age hostile to poetry is no longer convincing. Gray was capable of speaking out and often did so. But the second half of the 'Elegy' is a failure not because Gray could not make himself clear but because he was not himself clear as to what he meant to say.

The fact, of course, is that the age of the illuminati was over. It was the age of Enlightenment. Men no longer tried to

> *unsphear*
> *The spirit of Plato to unfold*
> *What Worlds, or what vast Regions hold*
> *The immortal mind . . . .*[5]

It was the age of inductive reasoning, of Locke, of the Royal Society for the Advancement of Science, and, above all, of Newton. Gray himself as a young man had been a student of Locke's philosophy and at one time had tried to summarize it in an elaborate Latin poem called 'De Principiis Cogitandi'. Though in his later life one hears less in his writings about Locke, yet his meticulous note-taking, as I observed it in the book in the storeroom at Pembroke College, and his careful botanical observations all indicate empiricism rather than the semi-mysticism of Milton. He was an industrious student, rather than a prophet. Gray was not of the stuff out of which mystics are made. There is something theatrical and unconvincing about the prophetic strain in his later poems. He lacked Milton's sublime sense of mission. The third stanza in the speech of the hoary-headed swain contrasts oddly with Milton's lines:

'Hard by yon wood, now smiling as in scorn,
'Muttering his wayward fancies he would rove,
'Now drooping, woeful wan, like one forlorn,
'Or crazed with care, or crossed in hopeless love.'

(ll. 105-8)

Those have no counterpart in Milton, whose melancholy mood was self-reliant and optimistic. They refer instead to melancholy in the pyschiatrist's sense of the word – the craziness of the man who has gone over the edge through anxiety or unrequited love. They seem strangely out of place, and perhaps it is not far-fetched to say that they express Gray's sense of defeat in his quest for illumination. It is ironic that in the 'Ode for Music', when Milton is brought down by Gray from the 'realms of empyrean day' to make his speech, Newton himself bends down his head from the opened heavens, 'And nods his hoary head and listens to the rhyme' (l. 26). But he says nothing, and one may well wonder what he is thinking about and how those two ex-Cantabrigians – Newton and Milton – get on together in the other world. Was Gray aware of the gulf that separated them in the pattern of human thought? His failure to develop convincingly in the 'Elegy' the concept of the contemplative life may have been due to the impossibility for him of living according to Milton's plan in the age of rational scepticism.

The common reader, to whom in conclusion I must return, has expressed himself by choosing all the quotations so dear to his heart from the earlier part of the poem. Those superbly phrased generalities about life, death, and immortality have caught his attention and stuck in his memory. In a world in which so many millions of words are wasted daily, dying like ephemerids almost as soon as they are born, the marvellous thing is that so many of Gray's words are as fresh today as when they were first written. But the poet's private defence of his way of life has not often been understood, least of all by the common man. Even if it had been understood it would hardly have made much appeal and would make none at all today. Gray's ethic of withdrawal and non-commitment, his distrust of human nature, and his absorption in his own intellectual gratifications offend our uneasy social consciences. The poem, of course, is not nearly so widely read as it was even fifty years ago, and although it has long outlived the hundred years that Johnson fixed as enough to make a work a classic, it survives now only in a few lapidary phrases remembered out of context and only partly understood.

Acadia University

Notes

1. I had written this paper before I read Roger Lonsdale's authoritative commentary on the 'Elegy' in his *Poems of Thomas Gray, William Collins, and Oliver Goldsmith*. I am glad to have his support for several of my points, and where I differ from him, or go beyond him, I do so with apprehension. With another recent commentator, Morris Golden, I cannot agree so fully, especially with his statement that in the 'Elegy' Gray 'achieves the fusion of the species in the individual'. ('The Imagining Self in the Eighteenth Century', *Eighteenth-Century Studies* 3 [1969], 25.)

2. Roger Lonsdale (p. 139) reminds one that 'The favourable sense of "melancholy", implying a valuable kind of sensibility ... , was becoming fashionable', and cites parallels from James Thomson's 'Autumn' (1730) and T. Warton's 'Pleasures of Melancholy' (1747). The parallels between Gray and Milton on which I rely heavily are, of course, not original with me; many of the earliest critics and reviewers noticed them, but their logic has not before been fully obeyed.

3. Some critics have busied themselves with a Poet-Spokesman, a Stonecutter-Poet, a Kindred Spirit, a Swain, and a Friend, and have worked out an elaborate and unconvincing story-line for them all. Odell Shepard, 'A Youth to Fortune and to Fame Unknown', *Modern Philology* 20 (1923), 347-73; Herbert W. Starr, 'A Youth to Fortune and to Fame Unknown: A Re-estimation', *Journal of English and Germanic Philology* 48 (1949), 97-107; F. H. Ellis, 'Gray's "Elegy": The Biographical Problem in Literary Criticism', *Publications of the Modern Language Association of America* 66 (1951), 971-1008; Morse Peckham, 'Gray's "Epitaph" Revisited', *Modern Language Notes* 71 (1956), 409-11. John H. Sutherland, in his 'The Stonecutter in Gray's "Elegy" ', *Modern Philology* 55 (1957), 11-13, has brought us back to earth.

4. *The Poems of John Milton*, ed. H. Darbishire (London, 1961), p. 38.

5. Ibid., p. 426.

ARTHUR JOHNSTON | *Thomas Gray:*
Our Daring Bard

When Henry Fuseli at the age of twenty-four had been in England a little over eighteen months he wrote to a friend in Switzerland, in November 1765: 'The Englishman eats roast beef and plum pudding, drinks port and claret; therefore, if you will be read by him, you must open the portals of Hell with the hand of Milton, convulse his ear or his sides with Shakespeare's buskin or sock, raise him above the stars with Dryden's Cecilia, or sink him to the melancholy of the grave with Gray. Intermediate tones . . . send him to sleep.'[1] Although Fuseli – 'his temperament passionate and audacious, his mind acute and restless, his wit dazzling and ruthless, a delight and a terror to all who knew him'[2] – wrote grandiose unrhymed odes himself, he thought that Gray 'fell off, when he tried writing odes'. Ten years later, he wrote to Lavater that 'the English don't boast they have produced a poet yet in this century, unless it be Richardson. Thomson's tame catalogue . . . Young's pyramids of dough, Pope's metrical and rimed prose – they don't call them poetry by a long chalk.'[3]

For Fuseli, who thought of poets and artists in terms of giants and dwarfs, there were only Homer, Dante, Shakespeare, and Milton. But among the dwarfs was Gray, 'although he has written but little, that little is done well'.[4]

It is interesting that it was the 'Elegy', and not the Odes, that Fuseli regarded as having that element of the extreme that Shakespeare, Milton, and Dryden had, and which was necessary to impress an English reader.

For Blake, who for a time was a friend of Fuseli, Gray's boldness lay elsewhere. Describing his painting of 'The Bard' in 1809, Blake wrote: 'Weaving the winding sheet of Edward's race by means of sounds of spiritual music and its accompanying expressions of articulate speech is a bold and daring, and most masterly conception, that the public have embraced and approved with avidity. Poetry consists in these conceptions.'[5] Blake, who had only a limited verbal sensitivity, found boldness and daring in the conception of artistic energy, completely un-self-regarding, opposing the armed might of the tyrant.

Between Fuseli and Blake there was Johnson's commentary. Johnson was disapprovingly aware of Gray's daring. With his wide reading and tenacious memory, Johnson must have known that nothing in previous poetry had prepared him for 'The Bard', and certainly not Horace's ode on the prophecy of Nereus. In lightly accepting Algarotti's suggestion that 'The Bard' is an imitation of Horace's poem, Johnson is doing what he had condemned as a critical manoeuvre, in *Rambler* 143. There he had said that the charge of plagiarism was one commonly used 'when the excellence of a new composition can no longer be contested'. He had carefully shown that even a false accusation of this kind could be 'urged with probability' when even 'in books which best deserve the name of originals, there is little new beyond the disposition of materials already provided'. It was the very daring of the poem that made Johnson unwilling to be pleased – the revival of the fiction of prophecy, the 'fabulous appendages of spectres', the forsaking of the probable, the lack of 'any truth, moral or political', the conclusion with a suicide. But the boldness of Gray that Johnson with his usual percipience recognized, though without approval, lay in the area that Gray was most aware of – the language. Johnson at least pays Gray the tribute of verbal criticism. The language of the Spring ode is 'too luxuriant'. When Gray wrote 'honied spring' he was surely as aware as Johnson that he was giving a participial ending to an adjective derived from a noun, and that this was not something new, but Shakespearian and Miltonic. Gray, like Johnson, must have felt the 'violence both to language and sense' in calling Selima the cat *a nymph*, though Gray delighted in the violence. Johnson comments on Dryden's phrase, 'honey redolent of spring', that it is 'an expression that reaches the utmost limit of our language'; Gray, in making 'gales' 'redolent of joy and youth', 'drove it a little more beyond apprehension'. Gray, like Shakespeare, stands condemned by Johnson's sense of where 'the utmost limits of our language' are. Johnson's proprietary sense of our language leads him to condemn Gray's fondness for words 'arbitrarily compounded', such as 'many-twinkling'. He notices that the language of Gray's translations of Old Norse and Welsh poetry is 'unlike the language of other poets', that in the odes 'the language is laboured into harshness' and that Gray's mind 'seems to work with unnatural violence'. These comments surely imply a recognition of qualities in Gray's language that we must call 'daring' – even though Johnson told Boswell that Gray 'had not a bold imagination' (*Boswell's Life*, I, 402).

There are three kinds of boldness here. First there is Fuseli's recognition that the 'Elegy' is a poem of concentrated melancholia, a poem that deals with the human condition in its most fundamental term – the grave. The emblems on the title pages of the first twelve editions symbolize the poem's subject – *skull, bones, crown, bones, hour-glass, bones, spade, skull*.[6] James Langhorne, reviewing an imitation of the 'Elegy' in 1762, clearly read the poem in the same way: 'here is another Gentleman in black, with the same funereal face, and mournful ditty; with the same cypress in his hand, and affecting sentence in his mouth, viz. *that we must all die!*'.[7]

Gray's daring lay in part in being quick off the mark, in being up with the leaders of taste, in beating them to the post. However long their ancestry, Young's *Night Thoughts* (1742-45), Robert Blair's *Grave* (1743) and Harvey's *Meditations among the Tombs* (1746) are surprisingly clustered together, and Gray's 'Elegy' was certainly written between 1742 and 1750.[8] Gray's poem, in its memorable perfection, is the quintessence of this new taste, and so powerful that it tyrannized later poetasters.

There is much that is daring in the 'Elegy'. One aspect of it that we are less aware of today than Gray's contemporaries were is noticed by a writer in 1787. Commenting on the lines

> *Ev'n from the tomb the voice of nature cries,*
> *Ev'n in our ashes live their wonted fires.*

> (ll. 91-92)

he wrote: 'the last two lines of this stanza are somewhat ambiguous; neither the truths of revelation, nor the dictates of right reason, support the sentiments, or countenance the extravagant ideas they hold out. Well may they be said by the author of the criticism of this Elegy, to contain a position at which *Experience* revolts, *Credulity* hesitates, and even *Fancy* stares.'[9] One cannot write so about a timid imagination.

Blake's awareness of the daring of the concept of 'The Bard' is the most perceptive of the responses to Gray's boldness. For Blake is the only poet to recognize that here is the great assertion of the power of the poet and his imagination, comparable to Blake's own statement

> *I will not cease from Mental Fight,*
> *Nor shall my sword sleep in my hand*
> *Till we have built Jerusalem*
> *In England's green & pleasant Land.*

'Would to God that all the Lord's people were Prophets.'[10] Not 'Greek and Latin slaves of the sword', but a British bard in British scenery; not Brutus slaying the tyrant Caesar with a sword, but a poet, allied to the powers of nature and of the spirit world, destroying tyranny and evil by the poet's own powerful weapon, 'spiritual music'. Blake would have appreciated Gray's note on 'The Alliance of Education and Government', that the 'warlike Northern nations' 'revived the spirit of mankind' and 'restored them to their native liberty and equality'.[11] He would have wanted to add 'and fraternity' and so complete the revolutionary triad.

The third kind of daring, disapprovingly noticed by Dr. Johnson, Gray's boldness of language, requires more space than I can give it here, though fortunately it is not in doubt. Gray begins where a poet must begin, with an interest in words, and one that West thought too daring. In his letters Gray will astonish by his Shakespearian hit-or-miss – though usually hit – inventiveness. Such things as the sun rising over the sea – 'all at once a little line of insufferable brightness' *(Corres.*, II, 854n). Or writing to Brown about getting his room ready for his return to Cambridge: 'Pray let Bleek make an universal rummage of cobwebs, and massacre all spiders, old and young, that live behind window-shutters and books.'[12] There is linguistic daring in the 'universal rummage of cobwebs', if no other kind of daring in the sentence! Throughout the poems, if one can clear one's mind of familiarity, there is that incalculable element of strangeness that is characteristic of Gray. Waves creeping 'in lingering labyrinths', 'The Attic warbler *pours* her throat', the Zephyrs 'their gathered fragrance *fling*', 'the sunshine of the breast', a 'mute, inglorious Milton', 'papers and books, a huge imbroglio', Elizabeth's 'lyon-port', the sword of Conan mowing 'the crimson harvest of the foe'. One would hardly know where to stop, for Gray is daring in his use of unusual words no more than in his surprising use of the familiar – 'thoughts that breathe, and words, that burn'. He goes, of course, for his language to the most daring contexts in the most daring poets – Lucretius, Homer, Pindar, Shakespeare, Milton, Job, and Ezekiel.

But in considering Gray as 'our daring Bard' I am aware of another aspect of his work, which necessitates seeing that work as a whole. There is a sense in which the separate works of a poet are all fragments of one long poem. The poets we remember – and this is one reason why we remember them – have, however, a sense of form and unity, and break their work into organized fragments that we recognize as poems. Certainly in the eighteenth century the power of a poem's genre was intense – so intense that there was an inevitable longing for the 'loose, baggy monster' of a poem that would allow the poet to wander through subjects and styles. Young, in the *Night Thoughts*, deliberately meditated on life, death, and immortality, his method, he said, being 'rather imposed, by what spontaneously arose in the author's mind, on that occasion, than meditated or designed'.[13] Thomson in *The Seasons*, Akenside in *The Pleasures of Imagination*, Churchill in his satires, Robert Lloyd in his verse epistles, Smart in *Jubilate Agno*, Cowper in 'The Sofa', are all trying in their different ways to find ways of making poems that will allow them to talk of anything that interests them as thinking men. An interesting and unusual attempt was made by Thomas Otway in the seventeenth century. Writing in the varied verse of the free ode, in 'The Poet's Complaint of his Muse: or, A Satyr against Libells' (1680), he depicts himself as 'A wandring Bard, whose Muse was crazy grown',[14] and after a lengthy account of his life as a poet among poets whom he despised (a sort of 'Epistle to Arbuthnot' in the metre of the 'Immortality Ode'!), he goes on to a vision of the birth of libel, the civil war, and the departure of the Duke and Duchess of York into exile. We are accustomed to saying that a lyric mode cannot carry such disparate freight. And indeed to a poet such as Gray, who like Johnson was born a lyric poet, the habit of careful polishing of every part made the long poem impossible. But there is a sense in which it is true to say that the poems Gray wrote between June 1742 and June 1750, between the 'Ode on the Spring' and the 'Elegy', are finished segments of a single poem. When, however, one begins to show this in detail it becomes clear that the origins of the sequence and its culmination lie outside the work of that decade, and that there is an interesting development to be found in the whole body of work.

Gray wrote very little – a few original poems and a few translations. He wrote with difficulty, and would never, like many of his contemporaries, have settled down to a verse translation of some voluminous writer, Homer, Virgil, Statius, Lucan, or even of a lyric poet, Theocritus, Pindar, Horace, Tibullus. I assume that when Gray chose to translate a poem, it was because he could see in the original something that he himself wanted to express. Certainly, when West wanted to speak movingly to his Cambridge friends about his illness and his fears of an untimely death, he imitated an elegy of Tibullus and added a versified passage from one of Pope's letters. Gray's translations are never so close to his original that one cannot see him making his own poem out of the material. But there is always enough of the original to ensure that the poem is distanced.

If we look, for example, at his version of Propertius' *Elegies* III v, written in December 1738, we find a poem in which a young poet dedicates himself to the muse and to love. But he is aware of other possibilities – learning, which clearly attracts him but which he puts off until old age (though he spends the larger part of the poem describing this learning), and the nobler pursuit of the soldier. He ends by making very explicit what Propertius has said:

> *These soft, inglorious joys my hours engage;*
> *Be love my youth's pursuit and science crown my age.*
> *You, whose young bosoms feel a nobler flame,*
> *Redeem what Crassus lost and vindicate his name.*
>
> (ll. 55-58)

Crassus, the wealthy politician, was killed, with his son, leading an expedition against the Parthians in 53 B.C. For Gray in December 1738, the last couplet could well be an allusion to the clamour in England for a war with Spain, to protect British ships and to force Spain to compensate the South Sea Company for confiscations – redeeming what Crassus lost. But nothing hangs on the possibility of such an allusion. The important fact is that Gray is dissociating himself from the active life of the warrior, and selecting the withdrawn life of the poet and lover, the 'soft, inglorious joys', in a poem which includes thoughts about the transience of youth and pleasure and the coming of age and death. Two years earlier Gray had written facetiously to Walpole, 'if I cannot die like a Hero, let it be at least like a despairing lover' (*Corres.*, 1, 54). And he seems to have been very much aware of the contrast between the warrior and the 'silken son of dalliance'. It is there in Agrippina's description of Nero:

> *Has he beheld the glittering front of war?*
> *Knows his soft ear the trumpet's thrilling voice,*
> *And outcry of the battle? Have his limbs*
> *Sweat under iron harness? Is he not*
> *The silken son of dalliance, nursed in ease*
> *And pleasure's flowery lap?*
>
> ('Agrippina, A Tragedy', ll. 94-99)

And the passage of Shakespeare that came into his mind, in the famous letter to West of 8 April 1742, was the declaration of the warrior, Richard III:

> *But I, that am not shaped for sportive tricks,*
> *Nor made to court an amorous looking-glass:*
> *I, that am rudely stamped, and want love's majesty*
> *To strut before a wanton, ambling nymph.*
>
> (*Corres.*, I, 193)

Every word of that was a picture for Gray. It is the other side of the medal from that presented by Propertius, and was to be ultimately of more significance for Gray.

His version of the Propertius elegy is important in nearly all its detail. It was not merely the economy of a poet in love with the phrases he had culled that sent some of these early lines forward into his later verse. The couplet here

> *How flames perhaps, with dire confusion hurled,*
> *Shall sink this beauteous fabric of the world*
>
> (ll. 31-32)

suitably tightened appears in one of the last poems he wrote:

> *Till wrapped in flames, in ruin hurled,*
> *Sinks the fabric of the world.*
>
> ('Descent of Odin', ll. 93-94)

The image of 'The hissing terrors round Alecto's head' (l. 46) becomes, in the 'Ode to Adversity',

> *Not in thy Gorgon terrors clad,*
> *Nor circled with the vengeful band.*
>
> (ll. 35-36)

The torment in Hades, 'Famine at feasts and thirst amid the stream' (l. 51), becomes, in 'The Bard',

> *Fell Thirst and Famine scowl*
> *A baleful smile upon their baffled guest.*
>
> (ll. 81-82)

The fact that so much of the poem does go forward suggests the importance of it to Gray at the time when it was written.

In April 1742 he translated another Propertian elegy (IIi). The poem contains much the same kind of material, the poet choosing love yet describing also 'the hero's toil, the ranks of war' (l. 33). Here there is a youth who, in contrast to the youth of the later 'Elegy', is 'not unknown to fame' (l. 65). (As we shall see later, fame is an important topic for Gray.) While generally following Propertius, Gray elaborates the detail of some areas of his original. The poet imagines that he has lost his mistress, and as a result falls into an incurable decline and suddenly dies:

> *'Tis hard the elusive symptoms to explore:*
> *Today the lover walks, tomorrow is no more;*
> *A train of mourning friends attend his pall,*
> *And wonder at the sudden funeral.*
>
> (ll. 95-98)

This is hardly to be found in Propertius. But, dramatized, it becomes an element in the 'Elegy' later, when the youth, 'crazed with care, or crossed in hopeless love' is suddenly missed 'on the customed hill' and is borne 'through the church-way path'. Gray, like Propertius, ends the poem by imagining Maecenas chancing to pass the poet's tomb, reining in his horse, and, as he drops a tear, pronouncing the poet's epitaph:

> *When then my fates that breath they gave shall claim,*
> *When the short marble but preserves a name,*
> *A little verse, my all that shall remain,*
> *Thy passing courser's slackened speed retain*
> *(Thou envied honour of thy poet's days,*
> *Of all our youth the ambition and the praise!);*
> *Then to my quiet urn awhile draw near,*
> *And say, while o'er the place you drop a tear,*
> *Love and the fair were of his life the pride;*
> *He lived while she was kind, and, when she frowned,*
> > *he died.*
>
> (ll. 99-108)

This elegy of Propertius is as close an analogy as one is likely to find for the revised ending of the 'Elegy', which is anglicized and christianized Propertius. The most recent translator of Propertius, Mr. A. E. Watts, even echoes Gray here:

> *If chance should lead you near my tomb, stop there*
> *Your British chariot and rich-harnessed pair.*[15]

I am sure that if Gray could have read that he would have smiled and thought of Walpole.

Here in Propertius are many of the essential elements of Gray. The warrior and the lover would be familiar enough to him in Cambridge and London. One is reminded of the young Boswell coming to London twenty years later to get his commission and to make love. And of Boswell going to Oxford and on Monday 25 April 1763 meeting Richard Shepherd, a fellow of Corpus Christi College and author of *Odes Descriptive and Allegorical* (1761) and *The Nuptials* (1761), a didactic poem. Shepherd told Boswell that his fellowship 'kept him from active life, which was the sphere he loved most; in particular the Army'. Boswell sagely commented that 'Mr. Shepherd is exactly in the quiet serene life that is proper for him, and yet he has some fanciful ideas of the charms of the scarlet coat and the respect which is shown to a military man who has seen the world, as the phrase goes.'[16]

But even Adam Smith, professor of moral philosophy in Glasgow and author of *The Wealth of Nations*, thought 'that his friends had cut his throat in not allowing him to be a soldier'. Gray did not so mistake himself. But war and the warrior fascinated him. 'Some village-Cato', 'some Caesar', wading 'through slaughter to a throne', the 'thoughtless world' exalting 'the brave' and idolizing success, are aspects of the warrior that he cannot ignore. The 'charms of a scarlet coat' were surely in his mind when he wrote of the 'insect-youth' that 'some shew their gaily-gilded trim'. And he was poignantly aware of his own failure as lover also when he added:

> Thy joys no glittering female meets,
> No hive hast thou of hoarded sweets,
> No painted plumage to display.

('Ode on the Spring', ll. 45-47)

In 'A Long Story' it is significant that the ladies are seen as 'A brace of warriors' fully armed, while the poet is conveyed by the muses 'To a small closet in the garden'

> Where, safe and laughing in his sleeve,
> He heard the distant din of war.

(ll. 75-76)

Eight years have brought him to a full and amused acceptance of what Boswell diagnosed later for Mr. Shepherd, 'the quiet serene life that [was] proper for him'.

Selima the cat is destroyed by stretching out for what seem to be two angel forms dressed in 'scaly armour' of 'Tyrian hue'. The warrior attracts and repels Gray.

In his version of Propertius IIi, Gray had written that there was no cure for the unhappy lover. 'Here arts are vain, even magic here must fail' (l. 85). But in his role as Poet Gray in fact exercises the most potent magic, and in 'The Progress of Poesy' he celebrates its power.

> For ills unseen what remedy is found,
> Or who can probe the undiscovered wound?

(Elegies II i, ll. 91-92)

In the 'Progress' Gray answers:

> Enchanting shell! the sullen Cares
> And frantic Passions hear thy soft control.

(ll. 15-16)

The warrior is conquered by the poet.

> On Thracia's hills the Lord of War
> Has curbed the fury of his car,
> And dropped his thirsty lance at thy command.

(ll. 17-19)

Poetry is magic, 'thy magic lulls the feathered king' (l. 21),

> *Quenched in dark clouds of slumber lie*
> *The terror of his beak and lightnings of his eye.*
>
> (ll. 23-24)

Poetry controls, lulls, commands. In love, poetry — but Gray is not sure here. The 'rosy-crowned Loves' dance, and Venus glides regally among them,

> *O'er her warm cheek and rising bosom move*
> *The bloom of young desire and purple light of love.*
>
> (ll. 40-41)

But in Chile poetry's civilizing and liberating influence is felt in the poems on 'feather-cinctured chiefs and dusky loves' (l. 62), and when poetry revives in Elizabethan England its subject-matter is 'Fierce war and faithful love' ('The Bard', l. 126).

In 'The Bard' and the translations from Old Norse and Welsh, the attraction of the warrior is paramount. In 'The Bard' poetry is again magic:

> *Mountains, ye mourn in vain*
> *Modred, whose magic song*
> *Made huge Plinlimmon bow his cloud-topped head.*
>
> (ll. 32-34)

But whereas, in 1742, in the sonnet on the death of West, nature was portrayed as indifferent to the poet's grief, in this poem nature may mourn in vain, but it does mourn. The army of Edward represents political oppression, in which the arts cannot flourish, the arts which Gray had defined, in notes prepared for his poem on 'The Alliance of Education and Government', as 'eloquence, policy, morality, poetry, sculpture, painting, architecture'. As he showed in those notes, Gray's ideal in a society is a combination of 'contemplation and pleasure' with 'courage and discipline', or of 'hardship, action and war' with 'civility, politeness, and works of genius'. The citizen of a country without freedom is 'selfish and base-minded' (*Poems*, pp. 90-91). Gray has no one-sided attitude towards war and the warrior. He uses the image in 'The Progress of Poesy' in a significant passage when he wants to give his most profound statement of the value of poetry:

> *Man's feeble race what ills await,*
> *Labour, and penury, the racks of pain,*
> *Disease, and sorrow's weeping train,*
> *And death, sad refuge from the storms of fate!*
>
> (ll. 42-45)

Here is the Gray of the 'Spring Ode', the 'Eton College Ode', the 'Ode to Adversity' and the 'Elegy'. But he goes on:

> *The fond complaint, my song, disprove,*
> *And justify the laws of Jove.*
> *Say, has he given in vain the heavenly Muse?*
> *Night and all her sickly dews,*
> *Her spectres wan and birds of boding cry,*
> *He gives to range the dreary sky:*
> *Till down the eastern cliffs afar*
> *Hyperion's march they spy and glittering shafts of war.*

(ll. 46-53)

His note to this in 1768 merely explains the use of the images of night and Hyperion: 'To compensate the real and imaginary ills of life, the Muse was given to Mankind by the same Providence that sends the Day by its chearful presence to dispel the gloom and terrors of the Night' (*Poems*, p. 167n). The benevolent association of 'the glittering shafts of war' with Day and Hyperion is explained in a note for 'The Alliance of Education and Government':

> Those invasions of effeminate Southern nations by the warlike Northern people, seem (in spite of all the terror, mischief, and ignorance which they brought with them) to be necessary evils; in order to revive the spirit of mankind, softened and broken by the arts of commerce, to restore them to their native liberty and equality, and to give them again the power of supporting danger and hardship; so a comet, with all the horrors that attend it as it passes through our system, brings a supply of warmth and light to the sun, and of moisture to the air. (*Poems*, p. 91)

It is characteristic of the way in which Gray's poems are linked to each other that the phrasing of the lines in 'The Progress of Poesy' should have been suggested by two lines in Cowley's 'Ode to Brutus':

> *Or seen her* [i.e. morning's] *well-appointed Star*
> *Come marching up the* Eastern Hill *afar.*

For Cowley's ode is in praise of the opponent of the tyrant Caesar. Dr. Johnson would presumably have seen the 'truth, moral and political' which Cowley makes explicit in his poem:

> *From thy strict rule some think that thou didst swerve*
> *(Mistaken, Honest men) in Caesar's blood;*
> *What* Mercy *could the* Tyrant's *life deserve*
> *From him – who kill'd* Himself *rather than* serve?[17]

Gray's Bard is here in embryo, and shows more 'moral' than Brutus. The

Bard may 'kill himself rather than serve', but it is inexorable Providence that destroys Edward and the house of Plantagenet.

The 'nightly fears' that beset 'the secret soul' of Edward, after his massacre of the bards and conquest of their country, will not be kept at bay by helm and hauberk, nor even by the tyrant's 'virtues'. Edward's virtues and his qualities as a warrior are disparate, as they were not in 'Brave Urien'. Nor, though Edward III and the Black Prince are unwitting victims of the curse that is visited even to the seventh generation, are these warriors seen unsympathetically. Edward III is 'the scourge of heaven', the 'Mighty victor, mighty lord', one of those 'warlike Northern people' who seem 'to be necessary evils'. And when the Tudors ascend the throne they are accompanied by 'many a baron bold' and their poets celebrate 'Fierce war'.

Gray has come a long way from 'soft inglorious joys' and

> You, whose young bosoms feel a nobler flame,
> Redeem what Crassus lost and vindicate his name.

('Translation from Propertius, *Elegies* III v', ll. 57-58)

And his Bard is far from the inglorious poet hidden in a garden closet

> Where, safe and laughing in his sleeve,
> He heard the distant din of war.

('A Long Story', ll. 75-76)

And from the youth, 'to fortune and to fame unknown', whose epitaph records his learning, his melancholia, his generosity, his sympathy, his friendship. The withdrawn, inactive, luxuriating figure is replaced by the defiant, involved poet, for whom poetry is a kind of action, superior to that of the warrior. The erotic, heterosexual lover that Gray had found attractive in Propertius for a short time had never become a role that Gray could play. The 'kindred-spirit' and the friend he found are clearly masculine. In the poems of the 1750s the poet is a man lamenting 'my friend, my Hoel', or his 'Dear lost companions'. To express his love for them Gray transforms the words that Brutus used to his wife Portia:

> As dear to me as are the ruddy drops
> That visit my sad heart ....[18]

becomes 'Dear as the ruddy drops that warm my heart' ('The Bard', l. 41).

Gone is the self-indulgent poet who imagines himself dead and being remembered by patron or friend. Gone is the poet of *memento mori*, longing to warn men of the inevitability of suffering and death. Now the poet is a kind of warrior, in those Norse poems that were surely for Gray examples of the poetry of 'the warlike Northern people'. In 'The Fatal Sisters' he is weaving 'the crimson web of war', his 'Songs of joy and triumph' raise 'Clouds of carnage' that 'blot the sun', as Edward I thought that the 'sanguine cloud' raised by his breath 'had quenched the orb of day'. In 'The Descent of Odin' he is 'a Warrior's son', braving the 'dog of darkness' whose jaws are filled with carnage. The magic of poetry is his, 'father of the powerful spell'.

> *Thrice he traced the runic rhyme;*
> *Thrice pronounced, in accents dread,*
> *The thrilling verse that wakes the dead.*
>
> (ll. 22-24)

And if Gray read this Norse poem as Mason did, and thought of the virgins with flaxen tresses and snowy veils as the Norns, signifying Past, Present, and Future, then Gray's sense of the poet as prophet, which is present in 'The Bard', is reinforced.

It is a short step to Blake's

> *Hear the voice of the Bard!*
> *Who Present, Past, & Future, sees . . . .*[19]

In 'The Triumphs of Owen' Gray is celebrating an early British defiance of invasion, a warrior who preserved British liberty and freedom by his prowess. The heroes of classical Greek and Roman history are replaced by a British hero, acting, as the Bard does, in British scenery. Owen's qualities as a warrior defending his country's freedom are not separate from his qualities as a man; he is swift and strong, the centripetal point of the battle, the source of courage in other men, but also

> *Lord of every regal art,*
> *Liberal hand and open heart.*
>
> (ll. 7-8)

And finally, in the extracts he chose so carefully from the passages of the 'Gododdin' in Evan Evans's *Dissertatio de Bardis*, Gray has examples of the British Bard as the sole survivor of a warlike and poetic band. The weight is on him now to do what a poet can do. Not to act as a warrior, but to draw to himself the qualities of the warrior that are admirable; to act out his elegiac role, Hyperion-like dispelling gloom because his lament is an affirmation of noble qualities – 'Too, too secure in youthful pride', 'He asked no heaps of hoarded gold', decked with 'Chains of regal honour', 'Flushed with mirth and hope'. Here is no selfishness, no base-mindedness, but generous confidence and love. The surviving poet may be 'the meanest of them all'[20] but it is his sacred task to preserve the fame of the happy warrior:

> *Sacred tribute of the bard,*
> *Verse, the hero's sole reward.*
>
> ('Conan', ll. 3-4)

Such poems, preserving a warrior's fame, embody the ideals that a society needs. It was a topic that Gray expounded in one of his notes for the poem on 'Education and Government': 'Many are the uses of good fame to a generous mind: it extends our existence and example into future ages; continues and propagates virtue, which otherwise would be as short-lived as our frame; and prevents the prevalence of vice in a generation more corrupt than our own' (*Poems*, p. 91). As he wrote in another note, 'One principal characteristic of vice in the present age is the contempt of fame' (p. 91). And this for Gray was a sign of a nation ill-governed.

The concept of the poet shown in the poems written between 1752 and 1761 grows naturally if surprisingly from the opposing concepts he had entertained from 1738 to 1750, from the poet as hidden and remembered only by a kindred spirit, to the poet as the sole surviving voice of liberty and virtue, from the poet as *memento mori* to the poet as celebrator of the noble dead, from the poet 'at ease reclined in rustic state', to the anguished poet 'With haggard eyes' on a rock 'o'er old Conway's foaming flood', from the poet as a 'silken son of dalliance' to the poet as mental warrior. His pattern of life still urged him to leave 'church and state to Charles Townshend and Squire' ('Sketch of his Own Character', 1.6), but he did in fact write 'The Candidate' and the lines on Lord Holland's Seat. Even though he dare not publish them, he left them about, doubtless half hoping that like his other works they would creep into print. Gray, like Cowley, loved 'his old hereditary trees'. Sandwich and Holland, he would have said, had no country; they were therefore selfish and base-minded; they had no family, no posterity, no desire for fame – or if they had, one that turned not on its proper subject.

'Our daring Bard' is not, of course, Gray's description of himself. His words are

> *Oh! lyre divine, what daring spirit*
> *Wakes thee now?*
> ('Progress of Poesy', ll. 112-13)

'Our daring Bard' is Samuel Johnson, who so describes himself in 1749 in the prologue to his tragedy of *Irene,* a play which shows how a Sultan proves to his soldiers that he has not lost all manhood in the delights of love, by slaying his beautiful Greek slave, Irene. Here is, in another version, the story of the lover and the soldier, of moral struggle and the corruption resulting from absolute power. Gray in 1749 was learning what Johnson's prologue states:

> *Ye glitt'ring train! whom lace and velvet bless,*
> *Suspend the soft solicitudes of dress;*

> *From grov'ling business and superfluous care,*
> *Ye sons of avarice! a moment spare:*
> *Vot'ries of fame and worshippers of pow'r!*
> *Dismiss the pleasing phantoms for an hour.*
> *Our daring bard with spirit unconfin'd,*
> *Spreads wide the mighty moral for mankind.*
> *Learn here how Heav'n supports the virtuous mind,*
> *Daring, tho' calm; and vigorous, though resign'd.*
> *Learn here what anguish racks the guilty breast,*
> *In pow'r dependent, in success deprest.*
> *Learn here that peace from innocence must flow;*
> *All else is empty sound, and idle show.*[21]

University College of Wales, Aberystwyth

Notes

1. E. C. Mason, *The Mind of Henry Fuseli* (London, 1951), p. 111.
2. Ibid., p. 15.
3. Ibid., p. 114.
4. Ibid., p. 343.
5. Blake, *Descriptive Catalogue of Pictures* (London, 1809), p. 35.
6. See Lyle Glazier, 'Gray's *Elegy*: "The Skull beneath the Skin"', in *Twentieth-Century Interpretations of Gray's Elegy*, ed. H. W. Starr (Englewood Cliffs, 1968), p. 40.
7. *Monthly Review*, xxvi (1762), 356.
8. Blair says that he wrote most of *The Grave* before he was ordained in 1731. See 'Life of Blair', in *Works of the British Poets*, ed. R. Anderson (Edinburgh, 1793-1807), viii, 853.
9. [G. Wright], *The Grave, by Robert Blair, to which are added Gray's Elegy . . . with notes, critical and explanatory* (1787).
10. 'Milton', *The Complete Writings of William Blake*, ed. G. Keynes (London, 1966), p. 481.

11. For the text of Gray's notes for 'The Alliance of Education and Government', see *Poems*, pp. 90-91.

12. *Corres.*, II, 740. Although the verb 'to rummage', meaning 'to search', is common from the late sixteenth century, the noun, as Gray uses it here, is first used by Horace Walpole in a letter in 1753, according to the *OED*.

13. 'Preface', *Night Thoughts on Life, Death, and Mortality* (London, 1806).

14. *The Works of Thomas Otway*, ed. J. C. Ghosh (Oxford, 1968), II, 405.

15. *The Poems of Propertius*, trans. by A. E. Watts (London, 1966), p. 71. Gray was unusual in translating Propertius. Very little of Propertius was translated before John Nott's version in 1782.

16. *Boswell's London Journal, 1762-1763*, ed. F. A. Pottle (London, 1950), p. 248.

17. *Poems of Abraham Cowley*, ed. A. R. Waller (Cambridge, 1905), pp. 196, 195.

18. *Julius Caesar*, II, i. 289-90.

19. 'Introduction', *Songs of Experience*, Keynes, p. 210.

20. 'The Death of Hoel', II. 5, 8, 14, 19, and 23.

21. *The Yale Edition of the Works of Samuel Johnson*, ed. W. J. Bate and others (New Haven and London, 1958-), VI, 111.

ROGER LONSDALE | *Gray and Johnson:*
The Biographical Problem

The basic facts about the relationship between Thomas Gray and Samuel Johnson can be presented so rapidly that at first sight it may appear that there was never sufficient contact between them to reach the stage of becoming problematical. The closest they came to meeting was in 1769, according to a familiar anecdote preserved by Sir Egerton Brydges. Gray and his young Swiss friend Bonstetten were walking in London one day when they became aware that 'a large uncouth figure was rolling before them, upon seeing which Gray exclaimed, with some bitterness, "Look, look, Bonstetten! – the great bear! – There goes *Ursa Major!*" This was Johnson: Gray could not abide him.'[1]

Gray's bitterness at the sight of Johnson is not explained. His other statements about his great contemporary can be quickly summarized. In a letter to his friend Horace Walpole in 1748 Gray rather patronizingly praised Johnson's 'Prologue on the Opening of Drury Lane Theatre' as 'far from bad', but he also described 'London' as 'one of those few imitations, that have all the ease and all the spirit of an original' (*Corres.*, I, 295). The only other relevant information comes from the Rev. Norton Nicholls, a close friend of Gray in the 1760s, who recorded that the poet 'disliked Doctor Johnson, & declined his acquaintance; he disapproved his style, & thought it turgid, & vicious; but he respected his understanding, & still more his goodness of heart; – I have heard him say that Johnson would go out in London with his pockets full of silver & give it all away in the streets before he returned home' (*Corres.*, III, 1290). It is not clear whether Nicholls meant that Gray literally 'declined' to make Johnson's acquaintance (as Horace Walpole was to do) or that Gray merely made no positive effort to meet him. Spending so much of his life in Cambridge, Gray was not often in the vicinity of Johnson, although he could easily have sought him out when he was in London working at the British Museum between 1758 and 1760, at the end of the decade which made both men famous.

It will already be clear that the subject of this enquiry is not exactly a fruitful literary relationship. These two great men, the best known and most admired literary figures in England in the later eighteenth century, did not meet or correspond, and each expressed dislike of the other. Yet this very lack of communication between them is surely so striking as to deserve further investigation. Out of the rather miscellaneous and even trivial information which must be examined something may emerge not merely about Gray's reputation in the decades following his death two hundred years ago, but also about the conflict between Johnson's reaction to Gray and the taste of most of his contemporaries.

James Boswell offers himself as a convenient guide to what Gray meant both to Johnson and to the sophisticated reader in the 1760s. Gray's two 'Pindaric' Odes had met a rather mixed reception when they appeared in 1757, but by the time Boswell arrived in London for his memorable visit five years later 'The Progress of Poesy' and 'The Bard' were well on the way to becoming essential reading for men of taste. Boswell, still in his early twenties, had yet to meet Johnson, but he already possessed all the right feelings about Gray's poetry. On Christmas Day 1762 he joined in the conversation at Tom Davies's bookshop with Robert Dodsley the publisher and Oliver Goldsmith ('a curious, odd, pedantic fellow with some genius', Boswell noted). Goldsmith lamented the decline of English poetry from the great days of Dryden and Pope. Dodsley dutifully defended the contemporary contributors to his own famous *Collection of Poems*. And Boswell also eagerly challenged Goldsmith:

> BOSWELL "And what do you think of Gray's odes? Are not they noble?" GOLDSMITH "Ah, the rumbling thunder! I remember a friend of mine was very fond of Gray. 'Yes,' said I, 'he is very fine indeed; as thus –
>
> > Mark the white and mark the red,
> > Mark the blue and mark the green;
> > Mark the colours ere they fade,
> > Darting thro' the welkin sheen.'
>
> 'O, yes,' said he, 'great, great!' 'True, Sir,' said I, 'but I have made the lines this moment.' " BOSWELL 'Well, I admire Gray prodigiously. I have read his odes till I was almost mad.' GOLDSMITH 'They are terribly obscure. We must be historians and learned men before we can understand them.'[2]

Goldsmith's distaste was characteristic. He had been an early and grudging reviewer of Gray's Odes in 1757 and he consistently disparaged them and their imitators, no doubt heartened by the knowledge that his friend Johnson shared his attitude.[3] Boswell had now, in fact, encountered the views of the Johnson camp, if so sparsely occupied a position can be so described. Boswell realized this for himself a few months later. Not long after meeting Johnson in May 1763 he recorded his new hero's opinion of Gray, which he had no doubt eagerly sought: 'Sir, I do not think Gray a superior sort of person. He has not a bold imagination, nor much command of words. The obscurity in which he has involved himself will not make us think him sublime. His *Elegy in a Churchyard* has a happy selection of images, but I don't like his great things.' Johnson went on to criticize the abruptness of 'The Bard', using arguments and examples which were to reappear in the 'Life of Gray' some two decades later.[4]

The difference in literary taste between their generations (Johnson was some thirty years older than Boswell) is well brought out in the attitudes of the two men to Gray's poetry. It seems not to have been noticed that, even after hearing Johnson's uncompromising opinion, Boswell apparently held Johnson and Gray in something like equal esteem for a considerable period. When Boswell left London for Holland in August 1763, his friend William Temple presented him with a volume of the poems of William Mason, Gray's Cambridge friend and later his biographer, and a poet often linked with Gray as a lyric poet. Boswell in turn presented Temple with Gray's poems. He was later to recall the period when he and Temple had 'sat up all night at Cambridge and read Gray with a noble enthusiasm, when we first used to read Mason's *Elfrida*, and when we talked of that elegant knot of worthies, Gray, Mason, Walpole, &c.' Before long Temple was writing excitedly to tell Boswell that he had actually met Gray at Cambridge and had found him to be not merely a great poet but 'the best bred man and the most agreeable companion in the world'. (There may also have been an implicit contrast with Boswell's new friend, since Temple had met Johnson previously and had found him 'surly, morose, dogmatical, imperious'.) Boswell was impressed. He wrote back declaring loyally that 'Mr. Johnson is ever in my thoughts', but he also carefully urged Temple to cultivate the friendship of Gray, 'that when I return to dear England you will present me to him'. In the next few months there are many reverent references to Gray in Boswell's letters and journals: 'The contemplation of such a man must rouse every noble principle. . . . A genius like his can seldom arise to show humanity how high it may be'; 'Long live the bard of sublimity'; he congratulates Temple on having 'so great a bard' as his friend and counsellor; 'I revere Mr. Gray', he writes in December 1763. He plans to imitate Gray by keeping a commonplace book and Gray also, rather curiously, becomes a model for conduct: 'Be Gray. Be *retenu* and worship God. Think.' In Berlin in July 1764 he lists Gray with Johnson and Pitt as 'nobler beings'.[5]

After his return to England Boswell asked Temple for an introduction to Gray but was evidently unable to use it. But all his veneration for the poet is expressed in a letter to David Garrick in September 1771, shortly after Gray's death:

> I am affected with much melancholy on the death of Mr. Gray. His *Elegy* . . . has been long like a part of myself; and many passages in his other poems glance across my soul with a most enlivening force. I never saw Mr. Gray; but my old and most intimate friend, the Reverend Mr. Temple, Rector of Mamhead in Devonshire, knew him well. He knew his foibles; but admired his genius and esteemed his virtues. I know not if you was acquainted with Mr. Gray. He was so abstracted and singular a man, that I can suppose you and him never having met.[6]

By this stage Boswell had gathered from Temple that Gray was a more complex personality than had at first been apparent. Yet he was enthusiastically responsible for the publication in the *London Magazine* of a 'Character' of Gray which Temple had sent him and he was never to lose his sense of excitement over what he had called the 'elegant knot of worthies'. This is clear from his later account of meetings with Mason and Walpole, even when they expressed their dislike of Johnson to his face. A striking example occurred on Christmas Day 1785 after Boswell had met Mason in York Minster: he sat through a tirade against Johnson at Mason's dinner-table but was more than mollified to be told that 'Mr. Gray had read my *Account of Corsica* with great pleasure. This flattered me highly.'[7] Boswell would no doubt have been less enthusiastic had he known that in 1768 Gray had in fact cited the book in a letter to Walpole as evidence of 'what I have always maintained, that any fool may write a most valuable book by chance, if he will only tell us what he heard and saw with veracity' (*Corres.*, III, 1019).

Boswell is an early and well-documented case of the predicament which was to become common in the 1780s, when those who wished to admire both Johnson and Gray found themselves caught in a painfully polarized situation. To the end of his life Boswell never really knew why

Johnson felt so intensely about the Cambridge poet whom he had never met. In March 1790, when his *Life of Johnson* was already in the press, he wrote to Joseph Warton: 'If you can recollect the origin of Johnson's prejudice against Gray's poetry, pray let me have it.' But Warton could suggest only that Johnson's 'strange aversion' to Gray sprang from the confinement of his taste to 'that sort of poetry, that deals chiefly, in nervous, pointed, sentimental, didactic Lines'.[8] Such a purely literary explanation hardly accounts for the growing intensity of Johnson's reaction to the very mention of Gray's name in the years after the poet's death. The knowledge that William Mason had undertaken a biography of his friend came as exciting news to those like Boswell who admired both poets. He mentioned the forthcoming biography of Gray to Johnson in March 1772 and the response was ominous: 'I think we have had enough of [Gray].'[9] When Mason's *Memoirs of Gray* finally appeared in 1775, Boswell was highly elated, as he told Temple, that 'a character drawn by you should be placed by the hands of Mason upon the top of Gray's pyramid as a suitable apex':[10] in other words, that Mason had concluded his biography by reprinting Temple's account of Gray's character from the *London Magazine*. As so often, Boswell found himself on treacherous ground. Mason was not very gratified when Boswell revealed to him that the author of this 'character' of Gray was a friend of a friend of Johnson.[11] And Johnson himself soon felt obliged to repress Boswell's renewed enthusiasm for the poet.

On 28 March 1775 Boswell dined with Johnson at Mr. Thrale's: 'Mr. Johnson attacked Mr. Gray, and said he was a dull fellow. I said he was reserved and might appear dull in company. But surely he was not dull in his poetry, though he might be extravagant. "No, Sir", said Mr. Johnson. "He was dull in company, dull in his closet, dull everywhere. He was dull in a new way, and this made many people think him great. He was a mechanical poet.'[12] A few days later we find Johnson warmly and provocatively praising the 'Odes to Obscurity and Oblivion' published in 1760 by Robert Lloyd and George Colman as parodies of Mason and Gray. He also sneered at Mason's admired *Elfrida*, which, he said, contained 'now and then some good imitations of Milton's bad manner'. Boswell elaborately disowned these views when he printed them in the *Life of Johnson* in 1791 but one exchange in this conversation he could not bring himself to include even then. Talking of Pope's quarrels with the Dunces, Boswell had declared: 'They could not have a malignity against Pope without knowing him.' And Johnson had replied: 'Yes, Sir, very well. I hate Gray and Mason, though I do not know them.'[13]

Thomas Campbell recorded a conversation a few days later in which Boswell led Johnson to talk about Gray's poetry and put him into an inevitable bad temper.[14] Repeatedly in 1775 we find Johnson dismissing Gray and his biographer as 'but dull' and he was still at it when Boswell met him again in April 1776. Johnson was now letting it be known that he thought Akenside a better poet than either Gray or Mason. At about the same period Bennet Langton heard Johnson describe Gray's Odes as 'forced plants, raised in a hot-bed; and they are poor plants; they are but cucumbers after all'.[15]

Although more evidence could be adduced, it will already be clear that the terms in which Johnson wrote about Gray as both man and poet in the *Lives of the Poets* a few years later were perfectly consistent with the opinions he had been expressing so vehemently in private for almost two decades. His attitude can hardly be explained away as mere over-reaction to Boswell's enthusiasm for Gray, although an element of the same irritation as, for example, in his dismissal of Boswell's enthusiasm for the Corsicans may have been present. The tone of his pages on Gray in 1781 is provocatively ironic and even contemptuous in a manner which is rarely paralleled elsewhere in the *Lives*. Johnson admitted to some respect for Gray's intellect and learning, but he hardly bothered to disguise his contempt for the life Gray chose to lead at Cambridge or for much of his poetry, which seemed to Johnson to have precisely the characteristics he would have expected from so fastidious an aloofness from the real world. He explicitly dissociated himself from the 'zeal of admiration' for Gray in Mason's biography; mocked the early readers of the two Odes who had been deluded by stupidity or a desire to be fashionable into admiring them; praised the 'ingenuity' of the Lloyd-Colman parodies once more; and, above all, engaged in a detailed analysis of much of the poetry which is virtually satiric in tone. Like Mason he reprinted William Temple's generally eulogistic account of Gray, but with the dubious comment that he was 'as willing as his warmest well-wisher to believe it true', indicating that he neither believed it to be true nor counted himself as a well wisher (*Lives*, III, 429).

Johnson himself said very little that is particularly revealing about his attack on Gray. When Boswell met him in March 1781 he could not resist raising the matter: 'I said to the Doctor he might have been kinder to Gray. He very justly said he could not be kind. He was entrusted with so much truth. He was to tell what he thought; and if people differed from him, they were to tell him so.'[16] They did not hesitate to tell him so. The uproar, the cries of mingled pain and rage, sound clearly enough across the years.[17] To many readers who admired both Johnson and Gray the shock caused by the *Lives of the Poets* was intense. Egerton Brydges, who was about twenty at the time, later recalled that 'their captiousness, their hardness, their awkward humour, their affected raillery, and capricious contempt, seemed like the burst of discordant sounds upon fairy dreams'.[18] The first reviewers of the *Lives* in 1781-82 clearly respected and admired Johnson's total achievement as critic and biographer, but only the *Critical Review* had any sympathy for the assault on Gray and even this reviewer admitted that Johnson had 'boldly steered against the tide of popular opinion, by calling in question the transcendent excellence of our modern Pindar'.[19] The *Gentleman's Magazine* deplored Johnson's use of carping verbal analysis to 'fritter away' the beauties of the Odes, and other contributors in the correspondence pages of the magazine sound genuinely shocked and personally wounded by Johnson's attack.[20] Edmund Cartwright in the *Monthly Review* thought Johnson's discussion of 'The Progress of Poesy' 'a continued tissue of misrepresentation', his manner as a whole 'not only hostile, but malignant', his motive explicable only as 'a dogmatical spirit of contradiction to received opinions'.[21] The *London Magazine* was baffled: 'Some unknown prejudice has warped the judgement of the critic upon this occasion.'[22]

Gray's confessed champions had soon organized themselves, the way being led by the anonymous author of *A Cursory Examination of Dr. Johnson's Strictures on the Lyric Performances of Gray* (1781), who was pained by Johnson's 'unfair, and unusual mode of criticism' and by 'his total deviation from the common track of popular opinion'.[23] William Tindall's *Remarks on Dr. Johnson's Life, and Critical Observations on the Works of Mr. Gray* (1782) again defended the Odes, which had hitherto been 'considered as the only standards of taste, and the models of composition'.[24] Several pages of John Callender's *Deformities of Dr. Johnson* (1782) were devoted to abuse of the 'Life of Gray'. More reasonable and respectful in tone was Robert Potter's *Inquiry into Some Passages in Dr. Johnson's Lives of the Poets* (1783). Potter believed that 'The Bard' was 'the grandest and sublimest effort of the Lyric Muse'; that it was characterized by 'forcible conception, a fervor of enthusiasm, and a terrible greatness'. Johnson's objections were 'cold and tasteless', 'arbitrary and unmannered'. There is the familiar note of bewilderment: 'What could induce Dr. Johnson, who as a good man might be expected to favour goodness, as a scholar to be candid to a man of learning, to attack this excellent person and poet with such outrage and indecency?'[25]

The torrent of discussion and comment continued in pamphlets, satiric poems, periodical essays, biographies of Johnson, and editions of Gray well into the next century.[26] The immediate popular reaction was perhaps best summarized by a 'caricature of the nine muses flogging Dr. Johnson round Parnassus' which, we are told, was published to please the admirers of Gray.[27]

It is, however, when we examine the reactions of Johnson's own circle to his criticism of Gray that the extent both of Gray's reputation in the 1780s and of Johnson's isolation becomes clear. Goldsmith alone had shared similar views, but he had died in 1774 and even he had admitted in 1757 that 'the circumstances of grief and horror' and 'the mystic obscurity' in 'The Bard' 'will give as much pleasure to those who relish this species of composition, as anything that has hitherto appeared in our language'.[28] Garrick had also died recently, but he had been an early admirer of the two Odes, addressing a poem to Gray on their publication in 1757. According to Joseph Cradock, one of Garrick's party-pieces had been to mimic Johnson's 'uncouth manner' of 'growling' over passages from 'The Bard', 'without articulating many of the words'.[29] To what has been said above about Boswell's enthusiasm for Gray need be added only the fact that in 1791 he acknowledged that his *Life of Johnson* had followed the 'excellent plan' of Mason's *Memoirs of Gray*, an admission which, it may be supposed, would not have greatly gratified Johnson, but which seems to show Boswell making a final conciliatory gesture towards the Walpole-Mason group (*Boswell's Life*, I, 29).

Mrs. Thrale frequently noted and usually regretted in her journal Johnson's lack of taste for modern poetry and in particular for what he called Gray's 'unmeaning & verbose Language'. In October 1780 she recorded that Johnson's criticism of Gray 'displeases many people; Sir Joshua Reynolds in particular'.[30] Reynolds himself criticized both the content and the method of Johnson's critique in the prose 'Portrait' of his friend which remained unpublished until 1952;[31] but in his final Discourse to the Royal Academy in 1790 he had implicitly disowned Johnson's views by referring emphatically to Gray as 'our great Lyrick Poet' and to 'his sublime idea of the indignant Welch bard'. Similarly Joseph Warton had taken an early opportunity of dissociating himself from Johnson by praising 'The Bard' at the end of the second volume of his *Essay on Pope* in 1782, and did so even more warmly when he revised the volume a short time later.[32] Even Dr. Burney, one of Johnson's most devoted admirers, found his loyalty under strain. When his friend Thomas Twining wrote in 1781 to tell Burney that he thought Johnson's strictures on Gray 'unjust & narrow', Burney had to agree:

> What you say of Johnson's severity to Gray I join in. . . . For tho'
> I revere Johnson on many accounts, I think his severity here mis-
> chievous. . . . I have often had battles with him about Prior & Gray,
> & during the time he was writing the Character of the latter often
> begged he would spare him, & made M.rs Thrale join with me; but
> his opinion was rocky. – G. was a Cambridge man – a friend of
> Mason – & had been as he thought – I suppose – too violently
> praised.[33]

Open disagreement of the sort Burney had attempted could be rash.
Fanny Burney describes an argument about Pope and Gray between
Johnson and William Weller Pepys in October 1782. Johnson eventually
became so 'satirical and exulting' and Pepys was 'so roughly confuted,
and so severely ridiculed' that 'he was hurt and piqued beyond all power
of disguise, and, in the midst of the discourse, suddenly turned from him,
and, wishing Mrs. Thrale good-night, very abruptly withdrew.'[34] Other
friends more discreetly expressed disagreement after Johnson's death.
Arthur Murphy, who had reviewed Gray's Odes enthusiastically in 1757,
but who later seemed to agree with Johnson's strictures in conversation,
wrote in his *Essay on Johnson* in 1792 that 'there are, perhaps, few friends
of Johnson, who would not wish to blot out' passages in the 'Life of Gray'
on the 'Eton Ode' and 'The Bard'.[35]

When Johnson's friends were prepared to disown his views in this
manner, the bitterness with which Gray's friends and admirers reacted
can come as no surprise. In the chorus of voices expressing outrage and
demanding revenge there were none more strident than those of two
celebrated literary ladies. Mrs. Elizabeth Montagu, the Bluestocking
whom Johnson himself so much respected, at once 'dropped' him from
her society, as Johnson himself admitted. In November 1781 she referred
to 'the envy, and the malice, and the railing, of such writers as Dr. Johnson, who bear in their hearts the secret hatred of hypocrites to genuine
virtue, and the contempt of Pedants for real genius'. Pained also by his
comments on her friend Lord Lyttleton, she later went so far as to describe in a letter the Johnson of the *Lives of the Poets* as 'the vampire,
who violates the tomb, profanes the sepulchre, and sucks the blood of
sleeping men – cowardly, ungenerous monster!' She is said to have incited
Robert Potter to produce the *Inquiry* discussed above and rejoiced when
these 'reprehensions of the malignant Biographer and wretched Critick'
appeared in May 1783.[36]

An even more dedicated activist was Anna Seward, the Swan of Lichfield, who felt strongly that Gray's friend and biographer should retaliate to the arrogance and 'the absurd, yet plausible sophistry' of the 'Life of Gray'. 'Every month that rolled on,' she later recalled, 'rendered me more and more impatient of Mason's forbearance.'[37] Eventually she published a poem in the *Gentleman's Magazine* in October 1783, urging Mason to enter the fray:

> *Long have I seen the injur'd Muse of GRAY,*
> *At MASON's desk, angry and mournful stand,*
> *With asking eyes, that flash'd th' indignant ray,*
> *The pen extending with impatient hand.*

Mason was to go forth as a David against 'that Philistine critic, who defies/The chosen armies of the heavenly Muse':

> *Blush, loiterer, blush! that from thy able arm*
> *Truth's victor pebbles are not flung ere now,*
> *The giant's noisy prowess to disarm,*
> *And sink deep buried in his shameless brow!*[38]

Horace Walpole, Gray's earliest surviving friend, had by then already been trying to goad the wretched Mason into action for some time. They had watched the publication of the 'Life of Gray' with fascinated horror. In February 1781 Walpole told Mason that Edward Gibbon had reported that 'somebody asked Johnson if he was not afraid that *you* would resent the freedoms he has taken with Gray'. Johnson had replied, '*No, no Sir, Mr Mason does not like rough handling*'. Such messages were intended to rouse Mason's fighting spirit against the 'saucy Caliban', the 'tasteless pedant', 'Dagon', 'Demogorgon', as Walpole variously described Johnson. Mason agreed that Johnson's attack on Gray was 'certainly the meanest business that ever disgraced literature' and he did retaliate rather clumsily in his *Archaeological Epistle to the Rev. Jeremiah Milles* in 1782.[39] It was only after Johnson's death, however, that Mason became really violent in his *Memoirs of William Whitehead* in 1788, extravagantly dismissing the 'Life of Gray' as 'those acid eructations of vituperative criticism, which are generated by unconcocted taste and intellectual indigestion'.[40] Such abuse was very much to the liking of Miss Seward, although she was disappointed to have to admonish a young male friend, who thought it tasteless, by reminding him that Johnson was 'the greatest enemy the poetic science ever had, or ever can have; one, who has already, by his frontless sophistry, brought it into a degree of disgrace, fatal to the expectations of its rising votaries'.[41]

It must seem likely that some of the extra animus in the 'Life of Gray' sprang from Johnson's hostility to the Walpole-Mason group as a whole. That Walpole and his friends inspired such resentment is suggested by some remarks made in the *Monthly Review* in 1798 by Dr. Burney, who was normally anxious to be fair to both Walpole and Johnson: 'At this time, Gray, Mason, and Walpole, formed a party hostile to all around them. They certainly had great merit: but not *all* the merit in the kingdom. Yet the contempt and arrogance with which they treated every other candidate for fame, abroad and at home, was so offensive that many, who were disposed to admire their writings, unwillingly allowed them their due share of praise.' Earlier Burney had tried to explain the particular hostility between Johnson and Walpole (who, a few years before his death, had become Lord Orford): 'the Peer hated Johnson because he was rough in manners and conversation, unwieldy and uncouth in his figure, a Jacobite, and a Christian. Johnson had a natural antipathy to the noble Lord as being a Whig, the son of a Whig minister, effeminate and unmanly in his appearance, dainty and affected in his taste, a Cantabridgian, and a philosopher *à la Voltaire*. The elements of fire and water cannot be more hostile to each other than this pair.'[42]

It is paradoxical that the only recent study of the relations of Johnson and Walpole is concerned to stress their 'accords and resemblances',[43] since Walpole's letters and other writings are riddled with contemptuous if fascinated abuse of Johnson. As Gray may have done, Walpole literally 'declined his acquaintance', refusing to let Sir Joshua Reynolds introduce him to Johnson when they were in the same room. When Boswell on another occasion rather nervously came to ask Walpole for information about Gray for Johnson's forthcoming 'Life', Walpole refused. According to Walpole's account, Boswell 'hummed and hawed and then dropped, "I suppose you know Dr. Johnson does not admire Mr. Gray" – Putting as much contempt as I could into my look and tone, I said, "Dr. Johnson don't! – humph!" – and with that monosyllable ended our interview.'[44]

As we have seen, the Walpole-Mason circle never entirely lost its glamour for Boswell. In 1788, he noted after a visit to Walpole that 'Hory's constitutional tranquility, or affectation of it, and the *tout ensemble* of his connections and history, etc., etc., pleased me much'.[45] But 'tranquillity' was not the mental state in which Walpole normally contemplated Johnson. Gray must have been affected by exposure to Walpole's violent attitude to Johnson, especially in the 1760s: to what Walpole called his 'blind Toryism', his Government pension, his elaborate prose style, his 'brutal' manners and dominating social manner.[46] If Walpole's attitude changed in the 1780s, it was only to the extent of adding tastelessness and lack of critical judgement to Johnson's failings, after the appearance of the 'Life of Gray'. Eventually, with the publication after his death of Johnson's *Prayers and Meditations* and his letters to Mrs. Thrale, Walpole did come to realize more sympathetically something of what lay behind Johnson's rugged exterior, although to the end contemptuous exclamations mingle with his expressions of pity for Johnson's sufferings and grudging admission of respect for his intellect.[47]

The sparse evidence available suggests that, if anything, Gray always had rather more respect for Johnson than Walpole was prepared to admit. Yet he undoubtedly shared, or was influenced by, Walpole's literary, political, and temperamental antipathy to Johnson. Reserved and fastidious, Gray could not be attracted by what he heard about Johnson's rough, vigorous, sometimes coarse person and personality. What William Temple had written about Gray, in the 'Character' quoted by both Johnson and Mason, helps to explain such mutual suspicion. Temple thought Gray's 'greatest defect' was 'an affectation in delicacy, or rather effeminacy, and a visible fastidiousness, or contempt and disdain of his inferiors in science ... yet he could not bear to be considered himself merely as a man of letters; and though without birth, or fortune, or station, his desire was to be looked upon as a private independent gentleman, who read for his amusement' (*Lives*, III, 430-31).

Johnson would have had no sympathy for such defensive delicacy and snobbery, or for Gray's attitude to the publication of his poetry, which he so often left to others to arrange while concealing his own anxious sensitivity about it beneath an affected indifference. Johnson's dismissal of Gray's belief that he could write only at certain inspired times as a 'fantastick foppery' reminds us of the significant contrast between the amateur, dilettante, provincial character of the Gray-Walpole-Mason circle and Johnson, the professional, metropolitan man of letters. In 1782 Walpole reduced Johnson's professionalism to mere avarice: 'yet he has other motives than lucre, – prejudice, and bigotry, and pride, and presumption, and arrogance, and pedantry are the hags that brew his ink, though wages alone supply him with paper.'[48] In the same year Mason sneeringly referred in his *Epistle to Dr. Milles* to 'Dr. Johnson or any other writer in the trade'.[49] Certain similarities between Johnson and Gray – their relatively humble origins, their melancholy temperaments and defensive pride, their learning – may only have added to Johnson's irritation. Although he is often severe about Gray, he can at times be shrewd and even sensitive about the poet's character and predicament, as in his remarks on the famous and unexplained quarrel between Gray and Horace Walpole, the Prime Minister's son, in Italy in 1741: 'If we look, however, without prejudice on the world we shall find that men, whose consciousness of their own merit sets them above the compliances of servility, are apt enough in their association with superiors to watch their own dignity with troublesome and punctilious jealousy, and in the fervour of independance to exact that attention which they refuse to pay' (*Lives*, III, 422). More generally, Johnson may have felt that Gray had merely backed away from difficulties with which he had himself contended: his contempt for Gray's retreat into discontented academic isolation is clear throughout his biography of the poet.

At various times additional motives for Johnson's antipathy to Gray were suggested, ranging from the accusation that he was simply envious of Gray's poetic pre-eminence at this period, to antagonism on political grounds. Inter-university rivalry between Oxford and Cambridge was invoked more than once to explain some of the bitterness aroused in the 1780s.[50] Yet to reduce the whole affair to merely personal or political terms would be misleading. The intensity of feeling aroused by the 'Life of Gray' in 1781 had another cause. We should not forget that when Johnson launched his attack, Gray's poetry, and especially the two great Odes, seemed to most readers the supreme lyric achievement not merely of the age but of all time. For John Pinkerton, 'Gray is the first and greatest of modern lyric writers; nay, I will venture to say, of all lyric writers; his works tho few (alas, how few!) uniting the perfections of every lyric poet, both of present and former times.'[51] Anna Seward in 1796 still thought the two Odes 'the first lyric compositions the world has seen, of loftier subjects than Pindar's'.[52] In attacking the Odes with such 'audacious contempt', Johnson had assaulted with all the authority and trenchancy at his command the sophisticated poetic taste of the whole age, confusing or outraging all those who pretended to refined sensibility or a feeling for the sublime, undermining the self-confidence of the cultivated reader.

To Johnson himself Gray's poetry, and the Odes in particular, embodied in an acute and all too influential form all the deplorable tendencies which he saw in English poetry since the death of Pope: wilful abruptness and obscurity; puerile classical or primitive mythology; unnervingly rugged metres and unpredictable stanzaic forms; affected, exhibitionistic diction in which plain prose meaning was diluted or distorted; remoteness from central human experience and the absence of explicitly 'improving' concerns; the exclusion of the 'common reader' from the envisaged audience, especially in the case of the two Pindaric Odes, which Gray's own epigraph proclaimed to be 'vocal to the intelligent alone'. Considered in the perspective of the whole development of English poetry, it can be argued either that Johnson was courageously refusing to be deluded by temporary poetic fashions and preoccupations, or that he was obstinately resisting every sign of nascent Romanticism. The main purpose of the present enquiry is to argue neither case, but to establish Johnson's posture as it appeared to his contemporaries. And in their eyes there can be no doubt that Johnson seemed to be fighting a perverse rearguard action against inevitable developments and changes in taste to which he could not adjust himself.

Just how out of touch with his contemporaries he had become is clear, for example, from the repeated objections which were made to his derision of the 'marvellous' in 'The Bard', in reproof of which he had asserted that 'we are affected only as we believe; we are improved only as we find something to be imitated or declined. I do not see that "The Bard" promotes any truth, moral or political' (*Lives*, III, 438). More than one of the early pamphlets in Gray's defence in the 1780s reject the assumption that belief and improvement are involved in poetic experience. What matters is the emotional response aroused for its own sake, and 'The Bard' succeeds, we are told, in raising 'extremest anxiety' and leaves us 'thrilling with horror and amazement'.[53] It would no doubt be rash to adduce William Blake as representative of this generation, or of any generation, yet his enthusiastic response to Gray's poetry emphatically reminds us that, where we now may find restraints and inhibitions in Gray's poetry, his early readers found exhilarating verbal richness and powerful imaginative boldness. The 'great things' which Johnson so defiantly found 'but dull' were to Blake a repeated source of inspiration. His early poetry frequently echoes 'The Bard'. He exhibited a watercolour of the Bard himself at the Royal Academy in 1785 and in 1809, with reference to a second depiction of the Bard, referred in his *Descriptive Catalogue* to 'the bold, daring, and most masterly conception' of the device of the winding-sheet in the poem.[54] Above all there are the 116 illustrations to Gray's poems, first published in 1922, an idiosyncratic and uneven but often powerful response to the poetry, and not least impressive is Blake's willingness to illustrate so patiently and fully the more fanciful or grotesque poems with which one might have expected him to feel least sympathy:

> *Around the Springs of Gray my wild root weaves*
> *Traveller repose & Dream among my leaves.*[55]

Taste ineviably changed. To a new generation Johnson's formerly reactionary judgements, if not his assumptions and critical methods, came to be more or less acceptable. By 1818 William Hazlitt could say: 'Gray's Pindaric Odes are, I believe, generally given up at present: they are stately and pedantic, a kind of methodical borrowed phrenzy.'[56] Such a judgement takes Johnson's views for granted and this time there was no outcry. And now, two hundred years after Gray's death, while the rhetorical and technical accomplishment of the two great Odes (which had been at the heart of the furore) remains undeniable, it seems that we accept that Johnson had been right in some sense all the time. Perhaps partly from a fastidious distaste for the role of popular poet which the publication of the 'Elegy' had brought him in 1751, and yet partly from a desire to justify his new eminence, Gray seems to have tried in the two Odes to write by sheer will-power the kind of poetry which the more sophisticated readers of his age were looking for, or could be persuaded they were looking for. And, clearly, he succeeded in giving one generation at least a powerful and rewarding experience.

The 'Elegy' remains. For Hazlitt the 'Elegy' was still 'one of the most classical productions that ever was penned by a refined and thoughtful mind, moralising on human life'. And Johnson himself, we should remember, in a period when the Odes were more admired, had surely done justice to Gray's greatest poem. Having punctured, as he hoped, the spurious taste which had kept the Odes floating like barrage balloons above the contemporary literary landscape, an obstruction to all true poetic activity, Johnson ended the 'Life of Gray' – and, significantly, in their first published form the *Lives of the Poets* as a whole – with a memorable paragraph of condensed praise of the 'Elegy'. There was nothing casual about the terms in which he did so: this is no perfunctory compensation for what had preceded. Johnson was concisely summarizing and reasserting all his most firmly held literary values, which the Odes had so violently offended: his conviction that poetry is written for the ordinary reader and not the scholar; that the reader should find in poetry what is both natural and new, both surprising and just, should discover and recognize new clarity and order in his own experience. In these eloquent words Johnson made it possible for this protracted tale of antagonism and failed communication to close harmoniously and, here at least, to the credit of all concerned:

> In the character of his *Elegy* I rejoice to concur with the common reader; for by the common sense of readers uncorrupted with literary prejudices, after all the refinements of subtilty and the dogma-

tism of learning, must be finally decided all claim to poetical honours. The *Church-yard* abounds with images which find a mirrour in every mind, and with sentiments to which every bosom returns an echo. The four stanzas beginning 'Yet even these bones' are to me original: I have never seen the notions in any other place; yet he that reads them here persuades himself that he has always felt them. Had Gray written often thus it had been vain to blame, and useless to praise him. (*Lives*, III, 441-42)

Balliol College, Oxford

Notes

1. *The Autobiography, Times, Opinions and Contemporaries of Sir Egerton Brydges*, 2 vols. (London, 1834), II, 111. Brydges heard the story from Bonstetten himself.

2. *Boswell's London Journal 1762-1763*, ed. F. A. Pottle (London, 1950), pp. 105-06.

3. *Monthly Review*, XVII (1757), 239-43. See also *Poems*, p. 630.

4. *Boswell's London Journal*, pp. 282-83. The conversation was printed with small changes in *Boswell's Life*, I, 402-3.

5. *Letters of James Boswell*, ed. C. B. Tinker (Oxford, 1924), I, 41-42, 217; *Boswell in Holland*, ed. F. A. Pottle (London, 1952), pp. 14, 16, 32, 37, 60, 81, 242; *Boswell on the Grand Tour: Germany and Switzerland 1764*, ed. F. A. Pottle (London, 1953), p. 34.

6. *Letters of James Boswell*, I, 161, 183.

7. *Private Papers of Boswell from Malahide Castle*, ed. G. Scott and F. A. Pottle, 18 vols. (Mount Vernon, 1928-34), XVI, 149-50 (hereafter cited as *Private Papers*.

8. *The Correspondence and Other Papers of James Boswell Relating to the Making of the Life of Johnson*, ed. M. Waingrow (London, 1969), pp. 311-12.

9. *Boswell for the Defence*, ed. W. K. Wimsatt and F. A. Pottle (London, 1960), p. 77; *Boswell's Life*, II, 164.

10. *Letters of James Boswell*, i, 217.

11. Ibid, i, 234; *Correspondence of Horace Walpole*, ed. W. S. Lewis and others (New Haven, 1937–), xxviii, 209.

12. *Boswell: The Ominous Years 1774-76*, ed. C. Ryskamp and F. A. Pottle (London, 1963), p. 105; *Boswell's Life*, ii, 327-28.

13. *Boswell: The Ominous Years*, p. 116; *Boswell's Life*, ii, 334-35.

14. *Johnsonian Miscellanies*, ed. G. B. Hill, 2 vols. (Oxford, 1897), ii, 52.

15. *Boswell's Life*, iii, 31-32, 38; iv, 13; *Private Papers*, xi, 237; *Letters of Johnson*, ed. R. W. Chapman, 3 vols. (Oxford, 1952), i, 317. Johnson's preference of Akenside to Mason was shared by Percival Stockdale, *An Inquiry into the Nature, and Genuine Laws of Poetry* (1778). Stockdale was one of the few critics at this period who believed that Gray was overpraised by his admirers. Of Mason he stated that 'He would have been highly honoured if he had been Akenside's Amanuensis' (p. 121).

16. *Private Papers*, xiv, 174.

17. W. Powell Jones, 'Johnson and Gray: A study in Literary Antagonism', *Modern Philology*, lvi (1958-59), 243-53, gives a full account of the public reception of the 'Life of Gray' in the 1780s. The present enquiry has explored, as far as is sensible, different avenues, and merely summarizes the main reactions of the reviewers and pamphleteers.

18. *Autobiography*, i, 230.

19. lii (1781), 86.

20. li (1781), 276, 516; lii (1782), 19-20.

21. lxvi (1782), 124-26.

22. li (1782), 38.

23. pp. 1-2.

24. p. 6. The Bodleian copy (12.θ.1871) is inscribed 'supposed, By the Revd. Wm. Fitzthomas', but the ascription to Tindall is more common.

25. pp. 30-33, 37-38. Potter had more to say about Johnson and Gray in *The Art of Criticism* (1789).

26. A few of the more interesting items (by no means all pro-Gray) are: John Young, *A Criticism on the Elegy Written in a Country Church-yard. Being a Continuation of Dr. Johnson's Criticism on the Poems of Gray* (1783); *A Dialogue between Dr. Johnson and Dr. Goldsmith in the Shades* (1785); Joseph Towers, *An Essay on the Life, Character, and Writings of Dr. Samuel Johnson* (1786); John Courtenay, *A Poetical Review of the Literary and Moral Character of the late Samuel Johnson* (1786); Gilbert Wakefield's edition of Gray's *Poems* (1786), in which he feared that Johnson's attack 'might operate with malignant influence upon the public taste, and become ultimately injurious to the cause of polite literature' (p. iii); Robert Anderson, *The Life of Samuel Johnson* (1795), p. 204; Samuel Berdmore, *Specimens of Literary Resemblance* (London, 1801), p. 16; Sir William Forbes, *The Life of James Beattie*, 2 vols. (London, 1806), ii, 111, 122-23, which contains the views of John Scott of Amwell, whose *Critical Essays*

(1785) were also an attempt to counteract the tendency of some of Johnson's *Lives of the Poets*; *European Magazine*, L (1806), 292; *London Magazine*, VI (1822), 563; *Westminster Review*, XXVII (1837), 12; the Earl of Carlisle, 'Lecture on the Writings of Gray', in Gray's *Poetical Works*, ed. J. Mitford, 4th edn. (Eton, 1853), pp. LXVII-C, often reprinted; *The Letters of Hannah More*, ed. R. B. Johnson (London, 1925), p. 70.

27. *Johnsonian Miscellanies*, II, 470.

28. See note 3 above.

29. Joseph Cradock, *Literary and Miscellaneous Memoirs*, 4 vols. (London, 1828), I, 37.

30. *Thraliana*, ed K. C. Balderston, 2nd edn. corrected, 2 vols. (London, 1951), I, 172, 188, 459-60.

31. *Portraits by Sir Joshua Reynolds*, ed. F. W. Hilles (London, 1952), p. 72.

32. In revising the *Essay on Pope* Warton also reduced his quotations from Johnson. See W. D. MacClintock, *Joseph Warton's Essay on Pope: A History of the Five Editions* (Chapel Hill, 1933), pp. 62, 66.

33. Burney's undated letter to Twining, written in October 1781, is unpublished. There is an early copy of it in the Osborn Collection at Yale and I am indebted to Dr. James M. Osborn for permission to quote it. See also *Recreations and Studies of a Country Clergyman of the Eighteenth Century*, ed. R. Twining (London, 1882), pp. 120, 141.

34. *Diary and Letters of Madame D'Arblay*, ed. Austin Dobson, 6 vols. (London, 1904-05), II, 107-8.

35. *New Essays by Arthur Murphy*, ed. A. Sherbo (East Lansing, 1963), pp. 144-56; Boswell, *Private Papers*, XI, 237; Murphy, *Essay on Johnson* (1792), p. 174.

36. *Mrs. Montagu, Queen of the Blues: Her Letters and Friendships*, ed R. Blunt, 2 vols. (London, [1923]), II, 134, 157; John Wooll, *Biographical Memoirs of the late Revd. Joseph Warton* (London, 1806), p. 397.

37. *Letters of Anna Seward*, 6 vols. (Edinburgh, 1811), I, 54; II, 144. See also II, 307.

38. 'Verses Addressed to Mr. MASON, Written before the Appearance of Mr. POTTER's learned and ingenious Refutation of DR. JOHNSON's Criticism in his Life of Mr. GRAY', *Gentlemen's Magazine*, LIII pt. ii (1783), 871.

39. Walpole, *Correspondence*, XXIX, 97, 104, 106, 111, 117, 120, 144, 155.

40. *Works of William Whitehead*, 3 vols. (York, 1774-88), III, 129.

41. *Letters of James Boswell*, II, 144-45. Mason could not win. He was attacked for cowardice in waiting until Johnson was dead before retaliating, in some verses 'On Mr. Mason's Abuse of the Late Dr. Samuel Johnson', in *An Asylum for Fugitive Pieces*, III (1789), 253; and Dr. Burney, an old acquaintance of Mason, nevertheless felt obliged by greater loyalty to Johnson to write a slashing anonymous attack on Mason in the *Monthly Review*, LVIII (1788), 177-82. See my article, 'Dr. Burney and the *Monthly Review*', *Review of English Studies*, XIV (1963) 357-58.

42. *Monthly Review*, XXVII (1798), 56, 282.

43. W. S. Lewis, *The Accords and Resemblances of Johnson and Walpole*, privately printed for The Johnsonians, 1967; reprinted in *Eighteenth-Century Studies in Honor of Donald F. Hyde*, ed. W. H. Bond (New York, 1970), pp. 179-86.

44. Walpole, *Correspondence*, xi, 275-76.

45. *Private Papers*, xvii, 102.

46. e.g. Walpole, *Correspondence*, xi, 237, 275-76; xxviii, 41n., 166; xxxiii, 88; 'General Criticism on Dr. Johnson's Writings', in *Works*, 5 vols. (1798), iv, 361-62; *Notes on Mason's Satires*, ed. P. Toynbee (Oxford, 1926), pp. 32, 54-55, 99.

47. e.g. Walpole, *Correspondence*, xvii, 102; xxxiii, 493-94.

48. Ibid., xxix, 180.

49. pp. 5, 6n.

50. 'Johnson felt the superiority, and for that he hated him.' (*Letters of Anna Seward*, iv, 159.) Boswell had already thought the charge worth refuting, *Boswell's Life*, i, 404. Political motivation was often suggested: e.g. a ms. note in the Bodleian copy of William Tindall's *Remarks* (1782), p. 75, attributes Johnson's attack on Gray to 'political *party-spirit*. Mr. Gray was a whig, (I judge by my own personal acquaintance with him) and Dr. Johnson an intolerant Tory.' The note is signed 'J(?).H. 1805'. University rivalry is mentioned by Walpole, *Correspondence*, xxix, 117; by Dr. Burney, *Monthly Review*, lxxviii (1788), 177; and Boswell, *Boswell's Life*, iv, 64.

51. *Letters of Literature. By Robert Heron, Esq.* (1785), p. 131.

52. *Letters of Anna Seward*, iv, 159-60.

53. *A Cursory Examination* (1781), p. 15; William Tindall, *Remarks*, p. 58.

54. *The Complete Writings of William Blake*, ed. G. Keynes (Oxford, 1966), p. 576. I am indebted to Mrs. Irene Tayler of the City University of New York for pointing out to me that the two paintings of the Bard are distinct and not, as some Blake authorities have suggested, one and the same.

55. Keynes, p. 414.

56. *Works*, ed. P. P. Howe, 21 vols. (London, 1930-34), v, 118.

DONALD GREENE

The Proper Language of Poetry: Gray, Johnson, and Others

It was when I was an adolescent or younger that I first learned that English is not one but two languages. I learned this through an early addiction to crossword puzzles, then a comparative novelty – the simple-minded crossword puzzles of American and Canadian newspapers, which do not go in for the elaborate and learned allusions and puns and anagrams of their more sophisticated British brothers but plumb the depths of unabridged dictionaries for unusual words, preferably of two or three or four letters and with as many vowels as possible, to fill the interstices between longer words. It was there that, like countless other North American crossword addicts, I first learned of the existence of the *ai*, the three-toed sloth, and of the *oud*, a musical instrument of northern Africa. A large category of these words had definitions to which the rubric 'Poet.' was affixed, and one soon came to know them and appreciate their uses. There was, for instance, the familiar 'Before (Poet.)', which everyone knew from his school days was 'ere'. Some of them were really too simple – 'Often (Poet.)', rendered 'oft', and 'It is (Poet.)', rendered ' 'tis'. Some of them were a little harder but not much – 'Think (Poet.)', which was 'ween', or 'Also (Poet.)', the delightful 'eke'.

All this, of course, merely confirmed what we had already suspected from our encounters with English verse in our elementary school readers – there are two English languages, one reserved for the writing of poetry, the other for everyday use. Who could doubt it after grappling with such familiar school book gems as

It little profits that, an idle king . . .
Matched with an agèd wife, I mete and dole
Unequal laws unto a savage race

Much have I travelled in the realms of gold
And many goodly states and kingdoms seen;

Round many western islands have I been
Which bards in fealty to Apollo hold –
the crossword definition for 'bard' is 'Poet (Poet.)' – and
Hail to thee, blithe spirit!
Bird thou never wert.

From these we also learned the second great rule of 'poetic' English: not only does it use a vocabulary peculiar to itself, but in it you can – indeed, you should – ingeniously twist sentences out of their normal spoken order. You don't say, 'It profits little' – not that you would use 'profits' in this way in everyday speech anyhow – but 'It little profits'; you don't say, 'I have been round many western islands', but 'Round many western islands have I been'. Most of us, after a few years' exposure to this kind of thing, in the fourth, fifth, and sixth grades, accepted the rule without demur, even sympathetically. As for Keats's 'Round many western islands have I been', well, after all, the poor man had to end the line with a word he could get a rhyme for, and there aren't many rhymes to 'islands'. If some naively recalcitrant ten- or eleven-year-old should object, 'Why couldn't Shelley have said, "Hello, happy spirit, you never were a bird"?' he was quickly set to rights: 'You don't understand, dear. Shelley was writing *poetry*. If he had written it your way, it would only be *prose*, wouldn't it? In order to have poetry, we must do things differently from the way we do them in prose.'

If any were yet unconvinced, this argument convinced us; and those of us who, as adolescence approached, dabbled furtively in trying to write poetry of our own firmly obeyed the rules and introduced a fitting quota of *ere*s and *'tise*s and *oft*s and second-person singular pronouns and verbs, and assiduously inverted our sentences – as Keats had discovered, this certainly helped the problem of rhyming – in much the same spirit as English schoolboys two centuries earlier had industriously thumbed their *Gradus ad Parnassum* to select a suitable quantity of mythological personages and Virgilian turns of phrases to introduce into their required Latin verses. Indeed, this seemed to be regarded by many early critics as the spirit in which English poetry is normally to be written. Thus the Reverend Samuel Wesley (father of John), in his 'Epistle to a Friend Concerning Poetry', 1700:

A diff'rent Style's for prose and verse required,
Strong figures here, neat plainness there desired:
A diff'rent set of words to both belong:
What shines in prose is flat and mean in Song.
The turn, the numbers must be varied here,

> *And all things in a different dress appear:*
> *This ev'ry schoolboy lash'd at Eton knows.*[1]

The attitudes I have been describing date from several decades ago. Surely, having been educated in the meantime by people like Eliot and Pound and Donald Davie, we are no longer so naive as to believe in a special poetic English language. To confirm this optimism, I sat down, when beginning to prepare this paper, with half a dozen modern 'college' dictionaries in front of me to see what they now said about 'oft' and ' 'tis' and the rest. To my consternation, every one that I consulted, even the most recent, the highly touted *American Heritage Dictionary*, even that widely recognized arbiter of current British usage, the *Concise Oxford*, still carries 'Poet.' as a usage label. 'Oft. adv. *Poetic. Often*', says the *American Heritage Dictionary*. 'Oft. *Rare or Poetic*', says *Webster's New World*.[2] 'Ere. adv. and conj. (poet., archaic)', says the *Concise Oxford*. ' 'Tis. Archaic and poetic', says the *American Heritage*. To be sure, 'archaic' appears rather oftener than 'poetic'; but still 'poetic' occurs often enough to make one wonder just *what* poetry these dictionary-makers, who in their advertising pride themselves on being up to the minute, have been reading. Nothing published in the last fifty years, obviously.

Donald Davie has already treated on a much broader scale than I can do here, in his *Purity of Diction in English Verse*,[3] the problem of what linguistic principles – in particular, principles of choice of vocabulary – are applicable to the writing and criticism of English poetry. I am not sure that I have a great deal to add to what Professor Davie has said in his admirable book, one of the first, and still few, works by a practising poet and critic of poetry to take eighteenth-century poetry with as much seriousness as the poetry of other centuries. But when I was invited to take part in a program commemorating Thomas Gray it seemed appropriate to spend some time exploring in a little more detail than Professor Davie did there the important, indeed crucial, difference of opinion on these matters between Gray and Samuel Johnson. Not, I'm afraid, that this exploration will afford much comfort to the friends of Gray, since in my view, and in that of many modern students, including, I think, Professor Davie (unless he has drastically modified his stance in the twenty years since his book was written), Johnson had clearly the better of the argument. But since the organizers of the Conference were willing to take the risk of inviting an unreconstructed Johnsonian to participate in a Gray celebration, you will have to address your complaints to them.

And indeed, if this paper should stimulate aficionados of Gray to present whatever can be said on the other side of the question, it will have made a useful contribution to a subject which has surely been too little studied. In the vast library of criticism of English poetry, discussion of the question of the proper language of poetry really forms an insignificant proportion: critics and aestheticians have spent far more time worrying about matters such as genre and imagery and intention, about terms like imitation and the sublime and high seriousness, about the psychological response to poetry and the moral effect of poetry, than about what, one might think, would be a primary question – just what a poet's approach to vocabulary and syntax should be. In Scott Elledge's two-volume, nearly 1,200-page anthology of criticism written between 1697 and 1796,[4] there seems to be only one essay whose title proclaims it to be dealing with specifically linguistic matters. This is Leonard Welsted's feeble 'Dissertation Concerning the Perfection of the English Language, the State of Poetry, etc.', 1724. Welsted, after a few pages of perfunctorily retailing the usual remarks about the refinement, perfection, and inevitable decay of languages, arrives at a defeatist position. He is speaking about 'the numerous treatises, essays, arts, etc. . . . that have been written by the moderns' on poetic technique:

> The truth is they touch only the externals or form of the thing, without entering into the spirit of it; they play about the surface of poetry but never dive into its depths: the secret, the soul of good writing is not to be come at through such mechanic laws; the main graces and the cardinal beauties of this charming art lie too retired within the bosom of nature, and are of too fine and subtle an essence to fall under the discussion of pedants, commentators, or trading critics. . . . These beauties, in a word, are rather to be felt than described.[5]

When one encounters the word 'soul' in a piece of literary criticism, one's heart sinks. Welsted then goes on to address himself to such matters as 'By what precepts shall a writer be taught only to think poetically'. Presumably if he can, then he need not worry about the language in which his poetry is written – that will come automatically from 'thinking poetically'. Though Welsted is dubious that 'thinking poetically' can be taught: 'True conceptions of poetry can no more be communicated to one born without taste than adequate ideas of colours can be given to one born without sight.' So that the important thing for the would-be poet or critic to do is to arrange to be born with taste. And this leaves Welsted free to devote the rest of his dissertation to 'the State of Poetry, etc.', to the moral function of poetry and the like.

It is to be feared that Welsted represents the main stream of English literary criticism. That innate purity of heart is the key to purity of diction is a proposition that one finds appealing only too strongly to Ruskin and Arnold and even Leavis. The number of English critics who have devoted much space to an actual examination of the language in which English poetry has been written is small, though not undistinguished. There is Ben Jonson, grumbling about Sidney's not keeping 'a decorum, in making everyone speak as well as himself', and about Spenser, who, 'in affecting the ancients, writ no language', and advising teachers to beware of letting youth 'taste Gower or Chaucer at first, lest falling too much in love with antiquity, and not apprehending the weight, they grow rough and barren in language'.[6] There are Samuel Johnson, and William Wordsworth, and Ezra Pound – I will not mention the handful of students now writing, like Donald Davie, except to say that, though concern with the actual language in which poems are written is probably greater now than it has ever been in the past, thanks in large part to the 'new critics', now so old hat, it is still not one of the major preoccupations of the critical fraternity.

And perhaps English poetry has needed such concern more than any other. Has the poetry of any other major language involved so much deliberate use of archaism? I offer the observation subject to correction, but surely as one reads post-Renaissance French poetry, from Racine to Baudelaire, or German, from Goethe to Rilke, one seldom feels that deliberate distancing from contemporary speech that immediately strikes one — or would strike one, if one's ears were not habituated to it from childhood onward — in 'Hail to thee, blithe spirit! Bird thou never wert', an idiom which Shelley would never have dreamed of using in conversation with his contemporaries or in his pamphlet on *The Necessity of Atheism*.

One wonders what the reasons were for the extraordinary popularity of this kind of thing among the English. There was of course the example of at least two great poets, one of the sixteenth and one of the seventeenth century. There was Spenser, with his 'Chaucerisms', as Ben Jonson called them, which he thought were 'better expunged and banished', and which Pope amusingly burlesques in the *Dunciad*:

> *But who is he, in closet close y-pent,*
> *Of sober face, with learned dust besprent?*
> *Right well mine eyes arede the myster wight,*
> *On parchment scraps y-fed, and Wormius hight.*
> *To future ages may thy dulness last,*
> *As thou preserv'st the dulness of the past!*[7]

There was Milton, always a problem, even to the mild Welsted, who speaks of 'an uncouth, unnatural jargon, like the phrase and style of Milton, which is a second Babel, or confusion of all the languages, a fault that can never be enough regretted in that immortal poet, and which if he had wanted, he had perhaps wanted a superior'. In the eighteenth century, and beyond, there are the innumerable imitators, conscious or unconscious, of Spenser and Milton. It is odd how this fashion started, apparently with John Philips, who in 1701 composed his poem 'The Splendid Shilling' in Miltonic verse as a joke, to burlesque Miltonic pomposity – sublimity, if one prefers – when juxtaposed with a 'low' subject. It begins:

> *Happy the man, who void of cares and strife,*
> *In silken, or in leathern purse retains*
> *A splendid shilling: he nor hears with pain*
> *New oysters cried, nor sighs for cheerful ale . . . .*

The point is obvious, and the fun, if mild, is certainly there. Extraordinarily, however, it quickly caught on for serious purposes, much in the same way perhaps as Fielding, setting out to mock Richardson in *Shamela* and *Joseph Andrews*, was converted by what he was trying to put down and ended by writing a near-Richardsonian novel, *Amelia*. In literature, it seems, those who come to scoff often remain to pray.

The Miltonistic fashion is not hard to explain: blank verse is easily churned out – you don't have to bother to hunt for rhymes; it is also easy enough to throw in the occasional archaic or coined or erudite polysyllabic word and to begin your sentences with the object rather than the subject. And merely doing this, it seems, has the extraordinary consequence of persuading many readers that what they are perusing has true poetic sublimity, in the way that a piece of satiric verse by Pope or Swift, though composed in contemporary colloquial language with the most exquisite skill, has not, and thus by comparison cannot even be called poetry at all. For this, we have the testimony of that egregious ass, Joseph Warton: 'We do not, it should seem, sufficiently attend to the difference there is betwixt a man of wit, a man of sense, and a true poet. Donne and Swift were undoubtedly men of wit and men of sense, but what traces have they left of pure poetry? . . . The sublime and the pathetic are the two chief nerves of all genuine poesy. What is there transcendently sublime or pathetic in Pope?'[8] Warton makes a distinction which has plagued English literary criticism ever since: 'For one person who can adequately relish and enjoy a work of imagination', he laments, 'twenty are to be found who can taste and judge of observations on familiar life and the manners of the age.' Familiar life and the manners of the age, then, are not susceptible to the poetic imagination; for that, it appears, one must treat of unfamiliar life and the manners of other ages, and one can easily see why archaic English should come to be regarded as an indispensable ancillary to the poetic imagination, so defined. David Nichol Smith, in his *Oxford Book of Eighteenth-Century* [English] *Verse*, includes a short excerpt from Philips's Miltonic burlesque, 'The Splendid Shilling', but rather amazingly selects a passage in which, taken by itself, the burlesque is not apparent:

> *Me lonely sitting, nor the glimmering light*
> *Of make-weight candle, nor the joyous talk*
> *Of loving friend delights: distressed, forlorn,*
> *Amidst the horrors of the tedious night,*
> *Darkling I sigh.*

And so on. In its full context, the joke is easily discerned: the speaker's gloom is the result of his lack of a splendid shilling which would enable him to spend the evening convivially in a tavern. But Nichol Smith seems to have chosen the excerpt because of its adumbration of introspective, Romantic melancholy. His volume was published in 1926, when the chief task of the student of eighteenth-century poetry was to hunt for the barely discernible hints of future Romanticism in the sotto voce murmurings of those who, like Gray, 'never spoke out'.

To the popularity of the Miltonic and the Spenserian imitation must be added, as an explanation of the strange persistence of archaism in English poetry, the influence of the King James Bible and the Tudor Book of Common Prayer. The English of both comes from approximately the same time, the mid-sixteenth century, when the language was still in the process of transforming itself from Middle English to Modern English: it is at least as close to the English of Malory, a hundred years earlier, as to that of Dryden, a hundred years later. For the idiom of the King James Bible, as everyone knows, was deliberately archaic, essentially the idiom of Coverdale rather than that of Bishop Andrewes and the other members of King James's committee of translators. Modern theologians continue to abuse it, and rightly, since it effectively disguises from the modern reader that the matters it deals with are living issues, of the here and now – as the archaic idiom of much eighteenth-, nineteenth-, and early twentieth-century verse effectively disguises from the reader, and very often from the poet himself, that poetry may have the function of dealing with living issues of the here and now. Ronald Knox put it well: 'The truth is that Bible English is a language of its own; a hieratic language, deeply embedded in the English mind and perhaps indispensable to the ordinary Englishman's religion; but not a model to be imitated, because its idiom is foreign to us. I say a foreign idiom, not in the sense that it is unintelligible but in the sense that it is artificial. . . . So it is all through the sacred text, from the first chapter of Genesis, where we read "God saw the light, that it was good," down to the last chapter of the Apocalypse, where the phrase "Without are dogs and sorcerers" has to carry the meaning "Dogs and sorcerers are not allowed inside".'[9]

Modern translation after modern translation of the Bible is offered to the public in the hope of getting them to see that texts like 'Now abide faith, hope, charity, these three: but the greatest of these is charity' do have something of immense importance to say to modern man. But in vain. The churchgoer prefers to remain in what Evelyn Waugh wrote of as 'the splendid, luminous, tawny fogs of our early childhood. . . . We designed a city [London] which was meant to be seen in a fog. We had a foggy habit of life and a rich, obscure, choking literature. The great catch in the throat of English lyric poetry is just fog . . . on the vocal cords. . . . Then some busybody invents electricity or fuel oil or whatever it is they use nowadays. The fog lifts, the world sees us as we are, and worse still we see ourselves as we are.'[10] The highest function of poetry, it might be argued, as of the Bible and Prayer Book, is precisely that, to get us to see ourselves as we are; but the use of the obsolete second person singular and other archaisms of diction and syntax, with the willing cooperation of its audience, effectively hinders us from doing so.

Then too there was the spell cast on the writers of verse tragedy in the late seventeenth, eighteenth, and even nineteenth centuries by the Elizabethan dramatists, especially Shakespeare. On these matters it is amusing to hear Ezra Pound's advice on what an aspiring young poet should read: 'English poetry????? Ugh. Perhaps one shouldn't read it at all.' Like Ben Jonson, Pound warns against Chaucer: 'If you read Chaucer you will probably (as I did though there is no reason why you should be the same kind of imbecile) start writing archaic English, which you shouldn't. Everybody has been sloppily imitating the Elizabethans for so long that I think they probably do one more harm than good. At any rate let 'em alone.'[11]

Finally – and here at last we come specifically to Gray – there was the development, in the mid-eighteenth century, of interest in past and distant cultures, notably the mediaeval – in 'old unhappy far-off things, and battles long ago'. As long as this interest was confined to sober historians and archaeologists and philologists, it could do little harm. But when, in the hands of Horace Walpole and James Macpherson and, to a lesser extent, Gray, and, later, Walter Scott, it became a means of escape from the real and present into a fantasy world, the potential evil consequences for literature, and even for political action, could be great, as many have pointed out. Mark Twain, in a startling passage in *Life on the Mississippi*, even blames Scott for the American Civil War, while for Flaubert, Scott shares, along with Chateaubriand, a good deal of the responsibility for Emma Bovary and *bovarysme* generally. Leslie Fiedler lays the blame for what he feels to be the unsatisfactory history of the American novel – the limited insight of Hemingway and Faulkner, dealing with a world of 'men without women', where women are always the potential enemy – at the door of Horace Walpole and his fellow practitioners of Gothicism.[12] Some of Fiedler's charge against Walpole of a distorted homoerotic vision – a charge only too easily supported from the biography of Walpole's early childhood, his dubious parentage, and his mother's neurotic possessiveness toward him[13] – inevitably clings to the figure of his friend Gray. Whatever Gray's feelings toward his protégé Bonstetten, he, like Walpole, was an inhibited, frightened person: it is impossible to forget the story of the cruel prank played on him by the Cambridge undergraduates whose cry of fire brought him out of his bedroom window and down the rope ladder he had provided, or his rival Christopher Smart's inimitable characterization of him: 'Gray walked as if he had fouled his small-clothes, and looked as if he smelt it.'[14]

No more than Johnson would I think of denying that Gray is a competent poet. But more and more, readers tend to find the strength of his poetic talent in his excellent satires, 'On Lord Holland's Seat', 'The Cambridge Courtship', and similar pieces, neglected by his nineteenth-century admirers, rather than in what Johnson acidly called 'the wonderful wonder of wonders', the Odes. I cannot resist quoting Donald Davie's verdict: 'This poem ['On Lord Holland's Seat'] seems to me, together with the fragmentary "Education and Government" [which Johnson also praised], and (in the main) the "Elegy", the only writings of Gray in which the diction is chaste in Johnson's sense or any other. The effect of Gray's example (e.g. in his Odes) was decadent and disruptive; and I can find little of value in his other poems.'[15] From a psychological point of view, of course, the deep self-pity found in the 'Eton' ode and in the epitaph at the end of the 'Elegy' – and what an ungraceful occupation it is, after all, to write self-pitying epitaphs on oneself! – combined with the outbursts of vicarious violence in the Odes, violence that takes place in faraway times and lands, where the poet is free to indulge in it to his heart's delight, add up to a consistent and familiar pattern of neurosis, which would be of interest only to the psychologist and the biographer if it were not for their popularity and the example they set for succeeding generations of writers and readers. This was true poetry, Warton and many following him proclaimed; this was the exercise of the poetic imagination, unlike the inferior verse of Pope and Swift and Donne, which dealt merely with 'familiar life and the manners of the age'. And the point about it that concerns us here is that archaic and artificial English is its appropriate medium. It would have been impossible to write 'The Bard' and 'The Descent of Odin' in anything approaching contemporary colloquial English, in, say, the idiom of Pope's 'Epistle to Arbuthnot'; the effect would have been hilarious. In the 'Elegy', which Professor Davie finds satisfactory only in part, one notes the difference in diction between the nobly dignified stanzas of the opening section, in which there is little archaism:

> *The boast of heraldry, the pomp of power,*
> *And all that beauty, all that wealth e'er gave,*
> *Awaits alike th' inevitable hour.*
> *The paths of glory lead but to the grave . . . .*
>
> (ll. 33-36)

and the archaism of such a maudlin stanza as this, from the self-pitying conclusion:

> *Hard by yon wood, now smiling as in scorn,*
> *Muttering his wayward fancies he would rove,*
> *Now drooping, woeful wan, like one forlorn,*
> *Or crazed with care, or crossed in hopeless love.*
>
> (ll. 105-8)

It was Samuel Johnson, of course, who found the example of Gray dangerous enough to mount a full-scale attack on it. Gray had made his own position clear in a letter to his friend West, which, since it was published in Mason's *Memoirs*, 1775, Johnson could very well have known:

> The language of the age is never the language of poetry; except among the French, whose verse, where the thought or image does not support it, differs in nothing from prose.

Poor disadvantaged French!

> Our poetry, on the contrary, has a language peculiar to itself; to which almost every one that has written has added something by enriching it with foreign idioms and derivatives; nay, sometimes words of their own composition or invention.

And he goes on to show that Shakespeare and Milton, and indeed Dryden, used such exotic diction.

94

Our language not being a settled thing (like the French) has an undoubted right to words of an hundred years old, provided antiquity have not rendered them unintelligible.[16]

The force of this last legalistic argument is a little hard to see.

Johnson's view, at the opposite pole from this, has seldom been accorded the importance I think it merits. As so often, Johnson here is far in advance of his time, pioneering a position that later critics are normally given credit for taking. We all know, of course, his comment, which may well be a comment on the passage just quoted: 'Gray thought his language more poetical as it was more remote from the common use' (*Lives*, III, 435). We know his strictures on Milton: 'Through all his greater works there prevails an uniform peculiarity of Diction, a mode and cast of expression which bears little resemblance to that of any former writer, and which is so far removed from common use, that an unlearned reader, when he first opens his book, finds himself surprised by a new language' (*Lives*, I, 189). Though of course the same complaint is made of Milton by critics from Welsted to T. S. Eliot, such comments have sometimes been explained by Johnson's alleged hostility to Milton's and Gray's Whiggism or by general personal or temperamental antipathy. This theory is at once refuted by calling attention to Johnson's criticism of Collins, a close personal friend for whom he had much tender affection. Collins's was the weakest talent of the three poets, and Johnson's strictures are correspondingly the severest: 'His diction was often harsh, unskilfully laboured, and injudiciously selected. He affected the obsolete when it was not worthy of revival; and he puts his words out of the common order, seeming to think, with some later candidates for fame, that not to write prose is certainly to write poetry' (*Lives*, III, 341).

These later candidates for fame included one Robert Potter, whose translation of Aeschylus Johnson thought 'verbiage' – he probably used the word as a French one, *verbiage* – and whose style he parodied in a burlesque translation of a chorus from Euripides:

> *Err shall they not who resolute explore*
> *Time's gloomy backward with judicious eyes,*
> *And scanning right the practices of yore*
> *Shall deem our hoar progenitors unwise.*

Johnson's own serious translation of the same chorus is not great poetry, but at least it approaches more closely to English; it begins:

> *The rites derived from ancient days*
> *With thoughtless reverence we praise,*
> *The rites that taught us to combine*
> *The joys of music and of wine.*[17]

They also included some of Johnson's personal friends, notably the Wartons, indefatigable dabblers in newly revived, 'with it' verse forms, such as the sonnet and the ballad. Johnson sourly sums up the poetic situation as he sees it in 1777; and not many later critics, viewing the vast poetic wasteland of the 70s, would disagree too violently:

> *Wheresoe'er I turn my view,*
> *All is strange, yet nothing new;*
> *Endless labour all along,*
> *Endless labour to be wrong;*
> *Phrase that time has flung away,*
> *Uncouth words in disarray:*
> *Trick'd in antique ruff and bonnet,*
> *Ode and elegy and sonnet.*[18]

Johnson's ballad parodies are attacks on the same kind of gimmickism that accounts for the popularity of the archaism and inversion used by Potter and many others. Here it is necessary to digress for a moment and rescue Johnson from a most unjust accusation by Wordsworth. You will perhaps have surmised that I believe Johnson's view of the proper language of poetry to be essentially the same as that propounded by Wordsworth in the 1800 Preface to *Lyrical Ballads*. I do think so; nevertheless, this does not mean that Wordsworth understood, or wanted to understand, what Johnson's position really was; few young, original writers want to do such justice to the leading figures of the preceding generation – Johnson certainly didn't do so to Swift, nor Swift to Dryden. For Wordsworth, as for many of his contemporaries, 'Dr. Johnson' was a potent symbol of the past they were revolting against, and in such circumstances any stigma will do to beat a dogma. Wordsworth found one in what he says was Johnson's attitude toward Percy's *Reliques of Ancient English Poetry*: 'The compilation was ... ill-suited to the then existing taste of city society', he writes in the 1815 *Essay Supplementary to the Preface*; 'and Dr. Johnson, 'mid the little senate to which he gave laws, was not sparing in his exertions to make it an object of contempt.' Nothing could be farther from the truth. Johnson did everything in his power to promote the success of the *Reliques*, advising Percy in his negotiations with the publisher, Dodsley; spending two months in Percy's home shortly before its publication, helping him with the glossarizing; writing a fine dedication for it; advertising it by mentioning it with praise several times in his edition of Shakespeare, published later the same year.[19]

What Johnson did view with contempt was the attempts of Percy,

Thomas Warton, and others, to cash in on the publicity thus given the old ballads: when they saw that a ballad looked easy to write, to churn out modern ballads of their own composing. Wordsworth as much as Johnson was repelled by their ineptness and phoniness; Percy's ballad, 'The Hermit of Warkworth', was written, says Wordsworth, in 'a diction scarcely in any one of its features distinguishable from the vague, the glossy, and unfeeling language of his day'. The ballad parody by Johnson that Wordsworth quotes, in the 1800 Preface, is not, of course, guilty of archaism:

> *I put my hat upon my head*
> *And walked into the Strand,*
> *And there I saw another man,*
> *Whose hat was in his hand.*[20]

Its fault, as Wordsworth says, and this was surely Johnson's point in composing it, is want of 'matter' – 'It is neither interesting in itself, nor can lead to anything interesting'; like Gray's most famous poem, as seen by Johnson, it does not promote any truth, moral or political. But another ballad parody by Johnson takes off the diction of 'The Hermit of Warkworth' perfectly – except, of course, for the last line:

> *Hermit hoar, in solemn cell,*
> *Wearing out life's evening gray,*
> *Smite thy bosom, sage, and tell*
> *Where is bliss? and what the way?*

('*Boswell*: But why smite his bosom, Sir? *Johnson*: Why, to show he was in earnest (smiling).')

> *Thus I spoke; and speaking sighed,*
> *Scarce repressed the starting tear:*
> *When the smiling sage replied,*
> *'Come, my lad, and drink some beer.'*[21]

It is an interesting experience to turn from Johnson's literary criticism to Wordsworth's 1800 Preface and discover how very close the views of the two men are – it is a pity that for most students these events take place in reverse order. Wordsworth reprobates 'the gaudiness and inane phraseology of many modern writers'; his own practice in *Lyrical Ballads*, he says, 'has necessarily cut me off from a large portion of phrases and figures of speech which from father to son have long been regarded as the common inheritance of poets'. One thinks of Johnson's scathing account of late eighteenth-century writers – essentially the same writers Wordsworth is complaining of – by comparison with the Metaphysicals: 'To write on *their* plan it was at least necessary to read and think. No man could be born a metaphysical poet, nor assume the dignity of a writer, by descriptions copied from descriptions, by imitations borrowed from imitations, by traditional imagery and hereditary similes.'[22] To both men, Gray is the symbol of what they reprehend – 'the head of those', Wordsworth calls him, 'who, by their reasonings, have attempted to widen the space of separation betwixt prose and metrical composition, and was more than any other man curiously elaborate in the structure of his own poetic diction'. Wordsworth, like Johnson, had probably read in Mason the remarks quoted above from Gray's letter to West. 'Not only the language of a large portion of every good poem', Wordsworth says, in opposition to them, 'even of the most elevated character, must necessarily, except with reference to the metre, in no respect differ from that of good prose, but likewise some of the most interesting parts of the best poems will be found to be strictly the language of prose when prose is well written. . . . It may be safely affirmed that there neither is, nor can be, any *essential* difference between the language of prose and metrical composition.' (How perverse of Matthew Arnold, in the face of this, and in an essay which opens with a quotation recognizing Wordsworth's greatness as a critic, to stigmatize Dryden and Pope as 'not classics of our poetry', but 'classics of our prose', Gray being 'our poetical classic of that literature and age'!)[23] Johnson's sarcasms, 'Gray thought his language more poetical as it was more remote from common use' and 'Collins [seemed] to think . . . that not to write prose is certainly to write poetry', have already been noted. The classic modern restatement of Wordsworth's and Johnson's position, as against Gray's and Arnold's – and what also seems to be Coleridge's, in his attack on Wordsworth in *Biographia Literaria* – is T. S. Eliot's essay of 1930 on Johnson's poetry, one of Eliot's finest critical performances:

> Certain qualities are to be expected of any type of good verse at any time; we may say the qualities which good verse shares with good prose. Hardly any good poet in English has written *bad* prose. . . . This is not a sign of versatility but of unity. For there are qualities essential to good prose which are essential to good verse as well; and we may say with Mr. Ezra Pound, that verse must be at least as well written as prose. . . . One does not need to examine a great deal of the inferior verse of the eighteenth century to realize that the trouble with it is that it is not prosaic enough.[24]

Johnson and Wordsworth would have heartily agreed.

All three critics then believe essentially that the poet must use 'a selection of language really used by men'. It should never be forgotten –

though Coleridge seems to forget it – that Wordsworth heavily stresses, as Johnson would have, the word 'selection'.[25] The language of country-men, Wordsworth says, 'has been adopted (purified indeed from what appear to be its real defects, from all lasting causes of dislike or disgust)'; the selection is to be made 'with true taste and feeling'; the poet's language, 'if selected truly and judiciously, must necessarily be dignified and variegated and alive with metaphors and figures'. All this is highly Johnsonian.

There is much more in the 1800 Preface that is Johnsonian: the philosophical or moral grounds on which Wordsworth argues that the language of poetry *must* be based on 'the language really used by men' – his view of the function and the material of poetry. 'The passions and thoughts and feelings' which the poet expresses, he writes, 'are the general passions and thoughts and feelings of men'. They are connected 'with our moral sentiments and animal sensations . . . with loss of friends and kindred, with injuries and resentments, gratitude and hope, with fear and sorrow. These, and the like, are the sensations and objects which the poet describes, as they are the sensations of other men, and the objects which interest them.' This is very far from Joseph Warton's sneer against unimaginative 'observations on familiar life and the manners of the age', and very close to Johnson's 'I have often thought that there has rarely passed a life of which a judicious and faithful narrative would not be useful. . . . We are all prompted by the same motives, all deceived by the same fallacies, all animated by hope, obstructed by danger, entangled by desire and seduced by pleasure.'[26]

The material of poetry then is 'the general passions and thoughts and feelings of men'; and since 'the poet thinks and feels in the spirit of human passions, how then can his language differ in any material degree from that of all other men who feel vividly and see clearly? Poets do not write for poets alone, but for men'. 'An author', wrote Johnson, 'partakes of the common condition of humanity; he is born and married like another man; he has hopes and fears, expectations and disappointments, griefs and joys, and friends and enemies, like a courtier or a statesman' and 'The only end of writing is to enable the readers better to enjoy life or better to endure it.'[27] Again Wordsworth: 'To this knowledge which all men carry about with them, and to these sympathies in which, without any other discipline than that of our daily life, we are fitted to take delight, the poet principally directs his attention. He considers man and nature as essentially adapted to each other, and the mind of man as naturally the mirror of the fairest and most interesting properties of nature.' 'The poet converses with general nature', Wordsworth insists, unlike the scientist, who converses 'with those particular parts of nature which are the objects of his studies.' One thinks of Johnson's Imlac, who warns the poet not to number the streaks of the tulip (as the botanist does) – and indeed there is no numbering of the streaks of Wordsworth's very general daffodils.

One is irresistibly reminded of Johnson on Shakespeare: 'Nothing can please many and please long but just representations of general nature. ... This therefore is the praise of Shakespeare, that his drama is the mirror of life: he who has mazed his imagination in following the phantoms which other writers raise up before him may here be cured of his delirious ecstasies by reading human sentiments in human language.' It is a different ideal of poetry from Joseph Warton's or from that which a critic of the 1920s lamented that Johnson did not have – 'The conception of poetry as a chariot whirling us heavenward in glory above the commonplaces of daily life was not his'.[28] It was not Wordsworth's either, nor Eliot's, who could write of the evening 'spread out against the sky/ Like a patient etherized upon a table'. I don't know whether it was Gray's or not, but certainly neither Johnson nor Wordsworth felt that in his poems, except occasionally, as in the 'Elegy', they were reading human sentiments in human language.

University of Southern California

Notes

1. Facsimile reprint, Los Angeles: Augustan Reprint Society, 1947, p. 5. It is interesting to note that Wesley's own verse here exhibits the 'neat plainness' of prose, not 'strong figures' or 'a diff'rent set of words'. This of course is because he is using the 'unpolish'd, rugged verse' (Dryden's phrase) thought adequate to verse satire, the verse epistle, and the like. The popularity of such forms in the eighteenth century may reflect an unconscious shift of poetic taste in the direction of Wordsworth's 'language really used by men'.

2. That is, the older work, based on *Webster's Second International Dictionary*. It is gratifying to note that *Webster's Third International,* and its abridgement, *Webster's Seventh New Collegiate,* seem to have at last abandoned this usage label. The *Random House College Dictionary* uses 'Literary'; it is hard to say whether this is better or worse than 'Poetic'. The *Concise Oxford* referred to is the third edition; I have not seen the latest edition. Johnson's *Dictionary,* needless to say, recognizes no such classification. Under 'ween', he gives many illustrative quotations from Spenser, Shakespeare, and Milton, but flatly tags the word 'Obsolete'.

3. London, 1952.

4. *Eighteenth-Century Critical Essays* (Ithaca, New York, 1960).

5. Elledge, I, 326-27.

6. 'Timber, or Discoveries', in *Critical Essays of the Seventeenth Century,* ed. J. E. Spingarn (Oxford, 1908), I, 34. The comment on Sidney is from *Conversations with Drummond of Hawthornden.*

7. III, 181-86.

8. 'Essay on the Genius and Writings of Pope', in Elledge, II, 717-19.

9. 'On English Translation', in *Literary Distractions* (London and New York, 1958), pp. 38-39.

10. *Put Out More Flags* (London, 1942), p. 203.

11. *The Letters of Ezra Pound,* ed. D. D. Paige (New York, 1950), pp. 89-90.

12. *Love and Death in the American Novel* (New York, 1960).

13. Sir Robert Walpole's biographer, J. H. Plumb, thinks the old rumour that Horace was not Sir Robert's son, but Carr Hervey's, is probably correct. Plumb's tracing of the movements of Sir Robert and Lady Walpole at the time the child must have been conceived – they had been long separated, and Lady Walpole was staying in Suffolk, near the Herveys – is convincing (*Sir Robert Walpole: The Making of a Statesman* [London, 1956], pp. 258-59.) 'The supposed necessary care of me so engrossed my mother, that compassion and tenderness soon became extreme fondness', Horace later reported. (W. S. Lewis, *Horace Walpole* [New York, 1961], p. 11.)

14. *The Collected Poems of Christopher Smart,* ed. Norman Callan (London, 1949), I, xxi. Ketton-Cremer (*Gray,* p. 86), however, believes the story apocryphal.

15. *Purity of Diction in English Verse,* p. 37n.

16. *Corres.,* I, 192-93. Johnson read Mason's book and disapproved of it (James Boswell, *Letters,* ed. C. B. Tinker [Oxford, 1924], I, 222-23).

17. *The Works of Samuel Johnson* (New Haven, 1958-),VI, 304, 303.

18. *Works,* VI, 288. When Dorothy Wordsworth introduced William to Milton's sonnets in 1802, a handful of memorable ones presently resulted. Yet it can plausibly be argued, when one looks at the thousands of dreary sonnets that infest the nineteenth and early twentieth centuries, that the revival of this Renaissance form was as dubious a blessing as the eighteenth-century fashion of imitating Miltonic blank verse. Even competent poets like Wordsworth

and Arnold fell victim to its dangerous facility, as the *Ecclesiastical Sonnets* and 'Who prop, thou ask'st, in these bad days, my mind' amply testify. To what depths it could sink in the hands of a lesser practitioner can be judged by glancing at some recently discovered 'Democratic Sonnets' by W. M. Rossetti (*Victorian Studies*, XIV [March, 1971], 270-74) – e.g., 'Postal Reform, 1840-41', which begins, 'To speak with tongue untrammelled, and to write/ With pen which barely pays the state its due,/ This, Englishmen, is first achieved by you'.

19. Johnson, *Letters*, ed. R. W. Chapman (Oxford, 1952), Letter 134.2; Allen T. Hazen, *Johnson's Prefaces and Dedications* (New Haven, 1934), pp. 158-63; Johnson, *Works*, index to vols. VII, VIII under 'Percy, *Reliques*'.

20. *Works*, VI, 269. Puzzlingly, Wordsworth's version is the first edition of the correct text, preserved in MS. among Boswell's papers.

21. Ibid., 294-95; *Boswell's Life*, III, 159.

22. *Lives*, I, 21. Wordsworth's Preface is cited from *Modern Criticism: Theory and Practice*, ed W. Sutton and R. Foster (New York, 1963), pp. 14-27. The text is that of the 1802 edition of *Lyrical Ballads*.

23. 'The Study of Poetry', in Sutton and Foster, pp. 94-108.

24. Introduction to 'London' and 'The Vanity of Human Wishes' (1930). Reprinted in *English Critical Essays: Twentieth Century*, ed. Phyllis M. Jones (Oxford, 1933).

25. 'The poet's art is selection' (*Lives*, III, 356).

26. *Rambler*, no. 60. For Johnson, biography, at least, does not 'avoid and exclude all accident', to quote Coleridge. The best comment on his famous dictum here, 'The business of the biographer is often to pass slightly over those performances and incidents which produce vulgar greatness, to lead the thoughts into domestick privacies, and display the minute details of daily life, where exterior appendages are cast aside and men excel each other only by prudence and virtue', is surely the passage from 'Tintern Abbey', 'That best portion of a good man's life,/ His little nameless unremembered acts/ Of kindness and of love' – or perhaps *The Prelude* itself.

27. *Idler*, no. 102; review of Soame Jenyns, *A Free Inquiry into the Nature and Origin of Evil*.

28. Joseph Epes Brown, *The Critical Opinions of Samuel Johnson* (Princeton, 1926), p. xxxi.

ELI MANDEL

Theories of Voice in Eighteenth-Century Poetry: Thomas Gray and Christopher Smart

'There can have been no personal sympathy or liking between them' (*Gray*, p. 86). Thomas Gray and Christopher Smart, Gray's latest biographer reminds us, had little use for one another. But they did share a talent for a peculiar poetry, a kind with which we are still not entirely at ease. It is that talent and that poetry which occupy me in this paper. We can agree, I suppose, with Norman MacLean's remark that the eighteenth century 'regarded the highest form of the lyric – the Great Ode – as one of the supreme expressions of poetry and itself as a supreme epoch in the history of the lyric', though it is not entirely clear that his rather florid ranking of Cowley, Dryden, and Gray is one that would have received instantaneous and unanimous critical support in the period.[1] Perhaps there is reason enough to look again at the Odes. After all, Gray evidently regarded his Pindarics as his most significant poetic achievement, and the puzzles of language and form the Odes attempt to solve remain to engage contemporary poets, however differently after two hundred years they might put the question.

I attempt, then, to look at questions raised by Smart's 'Song to David' and his *Jubilate Agno* and by Gray's Pindaric Odes; more particularly, my purpose is to consider the implications of Gray's and Smart's metaphoric identification of music and poetry, an identification which, in the form of the opening images of 'The Progress of Poesy', Dr. Johnson, you will remember, believed to be nonsense.

The terms 'voice' and 'music' appear in Smart's *Jubilate*.[2] Among the many curious and delightful passages in that poem, there is one which celebrates in Smart's enthusiastic way the power of prayer and voice:

> *For the AIR is purified by prayer which is*
> *made aloud and with all our might.*
> *For loud prayer is good for weak lungs and*

for a vitiated throat.
For SOUND is propagated in the spirit and
  in all directions.
For the VOICE of a figure is compleat in all
  its parts.
For a man speaks HIMSELF from the crown of his
  head to the sole of his feet.
For a LION roars HIMSELF compleat from head
  to tail.
                                    (Bl, 223-29)

We know Smart prayed mightily and noisily – in good voice, as he would say. One reason for his difficulty with authorities seems to have been his loud voice. We know also that he consistently identified prayer with poetry. Following the passage I have just quoted, for example, a series of rapid and remarkable associations links 'voice' with musical instruments and with the harp of God, a harp possessing powers identical with those attributed to David's harp in 'A Song to David'. Meanwhile, alongside these associations, a kind of contrapuntal voice in the 'Let' section works out variations on the theme of Leviathan and the creatures of the deep. A passing pun, nimbly if outrageously, delineates Smart's theme throughout the two linked passages: the nature of a Christian poetics, whatever is implied by the sound links and disparities in 'Apollos' and 'St. Paul'. Elsewhere in Smart, as we shall see, this metaphorical identity of voice, music, and poetry is considerably elaborated.

In its most general sense, of course, the metaphor or parallel of music and poetry remains mysterious, at best an evocative comment on the nature or essential character of poetry; at worst, sloppy aesthetics and murky sentiment. The parallel may even be of only superficial interest in eighteenth-century poetics despite its appearance in Gray's 'Progress of Poesy' and in a host of eighteenth-century 'progress' poems, allegories, and – by implication at least – St. Cecilia's Day odes. Jean Hagstrum reminds us, in his invaluable study of the pictorial and iconic tradition of English poetry from Dryden to Gray, of the point at which we find 'the replacement of painting by music as the art most analogous to poetry' in Burke's and Lessing's attack on pictorialist doctrine.[3] The musical analogy, M. H. Abrams suggests, belongs more properly or at least seems to present itself more often to nineteenth-century poetry and criticism than to the eighteenth century, its culminating expression presumably Pater's dictum that 'all art aspires to the condition of music'.[4] And if we are willing to follow a suggestion of Northrop Frye's in the *Anatomy of Criti-*

cism – that in English poetry imitative harmony is invariably visual rather than musical[5] – it would appear that in diction as well as in imagery the great eighteenth-century progress or pageant of poetry is visual or iconic, not truly auditory or musical.

If, however, Smart's or Gray's parallel of poetry and music is intended not in a general but in a specific sense, it points in a different direction from wherever it is onomatopoeia means to lead us, and it intends, I think, a rather different meaning for music from that implied by isolating diction or imagery as the essential poetic element. Smart's *Jubilate* leads me to believe he used 'voice' in at least two major senses which I would want to observe in reading Gray's Pindaric Odes, at least as a guide to the dimensions of the critical question I have raised. One sense I can best describe as dramatic; the other, for want of a better word, lyric. Both terms I use in a somewhat restricted sense. In its dramatic sense, 'voice' implies something akin to T. S. Eliot's meaning in his discussion of the three voices of poetry. A roughly synonymous term, it might be thought, would be 'persona', though I take it an eighteenth-century equivalent is less a character than a style, or more precisely a variety of styles. I think there is a parallel in George Wright's notion of the dramatic character of grammatical structure and persons. 'It is appropriate', he says, 'that the distinction between grammatical persons should be dramatic distinctions, for both grammar and drama are formalizations of the dynamics of human speech.'[6]

The term 'lyric' unfortunately overlaps with one of Eliot's three voices, but as I use it here it connects only in the most tenuous fashion with that; it has even less to do with those other richly obscure notions, Eliot's 'auditory imagination' and Pound's 'melopoeia', since both tend towards an unconscious music, as in Pound's account, 'perhaps the bridge between consciousness and the unthinking sentiment or even insentient universe'.[7] If I understand Donald Davie's comments on Fenollosa correctly, lyric voice corresponds to certain features of ideogram, though in place of the word 'things' one would write 'landscape', or 'the picturesque': 'According to Fenollosa, the uniquely poetical value of Chinese rests in its combining this temporal (sequacious) feature with the density and angularity of "things", the peculiar contribution of painting and sculpture. It is thus, as it were, both music and painting.'[8] An eighteenth-century equivalent would be the oft employed term 'harmony', 'tout ensemble' as Gray would have it, though less misleading is the unusual term Bishop Lowth employs in his *Lectures* on Hebrew poetry, 'inflexion', and most precise of all is Smart's 'visible prayer'.

In Gray's Odes as in Smart's, then, the parallel of poetry and music is manipulated in two ways: one is literal, the other metaphoric; one, in the dramatic character and situation of the poem; the other, in its speech. In both poets, subject and situation are literally poetry as music, presented to us in the form of a bardic figure or composite of figures. Metaphorically, the same figure appears in a use of language – syntax and diction – that elaborates, in a sense that I think can be spoken of precisely as musical, the literal subject of the poem. Perhaps a simpler and more direct means of suggesting the complexity and aptness of the musical analogy, and of explaining its persistence as a means of articulating the patterns and structures of poetry, offers itself in an ancient phrase: not *ut pictura poesis* but a speaking picture; in other words, a paradoxical inversion that sees the pictorial as the musical, or at least the enormous tension involved in that oxymoron which confuses the spatial and temporal.

It was, of course, not only the 'glittering accumulations of ungraceful ornaments' that offended Dr. Johnson (*Lives*, III, 440), nor solely the harshness of the language under which Gray's Odes laboured, nor even the unnatural violence with which the mind of the writer seemed to work. As usual, Dr. Johnson knew a critical problem when he saw one. As he puts it, it is the relative position of art and nature that signifies: 'An epithet or metaphor drawn from Nature ennobles Art', he comments in his criticism of Gray's poem, 'an epithet or metaphor drawn from Art degrades Nature' (*Lives*, III, 436-37). The critical problem of the Odes, as indeed of a poetry like Smart's, is that of estimating the formative power of genres, how we understand that 'Nature and Homer are the same'. Apparently, there is some link between the doctrine of poetic kinds and the musical metaphor in Gray and Smart.

Reminding us that generic criticism derives logically from a mimetic theory of literature, Earl Wasserman describes the doctrine of kinds as a 'cosmic syntax', one of those enormous articulating or ordering principles in the public domain to be placed alongside 'the Christian interpretation of history, the sacramentalism of nature, the Great Chain of Being, the analogy of the various planes of creation, the conception of man as microcosm'.[9] Since these patterns are what is meant by 'nature', the poet's imitation of nature gives reality to nature's principles.

It is doubtful that generic criticism has elsewhere been more exalted, though Wasserman, I think, is right to see it not simply as the 'rules of old' but as a mode of articulation so pervasive and schematically powerful as virtually to constitute its own survey of reality and experience. It is equally important to distinguish, as Wasserman does, the mimetic from the creative conception of poetry and to see the change from the one to the other as 'more than a critical phenomenon'. Yet the temptation of intellectual history is uniformity. One rightly finds the great cultural metaphors suspect. Ascham, Puttenham, Sidney, Milton, Dryden, and Addison certainly shared the doctrine of poetic kinds but their views about reality could scarcely with sense be put into the same vocabulary. That is why it is important, as well as fascinating, to find that plainly undeluded philosopher Hobbes working out an appealingly concise critical schema of poetic kinds: the poetic universe divides into three, the celestial, aerial, and terrestrial; this triad corresponds to those divisions in mankind poets treat of in imitating human life: the court, the city, and the country; and those imitations in turn yield heroic, scommatic, and pastoral poems.[10]

If not an ontology but a literary tradition identifies poetic kinds, it is a tradition of extraordinary range and flexibility, perhaps properly a 'cosmic syntax', at any rate able to comprehend the ambiguities of 'nature' and 'art' in Pope's famous lines:

> *Learn hence for ancient rules a just esteem*
> *To copy nature is to copy them.*

Presumably the balance of art and nature must somehow be maintained, perhaps in the ambiguities Pope plays upon. But a peculiarity of generic criticism is that certain forms tend to tip the balance toward an implied superiority of art to nature. For a variety of reasons, most of which Norman MacLean discusses in his 'From Action to Image', the art poem or high ode is such a form. But the musical analogies for poetry must have presented themselves naturally enough in the doctrine of kinds, in the Pindaric and Psalmist models, for example, both linked, through the theory of the Longinian sublime, to the Miltonic mode and its revelatory moments. A miracle of compression condenses the vast and comprehensive plan of the epic into the flashing power of creative phrases or insights. Addison's version may be taken as typical, despite its perilous trembling at the edge of the worst effects of the inexpressible sublime or intense inane variety. As cultural definition it can scarcely be bettered. Addison's enormously influential essays sought, among other things, to normalize, as it were, the epic, an intention that led to an orderly display of the work according to appropriate critical method, but oddly enough gave to the poem a peculiar emphasis, converting it from epic to a series of lyrics and landscape description. So it is that Milton's poem is virtually defined in the vision of creation, when the Messiah 'looked down with pleasure upon his new Creation, when every Part of Nature seem'd to rejoice in its Existence; when the Morning-Stars sang together, and all the Sons of God shouted for joy'.[11] Epic praise and St. Cecilia's Day odes may sort oddly together in our scheme of things. But from Cowley to Smart, there was little disagreement that music as a heavenly power ought to be celebrated, as gods and heroes were celebrated, in great odes. It was a short step from the celebration of music and heroes, in poems *accompanied* by music, to the identification of the poem itself with its mode and subject. One of Mason's notes to the 'Progress of Poesy' is worth recalling here:

> It will not surely be improper, at the conclusion of this ode, so peculiarly admirable for the musical flow of its numbers, to mention one circumstance relative to English lyric poetry in general, and much to its honour, which has lately been communicated to me by an ingenious friend. It is this: That it can fully, at least when in the hands of such a master, support its harmony without the assistance of musick. For there is great reason to believe that in the Greek ode, of which we are taught to think so highly, the power of numbers was little perceived without the effectual aid of a musical accompaniment.[12]

Gray's lyrics, this ingenious friend declares, 'with the richness of imagery and the glow of expression, breathe also the various modulations of an intrinsick and independent melody'. Interestingly enough, he theorizes that 'this singular advantage', as he calls it, derives from rhyme, and he concludes 'whatever opinion may be formed of its true use in other kinds of poetry . . . it is a necessary support to the harmony of our ode'.[13] An intriguing comment, particularly when one recalls Gray's extensive study of rhyme, his 'Observations on English Metre', 'On the Pseudo-Rhythmus', his experiments in prosody and his devotion to Latin verse.

Gray, of course, believed his Odes to be regular and, if we are to judge from the guarded ironies of his letters, was much concerned that the regularity of his work be noticed. Charges of obscurity disturbed and irritated him. '. . . as to the notes', he said, 'I do it out of spite' (*Corres.,* III, 1002). The comment throws some light on Smart's bitter reaction to criticism of his own great poem: 'This Song', he said, 'is allowed by Mr. Smart's judicious Friends and enemies to be the best Piece ever made public by him, its chief fault being the exact Regularity and Method with which it is conducted.'[14] For Gray and Smart, no doubt, it still made sense to appeal to a doctrine of kinds as sanction for a poetry that seemed to them essentially traditional, if impressed with the poet's own language. The tradition, of course, was not solely a repository of diction and image or choice lines that might serve as bright glass in their mosaic; in a literal sense it was the subject, the progress of poetry, and it offered the means to speak as well: the gigantic figure of bard, prophet, hero, whose poetic form I consider next.

As dramatic figure or speaker of the poem, the eighteenth-century character, unlike, say, a Browning persona, can quite properly present himself, as he frequently does, in a bewildering variety of voices rather than one. He is, as it were, drama rather than dramatic character. Styles, not a style. This, at least, seems to be the implication of Pope's remark to Spence on the subject of kinds and appropriate styles: 'Though Virgil, in his pastorals, has sometimes six or eight lines together that are epic, I have been so scrupulous as scarce ever to admit above two together, even in the Messiah.'[15] Or again, "Thus, for language; if an elegy; "these lines are very good, but are not they of too heroical a strain?" '[16] Maynard Mack remarks that for the Augustans allusion is a form of metaphor;[17] so too couplets and quatrains are compressed dramas, a view recalling Professor Davie's comments about a sentence having a tragic plot.[18]

The rich suggestiveness of Gray's stanzas, one suspects, proceeds from this sort of metaphoric drama of voice, as in the 'Eton College Ode':

> *Ah, happy hills, ah, pleasing shade,*
> *Ah, fields beloved in vain,*
> *Where once my careless childhood strayed,*
> *A stranger yet to pain!*

(ll. 11-14)

The antithesis of 'happiness' and 'vanity' is perhaps obvious, but 'childhood' and 'stranger' is a less easy opposition, particularly since the force of 'stranger' is directed along syntactical lines toward and away from 'strayed' and 'pain' and back then, with peculiar force, to the word 'careless'. The effect, of course, is more noticeable as between stanzas than simply within, and it seems to have been this peculiar disjunctiveness that in part created for readers the obscurity of the Pindaric Odes and Smart's 'Song'. One might perhaps recall the Augustan poets' command of rhetorical devices by pointing to the variety of modes each is capable of (Horatian satire, georgics and pastorals, Pindarics) but it is not rhetoric that concerns me here. I want to suggest rather that in the 'Progress of Poesy' and in Smart's 'Song' the disjunctive particulars create a character or person who exists, disconcertingly, in the landscape of the poem.

David, for example, is described. He is not the speaker of the song. Yet it is virtually impossible to escape the sense that he is the poem, and I think it can be shown that he is identified by Smart with harp, temple, landscape, and seasons. He is Israel, a tribe, a land, a person.[19]

Something similar happens in Gray's 'Progress'. As Professor Hagstrum has so convincingly shown, the poem presents, in sequence, tableaux or pictorial arrangements from a Birth of Venus allegory or 'Dance to the Music of Time' to the manifestation of the poets, Milton 'like Raphael's representation of the God of Ezekiel's vision', Dryden as 'Guido's or Poussin's Apollo', Shakespeare as a Child of Nature, and the poet as harpist, and awakening youth.[20] It has been taken to be a difficulty in the poem that the connections between stanzas, between the various tableaux and landscapes, is loose and arbitrary, the plan without unity. I would suggest the connections are made in the last stanza and they are twofold: one is the visionary world of poetry, 'forms . . . unborrow'd of the sun', that identifies the light brightening the poem as the ideal light of Fancy; the other is the explicit equating of music and painting, the musical as the pictorial:

> *Hark, his hands the lyre explore!*
> *Bright-eyed Fancy hovering o'er*
> *Scatters from her pictured urn*
> *Thoughts that breathe and words that burn.*
>
> (ll. 107-10)

Through successive manifestations, from the watery source of poetry to the image of the god-poets, the poem turns into an image of the poet himself about to see, presumably, what the poem has already shown us. The stanza fuses the playing of David's harp with visionary language and with the poet's own premonition or prefiguring of what is about to be:

> *Such forms as glitter in the Muse's ray*
> *With orient hues, unborrowed of the sun . . . .*
>
> (ll. 119-20)

The stanza then looks back across the whole poem as musical structure and as well with the astonished sense that the vision of the poem is only about to be.

In 'The Bard' the same image is amplified, but whereas in the 'Progress of Poesy' the poem only seems to come into existence at its conclusion, the vision of 'The Bard' closes with an ironic dissolution of the images we have seen. In that poem, a poet confronts a king and sings gloomy prophecies to him, while inside the panorama of the poem, inside the Bard's song, is another scene of ghostly poets weaving further prophecies.

Another poet-prophet confronts a gloomy king-tyrant in Smart's 'Song to David' and like Gray's Bard displays panoramic cyclical visions of dazzling pictorial complexity. A further elaboration seems to have been introduced by Smart in the temple imagery which, it appears, identifies musical structure with architecture, a possibility put forward in early impressionistic criticism of the poem and given considerable plausibility by Smart's handling of the tribes of Israel figures in the *Jubilate*.[21] Moreover, David's song, like its Orphic parallel in the *Jubilate*, unites music with vision. Like God's harp, 'its tune is a work of creation'.[22]

Violent as these conjunctions are, they are by no means unusual. The figure of the prophet whose song is a structure recurs: Prospero, with strange music, conjuring up a masque; the devils, in a demonic version of God's creativity, building Pandemonium to the sound of pagan music; Kubla Khan weaving mystic circles, attempting with song to build a sunny dome in air; Merlin depicting Camelot as a city built to music and therefore never built at all and therefore always being built; Abt Vogler summoning Solomon's demons to build a palace of art to his extemporized music. As encounter of prophet-poet and king, the range is from Dryden's Timotheus shaping Alexander's spirit in strange ways, to Pope's profoundly ironic praise of his Augustus, to Browning's Cleon denying Protus the one answer his art should give.

I do not mean these examples to indicate historical connection but rather to clarify the form that identifies music and poem, spatial structure and temporal rhythm. We can call it Byzantium, or Peter Quince, or A Midsummer Night's Dream, or the Bard. As in Yeats's 'Sailing to Byzantium', the prophetic vision is both picture:

> . . . sages standing in God's holy fire
> As in the gold mosaic of a wall

and song, a metal bird piping to a drowsy emperor 'of what is past or passing or to come'. It is *that* bird, 'Miracle, bird, or golden handiwork./ More miracle than bird or handiwork', an ironic version of poet before the king, and equally all that poetry can be. It is all that is implied in the differences between 'sensual music' and 'artificial song' and in the ironic tension between them. Peter Quince's music at the clavier playing upon an indifferent woman turns into the story of Susanna's music playing upon the Elders who would have played upon her. 'Music', moralizes Peter, 'is feeling then, not sound.' But it is, as his name tells us, a play within a play, a dream within a dream. As in *A Midsummer Night's Dream*, it may be the play or dream of a king-poet and his demonic counterpart, but whatever its multiple ironies, it creates illusions, pictures of sound, temples built and never built. Of the conclusion to Gray's

'Bard', Professor Hagstrum remarks: 'the bard and the sun have disappeared. The impoverished world is left to darkness – to "endless night" and the sound of roaring waters. The last effect of the poem, which Gray intended to be his greatest and of which he said, "I felt myself the Bard" is thus to dissolve its own visual fabric and to leave not a rack behind.'[23] At the conclusion of *The Tempest*, Prospero appears, to ask for our applause, in words that tell us we have now become the play itself:

> *Now I want*
> *Spirits to enforce, art to enchant,*
> *And my ending is despair,*
> *Unless I be relieved by prayer,*
> *Which pierces so that it assaults*
> *Mercy itself and frees all faults.*

If the bard is a musical figure or icon, in the sense of one who as a work of art points to a work of art – successively alienating the reader from the representative—the question still remains whether his language may in any precise sense be said to be musical. The question returns us to the first stanza of Gray's 'Progress of Poesy' and one of the most perplexing comments in eighteenth-century criticism. Samuel Johnson, of course, objects to Gray's confounding the images of 'spreading sound' and 'running water', remarking of the metaphor, 'If this be said of Musick, it is nonsense; if it be said of Water, it is nothing to the purpose' (*Lives*, III, 436). Applied to the comparison of music and water, Johnson's comment seems to me perfectly just. The problem is to decide what sort of landscape Gray intends us to see. His own explanation is, of course, well-known: 'The subject and simile, as usual with Pindar, are united. The various sources of poetry, which gives life and lustre to all it touches, are here described; its quiet majestic progress enriching every subject (otherwise dry and barren) with a pomp of diction and luxuriant harmony of numbers; and its more rapid and irresistible course, when swoln and hurried away by the conflict of tumultuous passions' (*Poems*, p. 161). 'Stream of music' is not said of music but of the music of poetry, a distinction Johnson seems to have missed. The stream is not a literal stream. It is a stream of diction, harmony of numbers, and tumultuous passions. That cannot exist in a naturalistic landscape. As external imitation, then, the passage literally makes no sense. The spatial and temporal can only be fused in an inner landscape or internal imitation of the sort described in the eighteenth century by Bishop Lowth:

Poetry is said to consist in imitation: whatever the human mind is able to conceive, it is the province of poetry to imitate; things, places, appearances natural and artificial, actions, passions, manners and customs: and since the human intellect is naturally delighted with every species of imitation, that species in particular, which exhibits its own image, which displays and depicts those impulses, inflexions, perturbations, and secret emotions, which it perceives and knows in itself, can scarcely fail to astonish and to delight above every other.[24]

Elsewhere in Lowth's lectures, as in Addison's papers on Milton's epic, and Dennis's essays on the sublime, we are told of an appropriate language for this internal imitation, a language peculiar to itself, Gray said in one of his best known comments on poetry.[25] It is what James Thomson spoke of as 'the peculiar language of heaven' and what Smart termed 'Impression', a language he described variously as prophetic or Horatian, an 'unrivall'd peculiarity of expression', as he said of Horace's poetry.[26] It is difficult to improve on Robert Brittain's analysis of Smart's Hebraic and Horatian qualities, and his list of examples of the peculiar impress and extraordinary concentration of Smart's language is quite marvellous: 'quick peculiar quince'; 'ye that skill the flowers to fancy'; 'the blaze and rapture of the sun'; 'idly vague from his indulgent yoke'; or 'to supplicate the knee'.[27] And, of course, there is the much-quoted stanza:

> Spinks and ouzles sing sublimely
> 'We too have a Saviour born';
> Whiter blossoms burst untimely
> On the blest Mosaic thorn.[28]

I think it is possible to put alongside this an equally fine list from Gray. There are differences, no doubt, but the effect, Horatian or Hebraic, is the same, an exactness of compression: 'Quenched in dark clouds of slumber'; 'Their feather-cinctured chiefs'; 'sea-encircled coast'; 'ratify his doom'; 'the tissue of thy line'; 'birds of boding cry'; 'Exact my own defects to scan';[29] and this quatrain from the 'Eton Ode':

> To each his sufferings: all are men,
> Condemned alike to groan;
> The tender for another's pain,
> The unfeeling for his own.
>
> (ll. 91-94)

Lowth's inflexions, secret emotions, image of the mind, presumably appear in the complexity of response this language calls forth as well as in its precision. But Brittain insists on another element, a musical one, or at least one for which he finds a parallel in eighteenth-century music: 'rich elaboration upon a structurally solid framework', 'the art of baroque . . . of Handel and his English successors such as Arne and Boyce'.[30] Now this is not the sort of analogy of music and poetry I have proposed elsewhere, but the possibility that Impression is contrapuntal or fugal language is worth looking at.

In the *Jubilate*, this intriguing meditation on 'relation' appears:

> For the relations of words are in pairs first.
> For the relations of words are sometimes in oppositions.
> For the relations of words are according to their
>   distances from the pair.

(B2, 600-02)

By itself, mysterious. But in the poem it is placed between an exercise on the spiritual music, as Smart calls it, and a catalogue of the tribes of Israel and their virtues. The spiritual music passage is one of several sonic and ideogrammatic alphabets in the *Jubilate*. They have been taken to be mad ravings. They have been called 'ridiculous exercises';[31] they have been seen as a sort of hopeless turning-over of the poetic engine on a cold morning, 'sputters and sparks of the fusing intellect', as Frye puts it, 'the creative process in an interesting formative stage', subconscious paranomasia.[32] They are, I think, none of these.

One such alphabet spells out the language of flowers, another the gods within numbers, another the pictures inside letters, the most interesting, for our purposes, the one on spiritual music. The fact that it amuses does not seem to me proof of lunacy:

> For the spiritual musick is as follows.
> For there is a thunder-stop, which is the voice
>   of God direct.
> For the rest of the stops are by their rhimes.
> For the trumpet rhimes are sound bound, soar
>   more and the like.
> For the Shawm rhimes are lawn fawn moon boon and
>   the like.
> For the harp rhimes are sing ring, string & the like.

(B2, 584-89)

And so it goes to the marvellously mysterious line:

> For the Bassoon rhimes are pass, class and the like.
>   God be gracious to Baumgarden.

(B2, 594)

If the rhymes mean anything at all in this biblical orchestra, it is that paired voices speak to one another and then it becomes possible to work out in poetry such remarkable counterpointings as, say, the language of scripture and the language of natural science, or personal experience and biblical story, or England's green and pleasant land and Jerusalem, or the tribes, their virtues, the virtues of Englishmen, the city of God. The leap from spiritual music to a poetics of relation to the throne of Revelation taking shape in eighteenth-century England becomes, at the very least, a possibility. How much easier to counterpoint the visual and the auditory. 'For', says Smart,

> The VOICE is from the body and the spirit – and
>   is a body and a spirit.
> For the prayers of good men are therefore visible
>   to second-sighted persons.   (B1, 239-40)

To the second-sighted critic, then, poetry as music is visible prayer. It is that incredibly precise interweaving of two (or more) languages or metaphorical systems, as say, in Stevens's 'Peter Quince at the Clavier' where Susanna's music, the Elders' music, landscape, and story weave and interweave the poem's song:

> The body dies; the body's beauty lives.
> So evenings die, in their green going,
> A wave, interminably flowing.
> So gardens die, their meek breath scenting
> The cowl of winter, done repenting.
> So maidens die, to the auroral
> Celebration of a maiden's choral.
> Susanna's music touched the bawdy strings
> Of those white elders; but, escaping,
> Left only Death's ironic scraping.
> Now, in its immortality, it plays
> On the clear viol of her memory,
> And makes a constant sacrament of praise.[33]

To speak of this as onomatopoeia would seem to me a dreadful impoverishment in critical vocabulary. In so far as there is imitation here, it is not sound imitating sound, but mind imitating mind, a process Smart called variously 'relation', 'spiritual music', and 'visible prayer', not comparison but transformation. In the gradually brightening glance of Gray's 'Progress', the poet glimpses those same transformations:

> Thoughts that breathe and words that burn.

Such forms as glitter in the Muse's ray
With orient hues, unborrowed of the sun . . . .

(ll. 110, 119-20)

It would be silly, of course, to pretend Gray and Smart spoke the same words, thought the same thoughts. There are similarities. Both are disconcerting poets. Their presence is extraordinarily immediate and equally elusive. Both speak the difficult music of the high ode, from one point of view heightened, glittering, laboured, harsh. But even in the music of the odes there is a note which is distinctively Gray's, something tentative, as if what he heard were about to be taken away forever or is not yet to be, not to be realized. Smart spoke once of the 'nervously pathetic' quality of Gray's verse.[34] The voice I hear is nostalgic and prophetic, elegiac and visionary. Leslie Fiedler remarks that nostalgia and hallucination are psychologically identical,[35] a comment recalling Arthur Carr's that 'Tennyson . . . forged a poetic instrument out of the themes of loss and recovery through regression into dream and vision'.[36] It is, of course, not Gray's character but his poetry we speak of when we notice at the height of vision a dream of loss:

Dear lost companions of my tuneful art,
Dear as the light that visits these sad eyes,
Dear as the ruddy drops that warm my heart. . . .

('The Bard', ll. 39-41)

That is Gray's characteristic note, a music Tennyson must have heard.

Any effort to speak of poetry as music is, finally, I suppose, an exercise in pure futility. But if there can be sanction for it, it would be in a grand metaphor which has possessed poets from the time at least of Sir John Davies to Theodore Roethke, that the universe is not discord, but harmony, and that if the poet disciplines himself to the pure task of listening closely, intently, he will hear the sound of the great planets in their enormous paths, the force that moves his own blood in its motion.

That metaphor seems to have been somewhere in the background of W. H. Auden's meditations in his 'Notes on Music and Opera': 'Man's musical imagination seems . . . to have little to do with the experiences of the outside world brought to him through his senses'; it is not our ear, but our voice that makes music possible.[37]

York University

Notes

1. 'From Action to Image: Theories of the Lyric in the Eighteenth Century', in *Critics and Criticism*, ed. R. S. Crane (Chicago, 1952), p. 408.

2. *Jubilate Agno*, ed. W. H. Bond (London, 1954). See Fragment B1, 236-55; B2, 584-96; C, 51-57.

3. *The Sister Arts* (Chicago, 1958), p. 151.

4. *The Mirror and the Lamp* (New York, 1953), p. 50.

5. (Princeton, 1951), pp. 258, 262.

6. *The Poet in the Poem* (Berkeley, 1960), p. 10.

7. 'How to Read', in *Literary Essays of Ezra Pound*, ed. T. S. Eliot (New York, 1968), p. 26.

8. *Articulate Energy* (London, 1966), p. 34.

9. *The Subtler Language* (Baltimore, 1968), p. 11.

10. 'Answer to Davenant . . .', in *Critical Essays of the Seventeenth Century*, ed. J. E. Spingarn (Oxford, 1908), II, 54-55.

11. *Spectator*, no. 339.

12. *The Works of Thomas Gray*, ed. William Mason (London, 1814), I, 87.

13. Ibid., I, 88.

14. Cited in *Poems by Christopher Smart*, ed. Robert Brittain (Princeton, 1950), p. 295.

15. Cited in Ian Jack, *Augustan Satire* (Oxford, 1965), p. 7.

16. Ibid.

17. ' "Wit and Poetry and Pope": Some Observations on His Imagery', in *Pope and His Contemporaries*, ed. James L. Clifford and Louis A. Landa (Oxford, 1949), pp. 32, 36.

18. *Articulate Energy*, p. 33.

19. Compare the list of virtues in 'A Song to David', the Tribe-virtue listing in the *Jubilate Agno* (B2, 603-15), the virtue-directions listing (B2, 354-58) and the Biblical source: Genesis 30 and 49; Ezekiel 48.

20. *The Sister Arts*, pp. 304-6.

21. See especially the comments on 'the architectonic features of the poem' and 'the orchestral effects . . . guided by the many references to music' in Brittain, p. 295.

22. *Jubilate Agno*, C, 51-57 and B1, 245-49. Compare 'A Song to David', stanzas 27 and 28.

23. *The Sister Arts*, p. 314.

24. *Lectures on the Sacred Poetry of the Hebrews* (Hildesheim, 1969), I, 367-68.

25. 'The language of the age is never the language of poetry. . . . Our poetry . . . has a language peculiar to itself' (*Corres.*, I, 192).

26. Cited in Brittain, p. 71. See also Thomson's Preface to *The Seasons*.

27. Cited in Brittain, p. 72.

28. 'Hymn xxxII' of 'Hymns and Spiritual Songs', Brittain, p. 209.
29. 'The Progress of Poesy', ll. 23, 62, 82, 'The Bard', ll. 96, 48, 'Progress', l. 50, 'Ode to Adversity', l. 47.
30. Brittain, p. 74.
31. *Jubilate Agno*, p. 23.
32. *Anatomy of Criticism*, p. 276.
33. *The Collected Poems of Wallace Stevens* (New York, 1955), p. 92.
34. 'The Brocaded Gown and Linen Rag', *The Collected Poems of Christopher Smart*, ed. Norman Callan (London, 1949), I, 50.
35. *The Return of the Vanishing American* (New York, 1968), p. 175.
36. 'Tennyson as a Modern Poet', in *Victorian Literature*, ed. Austin Wright (Oxford, 1961), p. 320.
37. *The Dyer's Hand* (New York, 1962), p. 467.

IRENE TAYLER **Two Eighteenth-Century**
Illustrators of Gray

In my work on Blake's illustrations to Gray, I have come to see that the relationship of illustrator to author is one of the most sensitive and revealing of human encounters. We think visually as well as verbally – maybe never one without the other – and that is partly why people have always liked books with pictures, books that raise ideas through the eye as well as the mind. When author and artist are the same, as in the case of Blake's own illuminated books, word and picture usually take complementary, if sometimes quite different, paths toward the same end. For example, the opulence of the gift of life is expressed in Blake's plate 'Infant Joy' [pl. I] by verse and picture both. In the title page to his *Marriage of Heaven and Hell* [pl. II] even the lettering is put to use to suggest visually that the opposed states of heaven and hell have certain angularities in common that awaken into life when the two are joined in 'marriage'; even the 'and' that joins them might be thought, in its embracing circle, to illustrate its own meaning. But in plate seven of *America* Blake uses design to counter text. Albion's Angel is thundering at America's young spirit of revolt, demanding:

> *Blasphemous Demon, Antichrist, hater of Dignities,*
> *Lover of wild rebellion, and transgressor of God's Law,*
> *Why dost thou come to Angel's eyes in this terrific form?*

A glance at the plate [pl. III] demotes all those snarls to whimpers and suggests almost comically – though very beautifully – that the main thing Albion's Angel and his ilk have to fear is fear. Put in Blake's terms, the trouble is with the kind of eyes the Angel has: as the eye, so the object, Blake tirelessly insists.

But when author and illustrator are not the same, questions of tone and tact – not to say intention – grow more complex. This may be seen in the differences between the pictorial readings given Gray by what were surely his two greatest eighteenth-century illustrators: Richard Bentley and William Blake. Bentley was Gray's contemporary and friend (through Walpole), and it was in deference to Bentley's delightful designs to 'A Long Story' that Gray allowed what he considered so slight an occasional poem to be published. *Designs by Mr. R. Bentley, for Six Poems by Mr. T. Gray* was published by Dodsley at Walpole's instigation in 1753. For each poem there is a full-page illustration and facing headpiece with decorated initial letter, and at the end of the poem a tailpiece. Bentley later did a number of designs and illustrations for Walpole; but it was this more ambitious, early work for which Bentley was known in his own day and which drew from Gray the high praise of his 'Stanzas to Mr. Bentley'.

Blake's illustrations, on the other hand, were the last done in the eighteenth century (in 1797-98) and were done in watercolour on large folio sheets into the centre of which the printed text had been pasted. There are 116 of them in all, in the unique copy that was bought by Blake's friend the sculptor John Flaxman for his wife's private library. Gray was of course by then considered an English classic, removed in time by a quarter of a century. I should add that Blake knew Bentley's designs and often alludes to them in his own.

A brief example will set the tone of difference. In the 'Hymn to Adversity' Gray praises adversity for the way it nurtures virtue, saying Jove sent his 'darling Child' to be reared by that 'Stern rugged Nurse'. Bentley rather scarily portrays her departure for school and then in the tailpiece (set in a mossy grotto of the romantic graveyard mode) [pl. iv] summarizes Gray's sense of the quiet nobility to be gained from facing hardship with fortitude: if the resulting spirit is melancholy, it is in Bentley's view, as in Gray's, a melancholy suffused with strength and dignity. Gray himself found this design especially pleasing. But Blake believed that virtue raised on abstinence and denial too easily grows savage and accusing, blunting the spirit and finally killing the life within. So he counters both Gray and Bentley [pl. v] in picturing what he calls 'Grief among the roots of trees' – it might have been the title to Bentley's tailpiece, and uses the same basic formulae of design. But with what a wicked difference! For what Blake shows us is an ominous, rootbound wetnurse, offering lethal milk. This is perhaps less illustration than polemic, which goes to show, I suppose, that the Sister Arts are siblings in more than name.

In another example Blake chooses to urge his poetic host from comedy toward divine comedy. The details of Blake's reading of Gray's 'Ode on the Death of a Favourite Cat' are too complex to go into here,[1] but again the contrast between his vision and Bentley's will suggest the amazing range of possible response to what Gray doubtless considered a modest enough little fable. Bentley joined Gray in regarding the whole affair with amused detachment, and the result is a fine example of Bentley at his best. A glance at the full-page illustration [pl. VI] shows his details to be at once more realistic and more elaborately 'arty' than anything Blake ever does.

Bentley's cat is thorough cat: his bowl even reflects the windowpanes that light our view. But that little domestic scene is overwhelmed by the elaborate inventiveness, and indeed the sheer mass, of its surroundings. The scene is framed – the word 'framed' is insufficient – by a decorative entablature supported by caryatids of a river god stopping his ears to Selima's cries (so phrased in the accompanying 'Explanation of the Prints') and Destiny cutting the nine threads of her life; and the whole structure is further embellished by a mandarin-cat in a pagoda, fishing in a Chinese vase, another cat drawing up a massive net from another Chinese vase, various elegant flowers and draperies, and a number of jubilant mice. At the foot of the entire structure, and displayed with conscious pomp, are the signatures of Gray and his illustrator: the poet's initials inscribed on a lyre, the artist's on a palette.

Bentley, like Blake, worked up small hints from the language of the poem, making from Gray's mere mention of a Chinese vase a complete oriental setting with costumed cat, and of the 'wat'ry God' and 'malignant Fate' robust imitations of Greek architectural statuary. The picture is thus a paradigm of Bentley's technique: the household cat surrounded in mock solemnity by the rich culture of fashionable eighteenth-century England, its deference to Classical tradition, its vogue of Chinoiserie, its decorous but pervasive accolade to the artist as gentleman-maker.

Thus Bentley, perfectly catching Gray's stylish irony, returns the poem all the more forcefully to the public world of its social and literary context: we are safely located in time and space. Just as the cat's bowl reflects the light that illuminates our view of it, so too the framing figures are faithfully shaded for us, emphasizing our role as observers of a fixed scene; it is our familiar world, however fancifully played upon.

Not so with Blake [pl. VII]. No picture frame here, not even the social frame of the parlour. Rather Blake plunges us immediately into the first stages of his idiosyncratic visionary reading of Gray's beast fable, managing to parody at once the animals of the mock elegy and the ladies toward whom the moral is directed. In one more example [pl. VIII] we see the pensive Selima purring applause at the sight of her own reflection, and below, tenderly embracing in an echo of Selima's self-admiration, are the goldfish, Gray's 'genii of the stream'. Whereas Bentley had complied with Gray's sense of physical and ironic distance, Blake unrelentingly insists that we join the world of cat and fish. And I must add that it is a world Gray would hardly have recognized – though his analyst might have.

And now one last brief example of these differing responses, using Gray's widely loved 'Elegy Written in a Country Churchyard' as the text. Bentley this time [pl. IX] uses the elaborate border of his full-page design to emphasize Gray's own comparison of the barrenness of pomp and power with the earthy richness of simple village life; but through that framing doorway is still the death's-head, with the kindred spirit's own shadow cast across the grave he enquires about, rather movingly stressing by pictorial gesture the inevitable progression of life towards death which is perhaps Gray's central theme in the poem. The vigour of country life is again celebrated in Bentley's headpiece [pl. x], though the initial 'T' counters with a *memento mori* in the ruined gothic abbey and rising bird of night, and it is this darker vision that is taken up again in the tailpiece [pl. XI], where the funeral procession bears the coffin to its final resting place – the sepulchre pictured below, lit by a burning torch that soon will flicker out in analogy to man's brief and fragile life. In Blake's version [pl. XII], which I think again takes account of Bentley's view of Gray as well as of Gray himself, we still have the funeral procession, but reduced to bare stick figures in the distance. Down where Bentley had his sepulchre Blake has the life of his picture, and its subject is Life itself in all its physical beauty and warmth and colour, however subdued just now by the sad occasion. One should see this design in colour, because the vivid colouring of the foreground is a good part of Blake's point, namely that the bosom of one's father and one's God – to paraphrase Gray's final line – is within; it is one's own bosom, the living spirit of every human being, not something one must wait until death to find. Indeed, those who so mistakenly wait are already partly dead, whatever the state of the physical body.[2]

Blake's intention, I think, throughout his entire series of illustrations to Gray, was on the one hand to correct by pictorial emphasis what he felt to be a rather morbid turn in the poet – his pallid caution, his melancholy, his retreat from life – and on the other hand to pay homage to his very great if sometimes latent poetic power. The point can be shown pictorially by two of Blake's designs. In an illustration to the

'Ode on a Distant Prospect of Eton College' [pl. XIII] we see Gray's 'vultures of mind'; they are in Blake's view the product of the minds they prey on, the ugly embodiment of Gray's own mental misery. But in a resplendent design to 'The Progress of Poesy', Blake offers his corrective [pl. XIV]. The design illustrates Gray's lines about the flight of those very night creatures of the mind ('birds of boding cry') before 'Hyperion's march and glittering shafts of war' – the sunrise envisioned as the enlightening power of poetic genius. Blake has just those same glittering shafts of war in mind in his own famous lines:

> Bring me my bow of burning gold
> Bring me my arrows of desire
> Bring me my spear: O clouds unfold
> Bring me my chariots of fire.

Had Gray been willing to shoot his arrows of desire more freely (if I may, through Blake, so allude to Professor Hagstrum's paper) he might, with all that power of 'sensibility', have driven out his own night creatures and mounted a glorious chariot of fire.

These examples from Blake and Bentley are by no means offered as comprehensive, but are meant rather to suggest something of Gray's ability to elicit from his illustrators highly sensitive and personally revealing responses. Perhaps I have seemed to suggest that Bentley (in contrast to Blake) was a mere translator from word to picture rather than a really innovative interpreter of Gray, though the evident wit, polish, and authority of his designs should more than counter any Blakean bias. But in fact there is quite another sense in which Bentley did extraordinary service to Gray's words – and to English book art generally.

Through the mid-eighteenth century illustrations in published books tended to look something like plate xv: that is, they were rectangular boxes, closed off at the edges, either stamped onto some part of the printed page or else taking up the full page themselves. Title pages were often much more complicated in their format, with the title circled by design, or with a design inserted among the words; Rubens built up a nice personal library by dashing off decorations to be engraved for title pages [pl. XVI], in return for which he was sent copies of the finished books. But even ambitious publishers made little further attempt to incorporate illustration into text, either in England or on the continent.

That is, until 1745. In that year the Venetian publisher Albrizzi brought out his sumptuous edition of Tasso's *Jerusalem Delivered*, with engraved designs after Piazzetta. It made an immediate European sensation. When Goethe's father saw the proof sheets he 'beheld them with astonishment and admiration'. The novelty of the book did not lie in the title page or the full-page illustraions. What was new was the series of vignette-shaped headpieces and tailpieces 'tossed on the page with a casual airiness that had never before been seen in book illustration'.[3] In fact there are earlier examples of delicate vignette-shaped head and tailpieces – for example those of the elegant Parisian edition of Molière's *Oeuvres* (1734), with illustrations by Boucher. But in that edition the real 'illustration' exists in the full-page designs only. The head and tail-pieces and the decorated initial letters, while generally appropriate to the rococo elegance of Boucher's illustrations, are designed by other artists and are so generalized in their content that each is used repeatedly throughout the six volumes of the edition. They may thus be considered as especially elaborate printers' decorations rather than true illustration, in contrast to those of both the Albrizzi and the Bentley editions. Albrizzi certainly knew that he *had* something and took out a fifteen-year copyright on the copper plates. But of course what he had was not something that could really be copyrighted; it was in fact a fresh conception of the way text and illustration might be married on a printed page. Naturally the very process of printing precluded the kind of free integration one finds in earlier hand-illuminated manuscripts, or in Blake's hand-drawn plates. But in this double spread of full-page illustration on one side, headpiece and decorated initial letter on the other [pl. xvii], you can see at once that we are dealing with a notion of illustration quite different from that of the closed-off rectangular block.

Eight years after this landmark of publication in Venice appeared Bentley's designs to Gray in England, executed not only in the same spirit, but with the same format – the double spread of full-page design, headpiece, and decorated initial at the outset of each poem, and vignette-shaped tailpiece at the end, each individually conceived as illustration of the specific poem in question.[4] Notice, in the tailpiece to 'Ode on the Spring' [pl. xviii], the way the trees fan out airily to the sides, and the water spills right out of the picture below.[5] One might observe as well the gracious spacing of lines and letters in both Albrizzi's and Bentley's books, the openness and elegance of the letterpress matching that of the designs that accompany it.

It is possible, of course, that Bentley never saw the Tasso – rather surprisingly the book was not in Walpole's library – but the internal evidence is reasonably strong, and so is the circumstantial evidence: the English Consul in Venice, Joseph Smith, subscribed to the Albrizzi edition, and his many services as bridge between the Venetian and English art worlds are well known. If Bentley did produce the parallel unwittingly, we have a striking example of artistic coincidence, and Bentley's achievement is all the more to his credit. But assuming he did have the Venetian book as his model, what he achieved is hardly less remarkable, for he seems to have been the only illustrator in England for the next *forty years* to realize that a revolution in book design was taking place. From these beginnings grew the enormously popular 'livres à vignettes' in France, the work of such engravers as Marillier, Choffard, and Gravelot (the last a pet-hate of Blake's, by the way), but these did not appear until the 1760s and after. As nearly as I have been able to ascertain, Bentley's work is the first further sign of the remarkable new possibilities just beginning to unfold.

And not only was Bentley prompt, he was also strikingly innovative, for there is no precedent in the Albrizzi Tasso – or any other book I have seen – for the kind of grainy wit and stylish grotesqueries of Bentley's designs to Gray's 'Ode on the Death of a Favourite Cat' or 'A Long Story', for example, or for his sensitive and elaborate allusions to details of the poet's language. Bentley not only recognized the possibilities for innovation in format, he exploited those possibilities to form a fresh and highly personal style of illustration.

Part of the resonance and vitality of both Bentley's project and Blake's results from their use of the page, their insistence on the close interdependence of visual and verbal: Bentley liked to sign his full-page designs with the paired signatures of himself and Gray – in one case with crossed pen and engraving tool, in two others with bardic harp and artist's palette. And on his title page, as if announcing that in one sense the real subject of the book *is* the relationship of poet and painter, he pictures Gray as Apollo at the lyre and himself (with witty deference) as a busy little ape at the canvas [pl. xix].[6] Blake's commitment to the Sister Arts I hardly need go into here. And his compliment to Gray on this score resides in the simple fact of his 116 closely attentive illustrations. Surely it is a measure of Gray's genius that he possessed the poetic density to provoke two such sets of illustrations – the one so resourcefully consonant with Gray's own tone and manner, the other as disruptively critical and passionately interpretive.

City University of New York

Irene Tayler

Notes

1. A fuller treatment of Blake's designs to Gray's 'Ode on the Death of a Favourite Cat' (to which the present discussion owes several paragraphs) may be found in my *Blake's Illustrations to the Poems of Gray* (Princeton, 1971), pp. 55-70.

2. Blake almost employs Gray's phrasing in *Jerusalem* (plate five, ll. 17-20), saying that his 'great task' is to open men's eyes 'into Eternity/ Ever expanding in the Bosom of God the Human Imagination'.

3. For generalizations about the impact of the Albrizzi Tasso I am indebted to Anne Palms Chalmers, 'Venetian Book Design in the Eighteenth Century', *The Metropolitan Museum of Art Bulletin* (January 1971), pp. 226-35 and A. Hyatt Mayor, 'Italian xviii Century Book Illustration', *The Metropolitan Museum of Art Bulletin* n.s.8 (1950), pp. 136-44. The words quoted in my text appear in Mr. Mayor's article on p. 140.

4. The one exception is the full-page design to 'Ode on the Spring', which acts as frontispiece to the whole set of six poems and so includes allusions to each of the six.

5. The effect of airiness intended by Bentley is even clearer in his original drawings, which are in Mr. W. S. Lewis's Walpole collection in Farmington, Connecticut, and which Mr. Lewis has generously allowed me to see.

6. Bentley's figure of course alludes as well to the ancient view of artist as ape imitating Nature, the Art of God.

Blake on Gray:
Outlines of Recognition

The need for a paper on Blake and Gray became obvious when, in the early stages of our planning, we began to consider the design of the poster announcing the Conference. Our selection of possible designs included the usual rococo border surrounding an announcement set in eighteenth-century type, a plate from Bentley's designs, an eighteenth-century landscape, a view of Cambridge or Eton, and a contemporary abstract design of horizontal and vertical lines supposedly representing continuity and change. Then came Blake's illustrations of the 'Elegy', particularly the design of the reaper [pl. xx] which we finally accepted. Here was the homage to Gray, identifying a specific concern of his work, and presenting important stanzas from his best-known poem.[1]

The design, offering the contrast between the powerfully defined image of the reaper and the amazed, even puzzled, observer, works as a guide to Gray's poem. It articulates Blake's transformation of Gray's image into a strikingly fresh visual representation. Based on the specific line 'oft did the harvest to their sickle yield' the design brings out from Gray's words a powerful sense of physical strength and human identity. We note this in the sweeping lines of the form and the massive proportions of the anatomy. This representation of energy is an element which is undeveloped, if at all considered, in Gray's poem. If, as Ian Jack has suggested, the theme of the 'Elegy' is nostalgia, it is a theme incompatible with Blake's concept of 'energy'.[2] Irene Tayler has pointed out that Blake transforms Gray's images and situations into his own individualized interpretation. He accomplishes this in a variety of ways. One in particular is this transmutation of a general comment on the labour of the peasant, ennobling in its way and recognized as such by Gray, into a highly particularized symbol of human energy. The sickle is an instrument of energy, and in linear congruence with this the man's body takes on the

shape of the sickle.[3] The suggestion is obvious: the body itself becomes
the instrument of energy. The water carrier, if that is what she is, stands
in awe of this wondrous shape. She stands at the moment of discovery
of physical energy.

The composition is similar to the second plate, the title-page, of
Blake's *Book of Thel* [pl. xxi]. Thel as observer is awed, perhaps bewil-
dered, by the energetic activity of Lily and Cloud as they act out the
visionary drama of renewal. This perception of wonder establishes a
relationship not only between Blake's two visual representations, but
between *The Book of Thel* and the 'Elegy'. In each poem a melancholy
figure contemplates a grave plot and broods on imminent death.[4] Both
poems dramatize the melancholy theme. The idea of contemplating one's
own death is as strong in Blake's poem as it is in Gray's. But there is a
difference. Thel is granted an alternative; contemplation of death opens
the possibility of the life of vision. There is no such alternative for the
narrator in the 'Elegy'. Contemplation of death in Gray is not the beginning of visionary life. Thel broods on death, and this kind of brooding often takes places in Blake's poems. He knew the outlines of melancholy.[5] Working against the melancholy contemplation of extinction,
there is in Blake the possibility of renewal.

Blake, in the design of the reaper and the girl, offers a guide to our
perception of the poem, just as the 'voice' of the narrator might be a
similar guide. We are struck by the strength of the figure in Blake's
drawing. That the narrator in the poem has seen a reaper is clear
enough; it is not clear that he viewed the figure with the sense of amazement depicted in Blake's illustration. Is this sense of amazement what
Gray had in mind? The answer seems to be that Gray had no immediate
concern for the particulars of the reaper's shape or form. Compare the
emphasis on the specific line in the poem with that given to it in the
illustration. In Gray, the line 'Oft did the harvest to their sickle yield'
takes its place in a series of generalizing comments on the 'rude forefathers of the hamlet' who lie buried 'Each in his narrow cell'. The
whole passage is controlled by the melancholy reflection on the dead.
Like the poem itself, it is without a sense of amazement or wonder. The
illustration reverses the emphasis in the passage. What was in Gray a
reflection on death becomes in Blake a revelation of life. It does not
occur to one to say of the design that 'all this must pass away'. The
representations of energy which are constantly Blake's concern are per-
sistently absent from Gray. This example from the 'Elegy' marks the
pattern of tensions which one discovers throughout the illustrations,

tensions resulting from the disparity between Blake's 'open' and Gray's 'closed' world. In *Milton*, Blake gives us a statement of the possibilities inherent in his expanding world:

> *Thou perceivest the Flowers put forth their precious Odours,*
> *And none can tell how from so small a centre*
>   *comes such sweets,*
> *Forgetting that within that Centre Eternity expands . . . .*[6]

But for Gray, the world is enclosed. His imagination dwells on the termination of existence. The passage from *Milton* must be understood in the light of Blake's task in that poem, which is to restore to Milton his imaginative form, to renew his imaginative perception of the world. This is what Blake is hoping to do for Gray in the illustrations.

Both poets agree that man exists within the cycle of the changing seasons and within the moral codes of his time, that natural seasons and moral codes define the limitations of his existence. Gray, more than some of his contemporaries, accepts the limitations. He defines 'human' in these terms. To 'know myself a man' is to submit to the stern Goddess Adversity. To be 'civilized' is to be fastidious. Blake strives to break out of these limitations, or to define them in such a way that outlines of freedom may be recognized. The illustrations, which are highly articulate representations of Blake's complex response, offer us the opportunity of comparing the two poets, particularly on the theme of limitations, and of identifying Gray's images in contrast to or in conjunction with those of Blake.

In the 'Ode on the Spring', Gray states his views about the acceptance of change; or, more particularly, about the signs of human identity which can be drawn from the observation of the seasons. The interpretations of the cycle shift from hope to despair – from the possibilities of renewal to the inevitability of death. This is the cycle of 'nature', the 'circle of destiny'. In *There is No Natural Religion* [*First Series*] Blake describes it as the 'same dull round over again'. The mere cycle of nature is an image of the 'profane' world which Mircea Eliade has discussed and explicated.[7] Attempting to make sense out of the cosmos, Gray, like Thomson, perhaps like his age, 'desacralized' the human image. In Eliade's words: '*when it is desacralized*, cyclic time becomes terrifying: it is seen as a circle forever turning on itself, repeating itself to infinity'.[8] Time is either of 'evanescent duration' or it is a 'succession of eternities'.[9] Gray is oppressed by the threat of 'evanescent duration'. His genius is that he made poems out of his sense of such oppression. 'Ode on the Spring' sets out very clearly the dilemma of trying to make sense out of the profane world. What starts out as a celebration of the return of the 'purple year' becomes a meditation on the vanity or, at best, the evanescence of life.

Of the six illustrations, the first two are introductory, depicting the return of the Pindaric genius and the poet diligently at work on his poems. The remainder illustrate the text of the poem, showing a male figure representing the awakened 'purple year' [pl. xxii]; the poet 're-clin'd in rustic state' reflecting on the vanity of human wishes; 'rough Mischance' and 'Age' at their destructive tasks; and, finally, the poet re-proached by the summer flies [pl. xxiii]. The awakened 'year' is nude, the contemplative poet in the fourth illustration is clothed, and the final view of the poet shows him nude but without the joyfulness of the figure in the third illustration. This representation of the awakened 'year' and the poet is perfectly consistent with the convention of depicting sacred figures nude and profane figures clothed. The contemplative poet in the fourth illustration is draped in a robe, which, however, has been dis-carded in the final illustration. There is also evidence in the 'Ode on the Spring' illustrations of Blake's use of right-left symbolism.[10] The awakened 'year' [pl. xxii] sees the visionary act of renewal from the right, and divine, side; the melancholy poet observes from the left, the incapa-citated and profane, side. Plate xxii also presents a design which Blake often used, the emergence of life from the flower. The passage from *Milton*, the 'Vision of the lamentation of Beulah over Ololon', has al-ready been cited. A similar act is depicted in the 'Infant Joy' plate from *Songs of Innocence* [pl. i]. Oothoon begins her journey by plucking 'Leutha's flower', an act which is depicted as the taking of a child from 'the bright Marygold of Leutha's vale' (*Visions of the Daughters of Albion*, 'The Argument', Plate iii). Gray establishes in 'Ode on the Spring' the kind of allegorical pattern to which Blake could quickly respond. It is surprising to see how little Blake had to invent, in the way of his own vision, to provide an imaginative reading of Gray.

The poem ends with a somewhat reluctant return to the celebration with which it started, but we are left with the poet in a dilemma, not unlike Thel's, unable to sort out his place amidst the sacred and pro-fane. At best he is left with 'evanescent duration', his nudity perhaps suggesting his potential for renewal, but his facial expression signifying his failure. It is a failure implied in Gray's own text. This perception of the 'evanescent duration' of life is close to the attitude which we call 'sensibility'. We can compare this poem to Blake's 'Spring' from *Innocence*, which is pure celebration of the joyful return of the year.

But we should not say that Blake solved the dilemma, that he simply overcame 'sensibility'. The *Songs of Experience*, with sick roses and weary sunflowers, depict a profane world, as do the cycles of 'The Mental Traveller'. The same dilemma exists in Gray's poem that exists in Blake's, but the latter's articulation of it is richer and more complex. Blake sees and illustrates Gray in the light of this complexity. For his own poems Blake solves the problem of the voice of sensibility, a voice confused by the demands of sacred and profane, by recognizing the ambivalence and dividing it into separate voices. This is Blake's connection to the tradition of 'sensibility': he carried its content into new ideas of poetic form. His identification of the ambiguity of these voices shows the way out of 'sensibility', the way out of its confinements. The 'Ode on the Spring' offers the possibility of an alternative to the contemplation of death, but the final stanza is not strong enough, not clearly enough defined, to overcome the profane moralizing of the middle stanzas of the poem. Gray's daring is here restrained, and Blake's final illustration of the poet-moralizer depicts the restraint.

In the 'Ode on the Spring', it is Contemplation, with 'sober eye', who counters the theme of joyful renewal. Gray gives an even more sober view in the 'Hymn to Adversity'. In contrast to the 'rosy-bosom'd hours', Adversity is called 'Stern rugged nurse', and in contrast to the admonishing summer flies, there is offered a 'Dread Goddess' who will teach the poet to be a man. If there is some ambiguity in the conclusion to 'Ode on the Spring', there is none in the submissiveness of the poet in his final plea to Goddess Adversity:

> *Thy form benign, oh Goddess, wear,*
> *Thy milder influence impart,*
> *Thy philosophic train be there*
> *To soften, not to wound my heart.*
> *The generous spark extinct revive,*
> *Teach me to love and to forgive,*
> *Exact my own defects to scan,*
> *What others are to feel, and know myself a man.*

(ll. 41-48)

Gray provides a clear response to the inevitability of suffering: it must be endured, and the most that can be obtained from it is a spirit of love and forgiveness and a portion of self-knowledge. The final illustration [pl. xxiv] depicts the heavily draped forms of a 'profane' morality. The Dread Goddess lays a 'chast'ning hand', a left, and therefore, by implication, a sinister hand, on a shrouded poet.

The right-left symbolism, to which Irene Tayler has given particular significance in her comments on this poem, is not immediately clear. The sweeping design of the illustration, starting at the lower left, rising as it crosses the page to the poet's head, carried back across the page by the figure of Adversity, then sent upward by her pointing finger, may have been more important to Blake than the demands of a right-left symbolic pattern. Does the raised right hand have a particular significance for a poem? If Blake is consistent in the symbolism, the right hand should be an indicator of spiritual knowledge. This would be in keeping with Gray's intentions in the concluding lines of the poem. But the shrouded and dismal poet seems an unlikely receiver of spiritual truths as they might be understood by Blake. There are three possible interpretations of Blake's illustration. The first is that Adversity offers wisdom to the poet, signified primarily by the symbolic gesture of the right hand. This would be consistent with Gray's meaning. The second is that Adversity offers profane, worldly, and mistaken, guidance to the suffering poet, signified by the heavy shroud covering the poet and by his despairing facial expression. This would be in opposition to Gray, and would show Blake's repugnance towards Adversity's teachings. Such an interpretation would not, however, account for any symbolic value to Adversity's gesture. The third, and this is perhaps a variation of the second, is that the illustration is complete in its ironic representation of Adversity. She not only offers him mistaken guidance, but she intentionally deceives him. The illustration is a parody of spiritual truth. The right-hand gesture is, then, significant in the illustration, but in a negative way. It becomes an ironic and deceitful sign of the false morality of the poem. What Gray offers is the profane morality of his age. He documents a world filled with moral awareness, but emptied of 'religious content'.[11]

If in the 'Hymn to Adversity' Blake found it necessary to tamper with Gray's meaning, there is no such need in his illustrations to the 'Ode on a Distant Prospect of Eton College'. The poem takes its place in the setting of Blake's world of Experience. As with Blake's *Songs of Experience*, there is a doubling of voices in the poem. One voice we hear is the stern realist depicting a world of despair; the other the voice of a melancholy narrator himself in a state of despair seeing the world as despair. The world of Eton College is the world of Experience where human aspiration is cut short, where the potential energy of the child is taken into the 'dark Satanic mills' and there destroyed. Eton as Gray describes it is not to be confused with Blake's Innocence. Blake distinguishes clearly between Innocence and Ignorance: '*Unorganiz'd Innocence*: An Impossibility. / Innocence dwells with Wisdom, but never with Ignorance.'[12] Gray is disturbed by the pointless quest for wisdom at Eton, and in the famous final lines makes clear that it is the world of ignorance, not innocence, which he has observed. It is ignorance in the sense of incapacity to discern what one's situation really is. Blake found himself able to adapt the scene to his own views and to produce one of the finest sets of illustrations in the whole series. We are again presented with the Thel situation. The melancholy and alienated speaker is given a vision of terror and discovers the only alternative to be withdrawal into a false paradise.

Blake found in the 'Eton College Ode' material which could be adapted to his own mind and art, to his themes of disillusionment and alienation, and to his desire to bring mental images into real existence through his craft. The descriptive scenes and the personifications in the Ode gave Blake the immediate opportunity to present a reading of Gray congenial to his own views and to Gray's. The set scenes, the allegorical processions, the grotesquerie of the 'ministers of human fate', 'black misfortune's baleful train', and the 'vultures of the mind', are in their own pictorial quality ready for visualizing [p. xxv]. We ought, of course, to visualize the scene ourselves, to transform pictorial quality into imagination. What I am most concerned to show, however, is the adaptability of this poem to Blake's world of alienation. The nihilism of the poem is the nihilism of the world of Experience, a world where moral decisions and educational processes have taken on such immediate importance that they cease to have ultimate meaning. It is somewhat paradoxical that, according to the narrator, the only genuine activity the young scholars have is their play, and even that is as vain as their education. There is little hope that either will be productive: 'Gay hope is theirs by fancy fed, / Less pleasing when possessed.' But this may be the problem of the ambivalent, the unredeemed, narrator. He uses stilted language to describe their play. To the mind of the speaker the joys of youth are bound by the inevitable restraints of growing old. The failing of creative energy, documented in the 'Ode on the Spring', is repeated here. The adult speaker in the poem is restricted, in his vision and his voice, by the limits of his perception. We do not have in Gray the obvious dramatization of voices which we have in Blake, but Gray does establish a distinctive voice, at least in his more successful poems. It is one of the marks of success of the 'Eton College Ode'.

The illustrations show that Blake read Gray with care and that he recreated details and patterns in the poems with accurate insight. The comprehensiveness and completeness of the task affirm the seriousness of Blake's attitude towards Gray's poetry. He often improvised upon Gray's themes and images, and although the illustrations are centred on Gray, they can be seen as highly imaginative and independent statements of Blake's response. On many matters the two poets separate, holding opposing views. I have attempted to indicate some of the oppositions. 'Sensibility', as an awareness of 'evanescent duration', is a possible connection, but it is the way out of sensibility outlined by Blake that I should wish to emphasize in conclusion. If in Gray to be a man is to know pain, to be human in Blake is to know joy. But I should also wish to stress Blake's awareness of melancholy. Here we have, for all the differences, a nexus, a recognition by Blake of a shared response to the world, but a response which, unlike Gray, he struggled to transform into joy.

Carleton University

Notes

1. Blake's illustrations have recently become more widely known. The Trianon Press facsimile of the 116 designs has been announced, and Princeton University Press has published Irene Tayler's thorough study, *Blake's Illustrations to the Poems of Gray* (Princeton, 1971). Since the time of the Conference, the Tate Gallery has mounted an impressive exhibition of the illustrations. The catalogue for the exhibition is in itself a significant tribute to both Gray and Blake.

2. For a discussion of the theme of nostalgia in the 'Elegy', see Ian Jack, 'Gray's *Elegy* Reconsidered', in *From Sensibility to Romanticism*, ed. F. W. Hilles and H. Bloom (New York, 1965), pp. 139-69.

3. Tayler, p. 133.

4. Stoke Poges as a place for making poetry, or for inspiring it, has, perhaps, a counterpart in the pastoral Vales of Har to which Thel returns to continue brooding on her extinction.

5. Blake's term 'outline' designates definite and particularized form. 'The great and golden rule of art, as well as of life, is this: That the more distinct,

sharp, and wirey the bounding line, the more perfect the work of art; and the less keen and sharp, the greater is the evidence of weak imitation, plagiarism, and bungling. . . . The want of this determinate and bounding form evidences the want of idea in the artist's mind, and the pretence of the plagiary in all its branches. How do we distinguish the oak from the beech, the horse from the ox, but by the bounding outline? How do we distinguish one face or countenance from another, but by the bounding line and its infinite inflexions and movement?' Blake, from 'A Descriptive Catalogue', *The Complete Writings of William Blake*, ed. G. Keynes (Oxford, 1966), p. 585.

6. Keynes, p. 520.

7. Mircea Eliade, *The Sacred and the Profane*, trans. Willard R. Trask (New York, 1961).

8. Ibid., p. 107.

9. Ibid., p. 104.

10. See the discussion in Tayler, pp. 76-77.

11. Eliade, p. 107. The passage reads as follows: 'The perspective changes completely when the sense of *the religiousness of the cosmos becomes lost.* This is what occurs when, in certain more highly evolved societies, the intellectual élites progressively detach themselves from the pattern of the traditional religion. The periodical sanctification of cosmic time then proves useless and without meaning. The gods are no longer accessible through the cosmic rhythms. The religious meaning of the repetition of paradigmatic gestures is forgotten. But *repetition emptied of its religious content necessarily leads to a pessimistic vision of existence.'*

12. Blake, 'Notes Written on Pages of the Four Zoas', *Complete Writings*, p. 380.

*The Distant Way:
Imagination and Image
in Gray's Poetry*

Something perhaps baroque, something related perhaps to Locke's imagery of obscurity—there is a metaphor of water at work in Gray's writing. We see a good deal of this suggestion in the letters from Italy, a
country which especially clarified Gray's imagination, as it did his scene
of people and affections. One may remember his delight in Genoa the
harbour city of Andrea Doria, or recall a description of typical summer
evenings by the Arno in Florence, with everybody listening to music and
having supper on 'the marble bridge' in the moonlight (*Corres.*, I, 167).
Tivoli's thousand waterspouts amused him impolitely (characteristic-
ally), and this is the moment to recall that his informal expression for
'just a moment' seems to have been 'just a Water-while'. His attention at
Horace's Tivoli went to its river coming down from a crown of mountains (*Corres.*, I, 156-57). The river moved through a pair of these
mountains to become a waterfall, then along two miles further to become
a quadruple fall. From the Sibyl's temple above, Gray looked across a
Campagna landscape of castles on hillocks, to the round dome of St.
Peter's in the farthest distance. The double falls of Tivoli mirror a
doubling of design seen frequently in Gray, something very much a part
of writer, translator, friend. Returning, 'many a good old tomb we left
on each hand, and many an Aqueduct. . . .' He noted the two new aque-
ducts of the Popes, which added to the beauties of the Campagna. The
Roman regard for water he obviously shared. Voices of fate spoke on
ocean shores. The fields of elegy are plowed with waves. Sensations flow
like rivers into the ocean of the mind.

> And just as rivers flow down from distant mountains – the
> Thames studded with sails, the Indus full of yellow sand, and the
> Euphrates and the Tagus, and the Ganges with its fruitful stream:
> each one rolling its own waters – and burst with resounding flood
> into the sea; and welcoming Ocean receives them in its great basin

and recognizes as its own the gifts of its children coming in a long line and keeps its blue face calm and laughs in scattered ripples: not otherwise do sensations vie with each other in their haste to pour themselves into the fresh mind, and they crowd around the entrances in a fivefold procession.[1]

Often a river image is central in a Gray poem, modifying and in some ways remaking a formal poetry. River and road may alternate as in Wordsworth's designs. The Thames, moving through double towers as it were, controls the description of the first part of the 'Eton Ode'; a road of ambush the second equal part. In the 'Elegy' the image of an evening road becomes a stream descending into Browne-like oceans of gem, to become in the morning the slow path of melancholy and melancholy death. The 'Progress of Poesy' carries streams of earliest poetic mountains across the Latian plains to the fresh landscape of renaissance England, to the Avon.

The route of the river assumes associations with 'a way', a way of life, a way of the soul. Gray created mystic moods such as Keats will imitate and extend, and both poets used imagery of motion – a moving river, a flight of a bird – in approaching these still ideas. The 'way' was a special word in Gray. Its sound echoes through the 'Elegy' to make his churchyard a very single place. The 'Favourite Cat', ironic in conception and in itself (too long to be an epitaph, Gray said), does not miss the magic – with its enchantments of the nearer East, the blue enclosure, the golden pair moving the small stream. This is not a vase, a tub, in which you lose your life. It is a screen in which you see and find it. To those interested in his most future whereabouts, this compulsive and apprehensive writer might write at last: 'however (if I can) I will think of you, as I sail down the *River of Eternity*' (*Corres.*, I, 208).

The way in Gray was the way of imagination. In the Eton and Thames Ode (Father Thames is father of this child), he creates the imagination of childhood. A crown surrounds this childhood, which has its own intellectual throne – a circle of beauty. Not a Platonic circle perhaps: a quieter circle of earliest sensation that is itself bliss, now missed by older lesser eyes and ears.

> *These ears, alas! for other notes repine,*
> *A different object do these eyes require.*

('Sonnet on the Death of Richard West', ll. 5-6)

In touching the vision of childhood, Gray suggests the language of the unconscious, the almost unknown. Among English poets, he is an early visitant in these special scenes of imagination. Walpole, who too entered these moods, attached to the 'Eton Ode' this river image from Lucan's *Pharsalia*: 'Nor have the people been permitted to see thee, Nile, when thou art small.'[2] The 'Elegy', approaching the peasant, touches this same imaginative mind – the natural mind. (And it is of the mind that Gray is chiefly poet.) The hidden gems of ocean, the unobserved flowers of the desert are the withdrawn beauties and truths of an old agrarian mind, the 'sleeping fragrance from the ground' ('Vicissitude Ode', l. 6). Such country vision separates from the unrollings of knowledge, and the poet's voice itself rather falls below this. As darkness goes away, the 'Elegy' becomes a more rational, and a lesser, pastoral.

Child and peasant, in the idiom of imagination and unconscious, Gray particularly gave to an English culture, these essences from a Baconian and Lockian environment of simplest sensation and experience. Gray's poetry is the expression of an empirical spirit.

Locke was so suggestive to Gray, in all directions: for his study of mind, for his own distant prospects of childhood, for his delicate implicit naturalism, for those rising Mediterranean and antique associations he added to his empiricism, for the strongly written language of pleasure and pain that belongs to pleasing-anxious being. How perfectly through his metaphor Gray often establishes a utilitarian motion which presents the image in rotation, a gradual circling, which lets the side of pain turn over above pleasure and beyond, in a context at once structural, musical, seasonal. It is his beautiful imagery of vicissitude – continually, slowly, revolving in a liquid sky – a 'charity, that glows beyond the tomb' ('Ode for Music', l. 50). Down in Florence in 1740 Gray began his Latin poem presenting the mind of Locke. His is a closest reading of Locke: and it is a poet's reading, as he enters those scenes of earliest sensation – those experiences of touch which begin in the life of the womb. Locke and Gray and Wordsworth all plant these 'snowdrops among winter snows'. With Locke Gray entered the scene of innocence – the place of a child's seeing. Gray keeps the spirit of poetry very close to childhood. His English Shakespeare is a 'dauntless child', living within the screen of nature, of pleasure and pain, and space and time. Here perhaps we look at a Lockian Madonna:

> *In thy green lap was Nature's darling laid,*
> *What time, where lucid Avon strayed,*
> *To him the mighty Mother did unveil*
> *Her awful face: the dauntless child*
> *Stretched forth his little arms and smiled.*
> *'This pencil take,' (she said) 'whose colours clear*

Richly paint the vernal year:
Thine too these golden keys, immortal boy!
This can unlock the gates of joy;
Of horror that and thrilling fears. . . .

('The Progress of Poesy', ll. 84-93)

Milton evaded this empirical scene, but not Dryden, and not Gray himself, a poet-child.

Yet oft before his infant eyes would run
Such forms as glitter in the Muse's ray
With orient hues, unborrowed of the sun. . . .

('The Progress of Poesy', ll. 118-20)

How Lockian in another direction may be the accumulations of self-conscious and painful associations – the swarms, the grisly band, the family of pain, the vultures of the mind. The madding crowd could be of association and the scene of mind, an opposite of bliss, a face and countenance of pain replacing a composed body.

Nicely Gray brings to imaginative poetry that tempo of imagination which is itself languor and indolence. Half-sleep, half-poetry. Marvell struck this beat in the 'Coy Mistress', in his vegetable love, which is imaginative love. The eighteenth century, as it grew imaginative, seems to have entered the scenery of slow motion. Locke himself often stopped the clock as association dragged its slow pace along. Instant slow replay, recollected in tranquillity. It was a favourite pastime in the eighteenth century to watch how slowly things might happen: the growth of finger-nails, the motions of halting wit, old age mounting the saddle, the law's delay, a Richardson rape, the grieving of Mr. Shandy. The briskness of the eighteenth century has been much overstated. They were chiefly engaged in watching slow time, which was imaginative time. Gray was a deliberate observer of slowly moving objects:

The lowing herd wind slowly o'er the lea. . . .
Slow through the church-way path we saw him borne.

('Elegy', ll. 2, 114)

Where willowly Camus lingers with delight!

('Ode for Music', l. 29)

The current of the Avon he was delighted to discover was hardly visible (*Corres.*, I, 408). His century forewent the moment, the epiphany, the happening in favour of a seated Johnsonian observation of things almost unmoving. Gray got into his stride almost as soon as he came up to Cambridge.

I am got into a room; such [a] hugeous one, that little i is quite lost in it; so [that] when I get up in the morning, I begin to travel [tow]ards the middle of it with might & main, & with much ado about noon bate at a great Table, which stands half-way it: so then, by that time, (after having pursued my journey full speed); that I arrive at the door, it is so dark & late, & I am so tired, that I am obliged to turn back again: so about Midnight I get to the bedside. (*Corres.*, I, 5)

Wit is white powder, but this age had another, whiter meaning.

Around and beyond the passive and delicate (and disarming) themes of imagination attached to child and peasant, Gray developed attendant themes of a poetic imagination – the language of art. This, too, was an earliest theme, one closest to his tragic friend West, who may be the poet figure of the 'Elegy' and elsewhere. There is a special gentleness in a West aesthetic statement that will not be missed: 'but who can forget poetry? they call it idleness, but it is surely the most enchanting thing in the world' (*Corres.*, I, 43). The theme grew in the years to become the heroic 'Progress' and 'Bard', poems in which the images and energies of Blake are not unseen, and indeed his metaphor of Christ as the imagination.

Gray may be supposed to have used colour in the direction of poetic creation. Perhaps green belongs particularly to the unconscious rustic world, while brighter colours move towards poetry – of bird, of prism. Poetry

> *Waves in the eye of heaven her many-coloured wings.*
>
> ('The Bard', l. 124)

We see the prism of the insect wing. There is an essential trembling image in the poetry which may seem to be related to the colour margins of the rainbow. Gray seems to attach to this imagery the eighteenth century's understanding of colours as illusion in terms of real matter, using his special vocabulary of glitter and glister in these directions. He uses shadow with colour, in Keats's style.

> *Dispel, my fair, with smiles, the timorous cloud*
> *That hangs on thy clear brow. So Helen looked,*
> *So her white neck reclined, so was she borne*
> *By the young Trojan to his gilded bark . . . .*
>
> ('Agrippina', ll. 188-91)

Gray may glance ahead at a time without this image of poetry. It is a small observation that his later poetry of insects conspicuously ignores colour in the depiction of these symbols of a diminished future. In a new waste land the song of a bird may seed the waste of air.

> *There pipes the woodlark, and the song-thrush there*
> *Scatters his loose notes in the waste of air.*
>
> ([Couplet about Birds])

'Every thing resounds with the Wood-Lark, & Robin; & the voice of the Sparrow is heard in our land' (*Corres.*, I, 388).

Gray's colours – glittering, trembling – may be extended into the imagery of painting and tapestry. Sometimes from his pictured urn comes something like a painted Italian room, as in the series of panels which comprise the 'Progress'. The moral personifications of an 'Eton Ode' may suggest an Arena Chapel: his Cambridge ode, a ceremonial wall in Mantua. We seem to be in a room of historical tapestries in the 'Bard', with its imagery of weaving, the weavings of pleasure and pain:

> *Above, below, the rose of snow,*
> *Twined with her blushing foe, we spread:* ...
>
> (ll. 91-92)

The verges of the 'Bard's' tapestry include damnation scenes. And it is interesting to think that the fatal sisters, weaving a prophecy, were likely imagined as standing in shallow weaving cellars, working tapestry on upright looms.

Architectural forms are rather similarly an impression in the poetry of this student of architecture. There are simplest linear forms, as page, banded letter, and cut epitaph. There are motifs of lyre and shell. There are doors and portals: the memorable gates of joy and of mercy. (In the letters: 'The first entrance of Rome is prodigiously striking. It is by a noble gate, designed by Michel Angelo', *Corres.*, I, 146). Floor imagery may include suggestions of mosaic pavement. Directly, an Elizabethan greathall is beautifully sketched, with its dancer wearing 'shoe-strings green'. There is a visible-invisible building rising in Gray's poetry, a mansion of the fleeting breath – the fleeting breath of poetry. And the image of the mountain may blend into the architectural structures. Here is poetry reappearing in the West, in a moment of dawn (and childhood), of colour and cloth. The light moves down the cone of the mountain.

> *In yon bright track, that fires the western skies,*
> *They melt, they vanish from my eyes.*
> *But oh! what solemn scenes on Snowdon's height*
> *Descending slow their glittering skirts unroll?*
>
> ('The Bard', ll. 103-06)

Touching the aesthetic images and symbols, one may wish to suggest how much of the Florentine spirit is implied in this midcentury poet.

Bernard Berenson made a striking comparison between Verrocchio's handling of light and Gray's in the 'Elegy'. To quote:

A vision of *plein air*, vague I must grant, seems to have hovered before him [Verrocchio], and, feeling his powerlessness to cope with it in full effects of light such as he attempted in his earlier pictures, he deliberately chose the twilight hour, when, in Tuscany, on fine days, the trees stand out almost black against a sky of light opalescent grey. To render this subduing, soothing effect of the coolness and the dew after the glare and dust of the day – the effect so matchlessly given in Gray's 'Elegy' – seemed to be his first desire as a painter, and in presence of his 'Annunciation' (in the Uffizi), we feel that he succeeded as only one other Tuscan succeeded after him, that other being his own pupil Leonardo.[3]

The Evening and the Dawn of Gray's 'Elegy' we might think of as softly remembering the serene pairs which preside over the mood of a Medici chapel. A sculptured body and a *pietà* are here as well. And, in another way, the delicate child figures of the 'Eton Ode' may take one's thoughts to the Pontormo frescoes in the Medici Poggio villa. Reminding us again of Gray and his Florence, in 1772, the year following Gray's death, the widow of Robert Walpole, Earl of Orford, bought the Villa Medici at Fiesole, which she redecorated in the Chinese taste. To Fiesole (and to Florence), Gray had written a farewell: 'Never again shall I see you in the distance from the valley of the Arno, girt all around with porticoes and a chaplet of gleaming white villas, as you soar aloft on the shining ridge; never again shall I gaze in wonder at the ancient temple with its screen of aged cypress and the roofs hanging over roofs.'[4] To Italy Gray had a devotion like Milton's, always remembered. And it is significant that the 'Bard' and the 'Progress' both point towards the moment of the Renaissance, in a spirit like Pope's and Gibbon's, itself one of freshness and renaissance.

But leaving colours and painting and building, one must say quickly that the first image of the creative imagination must be the persistent one of water and river – the 'genial current of the soul', flowers growing beside a stream, the 'golden flood', a Venus (as for Wordsworth) rising from the sea. Wordsworth saw the moment of poetry as an offering of the unconscious mind, in a moment often of chance and surprise, of wonder and mystery. One should like to attempt to relate the theme of creation in Gray to the unconscious – to the darkness, caverns, and sleep of the Odin prophecy, and, more obscurely, to Gray as an historian.

And so one might say that Gray had two central concepts of the imagi-

1 Blake, 'Infant Joy'

11 Blake, *Marriage of Heaven and Hell*

In thunders ends the voice. Then Albions Angel wrathful burnt
Beside the Stone of Night; and like the Eternal Lions howl
In famine & war. replyd. Art thou not Orc, who serpent-formd
Stands at the gate of Enitharmon to devour her children;
Blasphemous Demon. Antichrist. hater of Dignities;
Lover of wild rebellion. and transgreſser of Gods. Law;
Why dost thou come to Angels eyes in this terrific form?

III   Blake, *America*

iv   Bentley, for 'Hymn to Adversity'

x   Bentley, for 'Elegy Written in a Country Churchyard'

v Blake, for 'Hymn to Adversity'

VI   Bentley, for 'Ode on the Death of a Favourite Cat'

VII   Blake, for 'Ode on the Death of a Favourite Cat'

VIII   Blake, for 'Ode on the Death of a Favourite Cat'

ix   Bentley, for 'Elegy Written in a Country Churchyard'

The EPITAPH.

HERE rests his head upon the lap of Earth
    A Youth to Fortune and to Fame unknown,
Fair Science frown'd not on his humble birth,
And Melancholy mark'd him for her own.

Large was his bounty, and his soul sincere,
Heav'n did a recompence as largely send :
He gave to Mis'ry all he had, a tear,
He gain'd from Heav'n ('twas all he wish'd) a friend.

No farther seek his merits to disclose,
Or draw his frailties from their dread abode,
(There they alike in trembling hope repose)
The bosom of his Father and his God.

XI   Bentley, for 'Elegy Written in a Country Churchyard'

156 ELEGY WRITTEN IN A

'Hard by yon wood, now smiling as in scorn,
'Mutt'ring his wayward fancies he would rove;
'Now drooping, woeful wan, like one forlorn,
'Or craz'd with care, or crofs'd in hopelefs love.

'One morn I mifs'd him on the cuftom'd hill,
'Along the heath and near his favourite tree;
'Another came; nor yet befide the rill,
'Nor up the lawn, nor at the wood was he;

'The next with dirges due in sad array
'Slow thro' the church-way path we faw him
  'borne,
'Approach and read (for thou canft read) the lay
'Grav'd on the ftone beneath yon aged thorn.'

XII Blake, for 'Elegy Written in a Country Churchyard'

5⸸ ODE ON A DISTANT PROSPECT

Theirs buxom Health, of rofy hue,
Wild wit, Invention ever-new,
And lively Cheer of Vigour born ;
The thoughtlefs day, the eafy night,
The fpirits pure, the flumbers light,
That fly th' approach of morn.

Alas ! regardlefs of their doom,
The little victims play !
No fenfe have they of ills to come,
Nor care beyond to-day :
Yet fee, how all around 'em wait
The minifters of human fate,
And black Misfortune's baleful train !
Ah, fhow them where in ambufh ftand,
To feize their prey, the murderous band !
Ah, tell them they are men !

Thefe fhall the fury paffions tear,
The vultures of the mind,

Difdainful

XIII   Blake, for 'Ode on a Distant Prospect of Eton College'

85   THE PROGRESS OF POESY.

O'er her warm cheek, and rifing bofom, move
The bloom of young defire, and purple light
        of Love.

II. 1.

Man's feeble race what ills await!
Labour, and Penury, the racks of Pain,
Difeafe, and Sorrow's weeping train,
And Death, fad refuge from the ftorms of Fate!
The fond complaint, my fong, difprove,
And juftify the laws of Jove.
Say, has he given in vain the heav'nly Mufe?
Night, and all her fickly dews,
Her fpectres wan, and birds of boding cry,
He gives to range the dreary fky;
Till down the eaftern cliffs afar
Hyperion's march they fpy, and glitt'ring
        fhafts of war.

        II. 2.

XIV   Blake, for 'The Progress of Poesy'

xv   William Hamilton, for 'Elegy Written in a Country Churchyard'

xviii   Bentley, for 'Ode on the Spring'

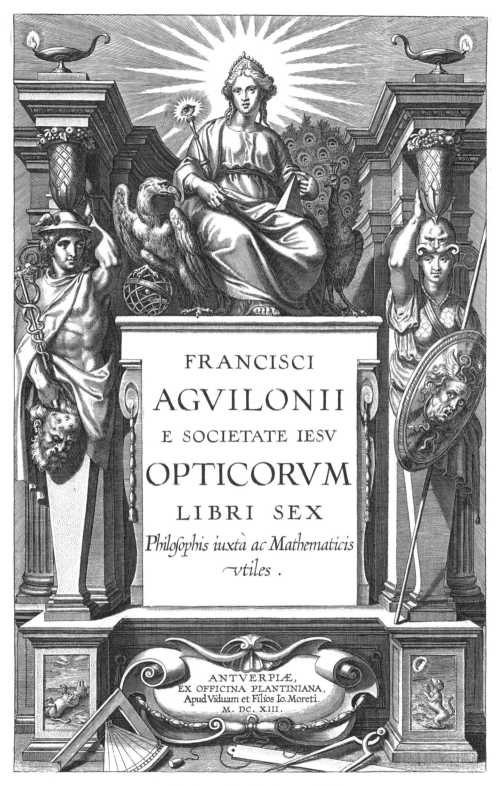

FRANCISCI
AGVILONII
E SOCIETATE IESV
OPTICORVM
LIBRI SEX
Philosophis iuxtà ac Mathematicis
vtiles .

ANTVERPIÆ,
EX OFFICINA PLANTINIANA,
Apud Viduam et Filios Io. Moreti.
M. DC. XIII.

XVI   Rubens, for *Opticorum libri sex*

A Sua   Eccellenza
Il Sig. Simon Contarini   Proccuratore di S. Marco,
e Proveditore Generale   in Terra Ferma.

Canto XV.

XVII

ARGOMENTO.

Dal Mago instrutti i duo guerrier sen vanno,
Dove il pino fatal gli attende in porto:
Spiegan la vela, e pria del gran Tiranno
D'Egitto i legni e l'apparecchio han scorto:
Poi tale il vento, e tale il nocchiero hanno,
Che ben lungo viaggio estiman corto.
All'Isola remota alfine spinti,
Da lor le forze sono, e i vezzi vinti.

CANTO DECIMOQUINTO.

I.

Ià richiamava il bel nafcente raggio
All'opre ogni animal che 'n terra
   alberga;
Quando venendo ai duo guerrieri
   il faggio
Portò il foglio, e lo fcudo, e l'aurea verga.
Accingetevi, diffe, al gran viaggio
Prima che 'l dì che fpunta, omai più s'erga.
Eccovi qui quanto ho promeffo, e quanto
Può della maga fuperar l'incanto.

(173)

XVII

Piazzetta, for *La Gerusalemme Liberata*

DESIGNS

BY

Mr. R. BENTLEY,

FOR SIX

POEMS

BY

Mr. T. GRAY.

LONDON:

Printed for R. DODSLEY, in Pall-mall.

MDCCLIII.

COUNTRY CHURCH-YARD. 151

Oft did the harveft to their fickle yield,
Their furrow oft the ftubborn glebe has broke:
How jocund did they drive their team afield!
How bow'd the woods beneath their fturdy ftroke!

Let not Ambition mock their ufeful toil,
Their homely joys, and deftiny obfcure;
Nor grandeur hear with a difdainful fmile,
The fhort and fimple annals of the poor.

The boaft of heraldry, the pomp of power,
And all that beauty, all that wealth e'er gave,
Await alike th' inevitable hour.
The paths of glory lead but to the grave.

Nor you, ye proud, impute to thefe the fault,
If Memory o'er their tomb no trophies raife,
Where thro' the long-drawn aifle and fretted vault,
The pealing anthem fwells the note of praife.

Can

xx   Blake, for 'Elegy Written in a Country Churchyard'

XXI   Blake, *The Book of Thel*

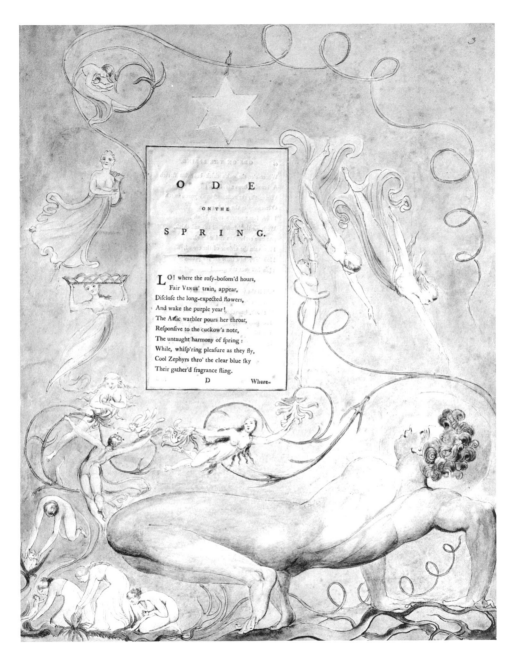

3

ODE

ON THE

SPRING.

L O! where the rosy-bosom'd hours,
    Fair Venus' train, appear,
Disclose the long-expected flowers,
    And wake the purple year!
The Attic warbler pours her throat,
Responsive to the cuckow's note,
The untaught harmony of spring:
While, whisp'ring pleasure as they fly,
Cool Zephyrs thro' the clear blue sky
    Their gather'd fragrance fling.
       D   Where-

XXII   Blake, for 'Ode on the Spring'

XXIII   Blake, for 'Ode on the Spring'

XXIV   Blake, for 'Hymn to Adversity'

60 ODE ON A DISTANT PROSPECT

Lo, in the Vale of Years beneath,
A grifly troop are feen,
The painful family of Death,
More hideous than their queen:
This racks the joints, this fires the veins,
That every labouring finew ftrains,
Thofe in the deeper vitals rage:
Lo, Poverty, to fill the band,
That numbs the foul with icy hand,
And flow-confuming Age.

To each his fuff'rings: all are men,
Condemn'd alike to groan:
The tender for another's pain;
Th' unfeeling for his own.
Yet, ah! why fhould they know their fate!
Since forrow never comes too late,

                                              And

xxv   Blake, for 'Ode on a Distant Prospect of Eton College' nation, the natural and the creative, and so realized and developed a pair of sentiments of special and abiding value to the romantic tradition. No traveller really, and hidden away so much of his life, like Emerson's scholar, he managed to calculate the obscure stars in his scene. His poetry lives in the double richness of his discoveries and attentions, and nature and art move evenly across his page, as do feeling and learning. He did not, to be sure, expand imaginative themes into the personal scene of association though exercising perhaps some of these freedoms (as did other fellow eighteenth-century figures) in the liberated form of the letter. Without such additions, still his poetry proceeds with fresh elemental theme, moving softly but strongly out of the past into new places of meditation and appraisal.

Wordsworth particularly inherited the spiritual concerns of Gray, and both quietly and joyfully he walked the routes of his imagination, in the Gray tempo of slow meditation and rapid excitement – 'luxuriant', 'hurried'. Gray was too immediate a part of Wordsworth's emotional and literary past to be allowed much direct mention. But Gray was close to him always, and particularly that August afternoon, as he returned from a visit to the grave of his young Hawkshead teacher of poetry, with its inscription from the 'Elegy'. There in this moving scene of waters and sands and architecture and level light (and of childhood, too), Wordsworth heard from travellers the word of Robespierre's death (and, in a sense, of the death of reason).[5] The magic private language of the soul and of its poetic reflector overwhelmingly spoke themselves, in this moment, in this scene:

> ... that very shore which I had skimmed
> In former days, when – spurring from the Vale
> Of Nightshade, and St. Mary's mouldering fane,
> And the stone abbot, after circuit made
> In wantonness of heart, a joyous band
> Of school-boys hastening to their distant home
> Along the margin of the moonlight sea –
> We beat with thundering hoofs the level sand.[6]

With Gray too Wordsworth trembled at the Chartreuse: and indeed in all ways he relived his sensibilities, with an even fuller philosophical attention, and an even more modern melancholy.

The river moves with Gray's beautiful tempo through 'Tintern' and through the *Prelude*, and childhood plays along its banks. Old country figures sleep beside flowing roads, or brood silently above pools. We know these first-born affinities, and Wordsworth's primary and first-born associations with the unconscious imagination of childhood – with the winds above Green-head Ghyll. Wordsworth widely expanded the symbolism of the unconscious mind, especially in early books of the *Prelude*, and always with Gray's magic proportions of the fresh and the mature.

With Gray too Wordsworth wrote of a rising and surrounding poetic imagination. Gray's imagery of weaving he particularly employed, perhaps with clearer threads of pleasure and pain. What tapestry in the scene of Gray's Cambridge – the frames of poetry fading into the garments of a minor courtly waste!

> *The surfaces of artificial life*
> *And manners finely wrought, the delicate race*
> *Of colours, lurking, gleaming up and down*
> *Through that state arras woven with silk and gold;*
> *This wily interchange of snaky hues. . . .*[7]

Perhaps colour and painting and removed architectural structures again rise as Wordsworth pursues his two worlds of the given and the achieved. Surely most central to his imagination is the invisible airy architectural structure of the mind which stands after builders, props and foundations all are gone – the building of the spirit.

Pleasantly, Gray and Wordsworth shared the Cambridge scene, both perhaps as celebrants and satirists. Agostino Isola, who was assistant to Gray in Italian languages in his professorship of modern history, was in a sense handed on to Wordsworth, acting as a tutor in Italian when Wordsworth ventured on his more independent college studies. In his letters, in the 'Installation Ode', and in many delightful scurrilous poetic scribblings, Gray created the mixed myth of Cambridge, which Wordsworth will enlarge in the third book of the *Prelude*. Gray's lifelong confinement in the Cambridge environment gave him not simply precocious senses of distaste and revenge which Wordsworth had less opportunity to develop: 'The quiet ugliness of Cambridge' (*Corres.*, II, 521) – for some readers their abiding love of Gray begins with their first reading in this poetic appendix. But for his longer (and earlier too) residence in Cambridge. Gray felt the surrounding old agrarian environment of this ancient place more fully than his follower. What Gray gave perhaps chiefly to Wordsworth's Cambridge book of the *Prelude* was the point of view – the Eton perspective of the young mind of youth. Wordsworth somewhat re-imagines in his Cambridge book the 'Eton Ode', beginning with 'circle' and 'wheel' and 'hoop'. Wordsworth read freshest boyhood back into the Cambridge he loved – finding the boy Milton there and the page Spenser, and finding too the ragged youth who came at the dawning of Cambridge humanism. Against an advanced Cambridge scene, Wordsworth played a simplest theme – the perspective of boyhood. This minor perspective he retained at intervals in the *Prelude,* as in the London scenes.

And finally, of course, Gray and Wordsworth share the Lake District. Gray made his journey to the Lakes in 1769 – the year prior to Wordsworth's birth in Cockermouth. To this scenery Gray brought the attentions of his early poetry, to peasant, to bird, to building. He also brought that increasing Baconian attention to the natural world which marks his changing mind. A first motif in the *Prelude* is that of the poet going to settle in a home, chosen in advance by the imagination. Such a choice Gray almost seems to make (and perhaps did) for a later residence in Grasmere:

> one of the sweetest landscapes, that art ever attempted to imitate.
> ... Grasmere-water. ... from the shore a low promontory pushes itself far into the water, & on it stands a white village with the parish-church rising in the midst of it, hanging enclosures, cornfields, & meadows green as an emerald with their trees & hedges & cattle fill up the whole space from the edge of the water & just opposite to you is a large farm-house at the bottom of a steep smooth lawn embosom'd in old woods, wᶜʰ climb half way up the mountain's side, & discover above them a broken line of crags, that crown the scene. not a single red tile, no flaring Gentleman's house, or garden-walls, break in upon the repose of this little unsuspected paradise, but all is peace, rusticity, & happy poverty in its neatest most becoming attire. (*Corres.,* III, 1098-99)

Victoria College, Toronto

Notes

1. 'De Principiis Cogitandi', trans. J. R. Hendrickson, *Complete Poems,* ed. H. W. Starr and J. R. Hendrickson (Oxford, 1966), pp. 163-64.
2. Starr and Hendrickson, p. 203.
3. Bernard Berenson, *Italian Painters of the Renaissance* (Garden City, N.Y., 1953), p. 63.
4. 'o Faesulae, amoena...', trans. J. R. Hendrickson, *Complete Poems,* p. 150.
5. *The Prelude,* ed. E. de Selincourt and H. Darbishire (Oxford, 1959), bk. x, 11. 481-552.
6. Ibid., 11. 596-603.
7. Ibid., bk. III, 11. 562-66.

Thomas Gray:
A Quiet Hellenist

As a rough old Coleridgean, with a palate a little coarse for Augustan nuances, I should offer my credentials before saying anything about Thomas Gray on so ceremonious an occasion. I must admit that my credentials are oblique, accidental, almost non-existent. My concern for Thomas Gray springs from a curious tissue of circumstances of a kind that Gray himself might take for an omen, or that might – for its gossipy inconsequence – induce him (if indeed this is permitted by the gods) to smile a little from the shades like one of Richard Bentley's cats.

For a year I lived on the winding Thames between Bourne End and Cookham, near Maidenhead, on the edge of a ten-acre water-meadow that in the spring was full of the cries and wings of courting curlews. Stanley Spencer was still painting in Cookham then; and at Cookham bridge we watched the Queen's red-bearded Swan-master set out for the yearly Swan-upping – just as Stanley Spencer had painted it – in an oared boat under banners, the men in splendid livery; and in the village street you could see some of the people who on the Last Day (in another painting of Spencer's) break out of their graves in the yew-lined churchyard of Cookham to greet their friends and lovers. If you cross the river at Cliveden Reach (the scene of *The Wind in the Willows*) and climb up into Burnham Beeches, and walk easterly with a little persistence, Stoke Poges will eventually disclose itself, very small and discreet; and given elevation enough a distant prospect of Eton College can be achieved. Other beech-trees more distant in time and place are also for me connected with Thomas Gray, almost as tenuously. I remember that in some summer before the war I found myself in Norfolk in Felbrigg Park. Here the beech trees are very ancient and of immense girth, their bark as grey and voluptuous as an elephant's hide; and antlered stags tiptoed in dainty disdain through the leaf-shadow. Here a great beech had been felled; and once the main splitting of it had been achieved with auger and black powder, and beetle and wedge, its wood under the bitt of a sharp axe had the texture of bone or boxwood and was speckled with pale mauve flecks like caraway seeds. Not very long ago I realized that that estate with the haunting Scandinavian name was owned by the man who twenty years later was to write a biography of Gray – a man learned, compassionate, and urbane enough to move easily in Gray's company.

Another chance pilgrimage took me more recently to the Cosin Feast at Peterhouse, where I discovered from a portrait hanging outside my bedroom in the Master's Lodge that there was once a Master of Peterhouse named John Whalley. The name, being familiar but uncommon, stirred my interest. I had always known about my regicide forebear Edward who married Cromwell's niece and, being a resolute soldier, became Master of Cromwell's Horse and his Quartermaster General; and how at the Restoration he was less vigorously hunted than most of the regicides and escaped with his son-in-law to New England and is still remembered in New Haven for his benevolence and a street named for him (though mispronounced). I had come to know too of another John Whalley, presumably some collateral forebear, who is succinctly described in *DNB* as a 'quack' on the preposterous grounds that he sold universal nostrums in Dublin, practised necromancy, and issued an astrological almanac entitled *Advice from the Stars*; and how, when Dublin got too hot for him, he settled in London and for the last ten years of his life lived off the proceeds of a libellous weekly called *Whalley's Newsletter*. Clearly a man of a different kidney from the Peter Whalley, contemporary of Gray, who preceded James Boyer as Upper Grammar Master at Christ's Hospital, edited Ben Jonson's plays (poorly), married an extravagant wife, and died in Ostend escaping from his creditors. Yet here, in the Master's Lodge of Peterhouse, there had lived a Whalley once, who spoke with Gray and sat at the same High Table when Gray was a fellow-commoner, being made Regius Professor of Divinity in the year of Gray's domestication in Peterhouse. He looks demure enough in his portrait; but he is remembered for an almost imperturbable indolence, notable even at a time when the universities expected that sort of thing. Gray however found that John Whalley, when roused from his lethargy, could be morose, mulish, and vindictive. I suspect that he was not very intelligent, or else had allowed his intelligence to lapse; I am not altogether happy about this. He was the sort of Master that only death could remove; and remove him it did, seven years before Gray's hasty translation to Pembroke.

Nothing but affection for the memory of Thomas Gray would have led me to open this reminiscent vein. To rehearse on this occasion the ways and words of this man, who was melancholy but not joyless, reticent but not untouched by passion, would be liturgically correct, and an elegiac mode would be appropriate, for the limpid movement of elegy can embrace at times the fact of death and at times the care of vine-plants and the nurture of bees. But elegy is a learned mode, not brief when cast into prose. I must limit myself to a theme less incantatory, less poignant, in order to raise certain questions about the constitution of Thomas Gray's mind and the relation between poetry and life. I wish to suggest that Gray's Hellenism places him in a peculiar position in respect of poetic sensibility; and that if there were some way of reconstructing and delineating the whole scope and quality of his mind and poetic intelligence – if we could come at the person living, thinking, writing, suffering, the whole man as distinct from that more analytic figure that psychology reconstructs to explain the more perplexing of his overt actions (his poems, for example) – then there might also be some way of dissolving the persistent but factitious distinction between 'classic' and 'romantic' as traditionally – and perhaps sometimes a little uncritically – applied in the history and analysis of English letters.

When the title of 'Humanist' is applied to Thomas Gray, and we think of him as a fastidious man, timid, hypochondriac, melancholic, withdrawn, and add to this his capacity for affairs when need arose, his compassion, the vulnerability of his so carefully concealed nature, and his capacity for love, the word seems to suit him like a stately but ill-fitting garment, a benevolent alternative to barbarism. The name Humanist however belongs properly – or should I say, historically – to the man whose mind is coloured by the Latin and Greek spirit as we have it in their literature, history, and philosophy. Latin *and* Greek: two very different cultures, two ways of mind almost irreconcilable. A knowledge of Greek has always been unusual among talented writers in English, and to possess the sense and spirit of the Greek mind is even rarer. For this reason I prefer the term 'Hellenist' to Humanist; then there can be no mistake that Greek is intended together with whatever else the word implies.

Greek has never been a dominant or shaping force in English letters, even though since its first tenuous introduction to England in the late fifteenth century a knowledge of Greek was the prized and distinctive mark of the early Humanist. Milton stands apart from all English writers of comparable stature for the strength of his Greek. His annotated copies of Pindar, Euripides, Lycophron, and Aratus survive as detailed testimony;

certainly his reading of the *Poetics* was more perceptive, more faithful to Aristotle, than was the reading of his Italian contemporaries that then prevailed and still largely prevails, and his understanding of tragedy is more truly Aristotelian in his conduct of *Samson Agonistes* than most of the commentators who have (in his absence) argued the point with him. Yet even in *his* poetry I hear little that I would identify as Greek in colour or instinct. During the eighteenth century the study of Greek had been firmly established in the universities as a necessary concomitant to Latin; even though the universities were moribund, no man could call himself then – or now – a classical scholar if he knew no Greek. To master that beautiful, direct, supple language is no small achievement; and beyond that is the way of shaping the mind sensitively to the lyrical power, the intellectual daring, and philosophical clarity that find their body in the monuments of Greek writing. Needless to say, a minute knowledge of Greek is not, and never was, a panacea; the history of scholarship does not persuade us that Greek provides an impregnable armour against pedantry or intemperance; it failed to make a reliable scholar of Gilbert Wakefield or an urbane man of Samuel Parr. But the lack of it can also induce thinness in the voice, and in the language unrefined rhythms and coarse textures. In a notable outburst B. Ivor Evans cries out against the absence of the Greek spirit in English literature.

> Chapman, though he translated Homer, wrote like a barbarian, whose great, tough genius involved itself in complexities far removed from any possible conception of a Greek ideal. Ben Jonson, despite his acquaintance with Greek, is Latin in his origins when those origins are not English. Shelley, who studied Greek closely and used Greek mythology for his most effective expression in *Prometheus Unbound*, has obviously departed completely from any adherence to Greek motives or values. Tennyson, Browning, Swinburne, and Landor, though they study Greek, employ that knowledge in verse to which classical principles have made only a minor contribution. Milton stands apart. . . . Dryden, who loved the classics as much perhaps as any English writer, was far happier with Latin than with Greek. He used Latin versions of Homer and Theocritus, and 'Longinus' he knew through Boileau and John Hall. Latin influences are again behind the eighteenth century, with Horace mainly in Pope, and Juvenal in Johnson.[1]

Some acquaintance with Greek was not uncommon among the literate of the eighteenth century and much of the nineteenth century; but Gray evidently had more than a tincture and did not lose it when he left school. In August 1750 he begins a letter to Wharton with the sly comment: 'Aristotle says (one may write Greek to you without Scandal) . . .' and quotes from the *Nicomachean Ethics* (*Corres.*, I, 327) – a somewhat different affair from Wordsworth's luxurious statement in the Preface to *Lyrical Ballads*: 'Aristotle, I have been told, has said, that Poetry is the most philosophical of all writing.'[2] Mathias's 1814 edition of the *Works* first printed some notes Gray had written on Plato and Socrates and all eleven of Aristophones' plays. Could Gray then have been an Augustan poet who had read beyond Virgil, Homer, Juvenal and Catullus, the *Poetics* in Italian, and the *Iliad* in Mr. Pope's ingenious translation? A list drawn from the catalogues of Gray's library and from his notebooks is impressive.[3] In Gray's library all the major Greek and Latin writers were represented, and many obscure ones too. In September 1746 when Pembroke College was thinking of doing something about its library, Gray sent Wharton from the alphabetical list of his own library 'a Page of Books: enough I imagine to chuse out of, considering the State of your Coll: Finances. the best Editions of ancient Authors should be the first Things, I reckon, in a Library: but if you think otherwise, I will send a Page of a different Kind' (*Corres.*, I, 241-42). He intended, but did not seriously embark upon, editions of Strabo, Plato, and the Greek Anthology (some poems from which he rendered in Latin elegiacs). His notebooks contain painstaking and continuous notes on his reading of Greek authors – not as copious or sharply focused as the notes in his interleaved Linnaeus, but much more than idle or trifling: on Plutarch, Sophocles, Fabricius's *Bibliotheca Graeca*, Diogenes Laertius, Athenaeus, Lysias, Isocrates ('the *Panegyrick*, the *De Pace, Areopagitic*, & *Advice to Philip*, are by far the noblest remains we have of this Writer, & equal to most things extant in the Greek tongue' [*Corres.*, III, 1121]), Andocides, Antiphon, Xenophon, Thucydides.

To have read carefully all these works, however, tells little about the manner of reading or the quality of sensibility. Even on grounds of plausibility van Hook's statement that 'Thomas Gray was perhaps the most learned man of his age' seems a little extravagant – certainly as far as Greek scholarship is concerned. Samuel Parr, it is true, considered Gray one of the few men in England who 'well understood' Plato;[4] and Samuel Parr – a coarse bombastic man, immodest in self-assessment, memorable to Coleridge for the 'dray-horse tread' of his prose style though celebrated as a composer of polished Latin epigrams – Samuel Parr was indeed a most learned man, a stupendous scholar. Gray does not walk with such a man; nor with Richard Bentley (whose eldest son made the illustrations for the *Six Poems*), nor with Thomas Tyrwhitt who was said to know 'almost every European tongue', who edited Chaucer, wrote perceptively on Shakespeare, was principal detector of the Chatterton forgeries, and made the first important edition of Aristotle's *Poetics* to be achieved by an Englishman; nor with Thomas Twining, tea-merchant *manqué*, who made almost the first and still one of the best English translations of Aristotle's *Poetics*; nor with Richard Porson, master of Euripides, restorer of the Greek inscription on the Rosetta Stone, whose beautiful Greek script has been one of the delights of classical study ever since types were cut from it for use in a series of Cambridge editions of Greek plays in 1810. Gray was not a classical scholar in the sense that any of these eighteenth-century English scholars was. He composed elegant Latin; he was an independent student of Greek, much more than a dilettante. He was not required – professionally or otherwise – to study or to teach Greek. To read the ancient literature, to enjoy it and understand it as best he could, was one of the absorbing preoccupations of his life.

Two or three extracts from his letters show with what eager enthusiasm he read his Greek. To West in May 1742:

> You see, by what I sent you, that I converse, as usual, with none but the dead: They are my old friends, and almost make me long to be with them. You will not wonder therefore, that I, who live only in times past, am able to tell you no news of the present. I have finished the Peloponnesian war much to my honour, and a tight conflict it was, I promise you. I have drank and sung with Anacreon for the last fortnight, and am now feeding sheep with Theocritus. Besides, to quit my figure, (because it is foolish) I have run over Pliny's Epistles and Martial ἐκ παρέργου; not to mention Petrarch, who, by the way, is sometimes very tender and natural. I must needs tell you three lines in Anacreon, where the expression seems to me inimitable. ... Guess, too, where this is about a dimple. (*Corres.*, I, 202)

West replied suitably: 'Your fragment is in Aulus Gellius; and both it and your Greek delicious. But why are you so melancholy?' Again, in September 1746, Gray writes from Stoke, this time to Wharton:

> I take it very ill you should have been in the twentieth Year of the War, & yet say nothing of the Retreat from before Syracuse [in Thucydides]: is it, or is it not the finest Thing you ever read in your Life? and how does Xenophon, or Plutarch agree with you? for my Part I read Aristotle; his Poeticks, Politicks, and Morals, tho' I

don't well know, wch is which. in the first Place he is the hardest Author by far I ever meddled with. then he has a dry Conciseness that makes one imagine one is perusing a Table of Contents rather than a Book: it tasts for all the World like chop'd Hay, or rather like chop'd Logick; for he has a violent Affection to that Art, being in some Sort his own Invention; so that he often loses himself in little trifleing Distinctions & verbal Niceties, & what is worse leaves you to extricate yourself as you can. thirdly he has suffer'd vastly by the Transcribblers, as all Authors of great Brevity necessarily must. fourthly and lastly he has abundance of fine uncommon Things, wch make him well worth the Pains he gives one. you see what you have to expect. this & a few autumnal Verses are my Entertainments dureing the Fall of the Leaf. notwithstanding wch my Time lies heavy on my Hands, & I want to be at home again. (*Corres.*, I, 241)

He must have persisted with Aristotle. In June 1757, when he sent Mason 'the breast & merry-thought & guts & garbage of the chicken, wch I have been chewing so long, that I would give the world for neck-beef, or cow-heel' (*Corres.*, II, 503) – the latest revision, that is, of 'The Bard' – he showed that he had read the *Poetics* more perceptively than most of his contemporaries, and had assimilated it for intelligent rather than prescriptive use.

I wish you were here, for I am tired of writing such stuff; & besides I have got the old Scotch ballad, on wch Douglas was founded [i.e. *Gil Morrice*]. it is divine, & as long as from hence to Aston. have you ever seen it? Aristotle's best rules are observed in it in a manner, that shews the Author never had heard of Aristotle. it begins in the fifth Act of the Play; you may read it two-thirds through without guessing, what it is about; & yet when you come to the end, it is impossible not to understand the whole story. I send you the first two verses. (*Corres.*, 504-5)

If we take a cursory muster of Gray's published poems something interesting emerges in support of his Hellenism. In 1756 at the age of forty-one he was offered the poet laureateship and declined it. The offer was based on the 'Elegy' principally; otherwise his reputation can have rested only upon the other five poems in the *Six Poems* (1753) – the three odes ('On the Spring', 'On Eton College', and 'To Adversity') that mark his first and most prolonged outburst of poetic energy in 1742 (if anything so slow-burning can be called an outburst), an ode on the death of Horace Walpole's favourite cat, and the 'Long Story', the facetious record of a flattering but inconsequent flirtation. To be offered the laureateship for so slender a harvest was a little embarrassing. 'I have nothing more, either nocturnal or diurnal, to deck his [Dodsley's] Miscellany with', he had told Walpole in 1751;[5] and when Dodsley had the book all ready, Gray protested about the title – 'to have it conceived that I publish a Collection of *Poems* (half a dozen little Matters, four of wch too have already been printed again & again) thus pompously adorned would make me appear very justly ridiculous' (*Corres.*, I, 371). Even with Bentley's illustrations and printed on only one side of the leaves, it made not more than 36 pages. When Whitehead picked up the laureateship that Gray had contemptuously put aside, there seems to have been no reaction, either of rejoicing or derision: England did not at that moment suffer from an embarrassment of poetic riches. The 'Elegy' had struck a commanding chord, and so had the Latinism of the three other grave odes. But Gray intended to move forward. When he started writing English verse in 1742 he stopped writing Latin verse and intensified his reading of Greek.

His next published volume came in 1757, the first-fruits of the *Officina Arbuteana*: the first two Pindaric Odes – 'The Progress of Poesy' and 'The Bard' – printed without titles and with virtually no notes, and addressed (with two words from Pindar's IInd Olympian Ode) 'to the intelligent alone'. When the 'Progress of Poesy' was seventeen lines short of completion and five years short of publication Gray had told Walpole that he might soon send Dodsley 'an ode to his own tooth, a high Pindarick upon stilts, which one must be a better scholar than he is to understand a line of, and the very best scholars will understand but a little matter here and there' (*Corres.*, I, 364). When it came to publication he declined to help his readers: 'I do not love notes, though you see I had resolved to put two or three. They are signs of weakness and obscurity. If a thing cannot be understood without them, it had better be not understood at all.'[6] Embarrassed at the praise of the 'Elegy' which had slipped into print by accident and might never have been acknowledged by its author but for the outrageous inaccuracies of the unauthorized printing, Gray was seriously attempting something more difficult, more exalted, more intricate and dangerous than he had before ventured in public. The composition had engaged him for almost five years; he placed greater store by those two Odes than even the 'Elegy'. 'They are Greek, they are Pindaric, they are sublime!' Walpole told Mann; 'consequently I fear a little obscure.'[7] Gray (as author) asked Walpole (as printer) to tell him 'what you hear any body say, (I mean, if any body says any thing)' (*Corres.*, II, 513). A few intelligent readers admired them for their eloquence and some admired the 'Progress of Poesy' for the rendering of Pindaric metres into English with a strictness never before attempted. But most readers found them insuperably obscure; and since that age was reasonably honest – unlike our own, in which the unintelligibility of a slipshod piece of thinking can be taken as grounds for acclaim – the poems failed. 'nobody understands me', Gray said; '& I am perfectly satisfied' (*Corres.*, II, 522). But he was not satisfied: he was bitterly disappointed. 'the Συνετοί [intelligent] appear to be still fewer, than even I expected' (*Corres.*, II, 518). He knew some readers would have difficulty with the subject matter; but they were objecting to the very reason for the Odes existing – their rhapsodic and incantatory style; and to this cry Dr. Samuel Johnson, never beloved of Gray, had added his portentous voice.[8] Gray stopped writing poetry for publication for many years and withdrew into his cherished privacy.

In the spring of 1767, almost ten years after the two Pindarics had been published, Gray yielded to Dodsley's desire to print 'all I have ever publish'd', and in December of that year he also agreed to James Beattie's request that the Foulis brothers of Glasgow be allowed to issue their own edition of the same collection. So the collected poems appeared – eight in number – almost simultaneously in two editions: an unlovely edition by Dodsley in London on 12 March 1768, and a handsome Scottish quarto printed by Foulis in types specially designed. 'The *Long Story* was to be totally omitted, as its only use (that of explaining the prints [by Bentley]) was gone: but to supply the place of it in bulk, lest *my works* should be mistaken for the works of a flea, or a pismire, I promised to send him an equal weight of poetry or prose: so, . . . I put up about two ounces of stuff; viz. The Fatal Sisters, The Descent of Odin . . . , a bit of something from the Welch [i.e. *The Triumphs of Owen*], and certain little notes, partly from justice (to acknowledge the debt, where I had borrowed any thing), partly from ill temper, just to tell the gentle reader, that Edward I. was not Oliver Cromwell, nor queen Elizabeth the witch of Endor. This is literally all; and with all this I shall be but a shrimp of an author.'[9] Despite the additional notes – there had only been four in the 1757 – he was not disposed to ingratiate his readers, extending the Pindaric epigraph to read: '[shafts] that speak clearly to the intelligent; but for the generality they need interpreters.' The three new poems were impenitently in the voice of 'The Bard', drawn from Icelandic and Welsh originals by way of Latin with greater rhapsodic assurance than the first two Pindaric Odes had shown. Walpole had urged Gray to write more, but Gray replied firmly: 'To what you say to me so civilly, that I ought to write more, I reply in your own words (like the pamphleteer, who is going to confute you out of your own mouth), What has one to do, when *turned of fifty*, but really to think of finishing? However, I will be candid (for you seem to be so with me), and avow to you, that till fourscore-and-ten, whenever the humour takes me, I will write, because I like it; and because I like myself better when I do so. If I do not write much, it is because I cannot.'[10] But he never broke silence in public again – except for the 'Installation Ode' (1769), an unhappy episode to do with human pride and the vanity of human wishes.[11]

The copious notes added in 1768 help us to pick up what Gray thought were his tracks. In the *Six Poems* he acknowledges debts to Shakespeare, Milton, Green, and Dryden (including Dryden's translation of Ovid) – for Gray was after all an *English* poet – and to Dante and Petrarch, because he read Italian as well as French; but among the classical authors he recognizes only Virgil, unless there is a distant echo of Sophocles in the 'Eton' ode. The acknowledged debts in 'The Bard' are to Shakespeare, Dryden, Milton, and Spenser; and in 'The Fatal Sisters' to Milton and Shakespeare. 'The Progress of Poesy' draws heavily on English and Latin and for the first time on Greek: Shakespeare and Milton are joined by Cowley, Ossian, and the Authorised Version of the Bible; from the Latin, Virgil, Lucretius, and Juvenal; from the Greek, beyond the overarching presence of Pindar, there is Homer and Phrynichus.[12] In his first period of fluent composition in 1742 Gray had turned to Greek – Pindar and Lysias particularly – with a zest that was never to be quenched. Whatever was specifically Greek in 'The Progress of Poesy' had been carried over, by transformation of rhythm, tone, and energy, into three later bardic poems. His knowledge of Icelandic and Welsh was scanty; but the Latin versions he had to use to make sense of the originals did not deflect him from the Pindaric urgency and intricacy that he sensed in the Icelandic and Welsh. A conclusion might be ventured: that the three odes of 1742 and the 'Elegy' are dominantly Latin; that 'The Progress of Poesy' and 'The Bard' are consciously Pindaric, although only 'The Progress' seeks to reproduce Pindar's metrics in detail; and that the three later bardic odes, despite their Nordic and Celtic origins, are Greek in inspiration, shaped to the lyrical texture and impetuosity of Pindar's odes – a tune now fully assimilated and perhaps no longer consciously sought.

Matthew Arnold seems to be quite clear about Thomas Gray. Gray, he tells us, fell upon an age of prose; 'a sort of spiritual east wind was blowing'; his genius could not flower; he would have been 'another man' if he had been born in the same year as Milton, or in the same year as Burns.[13] Perhaps Arnold was not seriously applying to Gray the 'mute inglorious Milton' proposition so dearly (if only intermittently) beloved by Ontario Ministers of Education. Perhaps Arnold was saying in his roundabout importunate way that Gray was a greater poet than his poems would lead us to suspect. In fact Shakespeare was born when he was born; Milton was born when he was born; Gray was born when he was born. It is a critic's business to take what happens to be given and to look at it carefully, and if possible with a sense of wonder. We are given Gray's poems, his letters, some annotated books, some notebooks. What happens if we try to sketch out his poetic capacity on evidence other than simply the poems themselves? For in speaking of Gray's Hellenism – which is not perhaps very prominent in his poems – we wish to get at his sense of language and his sense of the textures of feeling and thinking.

Gray not only had an excellent ear for verse; he was also a musician of some accomplishment and much learning, as his letters bear almost Pepysian witness.[14] Also he had, if any man ever had, a poet's eye, the 'armed vision':[15] when he looks at a beetle it is like Aristotle looking at a dogfish. Only in some neutral and abstract sense are eye and ear merely *recording* faculties; the ear is one sense, the eye is another; and both are profoundly affected, each in its own way, in their acuity and discrimination, by the mind behind the ear, the feeling behind the eye, and by the generative reaction of the whole person in any moment of perception. Gray's interest in natural history – and here Ketton-Cremer puts it so well that I must read from his pages –

> Gray's interest in natural history had been a constant resource to him, ever since he first watched the flowers and insects in the Buckinghamshire meadows. He loved to grow plants in water or damp moss in his rooms, and sometimes extended his researches to the animal world, as when he reared the larvae of insects in a cup of water, and kept an owl, 'as like me as it can stare', in the college garden. His microscope was as often in use as his harpsichord; and during his summer tours he delighted to collect all kinds of herbs and roots, butterflies and beetles and the creatures of the rockpools by the sea. His observations and experiments were recorded in Latin in his pocket notebooks, and most of them were later transferred to the interleaved Linnaeus – details of the hermit crab whose behaviour he watched on the beach at Hartlepool, and the

young pelican which he saw at Glamis, and the eggs of the scaven-
ger beetle which he discovered in the dead body of a mole at Cambridge. (*Gray*, p. 213)

To be more particular: to read Gray's letters at random is like reading
his contemporary Gilbert White, although Gray never knew White and
the *Natural History and Antiquities of Selborne* was not published until
1795, two years after White's death and almost twenty-five after Gray's.
Birds, plants, insects, the temperature of the ambient air, the look of the
sky, the feel of the weather; the dates and seasons of crops, flowers, fruit –
these are the ground bass to the passacaglia of his quotidian awareness, an
intricate and grave liturgy of wonder, the requisite and clarifying engage-
ment of the senses in his knowing of the world and his knowing of himself. To Wharton on 31 January 1761:

the 18th of Jan: I took a walk to *Kentish-Town*, wind N:W:, bright
& frosty. Therm: at Noon was at 42. the grass remarkably green
& flourishing. I observed on dry banks facing the South that Chick-
weed, Dandelion, Groundsel, Red Archangel, & Shepherds-Purse
were beginning to flower. (*Corres.*, II, 729)

Again to Thomas Wharton, on 18 April 1770:

our weather till Christmas continued mild & open. 28 Dec: some
snow fell but did not lie. the 4th of Jan: was stormy & snowy, wch
was often repeated during the month, yet the latter half of it warm
& gentle. 18 Feb: was snow again, the rest of it mostly fine. snow
again on 15th March, from 23 to 30 March was cold & dry, Wd E:
or N:E:. on ye 31st rain. from thence till within a week past, Wd
N:W: or N:E: with much hail & sleet; & on 4 Apr: a thunder-
storm. it is now fine spring-weather.

1 March. first violet appear'd. frogs abroad.
4 ——— Almond blow'd, & Gooseberry spread its leaves.
9 ——— Apricot blow'd.
1 April. Violets in full bloom, & double Daffodils.
5 ——— Wren singing. double Jonquils.[16]

These preoccupations in the later years vexed Walpole – the copious
naturalist's notes, the detailed drawings in a most delicate hand: here,
thought Walpole, was the greatest poet of his age 'heaping notes on an
interleaved [copy of] Linnaeus, instead of pranking on his lyre'.[17] Gray
was not easily roused: 'to be employed', he might have said, 'is to be
happy'. One of the last things he wrote (again in his copy of Linnaeus's
Systema Naturae) was a set of eight beautifully turned Latin verses on
the *Orders of Insects* and death seems to have interrupted him at the first

line of a ninth. Even with a friend as intimate as Walpole, Gray must
be allowed a degree of ironic reticence; for Walpole to search farther
would be to probe at the roots of the man's poetic nature. Perception of
this order is not only rarely achieved and more rarely sustained; whether
as highly developed as Gray's, it is the physical and vital root of poetry
itself. In such perception the senses merge and resonate: the eye loses its
abstractive cunning, the ear engages rhythms, the pulsed and pulsing
sounds that are the mark and movement of life; and in this state all
things become tactile – even sounds, colours, light, words. In Gray's *De
principiis cogitandi* (I, 62-78) there is a remarkable passage on the sense
of touch.[18]

> [When] sensations . . . pour themselves into the fresh mind, and . . .
> crowd around the entrances in a fivefold procession, the sense of
> touch plays the leading role; it goes first, widening the dark path
> for the lesser crowd, and restrains its headlong rush. This sense is
> not subject to the same restrictions that its brothers are: since it is
> the first-born, it asserts a wider sway, and has its dwelling deep in
> the marrow of the bones and throughout the viscera, and is widely
> diffused and has its being in the warp and woof of the skin. Indeed,
> even the child that has not yet struggled forth from its mother's
> womb dissolves the many layers of covering and bursts the chains;
> although it is as yet wrapped in soft slumber and bathed in warm
> fluid, nevertheless a very slight breeze has already been stimulating
> the sense of touch and opening the way for the breath of life. This
> activity is intensified the moment the child has exchanged the
> soothing warmth to which it has grown accustomed for the chill
> of the outer air, which assails its untried limbs with savage fury.
> Then a more excruciating sense of touch begins to function, and
> Pain, the constant companion of human life, takes possession.

Mason first published this in 1775. Whether Coleridge ever read it with
attention I do not know (though he annotated a copy of the 1814 *Works*);
the connection with Locke would certainly temper his interest. But much
of what Gray says here is also said by Coleridge in a fragmentary way in
many places and at dates much earlier than 1814; and he has much else
to say about the sense of touch, being a more perceptive and original
psychologist than Thomas Gray was. What is most striking in the unexpected coincidence between Gray and Coleridge is the possibility that
touch is the first and radical of the senses, that touch is somehow the
key to the synaesthesic mode in which feelings are embodied and in
which even the play of intellect can be transfigured. *Tact* is a central

word for Coleridge when he is thinking about poetry and about critical judgement; he used the word fastidiously and so preserved its delicate cutting-edge; the poet's tact is 'the *Touch* of a Blind Man feeling the face of a darling Child'.[19] Which is not to say anything about the relation between Gray and Coleridge. But Coleridge knew a great deal about the nature and origins of poetry – not only his own 'kind' of poetry, but of poetry simply – more perhaps in philosophical, psychological, and experiential detail than any Englishman before him; and Coleridge knew well that a sound theory of poetry must stand upon a sound theory of perception. It is startling to find that Thomas Gray had found out some of these things about the senses in his own way and for himself. He might conceivably have learned these things from his reading; he is more likely to have known them affirmatively from inside himself, from his own 'inner goings-on'. That same Antrobus uncle who had used his influence to carry Thomas Gray from the household of a ferocious father and an industrious (but not unaffectionate) shopkeeping mother into Eton College and then to Peterhouse, and had so brought him to the friendships that were to keep him rejoicing and grieving for the rest of his life, had also taught him to be a naturalist, encouraging in him a fascination with growing things and small creatures. Like his acquaintance Christopher Smart until imprisonment in a madhouse drove him to *A Song of David* and *Jubilate Agno*, Gray was probably most at his ease in humorous and topical verse. We know he was endowed with the fastidious sense of accuracy of a true scholar – and with a good deal of the scholar's delicate malice. Beyond that, his patient, brooding, finely discriminate power of observation suggests the potential of a fine poetic sensibility; yet that sensibility is seldom if ever clearly or at first hand realized in his poetry.

Poetry however is made of language, not of natural history; it is made by fitting language to the mind as much as fitting the mind to the world. If we turn again to Coleridge, himself a Hellenist, there may be other evidence for finding in Gray a Greek way of mind. Coleridge, born the year after Gray's death, inherited Gray's poetry at school and university, and much of his early verse resounds to it. As a nineteen-year-old undergraduate he sent his elder brother a transcript of two 'little odes of G[ray]' – unidentified – which he says were 'never published' and which he may have seen in manuscript at Pembroke College.[20] Six weeks later he entertained his girl-friend with an account of a visit from 'the ghost of Gray' who gave him stern advice: to send her a copy of his works and to 'write no more verses' because 'your poetry is vile stuff; and ... all

Poets go to [he]ll'.[21] In 1794 in his first published review he quoted half
facetiously from 'The Progress of Poesy', and in the same year sent
Southey strictures on a poem of his as too reminiscent of 'The Descent
of Odin' and noticed that another inflated poem was on a theme which
is 'so much better expressed by Gray'.[22] A list of projected writings
drawn up by Coleridge in 1796 includes 'Edition of Collins & Gray with a
preliminary Dissertation' – a title repeated in a slightly later list but
never completed.[23] Though he quotes from the 'Ode to Vicissitude' in
the same year, and is self-mockingly pleased that some people thought his
'Ode on the Departing Year' 'superior to the *Bard*', Gray's name disap-
pears from both the letters and notebooks in 1797 until in 1804 he spotted
a parallel to 'The Progress of Poesy' in Matthew Smallwood's 'Poem on
the Death of Cartwright'.[24] Hazlitt may well have remembered correctly
that in 1798 Coleridge 'spoke with contempt of Gray, and with intoler-
ance of Pope'.[25] If Coleridge had ever written the edition of Collins and
Gray, he would have argued for Collins's pre-eminence; for he says in
Biographia Literaria that during his first Cambridge vacation he wrote
an essay in which he 'assigned sundry reasons, chiefly drawn from a comparison of passages in the Latin poets with the original Greek, from
which they were borrowed, for the preference of Collins's odes to those
of Gray'. This comparison, and later conversation with Wordsworth, led
him (he said) to see that 'this style of poetry which I have characterised
[he had quoted from 'The Bard'], . . . as translations of prose thoughts
into poetic language, had been kept up by, if it did not wholly arise from,
the custom of writing Latin verses, and the great importance attached to
these exercises, in our public schools'.[26] What looks like outright dismissal, however, is illuminated a little by a notebook entry of early 1799.

> The elder Languages fitter for Poetry because they expressed only
> prominent ideas with clearness, others but darkly – Therefore the
> French wholly unfit for poetry; because [Poetry] is *clear* in their
> Language – i.e. – Feelings created by obscure ideas associate them-
> selves with the one *clear* idea. When no criticism is pretended to,
> & the Mind in its simplicity gives itself up to a Poem as to a work
> of nature, Poetry gives most pleasure when only generally & not
> perfectly understood. It was so by me with Gray's *Bard*, & Collins'
> odes – *The Bard* once intoxicated me, & now I read it without
> pleasure. From this cause it is that what *I* call metaphysical Poetry
> gives me so much delight.[27]

For Coleridge (unlike Gray's contemporaries) Gray was not too obscure:
he was too *un*obscure. By securing what to Coleridge's ear was uniform

semantic clarity, Gray had taken the timbre out of the song, the muscle out of the dance; the mysterious self-declarative directness of pure action of mind had been replaced by contorted meaning. Gray may have translated prose thoughts into verse, but the Greeks didn't; and when Coleridge first read John Donne's poems his heart leaped up instantly. What he recognized there was not simply a kind of poetry that he liked – for he had catholic tastes; he recognized the action of poetry declaring itself, the power declared by the intricacy of the containing resistance offered by language and structure. When Coleridge discussed Gray again in the *Biographia* his view was perhaps a little more kindly. 'I had long before [in discussions with Wordsworth] detected the defects in "the Bard"; but "the Elegy" I had considered as proof against all fair attacks; and to this day I cannot read either without delight, and a portion of enthusiasm. At all events, whatever pleasure I may have lost by the clearer perception of the faults in certain passages, has been more than repaid to me by the additional delight with which I read the remainder.'[28] But by 1833, with *Lyrical Ballads* and the 'Ancient Mariner' thirty-five years behind him, he could only say, a little perversely perhaps: 'I think there is something very majestic in Gray's Installation Ode; but as to *The Bard* and the rest of his lyrics, I must say I think them frigid and artificial. There is more real lyric feeling in Cotton's *Ode on Winter*.'[29] This was not a new position; as early as April 1811 he is reported to have said that he thought 'Collins had more genius than Gray, who was a singular instance of a man of taste, poetic feeling, and fancy, without imagination.'[30]

Gray wrote in his 'Stanzas to Mr. Bentley':

> . . . *not to one in this benighted age*
> *Is that diviner inspiration given,*
> *That burns in Shakespeare's or in Milton's page,*
> *The pomp and prodigality of heaven.*
>
> (ll. 17-20)

Coleridge singled out the word 'prodigality' in these lines as an instance of the untranslatableness of English: 'English may be called the harvest of the unconscious wisdom of various nations, and was not the formation of any particular time, or assemblage of individuals.'[31] Yet in 1811, when he had allowed no high merit either to Johnson or Gray and had complained that Gray's personifications 'were mere printer's devils' personifications', he had also said that 'the excellence of verse was to be untranslatable into any other words without detriment to the beauty of the passage; the position of a single word could not be altered in Milton without injury.' Was Gray's failure to match his poetic sensibility to his practice as a poet a failure in the sense of language? In a letter to West in April 1742, during his first poetic flowering, Gray had put his position clearly on the matter of poetic diction.

> As to matter of stile, I have this to say: The language of the age is never the language of poetry; except among the French, whose verse, where the thought or image does not support it, differs in nothing from prose. Our poetry, on the contrary, has a language peculiar to itself; to which almost every one, that has written, has added something by enriching it with foreign idioms and derivatives: Nay sometimes words of their own composition or invention. Shakespear and Milton have been great creators this way; and no one more licentious than Pope or Dryden, who perpetually borrow expressions from the former.

He then cites a number of examples from Dryden 'whom every body reckons a great master of our poetical tongue'.

> And our language not being a settled thing (like the French) has an undoubted right to words of an hundred years old, provided antiquity have not rendered them unintelligible. In truth, Shakespear's language is one of his principal beauties; and he has no less advantage over your Addisons and Rowes in this, than in those other great excellencies you mention. Every word in him is a picture. Pray put me the following lines into the tongue of our modern Dramatics: [from *Richard III* I i]. To me they appear untranslatable; and if this be the case, our language is greatly degenerated. (*Corres.*, I, 192-93)

Coleridge had been trained, he said, by James Boyer at Christ's Hospital long before he ever talked diction with Wordsworth, 'to leave out as many epithets as would turn the whole into eight-syllable lines [rather than ten- or eleven-syllable lines], and then ask myself if the exercise would not be greatly improved. How often have I thought of the proposal since then, and how many thousand bloated and puffing lines have I read, that, by this process, would have tripped over the tongue excellently.'[32] This stern discipline was not easily mastered. His distaste for abstractions and personifications came in the wake of Wordsworth; certainly there is no lack of personifications or abstractions or epithets or compound epithets in his own poems before 1796, and when he came to belabour Southey in 1814 for using typographical personifications in the juvenile 'Joan of Arc' he was being the executioner of his own early poetry too. By then he had had to make his own discoveries about the life of language – as every single poet has to. For him that central question was: what happens to language in the state of imagination? There is a hint of an answer in a notebook entry of 1829:

> Even the Dreams of the Old Testament are for the greater part evidently *poetic*, the beseeming Drapery of Wisdom either for prudence or for livelier impressions. Only we need not suppose, that the Hebrew Nabim set to work out a cold-blooded carpentry of ⟨Dreams⟩ Furors, like ⟨Grays⟩ The Bard or [Southey's] the Vision of Judgement – In those times and in that country Men reasoned with the organ of Imagination, and vivid Images were supplied the place of words, and came more readily than words in a language so limited & scanty as the Hebrew.[33]

So slight is Gray's poetic canon that when the ballistas, tortoises, and scaling-ladders of modern critical technique are mounted to assault this little handful of verses, the labour seems ill-expended, the booty not profitable: we come to much the same conclusion that Coleridge came to, though no doubt with more detailed supporting evidence than I have quoted. The 'Elegy' stands up well; the Pindarics are impressive for the meticulous attempt to match the details of Greek prosody, but on the whole they don't *feel* much like Pindar; the barbarous later pieces are vigorous but a little strait-laced. Yet what first had struck me forcibly in Gray's poetry was the strong contrast between the marmoreal sententiousness of the 'Elegy' and the rhapsodic if decorous abandon of the Pindaric and bardic odes; *and* the fact that both were the necessary utterance of the one man. Although Gray's Pindarics are not themselves much more rhapsodic than any other deliberately contrived Pindaric ode, Gray himself evidently *needed* to be rhapsodic in these poems, and went on being even more securely rhapsodic after his readers had said they didn't like what he was doing. Here at least the horse was going before the cart; the poetic genesis was necessary and correct no matter what, *sub specie aeternitatis*, the outcome. Given Gray's ear, his knowledge, his command of poetic resources – given also his passion and some strong if indefinable need to write — I could see no *prima facie* reason why he should not have made poems that declare to us beyond doubt from what depths of need or vision they had sprung. If we notice the vitality covert in his work, it is no more satisfactory to say that the vigour of the odes comes from Gray's use of exotic materials than is any other reference to a standard checklist of allegedly 'romantic' characteristics: the vigour must be in Gray himself and must call to itself the body it needs – exotic, it may be – to shape language to its force and purpose. Exoticism is often no more than a decorative or mannered confection, as we know from certain Persian eclogues fashionable in the eighteenth century and from Southey's Mexican and Welsh epics; it is sometimes as enchanting as Brighton Pavilion. But when exotic detail functions deftly, not only in a geographical and historical sense but also psychologically and linguistically, it can become an indispensable resource of distancing if the poet is to trace the movements of mind in psychic space. This, for example, might account for the pastoral convention in elegy. For conventional modes, metrical intricacy, and the structure of language itself are all shaping limitations in the making of poetry; a poet must explore them and use them almost as though they were not present if he is to discover in his poem the self-shaping and self-declarative dynamic of language.

The dispute about poetic diction in which Johnson and Wordsworth play so bludgeonly a role is, I think, too often uncritically cast as a simple question of the history and variability of literary taste. Poetry surely is *one*, not many – no matter how numerous its manifestations. Perhaps the only tenable objection to any particular diction is that it doesn't do effectively what the poet wants it to do. In general, poetic power calls into use – or fashions for itself – the resources of language it needs. What is puzzling about Gray's poetry is that, from what we can infer about his poetic sensibility and technical resources, he seems never quite to have fashioned for himself the words and rhythms he needed to declare the force and subtlety of his inner life or of his poetic intelligence. Which is not to say that he wrote no good poems, but that most of them have not realized the forces that called them into existence. The 'Elegy' is the most successful. Here he was writing an elegy, not a threnody – a grave and muted reflection upon mortality rather than an uncontrollable outcry against the indignity of death or the desolation of grief. The 'Elegy' falls comfortably within the Latinistic mentality, convention, and syntax; the deliberately contrived diction admirably suits the formality of the thought; he has discovered a beautiful solution to the movement of the Greek or Latin elegiac verse by not attempting to reproduce the classical metric. But the demands made by the Pindaric poems are emotionally much greater. The intricate limitations of structure and a certain intractability of diction are present to contain and pattern great force. Yet 'The Progress of Poesy', the only deliberately Pindaric of the poems, is perhaps the least Pindaric in feel. The bardic odes, departing from the mechanics of Greek prosody, discover their force in a wholly conceived rhythmic movement, as had been the case in the 'Elegy'; they *feel* more Greek, more Pindaric, though their origins are not Greek but Icelandic and Welsh through Latin. Yet even here Gray has not discovered the resonant tone and muscular rhythm that his known excitement over certain ballads and bardic poems aroused in him. The failure – and it is at most a subtle failure – is not, I think, primarily a failure either of energy or in appropriate structure, but a failure in the sheer dynamics of language itself. The racy flexibility, the sinewy variety of tone, pace, and emphasis that informs the prose of his letters has for some reason not overflowed into the movement of his verse, in the same way that the tactile delicacy and precision of his naturalist's vision never overflowed into the texture and imagery of his reflective odes. The Greek sensibility is present and active, but it has not found itself fully in his language. It is true also that nobody encouraged him to persist in so delicate and submissive a task. The poems he prized most highly were coolly received by the public. That he continued to labour at the bardic poems is a mark of his courage in facing a Latin world in a Greek spirit.

If I had to say what in English poetry feels truly Pindaric in the Greek sense, I can think only of 'Kubla Khan' and perhaps 'The Wreck of the Deutschland' – poems written by highly skilled metrists, both good Greek scholars, both with an exceptional sense of the intrinsic vitality of language, of language as something with a life of its own. To say that both are in some sense 'romantic' is, I think, to sound a cuckoo-cry rather than a trumpet-call. The question is not one of 'romantic' and 'classic' but of Greek and Latin. 'Romanticism is disease; classicism is health', Goethe said; 'the point is for the work to be thoroughly good, then it is sure to be classical.' By 'classical' Goethe could not have meant the cramped Latinistic neoclassicism in the England of the late seventeenth and the eighteenth century that achieved momentous force in Dryden and the clarity equally of delight and venom in Pope, and otherwise ran much to the unfocused and unsymbolized expression of feeling that (since Eliot) is properly called sentimentality. It was sentimentality that Goethe deplored, being as a young man capable of it himself. When Wordsworth's critics after some fifteen years got tired of abusing him, some in praising him called him a 'classical' poet – which in those days, as for Goethe, was a word of high if uncritical honour. Yet Wordsworth, compared with Coleridge, is radically a Latin, not a Greek mind, very much of an eighteenth-century temper as his later poetry shows. If Wordsworth is Greek at all it is in a certain Aristotelian specificity that can deflect abstractions into substance; but when he reflects, as reflect he almost inevitably does, the movement of the verse is not rhapsodic but elegiac.

To move from one language to another is not only to change the shape of the mouth and the features but also to move from one pattern of thought and feeling to another, to think differently in a different syntax, to feel differently. Greek and Latin, as modes of thought and sensibility, are almost irreconcilable; English is closer, as a language and a way of mind, to Greek than to Latin; and English has suffered terrible violence from the rigours and inflexibilities of the Roman mind. Once Latin had become the *lingua franca* of the learned world the force and delicacy of the Greek mind and language became systematically distorted and coarsened, in the same way that Roman copies of Greek sculpture become purposeful, muscle-bound, and haunted – changing Aristotle's *Poetics* (for example) almost beyond recognition, and earlier, in the middle ages, stripping the presocratic philosophers and the neoplatonists – and even Aristotle – of a certain oriental subtlety and ambivalence. This was achieved progressively not only by those who, knowing no Greek, had to read in Latin, but also by those who read their Greek in a Latin mode – as I suspect Milton largely did, and Pope and Johnson certainly did. There have been very few English poets whose work is commanded by the *classical* spirit – that is, by the spirit of *both* Greek and Latin. There is no truly classical *period* of English poetry. Those writers and periods that are commonly regarded as 'classical' are notably Latinistic and in certain important respects spiritually limited. Hence the otiose artificiality – in English usage anyway – of the romantic-classic distinction; it turns almost entirely upon superficies and artificials. The brothers Schlegel, who started that hare, were learned in Greek, imbued with its spirit, and could not conceive of the term 'classical' other than as including, if not dominated by, Greek. Hence the subtlety of their distinction, and the speed with which – even among their learned poet-friends and disciples in Germany – the distinction eroded into the banality of self-conscious cults and the make-work of professional polemics.

After all, it was Wordsworth who learned from Gray, not Gray who heralded Wordsworth. Wordsworth knew Gray's work early, and on the whole admired it much more than Coleridge did; and he acknowledged with gratitude that his very characteristic 'Ode to Duty' was drawn from Gray's 'Ode to Adversity'. In 1794 when Wordsworth was walking through the Lakes with his brother John he was reading Gray's journal of the Lakes. And when Coleridge and Wordsworth came to the head of Bassenthwaite on 10 November 1799 they chose to sleep at an inn at Ouse Bridge (now vanished) possibly because they knew Gray had once dined there. Many years after he had left Dove Cottage, Wordsworth remembered Gray's beautiful description of the Vale of Grasmere; he may even have chosen Dove Cottage in the autumn of 1799 because he looked at Grasmere for an instant through Thomas Gray's eyes.[34] It would be interesting to be able to define exactly how far and in what way Wordsworth's poetic sensibility was directly affected by Gray's feeling for the countryside and its creatures; for Gray's way of looking is more Coleridge's way than Wordsworth's.[35]

Thomas Gray was a very secret man, except to his intimate friends. For many years he had an ambition to be Cambridge Professor of Modern History, a subject in which he was almost as learned as in natural history. When his hope was eventually realized he gave no lectures and is not known to have supervised the studies of any undergraduate. His inaugural lecture, elaborately planned and partly composed in Latin, was never delivered. He intended to prepare some lectures and even to read them; he would resign his chair (he said) if he could not show some sign of fulfilling what was expected of him. Perhaps nothing was expected; he neither lectured nor resigned. This – and much else – is cause for wonder. If in the end Gray's Hellenism was not impetuous enough to allow him fully to realize the poetic force of his remarkable perceptual and intellectual endowments, it may also be that Greek language and literature can no longer – in the general ignorance of our times – fertilize our poetry, except in very rare individuals. Our sense of the beautiful vitality of Greek may almost totally have vanished. If that is so, we should expect to seek nourishment in our own language, now greatly developed since Thomas Gray used it, and in our literature so immensely rich and varied that it may now encompass even the suppleness and concentration of Greek (though seldom its superb clarity of tone and movement). Our poets have a momentous task now in discovering and rediscovering the integrity of language, greatly menaced as it is by widespread habits of indiscipline – habits that would appal Gray both as scholar and poet. As critics, however, we must also look back, as Gray looked back, towards the sources, both historical and personal. In considering the tantalizing anomaly of Gray's poetic destiny, we might find there some critical discriminations that would release us from the tyranny of habitual categories and self-justifying procedures. As we study the 'monuments of our own magnificence' we should also do well to turn back to the Greek way of mind and language, by whatever means we can; for in many hidden ways it has given nerve, precision, and grace to our own language. Certainly it was in the secret places of Gray's genius. We should be ill-advised to neglect the traces of it there.

Queen's University

George Whalley

Notes

1. *Tradition and Romanticism* (London, 1940), pp. 17-18.

2. *The Poetical Works of William Wordsworth*, ed. E. de Selincourt and H. Darbishire (Oxford, 1940-49), ii, 394.

3. See William Powell Jones, *Thomas Gray, Scholar* (Cambridge, Mass., 1937), and LaRue van Hook, 'New Light on the Classical Scholarship of Thomas Gray', *American Journal of Philology*, lvi (1936), 1-9.

4. Sir John Sandys, *A History of Classical Scholarship* (New York, 1958), ii, 417.

5. *Corres.*, i, 348. Cf. 364, to Walpole: 'You have talked to him for six *odes*, . . . He has reason to gulp when he finds one of them only a long story.'

6. Ibid., ii, 508. Cf. 522, to Mason: 'I would not have put another note to save the souls of all the *Owls* in London. it is extremely well, as it is.'

7. *Correspondence of Horace Walpole*, ed. W. S. Lewis and others (New Haven, 1937–), xxv, 120.

8. Johnson was to write: 'These odes are marked by glittering accumulations of ungraceful ornaments; they strike, rather than please; the images are magnified by affectation; the language is laboured into harshness. The mind of the writer seems to work with unnatural violence. . . . He has a kind of strutting dignity, and is tall by walking on tiptoe. His art and his struggle are too visible, and there is too little appearance of ease and nature.' Johnson also objected that Gray 'did not write his pieces first rudely, and then correct them, but laboured every line as it arose in the train of composition'; and found it 'a fantastick foppery' that Gray 'could not write but at certain times, or at happy moments' (*Lives*, iii, 440).

9. *Corres.*, iii, 1017-18, to Walpole. The letter to Beattie, with instructions for Foulis, is at iii, 982-84.

10. Ibid., iii, 1018. Elsewhere, for 'whenever the humour takes me' he uses the agreeable phrase 'just as the maggot bites'.

11. Coleridge seems to have been one of the few to speak kindly of the 'Installation Ode': he found 'something very majestic' in it (*Table Talk*, 23 Oct. 1833; also quoted at p. 161 below).

12. There were, as Roger Lonsdale's edition of the poems shows, many more debts and echoes than these, many of them no doubt submerged below the threshold of Gray's recognition. Gray presumably pointed out the debts that he thought might help the (uninstructed) reader; he was not interested in reconstructing the genetic process.

13. 'Thomas Gray', *The Works of Matthew Arnold* (London, 1903-4), iv, 68-69, 67.

14. See the index entry for 'Music' at *Corres.*, iii, 1319. In addition to 9 entries for music in general, 14 for opera, and reference to 6 named operas (including Purcell's *King Arthur*), there is mention of an 'Acoustic warming-pan', a 'Haspical', a lyricord, and several references to 'musical glasses'. The harpsichord may be taken for granted.

15. 'armed vision' is Coleridge's phrase, in *Biographia Literaria*, ed. J. Shaw-cross (Oxford, 1907), I, 81.

16. *Corres.*, III, 1126-27 at the end of the account of the Lake Tour. Just before the end of the letter Gray shows his Gothic enjoyment of the 'variety of chappels & remnants of the abbey' in ruins, at Kirkstall on the river Aire. The terse entries in W. Keble-Martin's *The Concise British Flora in Colour* (1965) have a similar quality of affectionate incantation: these at random — of *Cuculus baccifer*, 'In copses and bushy sea cliffs, very rare, perhaps intro-duced by migratory birds'; of *Frangula alnus*, 'On peaty heaths and damp hedgerows in England'; of *Conyza canadensis*, 'Alien in cultivated and waste ground'; of *Achillea ptarmica* (or Sneezewort), 'Common in wet meadows and on moors'.

17. Walpole, *Correspondence*, XXXIV, 123.

18. Also cited to great effect by Professor Jean Hagstrum in the first paper of the Conference: see p. 13 above. The translation of Gray's Latin is taken from *The Complete Poems of Thomas Gray*, ed. H. W. Starr and J. R. Hendrickson (Oxford, 1966), p. 164.

19. *Collected Letters of Samuel Taylor Coleridge*, ed. E. L. Griggs (Oxford, 1956, 1959) [hereafter *Coleridge Letters*], II, 810. The whole passage is of interest: 'a great Poet must be, implicitè if not explicitè, a profound Meta-physician. He may not have it in logical coherence, in his Brain & Tongue; but he must have it by *Tact/* for all sounds, & forms of human nature he must have the *ear* of a wild Arab listening in the silent Desert, the eye of a North American Indian tracing the footsteps of an Enemy upon the Leaves that strew the Forest — ; the *Touch* of a Blind Man' (to William Sotheby, 13 July 1802). For a few notes on the sense of touch, see for example *The Notebooks of S. T. Coleridge*, ed. Kathleen Coburn (New York and Lon-don, 1957, 1961) [hereafter *Coleridge Notebooks*], I, 924, 979, 1297, 1414, 1568, 1812, 1826, 1827; II, 2152, 2398, 2399, 2403, 2468, 2495. In 2152 he asks 'Do not words excite feelings of Touch (tactual Ideas) more than *dis-tinct visual Ideas* — i.e. of *Memory?*'; in Appendix B to *The Statesman's Manual* (1816) he says that 'To the touch (or feeling) belongs the proxi-mate; to the eye the distant'. The subject is large and intricate, and much of the material unpublished; there is however an important but obscure marginale on touch and its relation to the other senses in *The Works of Jacob Behmen* (1764-1781), I, i, 49-50. A marginal note on John Petvin's *Letters concerning Mind* explains my hesitation in expecting Coleridge to have read *De principiis cogitandi* with enthusiasm: 'Yet still there were many of a better mould, who retaining their love and veneration of the Ancients were anxious to combine it with the new Orthodoxy by explain-ing Aristotle and even Plato *down* into John Locke. Such was that excellent man, and genuine *Classic* Scholar, the Poet Gray.' Petvin, understanding the ancients better though not loving them more, was one of those who tried 'pully—ing John Locke up to Plato & Aristotle'.

20. *Coleridge Letters*, I, 18.

21. Ibid., 27-28.

22. *Coleridge's Miscellaneous Criticism*, ed T. M. Raysor (Cambridge, Mass., 1936), pp. 91-94; *Coleridge Letters*, I, 116, 133.

23. *Coleridge Notebooks*, I, 161 (6), 174 (15).

24. *Coleridge Letters*, I, 278, 309; *Coleridge Notebooks*, II, 1919.

25. 'My First Acquaintance with Poets', *The Complete Works of William Hazlitt*, ed. P. P. Howe (London, 1930-34), XVII, 121.

26. *Biographia Literaria*, I, 12-13; cf.27n.

27. *Coleridge Notebooks*, I, 383. Cf. I, 1016: 'Whether or no the too great definiteness of Terms in any language may not consume too much of the vital & idea-creating force in distinct, clear, full made Images & so prevent originality – *original* thoughts as distinguished from positive thoughts – '. See also I, 921.

28. I, 27n.

29. *Table Talk*, 23 Oct. 1833.

30. *Table Talk*, 'Oxford Edition' (1917), pp. 318-19: from John Taylor Coleridge's 'Reminiscences of Mr. Coleridge'.

31. *Coleridge's Shakespearean Criticism*, ed. T. M. Raysor (London, 1960), II, 88.

32. *The Complete Poetical Works of Samuel Taylor Coleridge*, ed. E. H. Coleridge (Oxford, 1912), I, 3n.

33. Coleridge's Notebook 41, entry 28. The words ⟨Dreams⟩ and ⟨Grays⟩ have been scored out.

34. Gray's 'Lake Journal' had been accessible in Mason's version, tidied and cut, since 1775. Gray's description of Grasmere deserves to be quoted entire (*Corres.*, III, 1098-99). 'Past a back near *Dunmail-raise*, & . . . now begin to see *Helm-Crag* distinguish'd from its rugged neighbours not so much by its height, as by the strange broken outline of its top, like some gigantic building demolish'd, & the stones that composed it, flung cross each other in wild confusion. just beyond it opens one of the sweetest landscapes, that art ever attempted to imitate. (the bosom of yᵉ mountains spreading here into a broad bason) discovers in the midst Grasmere-water. its margin is hollow'd into small bays with bold eminences some of rock, some of soft turf, that half conceal, and vary the figure of the little lake they command, from the shore of low promontory pushes itself far into the water, & on it stands a white village with the parish-church rising in the midst of it, hanging enclosures, corn-fields, & meadows green as an emerald with their trees & hedges & cattle fill up the whole space from the edge of the water & just opposite to you is a large farm-house at the bottom of a steep smooth lawn embosom'd in old woods, wᶜʰ climb half way up the mountain's side, & discover above them a broken line of crags, that crown the scene. not a single red tile, no flaring Gentleman's house, or garden-walls, break in upon the repose of this little unsuspected paradise, but all is peace, rusticity, & happy poverty in its neatest most becoming attire.' It was 'the whole vale of Keswick' that in April 1794 recalled to Wordsworth Gray's description of it as 'the Vale of Elysium' (see *Wordsworth Letters*, 2nd edn. [1967], I,

114-15; cf. *Corres.*, III, 1079). For Wordsworth's – and Coleridge's – view of Grasmere in November 1799, see *Wordsworth Letters*, I, 271-72. In August 1841 Wordsworth wrote to Isabella Fenwick: 'I wish I could send you any pleasant news, but it is scarce; in small matters I must tell you that we hear that the Wishing Gate is destroyed, ... then, what is far worse, John Green, son of our late Butcher, is building a huge tall box of a house (right in the centre of the vale of Grasmere as you cross it) to the utter destruction of the primitive rustic beauty of the whole, as touchingly described by the Poet Gray in his journal written 70 years ago. This has hurt me more than, considering what human life is, it ought to have done.' (*Wordsworth Letters: The Later Years*, ed. E. de Selincourt [Oxford, 1939] III, 1089.) This recalls however a letter from Wordsworth to Richard Sharp *c* 7 Feb. 1805. 'Woe to poor Grasmere for ever and ever! A wretched Creature, wretched in name and Nature, of the name of *Crump*, goaded on by his still more wretched Wife ... this same Wretch has at last begun to put his long impending threats in execution; and when you next enter the sweet paradise of Grasmere you will see staring you in the face upon that beautiful ridge that elbows out into the vale (behind the church and towering far above its steeple) a temple of abomination, in which are to be enshrined Mr and Mrs. Crump. Seriously this is a great vexation to us, as this House will stare you in the face from every part of the Vale, and entirely destroy its character of simplicity and seclusion.' (*Wordsworth Letters*, 2nd edn., I, 534.) Dorothy thought that 'on that account chiefly for we do not set our hearts on spending all our days at Grasmere' (I, 539: cf.II, 23). Nevertheless, Wordsworth was the first tenant of this house, Allan Bank, and lived there from June 1808 until June 1811. The chimneys smoked incorrigibly. The index to Wordsworth's letters in the later years gives some indication of his detailed knowledge of Gray's poetry and his interest in Gray.

35. The 'Lake Journal' is to be found in *Corres.* No. 505, 508*, 511, 511A, 519. Considering how Gray in the Lakes was anxious, hypochondriac, and almost immobile, and Coleridge like a chamois-hunter on the fells, energetic and needlessly daring, it is interesting to consider how easily – with only a few changes in orthography – Gray's Journal would fit into Coleridge's notebook record of his scrambles through the same country: see for example *Coleridge Notebooks*, I, 1204-28 or *Inquiring Spirit*, ed. Kathleen Coburn (1951), §186 (pp. 225-42).

ALASTAIR MACDONALD

Gray and his Critics: Patterns of Response in the Eighteenth and Nineteenth Centuries

Gray has always been a challenge to his critics, not to say an embarrassment sometimes: how to place him, how to reconcile conflicting elements in his work. But he has never been ignored. Most literary histories, and critical assessments of periods and movements have, in one way or another, taken account of him. Since his time, there are few great names in English literature who have not left some recorded judgement, from the extended consideration to the comment written in letters and journals, or spoken in private to friends. He has earned for himself a good share of complimentary comparisons: 'worth more's', 'the only's', 'would rather's'. To Hazlitt, a single letter from the pen of Gray was 'worth all the pedlar-reasoning of Mr Wordsworth's Eternal Recluse'.[1] Matthisson, friend and correspondent of Bonstetten, said that Gray 'with less than a hundred pages, travels much more securely on the road to immortality, than the Polygraph of Ferney with his seventy volumes'.[2] Edward Fitz-Gerald felt sure 'that Gray's Elegy, pieced and patched together so laboriously, by a Man of almost as little Genius as abundant Taste' would 'outlive all these hasty Abortions' of certain contemporary poets.[3] Byron implied that Gray's 'Elegy' was worth all Gray.[4] Wordsworth said the latter part of the epitaph on Mrs. Clerke was almost the only instance he recollected of an eighteenth-century metrical epitaph in English which had 'affecting thoughts . . . pure from vicious diction'.[5] It is well remembered what General Wolfe would rather have done. Tennyson would rather, it is reported, have written the 'Elegy' than all Wordsworth.[6]

Remarkable, certainly, is such tribute to one who composed only a limited amount, and published not all of that. Many, whose contribution was greater in quantity, and perhaps in quality also, and many others who could be said to be on a par, have received less continuing attention. For more than two hundred years, the interested have been offering reasons; and it is unnecessary here, even if it were possible, to recapitulate their findings. But it might perhaps be said that Gray did two things which may ensure that success of capturing the notice of a reading public. He first moved and pleased them in a way all kinds and classes of reader could and did appreciate, in a compelling and subsequently immortal work. And secondly, not so long after, he challenged, baffled, and, as it might have seemed, flouted this same public, and had the reviewers and critics squabbling over him, with two demanding and unconventional poems. The combination of the caress and the whipping. And, as a further point, it might be added that he had the good fortune, for his continuing life in literary history and criticism, to elicit an estimate from one of the most authoritative critical voices of the day. This seemed to many so provocatively adverse and partial, and so challenging to the poet's already established fair fame, that it ensured for Gray another twenty years or so of critical attention on that score alone. In the meantime, his currency was further stiffened when he was taken by two vocal advocates of a new kind of poetry as exemplifying some causes of their revolt. Until he was carried, beyond heat, to another age when he could be more objectively regarded, though with memory of his not untroubled progress into posterity, and his virtues and shortcomings assessed by the standards of a changing taste.

And so, contention helped keep him alive. Sheer merit, too; although merit by itself is not an invariable guarantee of contemporary recognition or subsequent survival. But excellence there was. An unusual care and finish in the writing. A felicitous choice of theme, to what extent inadvertent or calculated may be debated, which met the taste of the times, which in some of his poems gave the poetry-reading public what it knew, and wanted, in more excellent measure; gave it itself as it then was. Wordsworth, elsewhere sometimes a detractor, said in a letter to Quillinan ([1837]) that it was 'worthy of note how much of Gray's popularity is owing to the happiness with which his subject is selected in three pieces – his Hymn to Adversity, his ode on the distant prospect of Eton College, and his Elegy'.[7]

Gray's personality, too, ensured a certain attention. In Gray, wrote Bulwer Lytton in 1837, 'the man and the poet appear in perfect harmony with each other'.[8] The poetry gave tantalizingly intermittent glimpses of a life, aspects of which were clearly reflected in it, sensed to be of fascination. The reclusive savant, emitting in print periodical flashes of manifest worth, and then withdrawing into the darkness of a guarded privacy, is often an object of interest and curiosity, for he at once stimulates the one, and never wholly satisfies the other. With Gray, the public had to be content with the sparingly released evidence; and the further reputation from other sources for taste and learning: the polymathy rumoured, but never allowed public display. No deliberate seeker after fame could, perhaps, have devised a more effective means of building a reputation than this, almost certainly uncontrived, procedure of Gray.

By the nature of his work, also, he became a measure, a touchstone, in appraisal and dispute, when wider critical issues were being viewed. And so it is that certain patterns, themes or motifs of response occur, recur, fade away, reappear in altered configuration in the succeeding years. In the changing vocabulary of critical response, his name has been webbed by the sounds of 'pathetic, simple, sublime, obscure, laboured, harsh, artificial, fresh', and many more such words for qualities discerned. Gray has been a glass reflecting the literary ages' own faces: criticism's faces, and grimaces.

In his own lifetime, he had twenty years of public recognition. Joseph Warton said, quite rightly, that when 'Gray published his exquisite ode on Eton College, his first publication, little notice was taken of it'.[9] In print, at any rate. Nor did the three poems ('Ode on the Spring', 'Ode on the death of a Favourite Cat', and the 'Eton Ode', again) which appeared, still anonymously, the following year, 1748, in Vol. II of Dodsley's *A Collection of Poems*, excite particular remark. Attention began with the 'Elegy'; although there is not a great deal of published contemporary comment on that. It seems it was accepted; and that much discussion was at first unnecessary. An unsigned notice in the *Monthly Review* for February 1751 intimates succinctly that: 'The excellence of this little piece amply compensates for its want of quantity.'[10] John Hill in the first of his 'Inspector' papers for the *London Advertiser* (5 March 1751) said the poem came nearer the manner of Milton than anything published since that poet, and suggested it had the quality of 'Lycidas'. The 'Elegy' is 'full of Imagination, and as full of Sentiment; the Imagery is striking, and just; the Descriptive Part elegantly simple; the Expression concise yet clear, nervous yet smooth, and majestic without Pomp'.[11] Virtues expected from good poetry, in fact, at this time. Not much extended comment. The review of the edition of Gray's poems with Bentley's designs in the *Monthly Review*, June 1753, said that to enlarge in the praise of the ingenious author of these poems would be impertinence; 'as his church-yard elegy is in every one's hands, and not more justly than universally admired'.[12] And that is fairly typical of the passing acceptance.

Later, William Belsham was to say (1793) that the '*Bard*' and '*Church-yard Elegy*' were 'master-pieces of sublime enthusiasm, and plaintive elegance',[13] giving, in these phrases, two of the main contrasting, and perhaps complementary, responses to Gray at this time. Incidentally, it may be worth remembering that use of 'enthusiasm' in connection with some of Gray's poetry is one instance in the rehabilitation of this word. From the condemnatory term, in both religious and poetic reference, of the late seventeenth and earlier eighteenth centuries, it is gradually elevated to the name for a quality becoming increasingly regarded as a *desideratum* for poetry. The publication of the two Odes in 1757 brought the motif of 'sublime' fully into the criticism of Gray. Hitherto he had been 'sweetest of our elegiac poets', in a phrase from No. 22 of *The World* (1753);[14] the 'pensive GRAY' of Mason's ode 'On Melancholy' of 1756.[15] Now the Odes introduced splashes of much bolder colouring into the vocabulary of response. A Gray 'in thunder clothed'[16] had startled the world of poetry and criticism into a different kind of attention. Two amazing Odes, said Horace Walpole to Mann (1757), 'they are Greek, they are Pindaric, they are sublime'.[17] Lord Lyttelton wrote of the 'bright & glorious flame of poetical fire in Mr Gray's Odes'.[18] The *Critical Review* said what follows ('The Bard', l.3 onwards) 'is all enthusiasm, exstasy [*sic*], and prophetic fury, that alarms, amazes, and transports the reader'.[19] Joseph Warton said Pope had written nothing 'in a strain so truly sublime' as 'The Bard' of Gray.[20] Adam Smith, later, wrote that Gray 'joins to the sublimity of Milton the elegance and harmony of Pope'.[21] Cowper said he thought Gray 'the only poet since Shakespeare entitled to the character of sublime'.[22] The vocabulary of response to these Odes borrowed something from the vocabulary of the poems themselves: 'terror, glitter, glittering, awful, horror, thrilling, sublime, Ecstasy, flaming bounds, sapphire-blaze, burn, daring spirit, prophet's fire, awful voice, terrors, Amazement, Rapture, soaring'. These were also the conceptions, and the words for them, associated in the so-called Neo-classical mind with the Longinian Sublime.

In this flurry of often somewhat breathily ecstatic sounds, there had, of course, been cooler voices. Goldsmith, in his unsigned review of Gray's Odes in the *Monthly Review*, September 1757, thought it a pity the poet should have addressed only a minority familiar with classical and Pindaric precedent; that he would do better to study the people; that the qualities of Pindar caught by these poems, 'the seeming obscurity, the sudden transition, and hazardous epithet', though intended as beauties, would be regarded as blemishes by the 'generality of his Readers'.[23]

Terror was an associate of the Sublime. And Gray now seemed also to have appeared as a kind of purveyor of terror, horror, the violent. Even, however, in the pensive, elegiac Gray there had been signs of this propensity in the vocabulary and imagery of pain, sorrow, disease, violence, present from the beginning in the English poems; and as Professor Arthur Johnston has just shown, in some of the Latin poems and translations before them. The 'toiling hand of Care' of the 'Ode on the Spring'. The 'fury Passions', 'pallid Fear', skulking Shame, 'Grim-visaged comfortless Despair', 'grinning Infamy', 'keen Remorse', 'moody Madness', the 'painful family of Death' of the 'Eton Ode'. The 'iron scourge and torturing hour', the 'Gorgon terrors', 'screaming Horror', 'ghastly Poverty' of the 'Ode to Adversity'. And a number of the other papers we have heard have given important new insights into the use of such terms by Gray. This imaging of the terrible and the fearful is itself no doubt some projection of the secret or subconscious dreads of a physically, though not intellectually or morally, timid man. It is merely intensified, and made objective in appropriate external situation, with the poetry of prophecy and incantation to which Gray seemed later to be drawn. This new-seeming, and more terrible, kind of Gray received further emphasis from the 1768 edition of his poems, which included 'The Fatal Sisters', 'The Descent of Odin', and 'The Triumphs of Owen', with their heightening of situation and imagery of horror. The *Critical Review* for May 1768, made an association with Aeschylus (and Aeschylus had provided Gray with epigraphs for the 'Ode to Adversity'), saying that the imagery of these poems was everywhere strongly conceived, and strongly expressed, 'abounding with those terrible graces of which Aristotle tells us Æschylus was so fully possessed'.[24] John Langhorne, in his long review of Mason's *Memoirs* of Gray, 1775, in the *Monthly Review*, said that Gray's genius was not marked alone by that 'tender and melancholy sensibility so interesting in the Country Churchyard'. There was a 'Gothic grandeur' of the 'most striking and powerful effect' which 'could be felt, could be tasted only by the few, while the natural pictures of the former were caught by and melted in every eye'. Sublimity of genius, he said, 'has been generally attended with a strong affection for the dæmonry of the ancient northern fable'. Milton had been particularly fond of it. There was something sublime in the Celtic mythology, in the idea of ancient 'hardyhood'. In the mythology of the Greeks, everything seemed puerile in comparison. Hence Gray's 'strong attachment to every thing that breathed of the former'. The Hall of Odin was heaven itself to him, and Ossian ' "the very dæmon of poetry" '.[25]

A concomitant of Gray's 'sublime', and often mentioned with it in criticism, is the 'obscure'. From the start, Horace Walpole talked about this. The Odes were Pindaric, sublime, he wrote to Mann. He went on, 'consequently I fear a little obscure – the second particularly by the confinement of the measure and the nature of prophetic vision is mysterious'.[26] And from then on, there was much talk of 'obscurity' in both conversation and print. Leslie Stephen, in 'Gray and his School' (*The Cornhill Magazine*, 1879), said that contemporary critics 'complained grievously of its ['The Bard's'] "obscurity" – a phrase which seems ill-placed to us who know by experience what obscurity may really mean'.[27] And there were those, in spite of eighteenth-century conditioning to a poetry accustomed to say more or less directly what it meant, who denied this charge. Lord Lyttelton, though he found the first part of the last stanza of 'The Bard' obscure, yet he understood it at the first reading. From '*Fond impious Man*' to the end he found 'very sublime'.[28] Of 'The Progress of Poesy', the review attributed to Arthur Murphy in *The Literary Magazine* (1757) could not 'perceive in this ode any thing of that unintelligible obscure which has been in every body's mouth'.[29] George Campbell, in his *Philosophy of Rhetoric* (1776), knew of 'no style to which darkness of a certain sort' was 'more suited than to the prophetical'; and that when the prophetic style was imitated in poetry, the piece ought, as much as possible, to possess this darkness and prophecy. 'The Bard' 'is all darkness to one who knows nothing of the English history, posterior to the reign of Edward the first, and all light to one who is well acquainted with that history'.[30] But again, William Kenrick in the *London Review* of June 1775, writing of Mason's *Memoirs*, had said that some of Gray's Odes were 'too obscure even for that species of poetry, to which obscurity is pretended to be in some degree essential'. This was the cause of the 'little success' attending the first appearance of the two Pindaric Odes, 'even persons of very good sense and a good taste for poetry confessing they did not understand them'.[31] In a footnote to a line in his 'Elegy on the Death of Dr. Samuel Johnson', Richard Graves wrote: 'A new æra or school of poetry seems to have commenced with Mr. Gray, as different from the simplicity of Addison, Pope, and Parnel, as Pindar's or Horace's Odes from Homer or Virgil; and, as the *sublime*, which is the characteristic of Gray, often borders on *obscurity*, some pasages in his poems might, perhaps, be interpreted according to the *inclination* of the reader.'[32] Gray would have seemed obscure because his Odes were in a sense 'difficult' in comparison with the poetry of the generation of Addison, Pope, Parnell: having sometimes elliptical expression, and cryptic references to unnamed poets, literary and historical figures and situations: requiring notes. Not only this, but from the 1760s and '70s onwards, his poetry was before the public at a time when some feeling against imitation of the ancients and use of classical mythology and allusion was in the air;[33] and when a poetry more directly reflective of what we call 'real life' was beginning to emerge.

Raillery at obscurity there had been. Arthur Murphy, in his review of the Odes in the *Literary Magazine* (1757) gives an amusing representation of popular reaction to these poems, such as might have been heard in club, coffee-house, or salon.

'how do ye like *Gray*'s odes? – can't say? – don't you think they're very unintelligible? – damnably so – what do you think of *many-twinkling feet?* – very affected!' – and then, '*with arms sublime that float upon the air*' – was ever such an image? – only think of that – aukward enough! and then such *Spittle-fields* poetry as it is – *weave the warp and weave the woof*, &c.[34]

The celebrated parodies of Colman and Lloyd (1760) are perhaps the most imaginative form of questioning, or adverse response.

ODE I.
I. 1.

D A U G H T E R of Chaos and old Night,
Cimmerian Muse, all hail!
That wrapt in never-twinkling gloom canst write,
And shadowest meaning with thy dusky veil!
What Poet sings, and strikes the strings?
It was the mighty Theban spoke.
He from the ever-living Lyre
With magick hand elicits fire.
Heard ye the din of Modern Rhimers bray?
It was cool M-----n: or warm G---y
Involv'd in tenfold smoke.

And later in the poem:

IV. 1.

Man's feeble race eternal dangers wait,
With high or low, all, all, is woe,
Disease, mischance, pale fear, and dubious fate.
But, o'er every peril bounding,
Ambition views not all the ills surrounding,

> *And, tiptoe on the mountain's steep,*
> *Reflects not on the yawning deep.*[35]

A 'Chard Whitlow' of the eighteenth century. I don't know if Eliot's response is recorded. We do know Gray's. The parodies had made sufficient impression for him to mention them several times to friends in his correspondence. To Mason, June 1760, he wrote:

> so it is ... Mr Coleman, nephew to my Lady Bath, Author of the Connoisseur, a Member of some of the Inns of Court, & a particular Acquaintance of Mr Garrick. what have you done to him? for I never heard his name before. he makes very tolerable fun with me, where I understand him (wch is not every where) but seems more angry with you. least People should not understand the humour of the thing (wch indeed to do, they must have our Lyricisms at their finger's ends) he writes letters in Lloyd's Evening Post to tell them, who & what it was, that he meant; & says, that it is like to produce a *great combustion* in the Literary World: so if you have any mind to *combustle* about it, well & good! for me I am neither so literary, nor so combustible. (*Corres.*, II, 674-75)

To Wharton, June 1760, he said: 'there was a Satyr printed against me & Mason jointly. it is call'd *Two Odes*: the one is inscribed to Obscurity (that is me) the other to Oblivion.... The writer is a Mr Coleman, ... I believe his Odes sell no more than mine did, for I saw a heap of them lie in a Bookseller's window, who recommended them to me as a very pretty thing' (*Corres.*, II, 681).

Of Gray, Walpole said humour was 'his natural and original turn'.[36] Gray himself had a gift (some would think it might have been developed more fully and practised more often) for satire, parody, and burlesque. His response is beautiful. If, as R. A. Willmott suspects, in the *Church of England Review* (1837), Gray may have written his letters 'for the press',[37] he could hardly have shown reaction to the parodies in a more endearing light. But Willmott's view is debatable.

With Gray, it is often difficult to be sure of the real feelings under the brave and witty masks he presented to his various correspondents. The tendency to minimize self and his own accomplishment is one of his more characteristic – shall we say, defences: and it may well be working here. Parody is only one aspect of the general response to his Odes. There were cries of 'obscurity'. There was often a lack of real understanding of what he was doing in these poems. There were complaints that he was being different from the familiar, elegiac Gray. Many considered that dissatisfaction at the reception of his two (and in one sense) most ambitious poems put him off poetry more or less for good. Mason suggests that he was easily discouraged by adverse comments, and says he himself may have caused delay in finishing 'The Progress of Poesy' by telling his friend he did not think it would ' "hit the public taste".' When urged by him to continue, Gray always replied, ' "No, you have thrown cold water upon it".' And Mason says he mentioned this to show 'how much the opinion of a friend, even when it did not convince his judgment, affected his inclination' (Mason, p. 145n). Adam Smith wrote that Gray was 'said to have been so much hurt, by a foolish and impertinent parody of two of his finest odes, that he never afterwards attempted any considerable work'.[38]

There were doubtless other reasons, and many have often been discussed, why Gray did not produce much more poetry: slowness in finding and executing themes;[39] scholarly projects which made such claims upon his mental activity; a seeming lack of any regular compulsion, financial, professional, personal, to write for the world; latterly, anxiety about justifying his appointment to the Chair of Modern History; failing health and spirits. But he had shown interest in the response to his Odes. In his letters of the time there are frequent inquiries for news of reaction, and comments on reaction discovered.[40] In his own words to Wharton, the Συνετοί appeared 'to be still fewer, than even I expected'.[41] His epistolary attitude is the shrug of indifference. But we sense a real disillusionment.

This is quite typical of his general behaviour with his own productions. There was always the nervous fuss up to the time of publication: whether his name should appear or not, or how it should appear; injunctions about lay-out, punctuation, printing, quality of paper, and so on. Then there was the concern afterwards, thinly veiled by an assumption of detachment, about the reception by the reading public, and by (largely) despised reviewers and magazines.[42] And it all suggests a great sensitivity to that public exposure of himself he both needed and feared, when he was impelled at times to venture from the safe anonymity of the uncommitted life.

Criticism of Gray has clustered round the spaced events: publications in his lifetime; his death; Mason's *Memoirs*, revealing for the first time the letters and the more private Gray: Johnson's 'Life' (1781). For the last three decades of the eighteenth century, his reputation was high. The storm of criticism over Johnson's remarks broke harshly upon the afterglow of contemporary acceptance, which had approached sometimes a mindless adulation. Johnson whipped up the faithful to new heights of rapturous praise, sounding on, even into the next century. The familiar monuments rearing at once to Gray's defence include William Tindal's *Remarks on Dr. Johnson's Life* (1782); Robert Potter's *An Inquiry into Some Passages in Dr. Johnson's Lives of the Poets* (1783); and his *The Art of Criticism; as Exemplified in Dr. Johnson's Lives...* (1789); Gilbert Wakefield's edition of *The Poems of Mr. Gray* (1786). Wakefield, for example, wrote that a 'certain inelegance of taste, a frigid churlishness of temper, unsubdued and unqualified by that melting sensibility, that divine enthusiasm of soul, which are essential to a hearty relish of poetical composition; and . . . an invidious depravity of mind, warped by the most unmanly prejudices, and operating in an unrelenting antipathy to cotemporary merit, too often counteracted and corrupted the other virtues of his intellect'.[43] Potter perorates:

> What could induce Dr. Johnson, who as a good man might be expected to favour goodness, as a scholar to be candid to a man of learning, to attack this excellent person and poet with such outrage and indecency, we can only conjecture from this observation, 'there must be a certain sympathy between the book and the reader to create a good liking.' Now it is certain that the Critic has nothing of this sympathy, no portion nor sense of that vivida vis animi, that etherial flame which animates the poet; he is therefore as little qualified to judge of these works of imagination, as the shivering inhabitant of the caverns of the North to form an idea of the glowing sun that flames over the plains of Chili.[44]

These are representative comments and tones of voice in this defence of Gray against Johnson, which Hugh Sykes Davies has said 'became almost a genre of criticism in itself'.[45] Dr. John Young's anonymous *A Criticism on the Elegy written in a Country Church Yard* (1783), in imitation of Johnson's style and mode of verbal criticism in his 'Life of Gray', brought in an element of satire. The Glasgow professor writes, for example:

> Of inaccuracy in the formation of the thought, the fourth quatrain [of the 'Elegy'] furnishes some examples. It is more according to truth, as well as convenience, to suppose a Church-yard *hedged round* with trees, than *planted* with them. A Church-yard is not a thicket. A human body buried at the foot of a large tree, with strong spreading roots, is more consonant to poetry, than to practice. It is not true, that in an ordinary assemblage of graves, the "turf heaves in mouldering heaps." If the ground heaves, no doubt

the turf will heave with it: but the "heaps," if they are *"moulder-ing* heaps," must heave *through* the turf, not the turf *in* them. "Rude forefathers of the hamlet," is equivocal. The forefathers of a hamlet should mean other, ancienter hamlets. But of hamlets there are no genealogies. Among them no degrees of consanguinity are reckoned.[46]

Anna Seward said in a letter in 1785: 'I am charmed with that admirable sport of fancy, the pretended Continuation of Dr Johnson's Criticism on the Poems of Gray. I hope it will be generally read, exposing, as it does, in such exact imitation, the absurd, yet plausible sophistry, of that arrogant decider.'[47]

Dr. Johnson himself was not amused. Writing to Mrs. Thrale in 1783, he said:

Of the imitation of my stile, in a criticism on Grays Churchyard, I forgot to make mention. The author is, I believe, utterly un-known, ... I know little of it, for though it was sent me, I never ⟨cut⟩ the leaves open. I had a letter with ⟨it⟩ representing it to me, as my own work; in such an account to the publick, they (*sic*) [there] may be humour, but to myself it was neither serious nor comical. I suspect the writer to be wrong headed; as to the noise which it makes, I have never heard it, and am inclined to believe that few attacks either of ridicule or invective make much noise, but by the help of those that they provoke.[48]

It was usually accepted by partisans of Gray that Young was burlesquing Johnson. Although Horace Walpole makes the interesting remark in a letter to Mason that he rather thinks 'the author wishes to be taken by Gray's admirers for a ridiculer of Johnson, and by the latter's for a censurer of Gray'.[49]

The Johnson-Gray controversy was still alive in 1807 when Percival Stockdale published his *Lectures on the . . . English Poets*. He goes over old ground with the familiar vehemence in favour of Gray. Though by this time the issue was by no means so raw and tender. The *Edinburgh Review*'s account (1808) of Stockdale's *Lectures* says:

The author before us seems to have written the greater part of these remarks at a time when the subjects of criticism, on which he enters, excited a livelier interest than they do at present in the public mind. More than half of his pages is devoted to the refuta-tion of Dr Johnson's heretical dogmas on the merits of our best writers. There was a time when no true admirer of Milton or Gray could speak without a rapture of indignation of Johnson's blasphemies against those poets. We know not if any duels were fought in that fashionable controversy ... but if blood was not spilt, a great deal of gall was generated. ... Johnson's true glory will live for ever; his violent prejudices have already lost their authority. The refutation of his errors, therefore, is not now called for. Of all that was ever written against him, there is but one worthy of being preserved as a literary curiosity; we mean the continuation of his criticism on Gray's Elegy, being an admirable imitation of his style, and a temperate caricature of the unfairness of his strictures.[50]

It might be questioned, too, whether Johnson's criticisms were so entirely biased and unfair, although he was prejudiced, without a doubt. He said *some* good things in the 'Life'. Elsewhere ('Life of Parnell') he defended Gray against Goldsmith's implication that the 'Night Piece on Death' was a better poem of its kind.[51] Among other reasons, well discussed, for any prejudice, it might be added that, apart from the 'Life of Gray' and some letters, many of his pronouncements against the poet were made in the hearing of Boswell, a known Gray enthusiast. The element of Boswell-baiting over Gray, as over Scotland and the Scots, may have played some *small* part in the sum of Johnson's recorded response to Gray.

Johnson had his defenders. Even such an early champion of Gray against him as Robert Potter was to write in his *Art of Criticism* (1789): 'But our author's [Johnson's] remarks on Gray are not without some foundation; particularly that his language is encumbered and harsh; and that his poetry was in a manner the effect of industry and perseverance.'[52] And at the start, in 1781, just ten years after the death of Gray, the *Critical Review* had written of Johnson's *Lives* (August 1781):

Whether the whole of this free censure [i.e. of Gray] is strictly just and well founded, we will not pretend to determine. Certain it is, however ... that no man every acquired a high reputation at so easy a rate, or received such *great wages* for so *little work*, as Mr. Gray. — On his Elegy in a Country Church-Yard, we agree with Dr. Johnson, that too much praise cannot well be lavished; at the same time we think with him, that Gray's Odes, as well as his other little performances, have been much over-rated. ... Gray has been placed by his sanguine admirers by the side of Dryden and Pope. Dr. Johnson seems to have levelled him with the minor bards of a much inferior rank: half a century hence he may, perhaps, be fixed in his right and proper station,

'Behind the foremost, and before the last.'

In the mean time, as the twig inclined too much one way, we are obliged to Dr. Johnson for bending strongly towards the other, which may make it strait at last.[53]

After the turn of the century, in the eighteen-noughts, through the Regency decade, into the reigns of George IV and William IV, the 'Romantic Age', some of the heat of feeling about Gray goes out of discussion. So that John Aikin (1747-1822) writing the section on Gray in the *General Biography*, Vol. IV (1803), can produce as objective and balanced a view as we might wish today. So far, we may remember, the reading public knew only his poetry, and letters made available by Mason. Aikin considers that, as the learning of Gray was purely for his own use, it is exclusively as a poet that his name deserves to be transmitted to posterity. The small number of his poems, compared to the high rank he has attained, must indicate an uncommon degree of excellence. No one seems to have possessed more of that 'faculty of poetical perception which distinguishes among all the objects of art and nature what are fittest for the poet's use, together with the power of displaying them in their richest colours'. He continues: 'That many of these objects were derived to him from the works of other writers will not be denied by a judicious admirer; and if a distinction is to be made between the poet of nature and the poet of study, he is certainly to be ranged in the latter class.' His two principal Odes are addressed to prepared readers; and even with such preparation, 'the delight they afford will not be the same to all'. Gray, he continues, cannot be said to excel in 'pure invention', neither is he 'highly pathetic or sublime'; but he is 'splendid, lofty, and energetic; generally correct, and richly harmonious'. Though he excelled in lyric poetry, he could vary his manner to suit any kind of composition. Perhaps he was best qualified for the moral and didactic. The number of his fragments indicates 'a want of power to support a long-continued flight'. As a writer of Latin verse, perhaps few surpassed him in classic propriety. The letters are entertaining and instructive, 'free from all parade', having a 'fund of pleasantry, sometimes bordering upon quaintness'.[54]

The theme of obscurity begins to fade. Thomas Campbell writes in his 'Notice' of Gray in *Specimens of the British Poets* (1819) that the obscurity objected to in him has been exaggerated. 'He is nowhere so obscure as not to be intelligible by recurring to the passage.'[55] We hear less of the sublime, as the Lake Poets and others were voyaging into farther and stranger regions of this quality than Gray or the eighteenth century hazarded. Or Gray is said not to have been truly sublime. His sublimity was 'borrowed and mechanical', said Hazlitt.[56] Gray had often been praised before, in the later eighteenth century, for such qualities as accuracy, finish (Anna Seward);[57] classic brevity and terseness, classical correctness (Pinkerton);[58] accuracy of composition (Gilbert Wakefield);[59] 'highly-finished' work such as the 'Eton Ode' (Robert Anderson);[60] eclectic complexity. The rich poetry of Gray, wrote Isaac D'Israeli (1796), 'is a wonderful tissue, woven on the frames, and composed with the gold threads of others'.[61] This acceptance of carefulness, accuracy, finish, is a pattern of response which begins in the nineteenth century to reappear with emphasis shifted to another aspect of it, as taste and criteria for poetry change. Appreciation of what was regarded as admirably careful art modulates into complaint about artificiality, stiffness, laboured effect. Wordsworth, in the Preface to the second (1800) edition of *Lyrical Ballads,* singles out Gray as one 'more than any other man curiously elaborate in the structure of his own poetic diction'.[62] Coleridge thought 'The Bard' and the rest of Gray's lyrics 'frigid and artificial'.[63] Hazlitt said Gray's poetry was 'too scholastic and elaborate, and is too visibly the result of laborious and anxious study'.[64] Francis Jeffrey thought Gray and the small school beginning and ending with him 'far too elaborate and artificial'.[65] Byron, reported by Medwin, said that like Gray, 'Campbell smells too much of the oil: he is never satisfied with what he does; his finest things have been spoiled by over-polish – the sharpness of the outline is worn off'.[66] John Clare thought Collins's Odes superior to Gray's, because 'there is little pomp about them'.[67] Thomas Carlyle, in his review essay on Goethe (1828), saw Gray's poetry as a 'laborious mosaic, through the hard, stiff lineaments of which little life or true grace could be expected to look: real feeling, and all freedom of expressing it, are sacrificed to pomp, to cold splendour; for vigour we have a certain mouthing vehemence, too elegant indeed to be tumid, yet essentially foreign to the heart, and seen to extend no deeper than the mere voice and gestures.'[68] Arthur Henry Hallam used the phrase 'the tesselated mind of Gray'.[69] John Stuart Mill saw Gray's imagery as 'elaborately studied & artificial'.[70] And Bulwer Lytton wrote in 1837:

> Pindar's rapture never lived in the lyre of Gray, for Gray never knew what the rapture of poesy is. Painfully and minutely laborious ... weighing words in a balance, borrowing a thought here, and a phrase there, Gray wrote English as he wrote Latin. . . . Gray, from labour and research, surpassed them all [Young, Akenside, and Thompson [sic]] in artificial pomp and rhetorical melodies.

> In sustained and architectural splendour of diction he was the
> Gibbon of Poetry.[71]

The imagination of the age stretches itself in metaphor for this side of
Gray: one not so easily reconciled with contemporary aims for a poetry
which should draw less upon learning, literary precedent, the study, than
upon the free-ranging responses of man.

These quoted references to Gray are characteristic reactions of this
period. Gray was a little troublesome to the early nineteenth-century
Romantics. He had qualities they recognized to be something like their
own. But on the whole, he was too 'eighteenth-century', too 'classical',
stiff, and the rest of it. The eighteenth-century romanticisms which might
be discerned in him, predilection for the thrill and terror of the super-
natural, the Gothic, primitive vehemence of emotion in prophecy and
incantation, tended to be overshadowed by the many more aspects of
Romanticism developed by poets of these two generations. Wordsworth
and Coleridge were always uneasy with Gray, a poet on whom they had
been brought up, and had once loved, but whom their self-developed
taste for a different poetic required them to reject. Hazlitt, whose rational and in a sense eighteenth-century mind was more sympathetic, has
given perhaps one of the fairest and most balanced accounts of Gray
from a major critic in this epoch. He was an author of great pretensions,
he said, but of great merit. He aims at the highest things, and if he fails,
'it is only by a hair's-breadth'.[72] Collins, he thought, as one of his generation might tend to think, had a 'much greater poetical genius than
Gray', more of that 'fine madness' inseparable from it. Gray's Pindaric
Odes, he believed, were 'generally given up at present'.

> But I cannot so easily give up ... his Elegy in a Country Church-
> yard: it is one of the most classical productions that ever was
> penned by a refined and thoughtful mind, moralising on human
> life. Mr. Coleridge (in his Literary Life) says, that his friend Mr.
> Wordsworth had undertaken to shew that the language of the
> Elegy is unintelligible: it has, however, been understood! The Ode
> on a Distant Prospect of Eton College is more mechanical and
> common-place; but it touches on certain strings about the heart,
> that vibrate in unison with it to our latest breath. No one ever
> passes by Windsor's 'stately heights,' or sees the distant spires of
> Eton College below, without thinking of Gray. He deserves that we
> should think of him; for he thought of others, and turned a trem-
> bling, ever-watchful ear to 'the still sad music of humanity.'[73]

As Gray had passed beyond the heats of his own time and the following

thirty years, so he passed through those different prejudices and enthu-
siasms of the Romantic era, surviving changes of taste, having enough
variety of qualities to ensure acceptance in any period. With the Victorian Age, and the dying down, or modifying, of the special fervours of
the Romantics, he appears more and more a name established beyond
serious question. R. A. Willmott, in his review essay in the *Church of
England Review* (1837) of Prior's *Life of Goldsmith* and Mitford's *The
Works of Thomas Gray* (Pickering Edition), could write of these two
poets that they had both 'taken their place among the classics of our
literature'.[74] The feeling for craftsmanship in poetry was to receive new
emphasis. The elegiac side of Gray, at least, was readily adaptable to
Victorian taste and morality. Earlier, John Keble (1825) talked of the
'Elegy' as a specimen of the indirect species of sacred poetry.[75] And
farther into the nineteenth century, this remained an aspect ensuring its
continuing life. As knowledge of Gray and his work increased with successive editions, a scholarly approach also became more possible. Mathias, in his 1814 edition, had revealed new material, including some of
the prose from the Commonplace Books. Mitford, in his 1814 edition,
and in his subsequent editing, made available more information, both
scholarly and biographical. Sales of books Gray had owned stimulated
interest. He was much edited, both in major scholarly, and in more restricted, select editions. He was the subject of popular, of cabinet, and of
illustrated editions. Much ink flowed, in periodicals, on scholarly, bibliographical, and biographical detail; verbal criticisms, tracings of parallel
passages and possible sources of image and allusion in his poetry; the
actual identity of the churchyard of the 'Elegy', the authenticity of facts
of husbandry in the poem. Gray figured as a celebrity in works of topog-
raphy, in histories of Eton, and Cambridge University, in reference
books to London. He had indeed, as R. A. Willmott says, begun to speak
to us 'from every marble slab, from every little tomb with its osier bands,
from every straw-built cottage, and from every village church'.[76]

The earlier pattern of response to Gray's eclecticism which had occurred as complaint about unoriginality, stiffness, plagiarism, in the
Victorian Age tends to be traced in more favourable colours. He borrowed: but infused new life, or his own life, into what he took from
others. The tendency is to admire Gray as the artist; and here the artist
can be seen at work. Gray becomes interesting as the conscious craftsman,
the worker in the mosaic of language. The flowers might not indeed
grow in his own garden, said Willmott in the review article already mentioned, 'but no one ever combined their hues with more elegance and

skill'.[77] In his edition of Gray and other poets, Willmott again says: 'But even if he borrows the material, he invents the design; or if a former work suggested it, he so enlarges and embellishes it, that the copy breathes a new life.'[78] In the review of *Gray's Poetical Works*, edited by John Moultrie (1845), in the *Gentleman's Magazine*, there is a similar approving emphasis on this aspect of Gray. His language has been called a beautiful mosaic work of verbal elegance. But Gray, in looking to earlier poets, is in company with Virgil, Milton, Dryden, and Pope; and 'lyric poetry requires all the assistance which select language and harmonious numbers can bestow to support its bold and lofty flights'.[79] William Roscoe, one of the more interesting critics of Gray at this time, reviewing Mitford's *The Correspondence of Thomas Gray and William Mason* (1853) for the *Prospective Review* (1854), speaks of the essential unity of Gray's poems. 'The poet not only works in mosaic, but too often on a confused outline. Yet these poems have a unity.' Gray's pieces 'possess in general, in spite of their patchwork character as to ideas and composition, real unity of feeling'. To Gray, poetry was 'the art of adorning a thought'.[80] One of the worst features in modern poetry, Roscoe says, is a tendency to write 'word-poetry', poetry 'depending mainly on the beauty of sound, form, and association in words'. Tennyson has perhaps had a finer and more subtle appreciation of this sort of beauty than any poet. But his followers 'have seen half way into the secret of his power' and try to grasp his means 'without caring to have anything to convey'.[81] Gray may be said to have studied words more carefully than the things they represent. 'He had no thronging imaginations which required the vent of verse.'[82] And Roscoe says it is this 'over-balanced interest in details, acting under the influence of a highly-refined apprehension of beauty and fitness, that constitutes the peculiarity of Gray's poetry'.[83] Walter Bagehot (1859) saw Gray as a poet whose works abounded in 'semi-original conceptions'. One of those, who, 'musing on the poetry of other men, have unconsciously shaped it into something of their own: the new conception is like the original ... still it is sufficiently different from the original to be a new thing, not a copy or a plagiarism; it is a creation, though, so to say, a suggested creation'.[84] James Russell Lowell said: 'If his poetry be a mosaic, the design is always his own.'[85]

Historical perspective, distancing the eighteenth century, also begins to make criticism kinder to Gray. Leslie Stephen, in 'Gray and his School', says that while it seems to be now considered as unjustifiable plagiarism for a poet to 'assimilate the phrases of his predecessors', the eighteenth-century poets such as Goldsmith, and especially Pope, had 'no scruples in the matter'. Rather, it was a 'slow elaboration, with which it was perfectly allowable to interweave any quantity of previously manu-factured material so long as the juncture was not palpable'. Gray's adaptations seem sometimes 'to make the whole tissue of his poetry'.[86] Edmund Gosse sees the Pindaric Odes not as a class of poetry to be judged in terms of simplicity. In these 'elaborate pieces of poetic art' it is by virtue of originality of structure, varied music of balanced strophes, the extraordinary skill with which evolution of the theme is observed and restrained, that Gray shows himself, as an artist, to be far superior to Collins.[87]

There is thus an emphasis on this ability of Gray to make things his own. The Romantic conception of the poetic mind operating upon se-lected material works in favour of Gray here. At the same time, there is also that about him which pleases the Victorian artistic mind and eye for detail. The visual element in Gray was stressed also. R. A. Willmott in his review of Goldsmith and Gray talked about Gray's 'lively sense of the Picturesque', by which he said he meant here 'the peculiar effect imparted to the portraiture of any object by the mind of the author'.[88]

Feeling, pathos, warmth of tone were also desirable to the Victorian sensibility. And there was no doubt that Gray provided these. More and more, the 'Elegy' is dwelt upon as the most important of his poems. While Swinburne regarded Collins as much superior in lyric, he said that as an elegiac poet 'Gray holds for all ages to come his unassailable and sov-ereign station'.[89] To Edmund Gosse, it is 'unquestionable that the *Churchyard Elegy* stands first'.[90]

While a growing historical sense saved Gray from imputations of de-fectiveness in certain areas of his accomplishment, it did not altogether prevent some questionable views. Leslie Stephen and Matthew Arnold lay responsibility for the scantiness of Gray's production upon the cir-cumstances of his life. Stephen saw the environment of a college as an inhibition to creativeness.[91] Arnold, in his famous essay on Gray for Ward's *English Poets*, postulated that, being born at the wrong time, in an age of prose, blighted Gray, who was thus never able to speak out.[92] There were others who appeared to agree with this. Gosse says 'the steril-ity of the age, the east wind of discouragement steadily blowing across the poet's path' had much to do with this 'apparent want of fecundity'.[93] And Lionel Johnson, reviewing Bradshaw's (Macmillan) edition of Gray's poems for the *Anti-Jacobin* in 1891, says of Arnold's solution: 'That is as nearly the truth, in all likelihood, as any answer can be.'[94]

Duncan Tovey, on the other hand, takes issue with Arnold. The latter had worked Brown of Pembroke's remark that Gray 'never spoke out' into the substance of his essay as a leitmotiv for a wordless frustration in a general sense. Tovey points out, rightly, in *Gray and his Friends*, that, for one thing, there is little reason to believe these words meant more than that 'Gray did not acknowledge to his friends how near he felt his end to be'.[95] And he refutes Arnold's thesis that 'Gray, a born poet, fell upon an age of prose'; that with the qualities of mind and soul of a genuine poet, he was 'isolated in his century'.[96] Coleridge, like Gray, says Tovey, produced too little poetry; but we agree to find the explanation of this, not in the age, but in the man. Gray's *momentum*, he continues, 'comes from within; he writes to please himself; publicity is with him always quite a secondary matter, and his choice of subjects is absolutely his own; at the same time his own age welcomes him, and would gladly have had more from him'.[97] In Tovey's opinion, 'A mind searching in so many directions, sensitive to so many influences, yet seeking in the first place its own satisfaction in a manner uniformly careful and artistic, is almost fore-doomed to give very little to the world; it must be content, as the excellent Matthias says, to be "its own exceeding great reward".'[98]

Lastly, among the patterns or themes of response, it is interesting and perhaps encouraging, a little prophetic even, to find some in the later nineteenth century talking of 'freshness' in Gray: that qualities sometimes disparaged as outlandishness, artificiality, labour, smell of the oil, should, to a later and more modern generation, seem fresh. Leslie Stephen, in *Gray and his School*, sees Gray as standing apart from even his contemporaries, or near-contemporaries, Thomson, Young, Collins, Goldsmith. His poetry is like an oasis in the desert. It is 'a sudden spring of perennial freshness gushing out in the midst of that dreary didactic, argumentative, monotonous current of versification poured forth by the imitators of Pope'.[99] While Edmund Gosse said 'we are amazed at the originality and variety, the freshness and vigour of the mind that worked thus tardily and in miniature'. In the Pindaric Odes, Gray 'throws off the last shackles of Augustan versification, and prepares the way for Shelley'.[100]

So, with the later nineteenth-century critics, and editor-critics, Gray was brought to our own century. A growing knowledge has made us more cautious, less prone to entertain the sweeping, partisan response, for or against; fairer, possibly; more, one would like to think, understanding.

Weaving the web of criticism has continued. Gray has pleased, challenged, sometimes defied and outraged, passing criteria. Perhaps a feeling for him is more a matter of individual taste and temperament than with many other notable poets. But few though his works are, there is enough substance, it appears, to ensure continuing difference of opinion, threaded through the stuff of liking.

Memorial University of Newfoundland

Notes

1. [William Hazlitt], review of *Letters from the Hon. Horace Walpole to George Montagu, Esq.* (London, [1818]), *The Edinburgh Review* (December 1818), xxxi, 84.

2. Friedrich von Matthisson, letter to Bonstetten, 15 Mar. 1791, *Letters written from Various Parts of the Continent*, trans. Anne Plumptre, (1799), p. 208.

3. Letter to C. E. Norton, 22 Dec. 1876, *Letters of Edward Fitzgerald* [ed. W. Aldis Wright], 2 vols. (London, 1894), ii, 209. Morris, Swinburne, Browning. 'He [Tennyson] still admires Browning, for a great, though unshapen, Spirit; and acknowledges Morris, Swinburne, and Co., though not displeased, I think, that I do not.' (Letter to E. B. Cowell [1876], *More Letters of Edward Fitzgerald* [ed. W. Aldis Wright] [London, 1901], p. 186.)

4. For example: 'Had Gray written nothing but his Elegy, high as he stands, I am not sure that he would not stand higher; it is the corner-stone of his glory: without it, his odes would be insufficient for his fame.' (Byron, *Letter to **** ****** [John Murray], on the Rev. W. L. Bowles' Strictures on the Life and Writings of Pope* [London, 1821], p. 35.)

5. 'Upon Epitaphs (iii)' [first pub. Grosart, 1876], *Prose Works of William Wordsworth*, ed. William Knight, 2 vols. (London, 1896), ii, 179.

6. 'Tennyson I am told sets Virgil above Homer and thinks him for *Art* the first of poets – (he says moreover that he would rather have written Gray's *Elegy* than all Wordsworth).' (Arthur H. Clough, letter to William Allingham, 25 Jan. [1855], *Letters to William Allingham*, ed. H. Allingham and E. Baumer Williams [London, 1911], p. 155.)

7. *The Letters of William and Dorothy Wordsworth. The Later Years*, ed. E. de Selincourt, 3 vols. (Oxford, 1939), ii, 897.

8. [Bulwer Lytton] E. B., review of John Mitford, ed., *The Works of Thomas Gray*, 4 vols. (Pickering, London, 1837), *The London and Westminster Review*, v and xxvii, no. x and liii (July 1837), 14.

9. [Joseph Warton], *An Essay on the Genius and Writings of Pope*, i (1756); ii (1782), 292.

10. iv, 309.

11. [John Hill], *The London Advertiser, and Literary Gazette*, no. 2.

12. viii, 477.

13. *Memoirs of the Kings of Great Britain of the House of Brunswic-Lunenburg*, 2 vols. 1793), ii, 379.

14. [Edward Moore and others] Adam Fitz-Adam, *The World*, no. 22 (31 May 1753), p. 133.

15. 'Thro' this still valley let me stray, / Wrapt in some strain of pensive GRAY'. (W. Mason, *Odes* [Cambridge, 1756], p. 17.)

16. 'The Progress of Poesy', l. 106.

17. *The Correspondence of Horace Walpole*, ed. W. S. Lewis and others (New Haven, 1937–   ), xxi, 120.

18. *Supplement to The Letters of Horace Walpole*, ed. Paget Toynbee, 3 vols. (Oxford, 1918-25), ii, 100.

19. iv (August 1757), 169.

20. [J. Warton], *Essay on Pope*, ii, 481.

21. *The Theory of Moral Sentiments* (1759), sixth ed., 2 vols. (1790), i, 311. Does not appear in earlier eds.

22. *The Correspondence of William Cowper*, ed. Thomas Wright, 4 vols. (London, 1904), i, 141.

23. xvii, 240.

24. xxv, 367.

25. [John Langhorne], liii (August 1775), 102.

26. Walpole, *Correspondence*, xxi, 120.

27. [Leslie Stephen], xl (July 1879), 81.

28. *Supplement to The Letters of Horace Walpole*, ii, 101.

29. [Arthur Murphy], ii (September-October 1757), 426. See *New Essays by Arthur Murphy*, ed. Arthur Sherbo (East Lansing, 1963).

30. 2 vols. (1776), ii, 150-51.

31. [William Kenrick], i, 407.

32. [Richard Graves], *Lucubrations* (1786), p. 218.
> Unaw'd by names, if by too rigid laws
> *Some* bards he judg'd, who merit just applause,
> With equal candour, by a gentler test,
> He others tried, whom rival wits oppress'd.
> E'en Watts and Blackmore, whose flat strains abound
> With pious traits, in him a patron found.
Note on '*Some* bards . . .'.

33. Cf. Isaac D'Israeli: 'A REVOLUTION has taken place in modern Poetry, which is of the greatest importance to the lovers of the art. This is no less than a total banishment of the Heathen Mythology from our Poetry.... It is certain, that no order of beings have yet been found so agreeable to the imagination, when this poetic machinery is displayed by the address of superior genius. How admirably has *Gray*, in his Progress of Poetry, embellished with these beautiful forms the third stanza of the first Antistrophy.' (*Curiosities of Literature*, I [1791], 513-14, 516-17.)

34. II, 422.

35. [George Colman and Robert Lloyd], Ode I ['To Obscurity'], *Two Odes*, pp. 5-6, 13.

36. Walpole, *Correspondence*, I, 367.

37. [Robert Aris Willmott], review of James Prior, *The Life of Oliver Goldsmith* ([London], 1837), and John Mitford, ed., *The Works of Gray* (Pickering, [London, 1835-37]), *The Church of England Quarterly Review*, I (April 1837), 387.

38. *Theory of Moral Sentiments*, I, 311.

39. John Scott of Amwell said, 'whoever writes but as correctly as he has written, will not find himself able to write much'. (Essay VII, 'On Gray's Church-Yard Elegy', *Critical Essays on some of the Poems, of several English Poets* [1785], p. 243.)

40. See, for example, letters 246, 247, 248, 249, 251, *Corres.*, II. Of Goldsmith's review in the *Monthly Review* for September 1757, Gray wrote: 'the Review I have read, & admire it, particularly that observation, that the *Bard* is taken from *Pastor, cum traheret* ['The Author seems to have taken the hint of this subject from the fifteenth Ode of the first book of Horace.' – [Goldsmith]], & the advice to be more an *original*, & in order to be so, the way is (he says) to cultivate the native flowers of the soil, & not introduce the exoticks of another climate' (*Corres.*, II, 532-33).

41. *Corres.*, II, 518. Συνετοί, the intelligent, the wise.

42. Cf. Gray to Walpole, [21 Oct. 1757]: 'I have looked with all my eyes, & can not discover one error [possibly Garrick's verses, printed by Walpole], wch is the greatest misfortune, that can befall a Critick' (*Corres.*, II, 535). Gray to Mason, 23 July 1756:

> but I shall enquire after yours [Mason's verve], & why it is off again? it has certainly worse nerves than mine, if your Reviewers have frighted it. sure I (not to mention a score of your Uncles and Aunts) am something a better Judge, than all the Man-Midwives & Presbyterian Parsons, that ever were born. pray give me leave to ask you. do you find yourself tickled with the commendations of such People? (for you have your share of these too) I dare say not. Your Vanity has certainly a better taste. and can then the censure of such Criticks move you? I own, it is an impertinence in these Gentry to talk of one at all either in good or in bad, but this we must all swallow, I mean not only we, that write, but all the *we's* that ever did any thing to be talk'd of. (*Corres.*, II, 466-67)

John Langhorne, in his review for the *Monthly Review* of Mason's *Memoirs*, 1775, refers to this letter.

> From a letter of Mr. Gray to Mr. Mason, dated July 25, 1756, it should seem that the latter had expressed some dissatisfaction at the treatment he had met with from the Reviewers, and the former, to remove his chagrin, recommends it to him to despise the criticism of Presbyterian parsons, &c. *[* Man-midwives too are mentioned, possibly, not with reference to us.] Now, we remember that Mr. Mason's Odes were, about that time, freely criticised in our Review, but not by any Presbyterian parson. No person of that denomination ever presumed, in our Society, to approach the regions of Parnassus: as to the rest, we feel ourselves superior to anger on such occasions, and have no answer for the dead. One thing, however, we must not pass unnoticed: 'I own, says the Letter-writer, it is an impertinence in these gentry to talk of one at all either in good or bad; but this we must all swallow; I mean not only we that a write [*sic*], but all the we's that ever did any thing to be talked of.' The vanity of this passage may be indulged; the absurdity of it in a writer of Mr. Gray's character, is really wonderful, and how it should escape such an editor as Mr. Mason is equally extraordinary. *It is impertinent in us to* TALK *either in good or bad of a writer who has done something to be* TALKED OF! Could we possibly be serious in the face of an Hybernicism, we might enlarge upon the right of public criticism on whatever is exhibited to public sale – But neither can we treat the understanding of our Readers so much like that of children, as to think such an argument by any means necessary. Mr. Gray ought to have been so much of a Civilian as to have remembered, PUBLICI JURIS, ET PUBLICO SUB JUDICE. Let us contemplate him in a more amiable light, and see him equalling Sulpicius in his consolatory letter to Cicero, while he writes to his friend Dr. Wharton on the death of his only son.... (*The Monthly Review*, LIII [July 1775], 9.)

William Kenrick, in the *London Review* for June 1775, reviewing Mason's *Memoirs*, says: 'Of Mr. Gray's contempt for Reviewers, we have an instance in a preceding letter.' And he quotes from this same letter of Gray's: 'Sure I ... either in good or in bad' (I, 407-8).

43. p. 18.

44. *An Inquiry*, pp. 37-38.

45. *The Poets and their Critics. Chaucer to Collins*, rev. ed. (London, 1960), p. 221.

46. [John Young], *A Criticism on the Elegy written in a Country Church Yard. Being a Continuation of Dr. J——n's Criticism on the Poems of Gray*, p. 22.

47. *Letters of Anna Seward*, 6 vols. (Edinburgh, 1811), I, 54.

48. *The Letters of Samuel Johnson*, ed. R. W. Chapman, 3 vols. (Oxford, 1952), III, 48.

49. Walpole, *Correspondence*, xxix, 308. Boswell, discussing imitators of John-son's style, wrote of Young's work: 'But I think the most perfect imitation of Johnson is a professed one, entitled 'A Criticism on Gray's Elegy in a Country Church-Yard,' said to be written by Mr. YOUNG, Professor of Greek, at Glasgow, and of which let him have the credit, unless a better title can be shewn. It has not only the peculiarities of Johnson's style, but that very species of literary discussion and illustration for which he was eminent. Having already quoted so much from others, I shall refer the curious to this performance, with an assurance of much entertainment' (*Boswell's Life*, iv, 392).

50. xii (April 1808), 62.

51. 'The *Night-piece on Death* is indirectly preferred by Goldsmith to Gray's *Church-yard*, but, in my opinion, Gray has the advantage in dignity, variety, and originality of sentiment' (*Lives*, ii, 53).

52. [Robert Potter], *The Art of Criticism; as Exemplified in Dr. Johnson's Lives of the Most Eminent English Poets*, p. 184.

53. lii, 89.

54. [John Aikin] 'A', *General Biography*, 10 vols. (London, 1799-1815), iv (1803), 503-4.

55. (London, 1819), vi, 191.

56. 'Critical List of Authors', *Select British Poets* (1824), *The Complete Works of William Hazlitt*, ed. P. P. Howe, 21 vols. (London and Toronto, 1930-34), ix, 240.

57. For example: 'The accurate, the finished Gray'. (*Letters of Anna Seward*, i, 202.)

58. 'His mode of expression is truly lyrical; and has a classic brevity and terseness, formerly unknown in English, save to Milton alone.' ([John Pinkerton] Robert Heron, *Letters of Literature* [1785], p. 35.) 'I know of no writer before Gray whose works are of classic correctness, except Milton' (Ibid., p. 63).

59. 'a richness of phrase and an accuracy of composition, superior to all' ('Advertisement', *The Poems of Mr. Gray*, p. [iii]).

60. 'This highly-finished ode'. ('The Life of Gray', *A Complete Edition of the Poets of Great Britain* [1792-95], x [1794], 193.)

61. 'On Novelty in Literature', *Miscellanies; or, Literary Recreations* (1796), pp. 316-17.

62. *The Poetical Works of William Wordsworth*, ed. E. de Selincourt and Helen Darbishire, 5 vols. (Oxford, 1940-49), ii (2nd ed., 1952), 391.

63. *The Table Talk and Omniana of Samuel Taylor Coleridge* (London, 1917), p. 282.

64. *Edinburgh Review*, xxxi, 83.

65. [Francis Jeffrey], review of Walter Scott, ed. *The Works of Jonathan Swift, D.D.*, 19 vols. (Edinburgh, 1815), *The Edinburgh Review*, xxvii (September 1816), 7.

66. Thomas Medwin, *Journal of the Conversations of Lord Byron* (London, 1824), p. 111.

67. *Journal*, Sat. 25 Sept. 1824, *The Prose of John Clare*, ed. J. W. and Anne Tibble (London, 1951), p. 108.

68. [Thomas Carlyle], 'Goethe', review of *Goethe's Sämmtliche Werke. Vollständige Ausgabe letzter Hand* (Goethe's Collective Works, Complete Edition, with his final Corrections). *Zweite Lieferung, Bde.* 6-10 (Stuttgart and Tübingen, 1827), *The Foreign Review*, no. 3 (1828), ii, 92.

69. 'Oration, on the Influence of Italian Works of Imagination on the Same Class of Compositions in England', *The Writings of Arthur Hallam*, ed. T. H. Vail Motter (New York and London, 1943), p. 230n.

70. Letter to Edward Lytton Bulwer, [May or June (?) 1837], *Collected Works of John Stuart Mill* (Toronto and London, 1963–   ), xii, 336.

71. *London and Westminster Review*, v and xxvii, no. x and liii, 4, 14.

72. 'Critical List of Authors', *Works*, ix, 241.

73. Lecture VI, 'On Swift, Young, Gray, Collins, &c.' (1818), *Lectures on the English Poets, Works*, v, 118.

74. i, 361.

75. 'With regard to the indirect, and, perhaps, more effective, species of sacred poetry, we fear it must be acknowledged, to the shame of the last century, that there is hardly a single specimen of it (excepting, perhaps, Gray's Elegy, and possibly some of the most perfect of Collins's poems) which has obtained any celebrity.' ([John Keble], 'Sacred Poetry', review of Josiah Conder, *The Star in the East; with other Poems* [London, 1824], *The Quarterly Review*, xxxii [June 1825], 231.)

76. *Church of England Quarterly Review*, i, 361.

77. Ibid., 385.

78. 'Gray', *The Poetical Works of Thomas Gray, Thomas Parnell, William Collins, Matthew Green, and Thomas Warton* (London, 1854), p. 20.

79. xxiv (September 1845), n.s. 225-26.

80. [William C. Roscoe], x (August 1854), 396.

81. Ibid., 397.

82. Ibid., 398.

83. Ibid., 399.

84. [Walter Bagehot], 'John Milton', review of David Masson, *The Life of John Milton*, i [1859]; Thomas Keightley, *An Account of the Life . . .* of John Milton [1855]; Thomas Keightley, *The Poems of Milton* [1859], *The National Review*, ix (July 1859), 174-75.

85. 'Gray', *The New Princeton Review*, i (March 1886), 177.

86. *Cornhill Magazine*, xl, 81-82.

87. *A History of Eighteenth Century Literature* (London, 1889), p. 241.

88. *Church of England Quarterly Review*, i, 385.

89. 'William Collins', *The English Poets*, ed. T. H. Ward, 4 vols. (London, 1880), iii, 279.

90. *History of Eighteenth Century Literature*, p. 240.
91. *Cornhill Magazine*, XL, 78.
92. III, 303, *et passim*.
93. *History of Eighteenth Century Literature*, p. 239.
94. [Lionel Johnson], *The Anti-Jacobin*, no. 28 (8 August 1891), 671.
95. (Cambridge, 1890), p. 21.
96. *English Poets*, III, pp. 312-13.
97. *Gray and his Friends*, pp. 28-29.
98. Ibid., p. 31. 'With his high spirit strove the master-bard, / And was his own *exceeding great reward*'. ([T. J. Mathias], *The Pursuits of Literature*, Pt. I, ll. 76-77 [1794], p. 12. Note on 1.77: ' "I am thy exceeding great reward." *Genesis*, chap. xv, ver. 1.')
99. p. 72.
100. *History of Eighteenth Century Literature*, p. 239.

JAMES STEELE *Thomas Gray and the Season for Triumph*

Gray has been frequently described as a gentleman of modest means and middle-class background who led an intensely private life. Matthew Arnold insisted, on rather flimsy evidence, that he was also a melancholy man who never spoke out. Most latter-day critics have in one way or another followed Arnold in affirming – or assuming – that the subject-matter of Gray's poetry is essentially the feelings and passions, the moods and sentiments, the ecstasies and anxieties of one who withdrew from the world at least in spirit – a 'poetic' soul stifled by an age of prose. It will be argued in this essay that both Gray's poetry and certain bio-graphical facts suggest that such an assessment and reading of Gray is in need of some revision. There is reason for believing that Gray, by virtue of his family background, his wealth, and his wider social and economic connections, was very much a part of the *rentier* stratum of the capitalist ruling class in England. He was in fact a life-long whig with firm ideas about what constitutes true liberty and with a partisan's knowledge of its historic roots. He also had an enthusiastic appreciation of the origin and development of the British Empire and strong opinions as to how it might be most efficiently advanced in his own time. In the 1740s he wanted England to avoid armed conflicts with Spain in the Caribbean and to stay out of the fruitless war on the continent. By late 1754, how-ever, he had become an ardent admirer of Pitt, who was advocating a war with France for world colonial and commercial supremacy. Although Gray was critical of the Peace of Paris concluded in 1763 and lamented Pitt's retirement, he nevertheless continued to have high hopes for British imperial progress. These and related public matters are (as I shall try to demonstrate) as much a part of Gray's poetry as his subjective feelings and moods. Certainly an appreciation of the beauty of his poetry must be based on an understanding of both these elements. The argument of this essay will be primarily concerned with some of the more obvious relationships between the poet and the prosaic world of politics, business, and empire. What is offered below are suggestions for an interpretation of Gray which may be worth developing in greater detail.

Although the facts about the wealth and connections of the family into which Thomas Gray was born in 1716 are well known, their implications have not been fully appreciated. The poet's grandfather, Thomas Gray, was a merchant, and there is good reason for believing that he was very rich. He was a member of the Honourable Company of Coopers and was admitted to the Honourable East India Company in 1678.[1] In the 1680s the latter Company's shareholders consisted of 'a small clique of about forty persons closely connected with the Court' who wielded a vast capital of '£1,700,000, on which the dividends averaged 22 percent'.[2] In joining this Company, Thomas Gray (the poet's grandfather), a trader in wines and diamonds, was maintaining a family connection which had been carried on by his brother Matthew, who died before 1678 in the Company's service at Surat.[3] Such was the grandfather's influence in the Company that his second son, Thomas (uncle of the poet), was, upon his security, subsequently elected Factor at Fort St. George, Madras in 1678. There, according to his ornate tombstone, this son served 'seven years in quality of one of ye Wor[shi]p[ful]l Council' before his death in 1692 at the very young age of 23. The eldest son, Matthew, was a merchant who remained in London. The grandfather, we know, employed several servants, including 'an Indian black boy'. Since several of these servants died and were buried in London, and at least one died and was buried in Wanstead, Essex, it may be presumed that this Thomas Gray was prosperous enough to maintain houses in both places. He was in fact a 'citizen' of both London and Wanstead, and in the latter town he served for a time as churchwarden. Although Thomas Gray died in Wanstead, he was taken to London for burial in St. Olave's in the 'middle chansell', an interment appropriate for a merchant of much wealth and dignity. The family fortune was apparently large enough and its connections sufficiently strong to enable the third son, Philip – the allegedly irascible father of the poet – to carry on business as a financier. Philip Gray has been variously described as a 'money scrivener' and an 'exchange-broker' (i.e. a dealer in money, stocks, bonds, and investments), but at that time the two occupations were practically identical.[4] He was also known as a 'draper' (Corres., III, 1204, n. 1), possibly because of his wife's lucrative interest in a millinery shop which he owned and which was regarded as 'a kind of India warehouse' (*Gray*, p. 1). Mrs. Gray claimed that her revenue from a £240 investment in 'stock in trade' at the time of her marriage was large enough to enable her to be of no charge to her husband during nearly thirty years of marriage. In fact, her independent income gave her the means to clothe both herself and her twelve children, to provide most of the furniture for her husband's house, to pay £40 rent a year to her husband for the shop, and to provide almost everything for Thomas Gray first at Eton and later at Peterhouse, Cambridge (*Corres.*, III, 1195-96). About 1736, Philip Gray built Oak Hall, a country house in Wanstead, which was sold by his son Thomas between 1760 and 1763 to Frederick Bull, an alderman and future lord mayor of London (*Corres.*, I, 421, n. 9). A survey carried out in 1824 indicated that, in addition to the house, the estate then contained some four acres of walled grounds complete with an 'orangery, vinery, fountain, ponds etc. with gardens beautifully laid out'.

When Philip Gray died in 1741, he was described as a person 'of Reputation and Fortune'.[5] It was estimated that he left about £10,000 to his son Thomas.[6] Yet Ketton-Cremer notes that when Philip Gray's estate was settled about 1742, 'it was discovered that in the last few years, he had contrived to muddle away the greater part of his own capital' (*Gray*, pp. 66-67). At the height of his fortunes, therefore, Philip Gray must have been worth more than £20,000, from which he might reasonably have expected to have received an income of one to two thousand pounds a year. How much of this wealth Thomas Gray had access to before the death of his mother in 1753 is not known. When his own will was settled in 1771, his assets are said to have been worth some £6,000 or £7,000 (*Corres.*, III, 1277 and n. 4). In his later years, in addition to substantial *rente* from this estate, he also received £400 a year for his professorship at Cambridge (*Corres.*, III, 1048). In mid-eighteenth-century England approximately 1,300 families – not individuals – are said to have had an income of £1,000 per annum or more.[7]

Thus Thomas Gray was born into a rich and well established family. It was entirely appropriate that he should have attended Eton, which since the late sixteenth century had been educating the sons of commercial magnates along with those of the richer landed gentry; that he should have there consorted on a footing of equality with Walpole, West, and Ashton; and that he should have taken a casual attitude towards earning a degree. His grand tour in a very grand manner, his return to Cambridge with the rank of fellow-commoner,[8] his unwillingness to condescend to practise civil law, his gracious declining of a dutiful secretaryship to the British ambassador to Spain, and his refusal of the reputedly servile poet-laureateship (*Corres.*, II, 543-44) were characteristic of a man of his class. His acceptance of an unsolicited offer of the Regius Professorship of Modern History – a sinecure which Gray described as 'the best thing the Crown has to bestow (on a Layman) here [at Cambridge]' (*Corres.*, III, 1048) – evidently marked the lowest degree to which he would stoop.

Gray led the retired life of an independent gentleman. He chose to do so not because he considered himself unable to make his way successfully in the world but because he really believed what he once said in jest: that the happy man, like 'one of Lucretius' Gods, [is] supremely blest in the contemplation of his own felicity' (*Corres.*, II, 898). 'When the belly is full [he once wrote to Mason], the bones are at rest. you squat yourself down in the midst of your revenues . . .' (*Corres.*, II, 773). As he explained to West in a more serious vein:

> To me there hardly appears to be any medium between a public life and a private one; he who prefers the first, must put himself in a way of being serviceable to the rest of mankind, if he has a mind to be of any consequence among them: Nay, he must not refuse being in a certain degree even dependent upon some men who already are so. If he has the good fortune to light on such as will make no ill use of his humility, there is no shame in this: If not, his ambition ought to give place to a reasonable pride, and he should apply to the cultivation of his own mind those abilities which he has not been permitted to use for others' service. Such a private happiness (supposing a small competence of fortune) is almost always in every one's power, and the proper enjoyment of age, as the other is the employment of youth. (*Corres.*, I, 169)

Gray went on to acknowledge in this same letter that in seeking a private life for himself, even at a young age, his conduct was at odds with his own better judgement. In later years his conduct and his better judgement were thoroughly consistent with each other:

> to find oneself business (I am persuaded) is the great art of life; & I am never so angry, as when I hear my acquaintance wishing they had been bred to some poking profession, or employ'd in some office of drudgery, as if it were pleasanter to be at the command of other People, than at one's own; & as if they could not go, unless they were wound up. yet I know and feel, what they mean by this complaint: it proves, that some spirit, something of Genius (more than common) is required to teach a Man how to employ himself.[9]

Gray once wrote to Mason that he (Gray) 'was always a Friend to

Employment, & no Foe to Money: but they are no friends to each other. promise me to be always busy, & I will allow you to be rich' (*Corres.,* II, 655). By 'Employment', however, he meant the high activity of individual 'Genius' mentioned in the preceding quotation. Gray was as ready as Pope to 'leave all meaner things/To low ambition and the pride of Kings'.

Although Gray insisted on cultivating his own garden he did not do so in isolation. The company he kept provides ample evidence that his position in English society was one of some pre-eminence. Needless to say, he was neither as rich nor as powerful as the Duke of Newcastle, who once gave Gray 'a fine Complement' and 'a very affectionate squeeze' with a hand which 'felt warm, sweated a little' (*Corres.,* I, 377). Nevertheless, his friends and acquaintances included – besides Walpole – Richard West, the son of the Chancellor of Ireland; the Dowager Viscountess Cobham and her beneficiary Miss Speed, two society heiresses; William Mason, a one-time Chaplain to the King and private secretary to a Secretary of State for the Southern Department, which was responsible for the colonies; Thomas Wharton, the son of a Mayor of Durham and heir-apparent of the Old-Park estate; Richard Stonhewer, who at various times was under-secretary to a Secretary of State, private secretary to the First Lord of the Treasury, and Commissioner of Excise, Knight Harbinger, and Historiographer to His Majesty; John Chute, 'the last descendant in the male line of Chaloner Chute, Speaker of the House of Commons' in 1659 (*Corres.,* I, 184, n. 1), the inheritor of the Chute family estates and an intimate friend of Walpole; Charles Victor de Bonstetten, the 'only son of the treasurer of Berne, and of one of the six noble families which ... [bore] the chief sway in the aristocracy [of Switzerland]' (*Corres.,* III, 1085); Lord John Cavendish, a friend who invited Gray to sit in the box of his brother the Duke of Devonshire (who, as Lord Chamberlain, was the second highest dignitary at court) at the coronation in 1761; Frederick Montagu, a Bencher, Member of Parliament, and – after Gray's death – Lord of Treasury; Richard Hurd, an 'eminent Prelate' and son of an Auditor-General, who at different times was Preacher at Whitehall, Preacher at Lincoln's Inn, Bishop of Lichfield and Coventry, and Bishop of Worcester; James Brown, the son of a London goldsmith who became the Master of Pembroke College and Vice-Chancellor of Cambridge University; and John Lyon, the ninth Earl of Strathmore and Kinghorn, who, as well as being himself the heir to many large estates, married a woman deemed by Lord Chesterfield to be 'the greatest heiress perhaps in Europe' (*Corres.,* I, 417, n. 8). It is no wonder that Gray's noble Prussian friend Count Algarotti, Chamberlain at the court of Frederick the Great, should have been so willing to stand corrected in a matter of poetic taste by Gray, who, though a commoner, moved in such high circles (*Corres.*, II, 825-26). Also understandable is the opinion once cited by Gray's friend Norton Nichols: 'The learned world at Cambridge ... was divided into two parties; the polite scholars and the philologists. The former, at the head of which were Gray, Mason etc, superciliously confined all merit to their own circle, and looked down fastidiously on the rest of the world' (*Corres.*, I, 416, n. 4). When Gray alluded to himself as a 'youth to fortune and to fame unknown' he was describing with decorous modesty his relationship to the English ruling class.

A more prosaic – and truer – assessment by Gray of his wealth and reputation would appear to have been the silent premise underlying his affirmation that his 'Principles in Government' were 'those of every true & rational Whig' (*Corres.*, II, 469). With his rich and high connections, Gray could easily identify himself with a party which was essentially a coalition of large capitalist landlords and commercial magnates. This alliance of interests, which was supported, however reluctantly, by a mainly tory squirearchy in the countryside whose political notions Gray evidently held in contempt (*Corres.*, II, 832), ruled England for most of the eighteenth century. They were the dominant elements of a class which was in control of most of the English economy even by the middle of the seventeenth century, when, partly as a result of the heroic efforts of such men as Hampden, Milton, and Cromwell, it also gained control of the English state. Gray was well aware of the historic links between the whigs of his time and their seventeenth-century predecessors. An argument central to the historical treatise which he is said to have praised above all others, Mrs. Catherine Macaulay's *History of England from the Accession of James I to the Elevation of the House of Hanover*,[10] was that the enlightened sons of the English revolution should revere those patriotic 'partisans of Liberty'[11] who had beheaded Charles I with undeniable justice. Gray's strong aversion to Pretenders, Old or Young (*Corres.*, I, 146, 158, 166-67), his contempt for 'all the flattery & blasphemy of our old Law-books in honour of Kings',[12] and his feeling that there was much reason in the popular demonstrations against the disqualification of John Wilkes after his electoral victory in 1769 (*Corres.*, III, 1059), were indications that he continued to cherish the ideal of liberty for which the Civil War had been fought. Gray's own images for it were 'Freedom's holy flame' (l. 65) in 'The Progress of Poesy', 'celestial fire' (l. 46)[13] in the 'Elegy' and 'the fire that animates our frame' (l. 65) in the 'Alliance of Education and Government'. In the last of these poems, the fire is genetically related to the 'sparks of truth and happiness' which are given at birth by impartial heaven 'Alike to all' (ll. 29, 28). These spiritual sparks are not to be confused, however, with the much less egalitarian 'equal Justice' of a free government which strives to scatter 'Light golden showers of plenty o'er the land' so that the 'tender' but worldly hopes of young men will not be unfairly thwarted, as necessarily happens in the wealth-engrossing empire of 'Tyranny' (ll. 15-20). Gray's sense of distance from the common people (*Corres.*, II, 852), his amusement at the pretensions of a 'broken Tradesman' (*Corres.*, II, 758-59), and his political fear of the collective strength of petty-bourgeois craftsmen[14] were also in line with a bourgeois definition of liberty which ever since the crushing of the Levellers had formally excluded men not in possession of substantial wealth.

Gray's admiration for Montesquieu's *Spirit of the Laws* was likewise consistent with this whig idea of freedom. Citing the constitution of England as his ideal, Montesquieu argued in this treatise that in a country of medium size, political liberty could be best attained through a constitutional monarchy in which the conflicting interests of 'the common people' and 'persons distinguished by birth, riches or honours' would be discreetly recognized and reconciled through a separation of legislative powers corresponding to their respective interests.[15] As in England, such a state would also guarantee the security of private property[16] and deny the right of voting to 'such [persons] as are in so mean a situation as to be deemed to have no will of their own'.[17] Seen in this context, Gray's notion that the 'Mind born to govern the rest of Mankind' should be educated in accordance with the idealist and aristocratic principles suggested by Plato in his oligarchist *Republic* becomes understandable (*Corres.*, III, 1118). Gray's almost unlimited respect for Machiavelli was a prudent corollary of this attitude. 'I rejoice', he wrote, 'when I see Machiavel defended or illustrated, who to me appears one of the wisest Men, that any nation in any age has produced' (*Corres.*, III, 996). Machiavelli's idea that material interest and power are the driving forces of history, his observations concerning the conflict of interest between the vulgar mob and the ruling classes, and his call for a strong national state capable of 'keeping faith' by maintaining order were principles not inconsistent with those of Gray. '*Desperare de republica* [Gray once wrote] is a deadly sin in politicks' (*Corres.*, II, 856), and it appears to be the only one he categorized as such.[18]

Even some of Gray's statements about the nature of poetry seem to issue from his whig notion of liberty. While the poet argued that his only reward in writing was 'to give some little satisfaction to a few Men of sense & character' (*Corres.*, I, 447), he insisted that poetry fulfills an important public role as well. In the 'Progress of Poesy', the poetic Muse soars upwards 'beyond the limits of a vulgar fate' (l. 122) and seeks to reveal ideals which 'Great' men should strive for. Gray told Beattie that the 'use' of poetry would be made manifest if the bardic hero of 'The Minstrel' were to 'do some great and singular service to his country . . . such as no General, no Statesman, no Moralist could do without the aid of music, inspiration, and poetry' (*Corres.*, III, 1140). He encouraged the rich and cultured Court Chamberlain to King Frederick in his 'efforts to reunite the congenial arts of Poetry, Musick & the Dance, wch with the assistance of Painting & Architecture, regulated by Taste, & supported by magnificence & power, might form the noblest scene, and bestow the sublimest pleasure, that the imagination can conceive' (*Corres.*, II, 810). He agreed with Count Algarotti that in such endeavours poetry 'must lead the way, & direct the operations of the subordinate Arts' (*Corres.*, II, 811). He believed, however, that the happy union of the sister arts is often hindered because poetry 'implies at least a liberal education, a degree of literature, & various knowledge, whereas the others (with a few exceptions) are in the hands of Slaves and Mercenaries, I mean, of People without education, who, tho neither destitute of Genius, nor insensible to fame, must yet make gain their principal end, & subject themselves to the prevailing taste of those, whose fortune only distinguishes them from the Multitude' (*Corres.*, II, 811).

Much of Gray's own poetry is in one way or another thematically concerned with ideals appropriate for great men and particularly for powerful eighteenth-century whig leaders. In the 'Ode for Music', Gray himself tried to combine the sister arts with the tangible support of 'magnificence and power'. It should be noted too that his imitations of the haughty, politically minded, yet proudly independent and soul-searching Pindar were consistent with such a theory of poetry. His 'ancient aversion' to the 'state poem' (*Corres.*, I, 295) clearly stemmed not from an apolitical attitude but from an inbred whiggish unwillingness to eulogize either the state or the prince. Public ends could be better served by addressing the 'few' and the 'great'. Even some of the passages Gray chose to translate from Latin and Italian seem to reflect in part his whig idea of liberty. Two of the Argive warriors whose physical prowess is celebrated in the passages which Gray, with mild contempt, translated from Statius's *Thebiad* (*Poems.*, pp. 17-19), later in the poem direct their strength against Eteocles, an unconstitutional Theban monarch. When Gray translated and singled out for special commendation the lines from Dante's *Inferno* describing the horrible fate which awaits would-be sovereigns who betray their political allies (*Poems*, p. 23), he was probably not unaware of the fact that the Guelphic family of Count Ugolino lived on in eighteenth-century England in the royal House of Brunswick.

The whig principles to which Gray so closely adhered involved not only a commitment to a particular kind of 'liberty' but an equally strong enthusiasm for that 'glory' which, since the time of Elizabeth, had been accruing to the English nation as a result of the rapid growth of its mercantile and colonial empire. As every eighteenth-century public schoolboy knew, the basis for this empire had been laid in Elizabethan and Jacobean times: first by the sea-dogs who challenged the dominion of Spain over the high seas; then by Protestant 'undertakers' of virtuous and gentle discipline who made bold attempts to subjugate and pacify Ireland;[19] and finally by entrepreneurs, both merchant and gentry, who established trading posts and plantations in many parts of the world. By 1630, English companies had interests in East India, Africa, Bermuda, the West Indies, and North and South America.[20] In his schoolboy lines 'In 5tam Novembris', Gray referred to the England of this period as a country 'famous for innumerable triumphs in war' (l. 13), a land which could 'shine conspicuous for a double prize, in the Arts and in War' and be 'the glory of the world' (ll. 15-16). (As we shall see, these are themes which Gray was to take up again in his later poetry.) Although Charles I did little to enhance England's imperial glory, Cromwell's willingness to use the power of the state in support of English interests in the Far East, India, the Mediterranean, and the Caribbean, his support of mercantilist Navigation Laws, and his attacks on Spanish and Dutch interests were signal contributions to the development of a world-wide empire, as even his contemporaries well appreciated.[21] Perhaps his greatest imperial achievement was the conquest of Ireland and the defeat of the rebellious Scots at Worcester. Certainly this was the opinion of Gray's favourite historian:

> It was just after the battle of Worcester that the nation was arrived at the meridian of its glory and crisis of its fate: All iniquitous distinction, all opposition to the powers of democracy, were totally annihilated and subdued; the government of the country was in the hands of illustrious patriots, and wise legislators; the glory, the welfare, the true interests of the empire was their only care; the public

money was no longer lavished on the worthless dependants of a court; no taxes were levied on the people, but what were necessary to effect the purposes of the greatest national good; and such was the economy of the Parliament, that at this time, whilst they kept a superior naval force to any which the preceding sovereigns had maintained, with a land-army of eighty thousand men, partly militia and partly regulars, the public assessments in Scotland, Ireland, and England did not exceed one million a-year.

A government thus conducted on the true principles of public interest, with the advantages peculiar to the island of Great-Britain, could not but be formidable to foreign states. They felt the present strength, and trembled at the growing power of England, which bid fair to be the second mistress of the world.[22]

Such praise of Cromwell, however, did not prevent Mrs. Macaulay from detesting Cromwell's subsequent usurpation and all the fruits thereof, and from dissociating herself from what she described as the conventional whig assessment of the Protector which bestowed nothing but 'exalted commendation' on all his acts.[23] Her dislike of the later Cromwell has a rough parallel in young Gray's Latin verses on the Restoration 'In D[iem]: 29[am] Maii', where, while referring to the field of Worcester as a plain where the battle was won by the 'enemy' (l. 14), he refrains discreetly from commenting on the justice of the Cromwellian cause.

In the three decades which followed the Restoration, British entrepreneurs – and Gray's grandfather was among them – managed to develop their interests abroad through commerce and the exploitation of colonial plantations. Although England fought two more trade wars with the Dutch, by which she acquired New York and strengthened her position in the Far East, it soon became apparent that her main rival was not Holland but France. This country was threatening to upset the balance of power in Europe and was fast becoming England's strongest competitor for fragments of the rapidly disintegrating Spanish Empire. The alliance with the Dutch, cemented by the whig settlement of 1688, provided England with a strong continental ally. At home, the establishment of the Bank of England in 1694 by whig City interests and the subsequent creation of a national debt gave the government access to the vast capital resources necessary for economic development and the effective waging of war.[24] Gray, it should be noted, derived a substantial part of his income from his investments in Bank of England annuities, which at the time of his death were valued at some £2550 (*Corres.*, III,

1283-86). In the War of the League of Augsburg (1689-97) and the War of the Spanish Succession (1701-13), the balance of power in Europe was preserved. By the Treaty of Utrecht, Britain acquired Nova Scotia, repossessed the Hudson Bay Territory and retained Gibraltar and Minorca in the Mediterranean, where her navy was superior to that of France. She was also ceded 'the monopoly of supplying the Spanish colonies with slaves, and a virtual though not formally admitted freedom of trade in other goods'.[25] This trade with the Spanish colonies was carried on by the South Sea Company, another organization from which Gray, as an annuitant, derived a part of his income.[26]

Even as a young man, Thomas Gray had high hopes for the future development of Britain's expanding empire. This, in fact, was the theme of his first published work, the fanciful 'Luna Habitabilis' written in 1737. From a sound general premise about the state of the British Empire, the Muse in this poem draws certain utopian conclusions which reveal much about Gray's feelings on the subject. The plausible premise is that England, 'which for so long has held sway over the sea and so often set the winds to work and ruled the waves', has triumphed often on earth (ll. 92-94); she is now, in fact, the world's brightest light, brighter even than Germany or France (ll. 64-67). Therefore, it is argued, England is 'predestined' (l. 79) to conquer the moon with a belligerent 'flying fleet' (l. 84) emitting 'inimitable lightning' (l. 89). (The planet is a prize worth fighting for not only because it might support labouring inhabitants and cities but also because, through the Muse's telescope, it appears to be a rich world composed of dark blue seas and islands as well as 'vast regions and lands', l. 42.) England will then 'assume the symbols of power in the sky' (l. 94), send out colonists, and establish traffic and treaties with earth. Although war and gunboat diplomacy will provide the means of conquest, Gray's justification for such an action is not merely *force majeure* but the superiority of English scientific knowledge. Gray's Muse Luna is also the goddess of astronomy and geometry, and she naturally assumes in a post-Newtonian age that her citizenship is English (l. 79). As the moon freely and happily submits to telescopic scrutiny from England, the predestined conquest is but a confirmation and development of a relationship which already existed. The beauty of empire and the connection between human knowledge and imperial progress suggested by Gray's extravagant Tripos Muse were matters to which the poet would return in his seriously imperialist poems of the 1750s.

While a growing faction of City merchants called for more armed conflict in the years following the War of the Spanish Succession, the tory squirearchy was most unwilling to pay the high taxes necessary for the financing of such ventures. Moreover, many powerful whig supporters of the Walpole administration were more than content to continue to exploit the economic advantages gained by the Treaty of Utrecht. Accordingly, as trade increased, as profits flowed in from plantations in the West Indies and America, and as high returns reached England from merchants in India and the Far East,[27] Walpole's government sought to strengthen the peace through a collective security pact with France, Holland, and Spain – the so-called Quadruple Alliance. The approval of this Alliance by young Gray and his Etonian friends, however light-hearted, seems implicit in their adoption of the name to describe their own little club (*Gray*, p. 5). And when aggressive City traders, angered by increasing mercantile rivalry in the South Atlantic and Caribbean regions, were at last successful in getting Britain embroiled in hostilities with Spain in 1739 – the War of Jenkin's Ear – Gray, like many a whig and the ministry itself, still supported a peace policy which would avoid the expense of war and safeguard England's traditional – and much more lucrative – commerce with Spain.[28]

When Gray (while travelling in Italy in 1740) learned from West of Admiral Vernon's victory on the Isthmus of Panama, where Spain had withdrawn a petty trading concession from the South Sea Company, he referred to the affair with the jesting contempt of a high whig: 'I forget Porto Bello all this while; pray let us [i.e. Gray and Walpole] know where it is, and whether you or Asheton had any hand in the taking of it. Duty to the admiral. Adieu!'[29] About a month later, Walpole and Gray together asked Ashton the same kind of question: 'How goes your War?'[30] And Gray added in the same mocking vein: 'you do not know perhaps, that we have our little good fortune in the Mediterranean, where Adm[iral] Haddock[31] has overturn'd certain little Boats carrying troops to Majorca, drowned a few hundreds of them, & taken a little Grandee of Spain, that commanded the expedition: at least so they say at Naples: I'm very sorry, but methinks they seem in a bad condition.'[32] As the war went on, Britain continued to lose vast amounts of shipping to Spanish privateers in European waters,[33] and the great fleet which she sent to the West Indies failed miserably at Cartagena. Tobias Smollett, who sympathized with the war party, reported that 'the miscarriages of this expedition, which had cost the nation an immense sum of money, was no sooner known in England, than the kingdom was filled with murmurs and discontent, and the people were depressed in proportion to that sanguine hope by which they had been elevated'.[34] Gray, however, who had never been a supporter of the war, was not crest-fallen: 'as to Politicks [he wrote to Chute], every body is extreme angry with all that has been, or shall be done: even a Victory at this time would be look'd upon as a wicked attempt to please the Nation' (Corres., I, 186). Although Walpole's 'wicked' ministry resigned in 1742, a 'distilled Walpolianism' continued to be the basis of foreign policy in the new administration.[35] France was still regarded as England's main rival in trade and colonization, but economic expansion through peaceful trade was still deemed to be in the broad national interest. Carteret, therefore, sought to isolate France[36] and to maintain a balance of power in Europe by means of a series of alliances which were easy to make but costly to honour. Thus when Silesia, a province within the jurisdiction of Maria Teresa (Empress of the Holy Roman Empire, Queen of Bohemia and of Hungary and consort of Emperor Francis I of Austria) was invaded by Prussia, Britain was obliged by treaty – and the family connections of England's Hanoverian King strengthened the commitment – to assist the Austrian and Hungarian forces in the war. It was a conflict, however, which many Englishmen, and even Carteret,[37] believed to be irrelevant to British interests, and one which threatened to embroil many European powers including France, an ally of Prussia. Gray prophesied the outcome with a satiric gusto rarely found in his letters:

> if you have any hopeful young Designer of Caricaturas [he wrote to Chute in May, 1742], that has a political Turn, he may pick up a pretty Subsistance here ... we are all very sorry for poor Queen Hungary; but we know of a second Battle (wch perhaps you may never hear off, but from me) as how Prince Lobbycock [i.e. Prince Lobkowitz of Austria] came up in the Nick of Time, & cut 120,000 of 'em [i.e. Prussians] all to pieces, & how the King of Prussia narrowly scaped aboard a Ship, & so got down the Dannub to Wolf-in-Bottle [i.e. Wolfenbüttel], where Mr. Mallyboyce [i.e. the Marquis of Maillebois] lay incamp'd, & how the Hannoverians with Prince Hissy-Castle [i.e. Prince Frederick of Hesse-Cassel] at their head, fell upon the French Mounseers, & took him away with all his Treasure, among which is Pitt's Diamond, & the Great Cistern. all this is firmly believed here, & a vast deal more; upon the Strength of which we intend to declare War with France. (Corres., I, 207-08)

In the event, England sent troops and vast amounts of treasure to the continent without tangible returns, while at home she was challenged by Jacobite rebels. Elsewhere in the world, Britain was successful in wrest-ing Louisburg and Cape Breton Island from France and in greatly restricting French trade with the West Indies. In India, however, Madras was captured by a French naval squadron.[38] Smollett described the state of the English nation in 1746 as follows:

It may not be amiss to observe, that the supplies of this year exceeded, by two millions and a half, the greatest annual sum that was raised during the reign of Queen Anne, though she maintained as great a number of troops as was now in the pay of Great Britain, and her armies and fleets acquired every year fresh harvests of glory and advantage; whereas this war had proved an almost uninterrupted series of events big with disaster and dishonour. During the last two years, the naval expence of England had exceeded that of France about five millions sterling; though her fleets had not obtained one signal advantage over the enemy at sea, nor been able to protect her commerce from their depredations. She was at once a prey to her declared adversaries and professed friends. Before the end of summer, she numbered among her mercenaries two empresses, five German princes, and a powerful monarch, whom she hired to assist her in trimming the balance of Europe, in which they themselves were immediately interested, and she had no more than a secondary concern. Had these fruitless subsidies been saved: Had the national revenue been applied with economy to national purposes; Had it been employed in liquidating gradually the public incumbrances; in augmenting the navy, improving manufactures, encouraging and securing the colonies, and extending trade and navigation, corruption would have been altogether unnecessary, and disaffection would have vanished: The people would have been eased of their burthens, and ceased to complain: Commerce would have flourished, and produced such affluence as must have raised Great Britain to the highest pinnacle of maritime power, above all rivalship or competition. She would have been dreaded by her enemies; revered by her neighbours: Oppressed nations would have crept under her wings for protection; contending potentates would have appealed to her decision; and the world have shone the universal arbitress of Europe. How different is her present situation! Her debts are enormous, her taxes intolerable, her people discontented, and the sinnes [*sic* sinews?] of her government relaxed. Without conduct, confidence, or concert, she engages in blundering negociations: She involves herself rashly in foreign quarrels, and lavishes her substance with the most dangerous precipitation: She is even deserted by her wonted vigour, steadiness, and intrepidity: She grows vain, fantastical, and pusillanimous: Her arms are despised by her enemies; and her councils ridiculed through all Christendom.[39]

When the Treaty of Aix-la-Chapelle brought hostilities to an end in 1748, the desire among Britons for peace was strong in virtually every quarter. Gray alluded to the Treaty facetiously but knowledgeably as the 'Mother of Proclamations & of Fireworks, that lowers the Price of Oranges and Malaga-Sack, & enhaunces that of Poor-Jack [i.e. dried Newfoundland cod] and barrel'd Cod' (*Corres.*, I, 314), and suggested that it was less important than the election of a College fellow. In a more serious mood, Gray suggested in the 'Elegy' that a distinction should be made between true and false heroism.

As early as 1738, Gray had translated passages from Propertius in which the glories of love and science are preferred to those of empire (*Poems*, pp. 25-27, 44-47). Then in the 'Ode on the Spring', written in 1742, he had alluded to the vain ardour of 'the crowd', the real littleness of 'the proud' and the indigence of 'the great' (ll. 18-20), all characteristics which Gray saw good-humouredly as a fair match for his own fly-like condition. In the 'Ode on a Distant Prospect of Eton College', written that same year, he had commented in a more serious way on the lethal destructiveness of the 'fury Passions' (l. 61) latent in young Etonians. Later, in the 'Elegy', completed in 1750 but written over a number of years, Gray again suggested that the ambition and pride of persons in high places makes for a 'madding crowd' engaged in 'ignoble strife' (l. 73) and confined to 'paths of glory [which] lead but to the grave' (l. 36) – a lesson which the English nation had learned well after some nine years of fruitless wars. In this poem he contrasts the vices of the mighty with the homely virtues of the poor country folk who lead contented, industrious lives devoted to peaceful toil. But the speaker in the poem makes it clear that while he would like to link himself to their virtue as closely as he can, he must nevertheless be regarded as a disaffected member of that same 'madding crowd' from which he would dissociate himself first by retirement and then by death. Although he modestly professes he is 'of humble birth' and 'a youth to fortune and to fame unknown' (ll. 118-19), he is clearly not to be identified with 'Misery' (l. 123) or numbered among 'the poor' with their 'destiny obscure' (ll. 30-32). On the contrary, he is a literate man, acquainted with 'Knowledge' (l. 49) and 'Science' (l. 119); he is also a melancholy poet for whom pensive country walks are the labour of the day rather than weary ploughing. Indeed, his only wish in life is for 'a friend' (l. 124), and this heaven has provided. His position in society is such that he could decorously condescend to chastise verbally even the 'Proud' (l. 37). His own funeral he envisages as a simple burial among country folk but with 'dirges due in sad array' (l. 113) and twelve lines of poetry on a stone epitaph – the same number of lines Gray was to write for the monument of Sir William Williams. Clearly, the speaker in the poem is a person of some wealth and power, and those of Gray's contemporary readers who knew the poet would have sensed the understatement in his self-portrait. They would have known that Gray was a man of considerable wealth, who knew the world of pomp, heraldry, ambition, and grandeur from the inside. As a matter of fact, when he received a request for permission to publish the 'Elegy' in a 'recently established and undistinguished' periodical, *The Magazine of Magazines* (*Poems*, p. 111), he regarded the invitation as a most embarrassing 'Misfortune' (*Corres.*, I, 341-42). Although the publishers were described by their bookseller as 'gentlemen', who regarded Gray as '*the excellent Author*' of the poem and begged 'not only his *Indulgence* but *the Honor of his Correspondence*' (Gray's italics), Gray could apparently not condescend to reply (*Corres.*, I, 341-42).

As a member of a polite society, the poet knew that many of those virtues admired in the lives of the poor were not entirely appropriate for the rich, just as certain heroic virtues attainable by the madding crowd were not the 'lot' (l. 65) of the poor. Although the poor, Gray suggests, have had within them potentially a certain 'noble rage', which he associates more particularly with 'celestial fire' in the heart, the 'rod of empire', and the 'living lyre', its expression has been 'repressed' by 'Chill Penury' (ll. 46-52). Moreover, Gray associates this latent rage with the achievements of a past age, with the work of Hampden, Cromwell, and Milton respectively, and suggests that indigent, would-be imitators of these heroes are in fact rather ridiculous (ll. 57-60). Yet noble rage in great men freely expressed is even less attractive: its virtues are liable to be accompanied by immorality and hypocrisy, by great crimes, and by decadence (ll. 66-72). As Cleanth Brooks has cogently argued, the irony of Gray's diction emphasizes the hollowness of such heroism so strongly that the poem is in part a satire on noble rage gone wrong.[40] The experience of the 1740s had indeed taught everyone that the British Empire was not to be enlarged by wading 'thro slaughter to a throne' – especially a throne in the Holy Roman Empire. As for liberty, the English constitution guaranteed the right of all hearts 'pregnant with celestial fire' to burn as brightly as they wished. Another sort of virtue, one more appropriate for high whigs in the early 1750s, is suggested by the epitaph of the young Poet. This virtue is based on the cultivating of the arts and sciences by a gentleman of piety, zealous only to settle his accounts with God after a benevolent and retiring life. (This moral was also quite consistent with an idea Gray expressed in another postwar poem, 'The Alliance of Education and Government'. There Gray argues that national degeneration resulting from either thoughtless belligerence or luxurious softness is quite unnecessary as long as the 'growing powers' (l. 13) of man's God-given soul are guided educationally by appropriate ideals and are allowed to develop under a government guaranteeing the liberty of 'equal justice'.) Thus in exploring the meaning of death, the 'Elegy' celebrates the *mores* of a life of peace. In the context of its moment in history, the subject of the poem was such that it would have been popular, as Gray himself remarked, even if it had been written in prose (*Poems*, p. 113). Within five years, the theme of Gray's verse would change as world-shaking events overseas made him increasingly aware of the beauty of war and conquest.

The Treaty of Aix-la-Chapelle brought about a cessation of hostilities on the European continent but not elsewhere. In India, North America, and the West Indies, clashes between England and France continued to occur. It became increasingly apparent that the long-standing rivalry between these two powers would result in a war in which the theatres of decisive importance would be the high seas and overseas territories rather than Europe. At stake was nothing less than mercantile and colonial supremacy in the world, and this was a prize which even traditionally peace-loving, annuitant-holding whigs, if they were astute enough to know where their own self-interest lay, might regard as a prize worth fighting for. In the event, the Seven Years' War gave England, under the leadership of Pitt, her 'First Empire' and the greatest glory she had ever known. Looking back from the vantage point of 1765 when Pitt lay dangerously ill, Gray said of this bold warrior in whom he had placed unbounded faith: 'when he is gone, all is gone, & England will be old England again, such as (before his administration) it always was ever since we were born' (*Corres.*, II, 873). In a period when most Englishmen (except for a few insular tories like Dr. Johnson) could see that the paths of glory might lead not only to the grave but also to triumph, Gray turned from the poetry of peace and wrote five stern poems of war: 'The Progress of Poesy', begun in 1752 and finished in a militant mood in 1754; 'The Bard', begun in December 1754 and completed on a triumphant note in May 1757; 'The Fatal Sisters', written early in 1761; 'The Descent of Odin', also written early in 1761; and the 'Triumphs of Owen', written in 1760 or 1761. The first two celebrate the beauty of empire and the last three the beauty of conquest. All came from the pen of a man who had become a confirmed patriot and a diffident imperialist by December 1754.

These poems, as we shall see, speak clearly for themselves in this matter, although the fact that few of Gray's readers, especially in recent times, seem to have noticed their imperial theme perhaps requires a word of explanation. Gray's hopes for British imperial glory as early as 1737 have already been remarked upon,[41] but his tone then was levitous and the theme was soon more or less set aside. The emergence of a seriously imperial attitude in the 1750s therefore represents a new and quite unexpected departure from the substance of his earlier verse. Such a departure is also inconsistent with what many biographical accounts have suggested about Gray the man and Gray's interest in the *res publica*. Mason, Mitford, and Gosse say nothing about the enthusiasm for imperial triumph which Gray expressed in his letters after the mid-1750s. Ketton-Cremer is likewise silent on this point and, to the contrary, suggests by implication that Gray was uninterested in such matters. Gray's poetic 'flowering' between 1752 and 1757 is said to have occurred while his relations with society were characterized by 'studied aloofness' and 'fastidious withdrawal' (*Gray*, pp. 106, 116). While Lord David Cecil has recognized that Gray was 'a strong Whig . . . [and] a full-blooded patriot' who 'could hardly keep his temper when he thought of the contemptible French',[42] he also suggests that Gray was a kind of eighteenth-century Pater, one who revelled in the pleasures of the imagination as he tried to escape from the real world. There is, of course, some truth in these accounts, but they do not tell the whole story either about Gray the man or about his poetry. The fact of the matter is that Gray followed with great interest Britain's changing fortunes in the war overseas and related political developments at home. If he wrote relatively few words about these matters in his letters, he did so precisely because he deemed them of such importance that he did not want to risk revealing opinions and information to the wrong people. Gray was well enough informed about the operations of the government's intelligence apparatus to caution Wharton in 1753, from whom he was 'impatient to know many things', to 'remember, [that] this election time letters are apt to be open'd at the offices' (*Corres.*, I, 388). When Gray himself mentioned important affairs of state or delicate political subjects, he wrote sometimes allusively, sometimes ambiguously and often cryptically.[43] But most frequently he prudently refrained from writing about anything that was not clearly in the public domain. '. . . the rest [as he once wrote to Mason] is left to oral tradition' (Corres., II, 877). Gray's letters written during the period between 1754 and 1761, however, make clear the fact that he supported Pitt and Fox in their early attempts to rouse the nation to action in 1754 and 1755, and exulted as much as any other whig patriot over the victories won between 1757 and 1761. Evidently he also wanted the British to rule in Ireland with an iron fist after the demonstrations there in 1760. When the Treaty of Paris was negotiated in 1761, he was clearly embittered by what he believed to be a grave compromise of British interests.

The precise time at which Gray began to support a war policy can be ascertained with less exactness. His cousin Mrs. Foster, wife of the Governor of Fort William (Calcutta), probably kept Gray well informed of the continuing Anglo-French rivalry in India. Her visit to England in the summer of 1751 coincided with Clive's first great victory at Arcot. The fact that Gray's protégé and dear friend Mason became private secretary to Lord Holdernesse, Secretary of State for the Southern Department (which included the colonies) in January 1754, likewise suggests that Gray was maintaining an interest in colonial affairs. There might even have been a grain of truth in Gray's jest (reported by Mason) that he accompanied Mason to London at that time 'to put Mason apprentice to a Secretary of State' (Corres., I, 389, n. 4). Nevertheless, there is no reason for assuming that throughout the early fifties and until sometime in the latter part of 1754, Gray's views – and the mood of his one major poem of this period, the 'Ode on Vicissitude' – were anything but consistent with what Horace Walpole described as Prime Minister Pelham's 'system of lethargic acquiescence, in which the spirit of Britain, agitated for so many centuries seemed willingly to repose'.[44] As Walpole explained, it was a most 'un-British' age:[45]

> The pacific genius of the house of Pelham was not unknown to France, and fell in very conveniently with their plan of extensive empire. They had yielded to a peace with us, only to recover breath, and to recoil with greater force after a few years of recruited strength; yet even in the short term lapsed since the treaty of Aix-la-Chapelle, they had not been unactive. Complaisance in Europe was to cover encroachments in both Indies. Mr. Pelham was willing to be the dupe. If the nation demanded no redress, he would neither propose nor seek it. Redress could be procured but by arms;

armaments must be furnished by money; money to be raised might create murmurs; opposition might ensue – were national honour or interest worth hazarding that? And having had the merit of lessening the National Debt, he had the more justifiable and reasonable excuse of dreading to augment it again, when it was still so burthensome. In the East Indies we had lost Madras in the late war; and since the peace, under pretence of the two nations engaging on different sides in support of two contending Nabobs, hostilities had continued with various success.

During Mr. Pelham's rapid decline of health, a small fleet had been fitted out to protect a trade, which the numerous reinforcements dispatched by the French East India Company, with equal countenance from their Crown, had already rendered very precarious, indeed desperate. In Africa, they debauched our Allies, erected forts, and aimed at embracing the whole Gold Coast and Guinea trade. But their attempts in America grew daily more open, more avowed, more alarming, indeed extended to nothing less than by erecting a chain of garrisons from Canada to the mouths of the Mississippi, to back all our settlements, cut off our communications with the Indians west of that river, and inclose and starve our universal plantations and trade: it would not be necessary to invade them, they would fall of course. The discussions left unsettled by the precipitate peace of Aix-la-Chapelle, and proposed to be adjusted by those most ineffective of all negotiators, Commissaries, gave, not a pretence, rather an invitation to the French, to dispatch by force of arms the liquidation of an affair which might be explained to their disadvantage. The fatal treaty of Utrecht had left but too many of our interests in the West Indies problematic: the impetuosity of Lord Bolingbroke to betray Europe left him no moments, could inspire him with no zeal to assert our pretensions in America.[46]

When the unexpected death of Pelham in March 1754 was followed two months later by the defeat of Washington in Virginia – 'a trifling action [said Walpole], but remarkable for giving date to the war'[47] – Newcastle's cabinet contained no one capable of leading the nation in a great struggle for empire.[48] Within the larger ministry, however, there were two powerful critics who would soon rise to power. At first Newcastle, supported by Hardwick and Holdernesse who shared his narrowly continentalist outlook,[49] 'assumed the hero, and breathed nothing but military operations'.[50] He even gained unanimous parliamentary support for increasing expenditures on Britain's military forces.[51] But his efforts were deemed inadequate by his secretary-at-war Fox, and Fox, in turn, found a strong ally in the person of Pitt, who had oratorical powers in the House and strong City connections.[52] Apparently Newcastle's real policy was merely 'to mask economy and a minimum of activity under the semblance of great operations'.[53] Accordingly, in the autumn of 1754 Fox and Pitt began their struggle for power in the cabinet and for the adoption of a bold policy of war. On 26 December 1754, Gray wrote cryptically but most significantly to Wharton: 'your Politicks I don't understand; but I think, matters can never continue long in the situation they now are' (*Corres.*, I, 417). In the same month, after two years of hesitation, Gray was at last able to write a strong, hopeful conclusion to his poem on the necessary and beautiful relationship between poetry and the glory of empire.

The argument of the opening stanzas of the 'Progress of Poesy' is much easier to understand than its development in the remainder of the poem, for which a knowledge of Gray's changing attitude towards 'glory' is of critical importance. Gray begins by saying that poetry (which, according to his note, 'gives life and lustre to all it touches', *Poems*, p. 161, n. 3) is the ultimate source of music, song, and dance, and is thus a force of considerable strength. The power of harmony can control 'sullen Cares' and 'frantic Passions' (ll. 15-16), including the belligerent fury of Mars and the imperial eagle of Jove. It can also, in the words of Gray's explanatory note to stanza 3, 'produce all the graces of motion in the body' (p. 165), even the movements of desire and love in Venus herself. He then wonders whether or not poetry can also 'justify the laws of Jove' (l. 47), which necessitate labour, penury, pain, disease, sorrow, and death. Gray answers in the affirmative because the night of human sorrows is counterbalanced by the dawn of militant poetic light. In a note to these lines Gray suggests that such compensation is in fact providential. He then discusses the 'Extensive influence of poetic Genius over the remotest and most uncivilized nations: its connection with liberty, and the virtues that naturally attend on it'.[54] At the lowest level poetry brings 'cheer' (l. 57) to primitive northerners suffering in cold, polar darkness. (In his later translations of Norse poetry Gray regarded such people as the heroic progenitors of the British.) Among the more culturally advanced natives of Chile, where the 'savage youth' 'repeat[s]' (l. 60) (i.e. speaks of, or celebrates) the leaders and loves of his society, even crude attempts at poetry make life worthwhile. They focus attention on socially unifying, admirable, heroic figures, primitive imitations perhaps of the 'Lord of War' (l. 17) and 'queen' of love (l. 36) known to the more civilized world. Gray had, indeed, very good reason, quite apart from any love of the exotic, for cherishing primitive Creole art. Evidently he knew about Admiral Anson's voyage around the world from 1740 to 1744,[55] the purpose of which was to attack Spanish prizes in the South Seas and Spanish settlements in Mexico, Peru, and Chile. Anson reported after his return to England that the recurring theme of the Chilean natives' 'recitals and representations' was revenge against their tyrannical Spanish masters and their French allies.[56] As this was a subject which the Creoles relished with 'enthusiastic rage',[57] Anson argued that an alliance with the Creole natives would have enabled Britain to challenge Spanish tyranny and establish British law on the continent of South America. The argument of lines 63 to 65 is therefore entirely appropriate: even when the Muse 'roves' to such uncivilized parts of the world as Chile she is followed by four virtues: the desire for the attributes of supreme power ('Glory'); a moral sense ('generous Shame'); a faith in the power of individual human genius ('the unconquerable Mind') and a love of liberty ('Freedom's holy flame').

The historic migration of the Muses is then accounted for by their scorn for 'the pomp of tyrant-power' and 'coward Vice', especially servility, and by their love of the 'lofty spirit' (ll. 79-81) which would, of course, be strong in the four virtues – including that of 'glory' – mentioned in lines 64 and 65. Accordingly, the Muses have always made their home in centres of imperial power, and have thus moved from Greece to Rome and thence to England. There the great truths of nature and of human sensibility have been richly delineated by the "unconquerable Mind' of Shakespeare. Divine truth – the ultimate source of both 'generous Shame' and 'Freedom's holy flame' – has been revealed by Milton. Dryden, for his part, has sung of 'fields of glory' spread 'Wide' over the world (l. 104). Gray probably had in mind works by Dryden such as his 'Heroic Stanzas on the Death of Cromwell', which celebrates several of Britain's glorious imperial conquests; 'Astrea Redux', which touches on the same subject; and the 'Annus Mirabilis', much of which is concerned with the British victories over the Dutch.[58]

Although Gray had completed a draft of the first 106 lines of the poem by July 1752, he was unable to write the concluding seventeen lines of the poem until late in 1754 (*Poems*, p. 156). The real reason for this probably lies not so much in the critical remarks of his friend Mason (*Poems*, p. 156) as in the difficulty Gray must have had in coping before August 1754 with the great problem which is posed – and answered – in these concluding lines. In an authentically heroic age, Dryden's lyrics had inspired 'Thoughts that breathe and words that burn' (l. 110), particularly (Gray tells us in a note) 'Alexander's Feast', which explores the moods and character of a world imperialist of considerable glory. Even though such ideas of worldly 'Glory' constitute one of the four virtues accompanying the progress of poetry (ll. 64-65), this kind of theme, however, is after Dryden's time 'heard no more' (l. 111). Why not? Gray himself does not say, perhaps because he thought the answer would be known to intelligent contemporaries. One obvious and plausible explanation is surely this: whereas poetry that would inspire piety, morality, and individual genius can be based on traditional verities which are relatively independent of the national achievements of a particular epoch, verse which would arouse a desire for success on fields of 'glory', even when it celebrates the qualities of a hero long dead, requires a background of contemporary heroic achievements – or possible achievements – if it is to ring true and not seem bombastic. The fact of the matter is – and this was also the hard historical fact that Gray had to face – many years had elapsed since great men of Britain had provided the Muses with acts of glory worth singing about in a high Pindaric ode: they had certainly not done so in the War of Jenkin's Ear, nor in the War of the Austrian Succession, nor in the halcyon days between 1751 and the summer of 1754. It would have therefore been impossible for Gray to waken the heroic lyre of Dryden before the autumn of 1754. By that time, a few Britons – with Gray's approval – were once more pitching the tents of war, and winning on 'fields of glory' (l. 104) was again becoming at least a possibility. It was then – and not before – that the 'daring spirit' (l. 112) of Gray could modestly measure his powers against the Theban eagle 'Sailing with supreme dominion/Through the azure deep of air' (ll. 116-17); it was then that he could contemplate 'Such forms [including that of 'glory'] as glitter in the Muse's ray' (l. 119); and it was then that he could see the gap between 'the Good' – the ideal in *all* its virtuous forms – and the 'Great' (l. 123) of his society, who seemed to know so little about what 'the Good' then really involved. Soon after completing this poem Gray began writing that part of 'The Bard' in which the hero curses tyranny. Some two years later Gray's Bard would also be able to wager on nothing less than the triumph of Britannia in the world.

Newcastle attempted to cope with his two critics, Fox and Pitt, by separating them. Fox was given a place in the outer cabinet on 17 December,[59] and in the following September he was brought into the inner cabinet as a Secretary of State and Manager of the House of Commons.

In return for these preferments, Fox agreed in September 1755 to support openly the government's systematic subsidization of Britain's continental allies. In so doing, he apparently abandoned his own earlier, non-committal, if not cool, attitude towards making such subventions,[60] and concurred with a court-sponsored continentalist war policy which ran counter to the grand strategy of Pitt, who wanted British resources allocated to the struggle for a *British* empire overseas. As for Paymaster-General Pitt, who, in response to defeats abroad and weak war measures taken at home, was becoming even more insistent on 'a complete change in policy and full responsibility for the conduct of business,'[61] to him no favour was shown. Indeed, towards the end of September 1755 it was rumoured by Walpole that Pitt, along with a friend and supporter, Legge, the Chancellor of the Exchequer, would be dismissed from the ministry after parliament met on 13 November (*Corres.*, I, 442, n. 5). As it happened, Pitt invited dismissal in his famous Rhône-and-Soane speech, in which he denounced the German subsidies and outlined his own imperial strategy. Gray had reliable intelligence of this great struggle for power within the ministry and wrote to Wharton on 18 October as follows:

> I am told, it is the fashion to be totally silent with regard to the ministry. nothing [viz. the impending dismissal of Pitt and Legge] is to be talked of, or even suspected, till the Parliament meets [on November 13]. in the mean time the new *Manager* [Fox] has taken what appears to me a very odd step [i.e. his decision to support continental subsidies[62]]. if you do not hear of a thing, wch is in it's nature no secret, I can not well inform you by the Post. to me it is utterly unaccountable. (*Corres.*, I, 442)

It seems evident that Gray's unfashionable sympathies in this circumspect letter continued to lie with Pitt and his hard-line war policy, despite Fox's strange 'unaccountable' concession to Pitt's opponents. Gray had, however, been giving aesthetic shape to his feelings about French tyranny much more clearly, if less directly, in the first 100 or so lines of 'The Bard', which he had been writing during the first half of 1755 (*Poems*, p. 178).

The subject of these lines is the conflict between an oppressive, regal tyranny which leads to death, moral decay, and ruin, and the willingness of heroic individuals 'to celebrate [in the words of Gray's original argument] true virtue and valour in immortal strains, to expose vice and infamous pleasure, and boldly censure tyranny and oppression' (*Poems*, p. 178). The particular tyranny which the Bard must face was established by a line of kings running from the Angevin Edward I to the Yorkist Richard III, all of whom, however – as Gray pointed out in his 'original argument' – were of 'Norman race'. The fact that the first of these kings had married the Spanish Eleanor of Castile and the second had taken to wife Isabel, the 'She-wolf of France' (l. 57), would not, in the opinion of either the Bard or Gray, have made the blood of this regal line run purer. Although the Bard prophesies that this race will come to an end in England with the death of Richard III, no one had to remind Gray's contemporaries that it was still very much alive and threatening just across the channel in Bourbon France.

The ideal of liberty Gray of course associated with the proto-British Bard and with his own British, whig point of view. Yet in 1755 Gray's Bard could not express his noble British ardour except as a negation of tyranny and its concomitant evils rather than as an affirmation of Britain's ability to triumph. As long as the British successors of the Bard in Gray's own time – and these would have included statesmen and warriors as well as poets – were unwilling to take forceful measures, and as long as British forces abroad, in a state of disarray, continued to suffer defeats at the hands of the French, Gray's Bard lacked a firm basis for such glorious hopes. Indeed, Gray was so outraged by Admiral Byng's loss of Minorca in May 1756 that he talked half seriously about leaving the country. This was a defeat which according to W. E. H. Lecky 'discredited her [Britain] in the eyes of the world, and annihilated both her commerce with the Levant and her supremacy in the Mediterranean'.[63] 'The British Flag (I fear) has behaved itself like a Train'd-band Pair of Colours in Bunhill-fields. I think every day of going to Switzerland. will you [Gray wrote to Mason] be of the party . . . ?' (Corres., II, 465). It is worth noting, too, that Gray apparently still had an admiration for Fox,[64] who, as Secretary of State, was the only member of the cabinet to have urged that stronger British forces be sent to the Mediterranean.[65] By the spring of the following year, Gray was provided with a much firmer basis for keeping high his hopes for triumph.

William Pitt had at last been asked to form a government, and, as prime minister from December 1756 to April 1757, he had begun to implement his grand strategy for empire.[66] Although lack of confidence on the part of King and many members of parliament led to the temporary resignation of Pitt and his ministry in April, the Great Commoner was so strongly supported by the merchants of the realm and the town corporations that he had indeed become 'the emblem of the popular will and the symbol of natural resistance to France'.[67] Even out of office he was recognized by Gray's friend Walpole as the 'arbiter of Britain',[68] and his speedy return to power was a virtual certainty. It was less certain, of course, that his imperial policy would enable Britain to defeat France, but for the first time such an outcome, despite the loss of Minorca and other set-backs, seemed at least possible.

It seems probable that Gray's awareness of this possibility gave him the inspiration to complete 'The Bard' in late May of 1757, just a few weeks before Pitt resumed office. For at the heart of the Bard's vision lies the wager that it will be the destiny of post-Norman Britain to prevail in the world. The Tudors, the Bard says, will revive the spirit of Britain's 'long-lost Arthur' (l. 109), a figure whose reputation as an upholder of magnanimous Christian virtue was no greater than his renown as a conqueror of many nations.[69] The prototype for the new race of kings, however, is to be Elizabeth, who in modern times, as Gray well knew, had begun England's struggle for world dominion. According to the Bard, song and the poetry of Shakespeare and Spenser flourish at her court. Had not Gray already argued in the 'Progress of Poesy' that the arts are the handmaidens of greatness of empire? Was it not in fact also a part of Spenser's 'truth severe' that the 'Fierce war and faithful love' (l. 126) described in his fairy fiction should be considered an integral part of that same struggle for dominion?[70] The greatness of Elizabeth's court, however, is also prophetically linked with that of Gray's own time. For the Bard also hears the voice of Milton and the more 'distant warblings' (l. 133) of those whom Gray identifies in a note as 'The succession of Poets after Milton's time' (*Poems*, p. 199), which would obviously include Gray himself writing in 1757. In the context of this succession, the 'gorgeous dames', the majestic, old statesmen, and the many barons bold who surround Elizabeth (ll. 111-14) are, in a very important sense, potentially Georgian as well as Elizabethan, for Gray is insisting on the extension of an Arthurian-Elizabethan sense of purpose into his own time. It is also clearly implicit in the Bard's vision of Britain's ultimate destiny described in lines 135 to 138 that this ideal is an imperial one. Britain ('the orb of day'), after having purged itself of bloody tyranny (the 'sanguine cloud' of the bardic curse), in the future ('Tomorrow') restores to a peaceful condition ('repairs') the rich oceans ('the golden flood'), and inspires with affection and admiration ('warms') the other peoples of the world ('the nations'), who will appreciate the strong, purified light of its civilization (the 'redoubled ray'). The doom which the Bard can then 'see' (l. 139) is merely a corollary of this vision of glory revealing the practical means of its realization: 'to triumph, and to die' (l. 142) is the ordinance which Britons will adopt in their historic struggle to achieve a *pax Britannica*. That such a course of action involves conquest is connoted – if not denoted – by the verb 'To triumph', and the necessary heroism is exemplified in the brave resistance of the Bard, who acts according to this ordinance in the only way he can. In his give-me-liberty-or-give-me-death suicide, he triumphs in death by denying the tyrannical Edward control over his freedom-loving person. The Bard dies, however, not just so that liberty might prevail within Britain, but also in order that a Britain where liberty had been achieved might prevail in the world. Britain's alternative fate was to continue in a state of decadent tyranny sustained by the exercise of merely regal authority ('sceptered care') and an inability to hope for something better ('despair', l. 141). The Bard's vision of future history, however, belies the substance of this prediction. His linking of British progress with the divine form of Elizabeth and the heavenly voice of Milton – another architect of the empire[71] – enables him to denounce the proponent of this unholy fate as 'fond' and 'impious' (l. 135). That such a fate really was Britain's lot was, however, seriously believed in some quarters. Gray knew that many Londoners were apparently convinced by the despairing argument of Dr. John Brown's *An Estimate of the Manners and Principles of the Times*, published early in 1757, and seriously believed that Britain was about to be enslaved.[72] Clearly, the beauty of empire rapturously celebrated by Gray in 'The Bard' expressed the zealous hopes of a patriotic Pittite at a time when British forces were being mustered for their impending worldwide challenge to the *ancien régime* of France.

Many of Gray's readers did not grasp his meaning. But Goldsmith was undoubtedly aware of the substance of Gray's hopes when he compared the prophecy of the Bard to the foretelling of Greece's conquest of Troy by Nereus.[73] David Garrick also made it clear that he understood the contemporary significance of Gray's poem when, in his defence of the first two Odes, he wrote:

> *Tho nurst by these* [i.e. Homer, Plato and Pindar], *in vain*
>   *thy Muse appears*
>   *To breath her ardors in our souls;*
> *In vain to sightless eyes & deaden'd ears*
>   *The Lightning gleams & thunder rolls.*
>
> *Yet droop not, Gray, nor quit thy heav'n born art,*
>   *Again thy wondrous pow'rs reveal;*
> *Wake slumb'ring virtue in the Briton's heart,*
>   *And rouse us to* reflect *&* feel.

With ancient deeds our long chill'd bosoms fire,
Those deeds which mark Eliza's reign!
Make Britons, Greeks again – then strike the Lyre,
And Pindar shall not sing in vain.

(*Corres.*, II, 535-36, n. 1)

Although the triumph on which Gray's Bard wagered did not occur for nearly two years, Gray did not despair of victory in the intervening period. He must have soon been heartened by news of Clive's great victories at Fort William, Chandnernagore, and Plassey, which by June 1757 gave the East India Company control of three of the richest provinces in India and 'changed the future of a continent'.[74] He took an interest in the preparations for a 'secret expedition' against France (*Corres.*, II, 510), and when the project later failed he analyzed its abortive tactics in a letter to Brown (*Corres.*, II, 536-37). He followed closely the fortunes of England's Prussian ally on the continent in its war against Austria, Russian, and France. When conflicting reports of Prussian successes in battle reached England in December, he enquired of Wharton: 'What are we to believe about Silesia? am I to make bonfires, or keep a general fast? pray, rid me of this suspence, for it is very uneasy to me' (*Corres.*, II, 542-43). He appreciated the danger of a French invasion of Britain, and evidently wished that supplies might be increased for the strengthening of British forces (*Corres.*, II, 628, 630). Gray wrote almost despondently to Wharton in August of 1758, commenting on the strategically indecisive British gains at Louisburg and Cherbourg, her losses at Crown Point and Ticonderoga, and on Prussian set-backs on the continent: 'I congratulate you on our successes, & condole with you on our misfortunes: but do you think we draw the nearer to any happy conclusion of the war, or that we can bear so great a burthen much longer. The K: of Prussia's situation embarrasses me, surrounded as he is, & reduced to the defence of his own little Marquisate' (*Corres.*, II, 585). But when news reached England of the great Prussian victory at Zorndorf, where some 18,000 Russian troops were said to have been slaughtered, Gray wrote as follows to Brown, who had evidently been keeping him posted on developments in America:

It is always time to write, (whether Louisbourg be taken, or not) & I am always alike glad to hear from you. I am glad however to repay you with the King of Prussia: there is a Man for you at a dead lift, that has beat & baffled his three most powerful enemies, who had swallow'd him up in Idea! not that I look upon this last exploit, however seasonable, as his most heroick exploit; I suppose it was only butchering a great flock of slaves & savages, a conquest, that, but for the necessity of it, he would have disdain'd. (*Corres.*, II, 587-88)

Gray rejoiced in later Prussian successes, but to him they were no substitute for an independent British victory. 'The Season for triumph is at last come [Gray wrote to Brown upon hearing news of the Prussian victory at Minden on 1 August 1759]; I mean for our Allies, for it will be long enough before we shall have reason to exult in any great actions of our own, & therefore, as usual, we are proud for our neighbours' (*Corres.*, II, 632).[75] News soon reached England of British victories at Guadaloupe and Marie Galante, of Hanoverian victories over the French, and of Boscawen's destruction of a French squadron in Lagos Bay. This was balanced, however, by the shameful return to England of Lord George Sackville, who had disgraced himself at the Battle of Minden. Gray's reactions were appropriately mixed: 'what do you say to all our victories? the night we rejoiced for Boscawen, in the midst of squibs & bonfires arrived Lord G: Sackville. . . . he expects a Court-Martial. . . . I fear it is a rueful case' (*Corres.*, II, 644-45).[76] Nevertheless, the poet was soon given reason for unqualified rejoicing in 'great actions' by Britain. The successes of General Amherst at Niagara (25 July), at Ticonderoga (26 July), and at Fort Frederick (4 August), and the capture by Wolfe of Quebec (13 September) were all signal victories. Moreover they cleared the ground for the British conquest of the whole of French Canada the following year. Although Gray thought that Pitt's oration on the dauntless but dead Wolfe was too bathetically rhetorical to be moving, he observed that Pitt's eulogy 'about Gen[eral] Amhurst [*sic*], & in commendation of the industry & ardour of our American Commanders, [was] very spirited & eloquent. this is a very critical time [he added in his letter to Wharton], an action being hourly expected between the two great Fleets [of France and England], but no news as yet' (*Corres.*, II, 651-52). Later, when the report of the great British victory at Quiberon Bay reached England, Gray relayed details of the action to Mason and commented astutely on its strategic significance: 'You will have heard of Hawke's Victory before this can reach you (perhaps by an Express). . . . there is an end of the invasion [of Britain by France]. . . . it is an odd contemplation that *somebody* [i.e. George II] should have lived long enough to grow a great & glorious Monarch. as to the Nation, I fear, it will not know how to behave itself, being just in the circumstances of a Chambermaid, that has got the 20,000£ Prize in the Lottery' (*Corres.*, II, 654-55). Gray was aware, of course, that even the lately won Quebec

was a prize worth having. In fact, he repeated General Townsend's remark that it 'is much like Richmond-Hill, & the River as fine (but bigger)
& the Vale as *riant*, as rich & as well cultivated' (*Corres.*, II, 656). If
Wolfe would have preferred to have written Gray's 'Elegy' than to have
taken Quebec, Gray, for his part, would probably have rather taken
Quebec in 1759 than have been the author of the pacific 'Elegy'. The
poet, however, was not one to lose his sense of decorum even when
Britain's own season for triumph had come round at last.

Gray continued to follow the development of the war as this season for
triumph was extended well into 1761. He commented on the perilous
campaign in Canada as British forces, attempting to defeat the French
counter-attack on Quebec in 1760, converged on the French army from
the East, South, and West. 'We are in great alarms about Quebec', Gray
wrote to Wharton in June, and then proceeded to discuss the tactics of
the battle (*Corres.*, II, 679). A few days later he was able to report to
Mason:

> The bells are ringing, the Squibs bouncing. the Siege of Quebec is
> raised. Swanton got up the river, when they were bombarding the
> Town. Murray made a sally, routed them & took all their baggage.
> this is sum & substance in the vulgar tongue, for I cannot get the
> Gazette till midnight. perhaps you have had an Estafette. since I
> find, their cannon are all taken, & that two days after a French
> Fleet going to their assistance was intercepted, & sunk or burnt.
> (*Corres.*, II, 684)

He also had early intelligence from Sir William Williams of the preparations for the expedition which eventually captured Bellisle off the coast
of France (*Corres.*, II, 706-7). '. . . the news of the surrender of Bellisle is
daily expected [wrote Gray to Brown in May 1761]. they [the French]
have not, nor (they say) possibly can throw in either Men or provisions,
so it is look'd upon as ours. I know it will be so next week, because I am
then to buy into the Stocks' (*Corres.*, II, 739). After the victory, which
subsequently gave England a counter to exchange for Minorca in the
peace negotiations, Gray wrote an 'Epitaph' for the Bellisle monument
of Sir William Williams. 'Foremost in dangerous paths of fame', Williams 'scorn'd repose when Britain took the field' and thus both triumphed and died 'for England's fair renown'.

During Britain's season for triumph Gray wrote and translated several
other poems expressing 'thoughts that breathe and words that burn' with
a spirit of martial ardour. All of his translations of Welsh and Norse

poetry are in the same vein but have to do with proto-British heroes in all their primitive, gothic strength. Thus 'The Fatal Sisters' is the celebration of an early Norse-Scottish victory in Ireland, won by warriors who have been chosen to triumph and to die. Their fate is spun on a loom of which the warp is death and the woof, victory. These sisters are, of course, divine agents, and the brave warriors whom they select for death, according to a part of the poem which Gray did not translate, will live a happy, immortal life with the gods after death. Carlyle, writing some eighty years after Gray had translated this fragment, suggested that the essence of 'Norse Religion' was 'a rude but earnest, sternly impressive *Consecration of Valour*'.[77] Moreover, he said he regarded the valiant Northmen as 'progenitors of our own Blakes and Nelsons'.[78] Apparently Gray also saw a link between the heroic spirit of the Norsemen and modern Britons, as he tells us in the moralizing, penultimate stanza of this Ode:

> *Mortal, thou that hear'st the tale,*
> *Learn the tenor of our song.*
> *Scotland, through each winding vale*
> *Far and wide the notes prolong.*
>
> (ll. 57-60)

While Gray would have the 'tenor' of the song learned by everyone who hears it, he assigns to Scotland in particular the task of keeping it alive. 'Scotland', however, is not mentioned in the Latin version of the poem on which he based his translation; it did not exist as a polity in 1024; and the Orkney Islands from which Sigurd launched his invasion forms only a small fragment of the country. Why then should Gray, writing in 1761, have seen Scotland as the appropriate instrument for propagating the Sisters' song of conquest? The few English readers who heard the Sisters' tale would not have required annotations by the poet in order to know the answer to this question. The Sisters prophesy the defeat of 'Eirin' (l. 45). Gray in his 'Preface' to the poem refers more specifically to King Brian (who was supported by the native Irish) as nothing less than 'the enemy' (*Poems*, p. 215). In fact, in Gray's peculiar version[79] of the poem the Sisters prophesy that this victory marks the beginning of the conquest of the whole island by proto-British, Nordic-Scottish forces (Sictryg, the 'youthful King', l. 31, and Earl Sigurd of Orkney, l. 8):

> *They, whom once the desert-beach*
> *Pent within its bleak domain,*
> *Soon their ample sway shall stretch*
> *O'er the plenty of the plain.*
>
> (ll. 37-40)

Thus Gray sees the battle as an initial encounter in the struggle to enlarge the Pale, and both Gray and his readers were well aware this
struggle was still going on in 1761. 'You have heard of the Irish disturb-
ances[80] (I reckon). never [Gray wrote to Wharton] were two Houses of
Parliament so bepiss'd & shit upon: this is not a figure, but literally so'
(*Corres.*, II, 657-58). '. . . the Irish are very intractable [he wrote later],
even the L^ds J:^s themselves; great difficulties about who shall be sent over
to tame them' (*Corres.*, II, 728). It was also common knowledge among
Gray's contemporaries that the British forces conscripted for the Seven
Years' War had been greatly strengthened by the recruitment, at the be-
hest of Pitt, of two highland regiments. These troops had rendered
valiant service, as Pitt himself later said of them: 'I sought for merit
wherever it was to be found. I found it in the mountains in the north. I
called it forth . . . a hardy and intrepid race of men . . . who . . . had gone
nigh to have overturned the State [in 1745-46] . . . they served with fidel-
ity as they fought with valour, and conquered for you in every part of
the world.'[81]

Whereas 'The Fatal Sisters' originally seems to have been a self-con-
tained poem which was later incorporated into the *Njáls Saga* (*Poems*, p.
214), 'The Descent of Odin' is a fragment of a much larger work, the
Poetic Edda. The significance of Gray's translation cannot be understood
without some knowledge of both the *Edda* and of the traditional, conventional interpretation of the poem by Christian readers. Two facts in
particular are of considerable importance in this regard. One is that the
prophecy of Balder's death in the larger context of the *Edda* marks the
beginning of the end of the whole pagan, Nordic universe – the twilight
of the gods – out of whose ashes would arise an entirely new creation.
The second is that many Christians, particularly those who brought the
gospel to the Norsemen, regarded Balder as the most Christ-like of all
the Norse gods. Considerations such as these led Carlyle in 1840 to see a
certain historical significance in the whole Nordic apocalypse:

> That is also a very striking conception, that of the *Ragnarök*, Con-
> summation, or *Twilight of the Gods*. It is in the *Völuspa Song*;
> seemingly a very old, prophetic idea. The Gods and Jötuns, the
> divine Powers and the chaotic brute ones, after long contest and
> partial victory by the former, meet at last in universal world-
> embracing wrestle and duel; World-serpent against Thor, strength
> against strength; mutually extinctive; and ruin, 'twilight' sinking
> into darkness, swallows the created Universe. The old Universe
> with its Gods is sunk; but it is not final death; there is to be a new
> Heaven and a new Earth; a higher supreme God, and Justice to

reign among men. Curious: this law of mutation, which also is a law written in man's inmost thought, had been deciphered by these old earnest Thinkers in their rude style; and how, though all dies, and even gods die, yet all death is but a phoenix fire-death, and new-birth into the Greater and the Better! It is the fundamental Law of Being for a creature made of Time, living in this Place of Hope. All earnest men have seen into it; may still see into it.[82]

If Gray's understanding of the *Edda* was anything like Carlyle's, then it becomes much easier to understand the significance of the fragment which he translated. Like the Bard, Odin confronts death, the death of his son and of the virginal goddesses who will also weep in Hoel. Moreover, the coming death-struggle between himself and 'Lok' (l. 90) is alluded to, a struggle which is to result in the ruin of the whole fabric of his pagan world. And Odin, like the Bard triumphant, has an intimation, albeit vague, of a brighter future: He prophesies to Hela, 'Thou the deeds of light shall know' (l. 39). Odin is naturally unaware that the Christian world of Gray's Britain will ultimately replace his own, although – and the irony here is very strong – Gray's post-pagan readers could see the naively prophetic intimations of a future Christian world in the person and fate of the gentle and beautiful sun-god, Balder. He is one of the 'sons of Heaven', whose 'head to death is given', whom 'Pain can reach' and for whose life-after-death is prepared a 'glittering board', a 'golden bed', and the 'pure beverage of the bee' protected by a 'shield of gold' (ll. 41-48). It is also prophesied in the *Edda* that he will come again after the world has been recreated.[83] The theme of Gray's fragment, therefore, has to do with a valiant, proto-British warrior about to enter a struggle unto death for a cause which was not unrelated historically to Britain's rationale for war in Gray's own time: the defence and extension of a higher Christian civilization.

The martial themes in Gray's translations from Celtic verse speak for themselves, although their relationship to Gray's own feelings invites comment. At a time when Britain was seriously threatened by a French invasion, it is understandable that Gray, who greatly feared such an event, should revive 'The Triumphs of Owen'. In this piece, Gray writes about an heroic and successful defence of the homeland against transmarine Irish, Norman, and Danish invaders. The swift, strong, liberal Owen, leader of the Welsh, is 'Britain's gem' (l. 4), and, like Gray's other heroes, he leads his troops to triumph or 'honourable Death' (l. 36).

Of the passages from the Welsh poem *Goddodin*, two are about the mighty prowess-at-arms of the early British warriors, Carodoc and Conan.

A third passage, 'The Death of Hoel', also celebrates British bravery. Gray, departing from the sense of the Latin text, attributes the defeat of the Welsh warriors to Hoel's being 'Too, too secure in youthful pride' (l. 5). The nature of this pride which goes before the 'fall' (l. 24) of these troops is more precisely defined by the ironic undertones in lines 11 to 20. First, the relatively innocent Hoel virtuously expresses contempt for 'heaps of hoarded gold'. Gray then writes:

> To Cattraeth's vale in glittering row
> Twice two hundred warriors go;
> Every warrior's manly neck
> Chains of regal honour deck,
> Wreathed in many a golden link:
> From the golden cup they drink
> Nectar, that the bees produce,
> Or the grape's ecstatic juice.
> Flushed with mirth and hope they burn:
> But none from Cattraeth's vale return ....
>   (*Poems*, pp. 234-35)

The superficial splendour of the 'glittering' must be caused by the 'Chains' of 'regal' honour wreathed in 'many a golden link' around 'Every warrior's manly neck'. The cup holding the debilitating 'ecstatic juice' of the grape, which causes the warriors to be 'flushed' with 'mirth' and false 'hope' is then strongly associated with this regal pomp by its 'golden' quality. Gray seems to be saying that British warriors would be well advised to avoid being deluded either by the trappings of royalty or by the decadence which such enticements engender. His high whig principles were, as usual, irrepressible.

With North America and India secure, Pitt planned in 1761 to capture several major French bases in the West Indies and elsewhere. Meanwhile, France strengthened its position by making a pact with Spain, which, while unwilling to declare war prior to the safe arrival home of its treasure fleet, also had claims to make on Britain.[84] Gray summarized the issues at stake in a letter to Mason in September: 'Spain has supplied them [France] with money, & is picking a quarrel with us about the [Newfoundland] fishery and [Honduran] logwood. Mr. Pitt says, so much the better! & was for recalling Ld Bristol [the British ambassador to Spain] directly: however a flat denial has been return'd [by the British government] to their [i.e. Spain's] pretensions' (*Corres.*, II, 757-58). Pitt, indeed, was of the opinion that Britain should force the hand of the

Spanish by immediately attacking their homeward-bound treasure fleet if Spain did not withdraw her commercial claims. So strongly did he feel about this matter that when the cabinet refused to act upon his advice in the hope that Spain could be kept out of the war, he resigned immediately. In so doing, however, he accepted a pension of £3,000 a year for himself and a title for his wife.

Like many whig Englishmen who admired Pitt's proud independence of royal courts and courtly favours, Gray was put 'much out of countenance' by Pitt's willingness to accept such patronage (*Corres.*, II, 761). He thought, however, that the 'contempt' (*Corres.*, II, 763) which Pitt, even while out of office, managed to express for the French peace proposals would do much to restore his popularity. As for the war itself, Gray was at first uncertain whether or not Pitt's belligerent attitude was in the country's best interest (*Corres.*, II, 763), and when war against Spain finally did break out (with Pitt still out of office) he still had certain reservations:

> I take no joy in the Spanish War, being too old to privateer, & too poor to buy stock [which Gray had just been buying (*Corres.*, II, 739)]; nor do I hope for a good end of any war, as it will be now probably conducted. oh that foolishest of Great Men [Pitt], that sold his inestimable diamond for a paltry peerage & pension: the very night it happen'd was I swearing, that it was a damn'd lie, & never could be: but it was for want of reading Thomas a Kempis, who knew Mankind so much better, than I.
>
> Young Pitt [a nephew of the Great Commoner] (whom I believe you have heard me mention) is return'd to England: from him I hope to get much information concerning Spain, wch no body has seen: he is no bad Observer. (*Corres.*, II, 771-72)

Evidently, Gray believed that if Britain were to conduct a successful campaign, the leadership of Pitt would be required. When Britain managed even without Pitt to gain notable victories, particularly in the Caribbean,[85] Gray shared the widely held opinion that honours won in the fields of glory were needlessly relinquished by a pusillanimous ministry in the negotiations that led to the Peace of Paris: 'You see we have made a peace [he wrote to Wharton]. I shall be silent about it, because if I say anything antiministerial, you will tell me, you know the reason; & if I approve it, you will tell me, I have expectations still. all I know is, that the D: of Newcastle & Ld Hardwick both say, it is an excellent Peace; and only M^r. Pitt calls it inglorious and insidious' (*Corres.*, II, 788).

Gray's 'silent' meaning, however, was perfectly plain; and like many members of the trading classes[86] he remained highly critical of the ministries appointed over the next three years by George III. The alleged attempts of this King to wrest the control of state patronage from the whig party machine, and then to employ it so as to recover the powers of the Crown as they had been left by the Revolution Settlement of 1689,[87] apparently ran counter to Gray's notion of liberty. 'And I ask you [Gray wrote to Wharton in 1763], how you like the present times? whether you had not rather be a Printer's Devil than a Secretary of State ... ?' (Corres., II, 807). 'the Ministry are all together by the ears [he wrote to Wharton in 1764], so are the Opposition: the only doubt is wch will be the weakest: I am afraid, I know' (Corres., II, 853). Some of the grounds for Gray's fierce satire against his former hero Fox ('On Lord Holland's Seat at Margate') seem to have had their origin during this period: Fox was alleged to have used 'gross bribery and intimidations' (Poems, p. 259) in the House of Commons to ensure the passing of the Peace of Paris. In 'The Candidate', Gray showed his contempt for another minister, the Fourth Earl of Sandwich. The poet was equally critical of the government's unwillingness to protect Britain's imperial interests:

if the French [he wrote to Mason in 1764] should be so unwise as to suffer the Spanish Court to go on in their present measures (for they refuse to pay the ransom of Manilla [allegedly owing to the British], & have driven away our Logwood-cutters already [from the Honduras, where British merchants had been granted concessions]) down go their friends the Ministry, & all the schemes of Right Divine & Prerogative; and this is perhaps the best chance we have. are you not struck with the great similarity there is between the first years of Charles the first, & the present times? who would have thought it possible five years ago? (Corres., II, 839)

Although Gray was scornful of weakness and servility in high places, he nevertheless kept these failings in perspective. When told of the proposed visit of Count Algarotti, he wrote to Wharton: 'I am glad to hear, he thinks of revisiting England tho' I am a little ashamed of my country at this present. our late-acquired glory did not set becomingly upon us; & even the Author of it, that Restitutor d'Inghilterra, is doing God knows what! if he should deign to follow the track of vulgar Ministers, & regain his power by ways injurious to his fame, whom can we trust hereafter?' (Corres., II, 828). What Gray was really hoping for was in fact the return to office of the great leader Pitt, ailing though he was (Corres., II, 873, 875, 882). This man, Gray believed, could control the London weavers rioting against the importation of foreign silks (*Corres.*, II, 875). Pitt was also a firm supporter of John Wilkes,[88] with whom Gray also strongly sympathized. And Gray, still an 'Antigallican' (*Corres.*, II, 907), undoubtedly appreciated Pitt's advocacy of a strong, aggressive, anti-French, imperial policy.[89] Gray, it is true, regarded Pitt's assertion of 'the rights of the [American] Colonies in their greatest latitude' and the ministry's willingness to repeal the Stamp Act as 'unaccountable on any principles of common-sense' (*Corres.*, III, 920-21); yet that did not prevent him from comparing Pitt's visit to the House of Commons for the debate on this question to Aeneas's bold appearance in the Limbo of the Dead (*Corres.*, III, 922). And although he looked upon the Great Commoner's acceptance of a 'foolish title' for himself as 'the weakest thing, that was ever done by so great a Man',[90] he nevertheless felt relieved when Lord Chatham finally consented in August of 1766 to form a government (*Corres.*, III, 934). By that time, Gray was able to agree with Mason's contention that Pitt had in fact 'Preserv'd the Colonies, [and] convey'd Fresh Spirits to expiring Trade' in 'the Affair of Stamps' (*Corres.*, III, 934, 1250). He also concurred with his friend in hoping that the ailing Pitt would 'do his best to save from Fate/That leaky Skiff we call the State' (*Corres.*, III, 934, n. 7). Pitt, however, succumbing to his illness, soon had to relinquish all responsibilities, and the leadership of the government was assumed by his deputy, the Duke of Grafton. Grafton had long been a strong supporter of Pitt. In fact the invitation to Pitt to join the ministry had been made partly as a result of the insistence of Grafton, who had threatened to resign if Pitt were not brought in. Gray had then all but rejoiced at the prospect of a 'union' of the two men.[91] Although Grafton, frequently overruled in the ministry, was unable to translate many of his own views into public policy, he nevertheless remained a disciple of Pitt in matters of foreign affairs. It was therefore appropriate that Gray, who was still maintaining an interest in colonial affairs (*Corres.*, III, 959, 1057-58), should have eulogized Grafton. Indeed in the concluding lines of the 'Ode for Music', he links him with no less a figure than Cecil, a former Chancellor of Cambridge it is true, but one much more famous as an architect of British imperialism.[92] The 'watchful' and 'dauntless' Grafton has lineaments which combine not only a 'Beaufort's grace' but a 'Tudor's fire' (l. 70) as well. There was no need for Gray to inform his readers that the keeping to a 'steady course of honor' (l. 91) by this man would involve nothing less than protecting and advancing British rights and interests around the world – on the high seas, in the American colonies, in India, in the Caribbean, and elsewhere. This was the essence of

Grafton's Pittite ideal. In Grafton's Britain, as in Pitt's, the arts, divine blessing, and liberty are still very much in evidence: the final 'Grand Chorus' of the 'Ode to Music' is to be symphonically sung by 'spirits blessed above' (l. 87) and by a Cambridge which will not profane with 'courtly tongue refined' (l. 80) the 'inborn royalty' (l. 81) of Grafton's mind. The worldly guarantor for the country's maritime progress is the British crown, symbolized by the serene 'star of Brunswick' (l. 93) which 'gilds the horrors of the deep' (l. 94), presumably with treasure flowing in from all quarters of the globe.

Gray's world vision, then, was consistently that of a whiggish, imperialistic bourgeois, latterly a Pittite. The beauty of the poetry in which he expressed this vision is as tough and uncompromising in substance as it is gracefully intricate in form. Moreover, in the context of those particular forces and feelings – both national and class – in relation to which Gray's work should be dialectically understood, this beauty is progressive in certain respects and of some power. In an epoch when imperialists had a bloody but constructive contribution to make to the world, Mason's epitaph for Gray's monument in Westminster Abbey was not inappropriate:

> No More the Grecian Muse unrivall'd reigns,
> To Britain let the nations homage pay;
> She felt a Homer's fire in Milton's strains,
> A Pindar's rapture in the lyre of Gray.[93]

Carleton University

Notes

1. C. H. Crouch, 'Ancestry of Thomas Gray the Poet', *Genealogical Magazine*, vol. 3, no. 4 (December 1927), 74.

2. Morris Collis, *British Merchant Adventures* (London, 1942), pp. 23-24. See also Ramkrishna Mukherjee, *The Rise and Fall of the East India Company* (Berlin, 1958), pp. 76-77.

3. Crouch, p. 74. Unless otherwise indicated, all subsequent quotations in this paragraph will be from Crouch, pp. 74-78.

4. By the middle of the seventeenth century, scriveners had relinquished to lawyers and notaries the work of inscribing and conveyancing, and had assumed the role of investment dealers. 'Money-scrivening' by individual dealers was superseded by the rise of institutional banking in the eighteenth century. (H. C. Gutteridge, 'The Origins and Development of the Profession of Notaries Public in England', *Cambridge Legal Essays written in honour of ... Doctor Bond, Professor Buckland and Professor Kenney*, [Cambridge, 1926], pp. 128-33). See also R. D. Richards, *The Early History of Banking in England* (London, 1929), p. 15.

5. Crouch, p. 75.

6. *The Poems of Thomas Gray*, ed. John Mitford (London, 1814), p. xciii. There is some ambiguity in Mitford's statement as to whether the person who acquired the £10,000 was Thomas Gray or his father, but the reference to 'the fire in Cornhill' which occurred after the death of the father makes it clear that the poet Thomas had inherited this sum of money from his father.

7. This was Joseph Massie's estimate based on a survey carried out in 1759-60. See Peter Mathias, 'The Social Structure in the Eighteenth Century: A Calculation by Joseph Massie', *Economic History Review*, x (1957), 42.

8. This was a status accorded 'men of birth or wealth, for whom the rules of study and discipline were often relaxed' (*Corres.*, III, 1203).

9. *Corres.*, II, 666. For other comments by Gray on the contemptible meanness of the professions and of office-holding, see *Corres.*, I, 421; II, 545, 759.

10. Ibid., III, 925, n.11. Cf. *Boswell in Holland 1763-64*, ed. Frederick A. Pottle (Toronto, 1952), pp. 75, 81.

11. Macaulay, IV, 404, 406.

12. *Corres.*, II, 832. See also *Corres.*, III, 1158.

13. Roger Lonsdale (*Poems*, p. 125) notes that Spenser, among others, in his *Hymn in Honour of Love* also used the phrase 'celestial fire' (1.186). Spenser explains that, although this fire is of heavenly origin, it kindles a love which is 'lord of truth and loyalty' (1.176) in this world. Gray would have agreed.

14. In 1765, Gray hoped that Pitt would 'accept the uncontrolled guidance of the nation', and then use this dictatorial power to put down the Spitalfield weavers (*Corres.*, II, 875).

15. *Spirit of the Laws*, trans. Thomas Nugent and ed. Franz Neumann (New York, 1949), I, 155.

16. Ibid., 187.

17. Ibid., 155.

18. Gray was not alone in his respect for this early bourgeois ideologist. For discussions of Machiavelli's influence on Halifax and Bolingbroke, see Felix Raab, *The English Face of Machiavelli: A changing Interpretation 1500-1700* (London, 1964), pp. 218-54, and H. Butterfield, *The Statecraft of Machiavelli* (London, 1960), pp. 135-65.

19. *A Briefe Note of Ireland*, often attributed to Edmund Spenser, provides a concise contemporary account of the policy underlying this bloody conquest. For useful modern studies, which have rarely been included in bibliographies on the subject, see A. L. Morton, *A People's History of England* (London, 1968); T. A. Jackson, *Ireland Her Own* (London, 1946); Elinor Burns, *British Imperialism in Ireland* (Dublin, 1931); Alice Wigfall Green, *Irish Nationality* (London, 1911); and Howard Mumford Jones, 'The Origins of the Colonial Idea in England', *Proceedings of The American Philosophical Society*, LXXXV (1942), no. 5, 448-65.

20. For recent summary account of this expansion and a useful bibliography, see T. K. Rabb, *Enterprise and Empire: Merchant and Gentry Investment in the Expansion of England, 1575-1630* (Cambridge, Mass., 1967).

21. See, for example, Edmund Waller's 'A Panegyric to my Lord Protector, of the present greatness, and joint interest, of his highness, and this nation'.

22. Macaulay, v, 364-65.

23. Ibid., 191.

24. Morton, *People's History of England*, pp. 292-94.

25. Ibid., p. 297.

26. At the time of his death, his South Sea Annuities were worth about £1,200 (*Corres.*, III, 1283-86).

27. Sidney Pollard and David W. Crossley, *The Wealth of Britain 1085-1966* (London, 1968), pp. 163-69.

28. John G. Sperling, *The South Sea Company* (Boston, 1962), pp. 23, 46. The £1,200 of New South Sea Annuities which Thomas Gray bequeathed in his will were first issued in 1733, and so may have been in the family from that time. If so, Gray would not have been acting contrary to personal interest in opposing the war. The annuities, unlike the Company's 'trading stock' which was subject to fluctuations in value depending on trading conditions, bore a fixed and guaranteed rate of interest, and, as an integral part of the national debt, were 'equivalent to government stock' (Sperling, p. 37). As a matter of fact, the Company's court of directors was divided into two bitterly opposed factions of share-holding annuitants who favoured war and bond-holding annuitants who recommended that the South Sea Company abandon its speculative trading ventures altogether and become nothing but an annuities holding company (Sperling, p. 44). This it soon became (Sperling, p. 48).

29. *Corres.*, I, 151. According to Tobias Smollett, *The History of England from the Revolution to the end of the American War and Peace of Versailles in 1783*, 8 vols. (1791), III, 31-32, Admiral Vernon was a boisterous fellow who was extolled by the proponents of the war as 'another Drake or Raleigh'. The same historian suggests that the Walpole administration agreed to send him to the Caribbean perhaps with the hope that he would disgrace both himself and the pro-war party in England.

30. *Corres.*, I, 154. Sir Robert Walpole said much the same thing to the Duke of Newcastle. See Basil Williams, *The Whig Supremacy 1714-1760* (Oxford, 1962), p. 210.

31. Haddock had been sent to this theatre to strengthen the bargaining position of the British negotiators at Madrid.

32. *Corres.*, i, 155. See also i, 170-72.

33. Smollett, iii, 65.

34. Ibid., 55-56.

35. V. H. H. Green, *The Hanoverians 1714-1815* (London, 1948), p. 148.

36. Ibid., p. 152.

37. Ibid., p. 152.

38. Ibid., p. 164.

39. Smollett, iii, 191-92.

40. *The Well Wrought Urn: Studies in the Structure of Poetry* (New York, 1947), pp. 108ff. One cannot agree, however, with Brook's suggestion that Gray argues that 'many [of the lives] of the "rude Forefathers" would have ended in cruelty and empty vanity had they "learned to stray" into the "paths of glory",' thereby implying a severely realistic judgement on the part of the poet (p. 114). Such an indecorous excursion would have been unthinkable to Gray, and nothing in the poem itself really supports Brooks's point. All that can be reasonably assumed is that the 'sober wishes' of the poor have not learned to stray into insobriety, which is not quite the same as the 'paths of glory'. Likewise, Brooks's remark that the epitaph 'commemorates one of the literally poor' (p. 120) because 'all he had, [was] a tear' is surely unwarranted. One is reminded of the rejoinder Gray once made to Mason when his friend apparently intimated that he might be too poor to manage a visit to Gray: 'I have known purse-proud People often complain of their poverty, wch is meant as an insult upon the real poor. how dare you practise this upon me?' (*Corres.*, iii, 977).

41. See above, p. 208.

42. 'Thomas Gray', *Poets and Story-tellers* (London, 1949), p. 49.

43. See, for example, Gray's advice to Wharton about even such a relatively unimportant subject as a dispute within the medical profession (*Corres.*, I, 411-12).

44. *Memoirs of the Reign of George III*, 3 vols. (London, 1846), i, 373.

45. Ibid., i, 378.

46. Ibid., 392-94.

47. Ibid., 399.

48. Williams, p. 346.

49. Earl of Ilchester, *Henry Fox, First Lord Holland: his family and relations*, 2 vols. (London, 1920), i, 22.

50. Walpole, *Memoirs*, i, 100.

51. Smollett, iii, 404-5.

52. J. H. Plumb, *Chatham* (Hamden, Conn., 1965), p. 37.

53. Ilchester, i, 222.

54. This is Gray's own summary of lines 54ff., *Poems*, p. 168.

55. Gray's library included a copy of the *Account of other Loss of y*^e *Wager &c: by an Officer of Adm: Anson's Squadron* (1744). See William Powell Jones, *Thomas Gray, Scholar* (New York, 1965), p. 160.

56. See Richard Walter, *Anson's Voyage Round the World*, ed. G. S. Laird Clowes (London, 1928), pp. 265-66.

57. Ibid., pp. 265-66.

58. In a note to line 105, Gray identifies the 'Two coursers of ethereal race' with Dryden's 'rhimes', and Lonsdale suggests parenthetically that by 'rhimes' Gray means couplets. There seems to be no good reason, however, for so limiting Gray's meaning: some of Dryden's well balanced quatrain verse also rhymes and is more thunderous in content and 'long-resounding' (1.106) in pace than many of his couplets.

59. Williams, p. 348; Ilchester, i, 239.

60. Williams, p. 349.

61. Ilchester, i, 265; Walpole, *Memoirs*, ii, 42.

62. It has been suggested (*Corres.*, i, 442, n.7) that this 'very odd Step' might have been an allusion to Fox's endeavours to bring the Bedfords to court. The offer to Bedford of the Privy Seal, however, was certainly not 'in its nature no secret'. It was an informal sounding made privately and indirectly through Lord Bedford's brother-in-law, Lord Gower (Ilchester, i, 278), and secrecy was its essence. Fox's support of the subsidies was both 'public' and – in the light of his earlier conduct – 'very odd'.

63. *History of England in the Eighteenth Century*, 8 vols. (London, 1879-90), ii, 485.

64. Horace Walpole drafted a letter to Fox, which read in part: 'I know you think Mr Gr. the greatest poet we have & I know he thinks you the greatest man we have' (*Corres.*, ii, 469, n.13).

65. Ilchester, i, 329, 336.

66. Plumb, pp. 60-68; O. A. Sherrard, *Lord Chatham: Pitt and the Seven Year's War* (London, 1955), p. 172.

67. Green, p. 189.

68. Walpole, *Memoirs*, iii, 7.

69. According to Geoffrey of Monmouth, he conquered Scotland, Ireland, Iceland, the Orkneys and many countries on the continent of Europe.

70. See, for example, *The Fairie Queene*, ii, Proem and Canto x.

71. Hans Kohn, *The Idea of Nationalism: A Study of its Origins and Background* (Toronto, 1967), pp. 169ff. This matter has not yet been given the attention it deserves.

72. *Corres.*, ii, 499 and n.3. Much to Gray's satisfaction, Mason later ridiculed Brown as one who had tried to prove his 'Country's Nothingness' (*Corres.*, iii, 935, and App. R.).

73. Oliver Goldsmith, *Works*, 4 vols., ed. Peter Cunningham (London, 1854-78), iv, 318.

74. Plumb, p. 70.

75. In a subsequent letter (*Corres.*, ii, 634-35), Gray described the action of this battle in some detail.

76. Although Gray does not refer specifically to Britain's successes in the West Indies, it may be reasonably assumed that his dealings at this time in South Sea annuities (*Corres.*, ii, 610, 621) would have led him to follow events there rather closely. The victories of the Prince of Brunswick's army had been recently reported in the *Gazette* (*Correspondence of William Pitt*, ed. Gertrude Selwyn Kimball, London, 1906, ii, 172-73). Gray had probably not yet heard the news of Amherst's victories in America, which reached Pitt on the very day that this letter was written, 18 Sept. 1759.

77. 'The Hero as Divinity. Odin Paganism: Scandinavian Mythology', *On Heroes, Hero-Worship, and the Heroic in History* (London, 1908), p. 276.

78. Ibid., p. 269.

79. See Roger Lonsdale's note to lines 37-40 in *Poems*, p. 219.

80. These were demonstrations in Dublin by those who feared, apparently not without some cause, that the Irish Parliament was about to be completely abolished by England.

81. Cited by Basil Williams, *The Whig Supremacy 1714-1760*, p. 357. Of course, Protestant Scots had been sent to Ireland as colonists in the seventeenth century.

82. Carlyle, p. 275.

83. *The Poetic Edda*, trans. and ed. Lee M. Hollander, 2nd ed. rev. (Austin, 1962), p. 12.

84. H. W. Richmond, *Statesmen and Sea Power* (Oxford, 1946), p. 137.

85. Green, p. 221.

86. Ibid., p. 308.

87. G. M. Trevelyan, *A Shortened History of England* (Harmondsworth, 1959), p. 358.

88. Green, p. 311.

89. Ibid., p. 311.

90. *Corres.*, iii, 931. See also *Corres.*, iv, 933-34.

91. Ibid., iii, 931. The third member of this 'union' was a certain Mr. Conway who had been a general in the Seven Years' War.

92. A. L. Rowse, *The Expansion of Elizabethan England* (New York, 1955), pp. 87, 150, 159, 173-74.

93. *Poems of Thomas Gray*, ed. Mitford, p. ci.

LOUIS KAMPF ⦚ *The Humanist Tradition in Eighteenth-Century England—And Today**

Literary history was invented during the eighteenth century, though literature had a sense of its own history well before that. Why should one write literary history? There are many reasons or justifications, some less attractive than others. However, the history which should most concern those involved with the life and career of literature is rarely the object of historians. What else should the literary historian be concerned with but the transformations of consciousness? What effect, she or he should ask, does literature have on the way a society thinks and feels about itself? And ultimately on the way it acts? Consciousness, we all know, is a slippery subject. Slipperiest of all is the development of class consciousness: the way groups of people come to be aware of belonging to one kind of social grouping.

Literature may be important in this process. It may not. The issue is rarely raised. Chronicling the details of what happens to the minds of masses of people – rather than elites – is no easy matter. For England, the work of the Hammonds, E. P. Thompson, and a few others informs us about the development of working class consciousness during the late eighteenth century. As for the relationship of eighteenth-century humanism – the work of Swift, Pope, Johnson – to that development, there is no work of significance at all. And ourselves? We hardly begin to understand how a major tradition – Augustan humanism – relates to the development of our own consciousness.

But why should we worry about eighteenth-century humanism as a source? Marx once remarked that

the tradition of all the dead generations weighs like a nightmare on the brain of the living. And just when they seem engaged in revo-

* This paper provided the basis for discussion at a symposium on 'Humane Studies in the Modern University' held on the last day of the Conference.

lutionizing themselves and things, in creating something that has never yet existed, precisely in such periods of revolutionary crisis they anxiously conjure up the spirits of the past to their service and borrow from them names, battle cries and costumes in order to present the new scene of world history in this borrowed language.[1]

Our crisis is not revolutionary – yet. But already we hear the yelps of the watchdogs of civility guarding the peace of the Augustans. The eighteenth century's cultural costumes have become a disguise for hidden, unarticulated – even unperceived – interests. But what really happened during the eighteenth century? What are the civilized spirits being conjured up for us? And in what ways did those spectres become the substance of daily life for people in the eighteenth century and for us?

It would take a very large volume to draw even the sketch of an answer. I shall, instead, propose a few theses. Some of them will seem arbitrary; others merely commonplace; yet others contradictory. Their intention is to encourage the sort of literary history which attempts to understand what the written word does to people's lives in society.

Thesis I. Nature.

> *Look round our World; behold the chain of Love*
> *Combining all below and all above.*
>
> . . . .
>
> *All serv'd, all serving! nothing stands alone;*
> *The chain holds on, and where it ends, unknown.*
> – a humanist poet.

Man is born free, and yet we see him everywhere in chains.
– an eccentric.

Shut, shut the door, good John!
– same poet as before.

Thesis II. Authority. We are familiar with the major concerns of the literary history of eighteenth-century England: the definition of Augustan humanism; the misadventures of neoclassical doctrine and practice; developments in the hierarchy of genres; the shift to what we call Romanticism. But consider the history of the larger culture during that century: there is the violent intrusion of industrialism and enclosure; as the intrusion's corollary there is the development of the modern system of class relationships; in the cities an inchoate mass of the homeless and oppressed transforms itself – with the help of friends and enemies – into a self-conscious and disciplined working class.

Contemplating such a canvas, one asks why there was a political revolution in France, and none in England. The usual answer is to point to the English genius for compromise as exemplified in the politics of 1688 and in the spirit of Augustan humanism. However, the peace of the Augustans was not very peaceful. The consensus concerning the legitimacy of the state and the power of property broke down during the eighteenth century. The uncivilized became restless: rather they were forced into restlessness. Yet state power was not overthrown. A question for the literary historian: Did the humanistic tradition play a role in preserving the authority of those who ruled? Is the English genius for compromise a form of oppression dressed in Augustan clothes?

Thesis III. Class consciousness. We know it exists, and that material conditions relate to its development. But how? E. P. Thompson's account defines the problem:

> Class happens when some men, as a result of common experiences (inherited or shared), feel and articulate the identity of their interests as between themselves, and as against other men whose interests are different from (and usually opposed to) theirs. The class experience is largely determined by the productive relations into which men are born – or enter involuntarily. Class consciousness is the way in which these experiences are handled in cultural terms: embodied in traditions, value-systems, ideas, and institutional forms. If the experience appears as determined, class-consciousness does not.[2]

The *Memoirs* of Thomas Hardy (the shoemaker and founder of the London Corresponding Society) give us the feel of how working class consciousness developed during the decades spanning the eighteenth and nineteenth centuries. The London Corresponding Society – and the many others like it – allowed its members consciously to define their experience. That experience was dominated by work. But for those in the Society it also included the propagation of opinions about the nature of that work, and the organization of the converted. This activity led to Hardy's indictment in 1794 for high treason. The charge was so severe because the Society had defined fundamental social oppositions in a culture which pretended to have no divisions. The organization of the converted implied the end of politics as the preserve of an hereditary elite or of those with property – that is, those who supposedly represented what was highest and most universal in the society. Burke's 'swinish multitude' was developing its own cultural institutions. Burke saw them not only as a threat to property, but as a threat to the humanistic culture which gave ideological support to the notion of property.

But Burke's sentimentalities about the aristocracy were not entirely representative of the defence of property. Bourgeois class consciousness did, after all, develop during the eighteenth century. We analyze its progress in the novels of the period, and consider Steele and the sentimental drama to be important historical links. However, we rarely ask how the propagation of bourgeois class consciousness related to the bourgeoisie's quest for political power. In France sectors of the bourgeoisie allied themselves with the forces of revolution; the bourgeois intelligentsia formulated the analyses which were to heighten revolutionary consciousness. In sharp contrast, the dynamic of English radicalism during the decades beginning with 1790 derived entirely from artisans and labourers. The middle classes were so supportive of law and order that they abdicated much of their political power. The fear induced by the prospect of a fundamental challenge – Jacobin egalitarianism – to its culture led the bourgeoisie to affirm that culture through the raw power of the state – a power not yet wielded by the bourgeoisie itself. What role did the humanistic culture the bourgeoisie had tried so hard to absorb play in that surrender? How does a class become blinded to its own political interests in the name of civilization?

Large sectors of the bourgeoisie had, of course, refused to recognize themselves as a class. The attainment of an aristocratic culture, one would like to believe, removes one from the bonds of social class. Today's academic social science has given expression to this dogma of humanism by emptying the concept 'class' of consciousness, and substituting quantitative definitions for articulated beliefs. Once the members of a class are deprived of social consciousness, they lose the possibility of political cohesion. That is why the bearers of humanistic culture tried to define the developing working class as the 'swinish multitude' – an inchoate mass. The threat was real. Working class culture and its attendant political cohesion were enemies not to be treated lightly. The English working class has not yet recovered from the onslaught of the civilized. Neither, for that matter, has the English intelligentsia.

Thesis IV. Civilization. A. R. Humphreys has written that the foundation of Augustan civilization is property.[3] Few except literary historians would want to argue with him. Macaulay, in a speech on the Reform Bill, universalizes the subject. Property, he tells us, is 'that great institution for the sake of which chiefly all other institutions exist, that great institution to which we owe all knowledge, all commerce, all industry, all civilisation, all that makes us to differ from the tattooed savages of the Pacific Ocean'.[4] Earlier, for the eighteenth century, the civilizing force of property had already been codified in Locke's claim that the purpose of a commonwealth is to protect property. Adam Smith justly observed that government exists for the propertied.

Ownership is, of course, the guarantee of a settled existence. And the sense of permanence is the quality by which Augustan humanism most liked to identify itself. The elegant country house became the embodiment of this humanistic ideal. We are all familiar with Pope's *Epistle to Burlington*; and in Pope's own Twickenham the doors could be shut to the intrusions of the uncivilized. Building the houses and estates which transformed the English countryside during the eighteenth century was made possible by enclosure. Its direct consequence for the rural population was proletarianization; J. L. and Barbara Hammond have been our best chroniclers of its effects. 'For the first time', they write, 'there existed a vast proletariate with no property but its labour, and therefore in the eyes of its rulers bound by no ties to the society in which it lived except by the ties that discipline could create.'[5] Deprived of property, the proletariat was excluded from the civilized world. Indeed, its labour transformed into surplus value became an instrument of civilization.

No figure illustrates the matter with such immediacy as the chimney sweep. A writer in the *Annual Register* describes the old mansion he moved into in 1787:

> In most of the old houses in England the chimneys ... were ... extravagantly large. This method of building chimneys may perhaps have answered well enough while it was the custom to sit with the doors and windows open; but when the customs and manners of the people began to be more polished and refined, when building and architecture were improved, and they began to conceive the idea of making their chambers close, warm, and comfortable, these chimneys were found to smoke abominably, for want of a sufficient supply of air.

His solution was to contract the chimney to sixteen inches – just wide enough for a boy to crawl into. The solution was a common one for architects building the more elaborate and comfortable houses demanded by the Augustan arts of life. Chimney sweeps became, as a result, valuable properties. A master chimney-sweep is asked by a committee of the House of Commons, 'Is not 8 pounds a large price?' – 'Oh yes, very large.' – 'Why was so large a price asked for that boy?' – 'Because this is a free country.' – 'Was he a small boy?' – 'Yes, very small for his age.'[6]

Thesis V. Order. Enough has been said and written about the Augustans' sense of order, and the integrative nature of their literary forms. The major Augustans promote the sense of class unity; looked at appropriately, they contend, the experience of all classes reveals the same human core. Yet what is the source of such a perception? A. R. Humphreys has an answer worth considering: 'Augustan literature, even in its brighter moods, would be less mature if the national life it expressed had not often been rough and harsh, subjecting all men to strong experience which rendered qualities like 'order' and 'balance' things to be achieved not by dilettantism but by deliberate faith, asserting the humanist ideal over the often degrading real.'[7] Order as an act of faith in the face of 'strong experience'! Looking at the 'degrading' realities of Augustan life, I am convinced that only faith can act as a support for 'the humanist ideal'. But who suffers the strong experience? And who has the resources for faith?

Adam Smith (and the many whose feelings he expressed) was among those capable of superb acts of faith. Having looked a good deal more carefully at the social insanities of eighteenth-century capitalism than any of his contemporaries, he wrote these familiar words: 'By directing that industry in such a manner as its produce may be of the greatest value, he [the individual] intends only his own gain, and he is in this as in many other cases led by an invisible hand to promote an end which was no part of his intention. Nor is it always the worse for society that it was no part of it. By pursuing his own interest he frequently promotes that of society more effectually than when he really intends to promote it.'[8] The source of the social order and balance so cherished by the Augustans is free trade. Wealth generates humanism. Consider the following from William Hutton's eighteenth-century *History of Birmingham*: 'For the intercourse occasioned by traffic gives a man a view of the world and of himself; removes the narrow limits that confine his judgment; expands the mind; opens his understanding; removes his prejudices; and polishes his manners. Civility and humanity are ever the companions of trade; the man of business is the man of liberal sentiment; a barbarous and commercial people is a contradiction.'[9] The work of social integration goes on in spite of one's competitive acts. Even Dr. Johnson joined the chorus and said that 'an English Merchant is a new species of Gentlemen'.

The eighteenth century was faced by an incipient class struggle engendered by capitalism. Humanism's response was to make the tradesman the source of order. The benefits flowing from his activity are universal, and nourish all classes.

Thesis VI. Renaissance Humanism. Why fight the boredom of trying to read the Renaissance humanists? Besides, Professor Kristeller has warned us to lay off unless we share his expertise. Yet he has also told us that 'Renaissance humanism remained alive in the educational and literary traditions of Western Europe and in the study of history and philology'.[10] I take this to be an invitation to speculation.

Both the Augustans and the continental *philosophes* saw the Renaissance humanists as their precursors. With good reason. Renaissance humanists tended to see classical antiquity as an age of perfection. To study the classics, according to Machiavelli, was both useful and edifying, since human nature is a constant.

Modern scholarship has taught us that the Renaissance humanists were rhetoricians devoted to the study of the classics as the best examples of eloquence. Such studies spread to other professional sectors. The latter became devoted to the *studia humanitatis* for their own sake, separate from their professional concerns. The cultivation of the humanities became a mark of status. Pico in his famous *Oration* tells us: 'I have never studied philosophy for any other reason than that I might be a philosopher. . . . I have always been so desirous, so enamored of this, that I have relinquished all interest in affairs private and public and given myself over entirely to leisure for contemplation.'[11] Fine. Especially if one happens to be a nobleman with an income. Who, after all, are the lovers of rhetoric and philosophy? 'The Renaissance humanists', according to Kristeller, 'wrote their moral works for their fellow scholars, for their students, and for an elite of businessmen and of ubanized noblemen who were willing to adopt their cultural and moral ideas.'[12] It is a bit naive to assume that those with worldly power did the bidding of the humanists; the reverse was surely most often the case. Some humanists, for example, were teachers who tried to establish learning as the basis for a new elite. To make their point, they proposed the thesis that the nobility's status was based on virtue and scholarly abilities, rather than on heredity or wealth. Other humanists were secretaries to princes and cities, one of their functions being the celebration of civic life. Bruni's *Panegyric on the City of Florence* served to reassure the city's patricians about the virtues of their activities. He justified his lies by observing that the genre of panegyric 'exalts many things above what is true'.

Humanism and its practitioners were at the service of elites. Renaissance humanists made the classical tradition the property of particular social strata. Pico devoted himself to philosophy to loosen the chains of necessity, and to become a free agent capable of making rational moral choices. For Pico such privatization of morality and philosophy was real enough. For the humanist – then or now – who works for a living it is an abstraction which can only serve as an ideological mask. Here is the life of work and daily intercourse. And here is the civilized life of contemplation. The split haunts us to this day; and since the eighteenth century it has become even more deeply embedded in the class system.

A note with a moral: 'Humanismus' as a descriptive term for the scholarly practice of the Renaissance was apparently coined by nineteenth-century German scholars, who then used the concept to defend classical studies in the school curriculum. Considering the bureaucratic and oppressive social uses to which the German school system was put, the matter gives one pause.

Thesis VII. Stoicism. To live according to nature, Stoicism taught the humanists, is freely and rationally to choose one's fate. To the uninitiated, this may seem like a violation of logic: How can fate be chosen? No matter. Of importance is how such beliefs intruded on the social and political will of people.

Central to the moral practice of Stoicism is the notion that reason must control the passions and appetites. There are many ways of encouraging reason. Refinement of taste, Sir Joshua Reynolds tells us, 'if it does not lead directly to purity of manners, obviates at least their general depravation, by disentangling the mind from appetite, and conducting the thoughts through successive stages of excellence, till that contemplation of universal rectitude and harmony which began by Taste, may, as it is exalted and refined, conclude in Virtue'.[13] It is a comfortable way of laying the devil to rest. But consider Dr. Johnson's warning to Boswell: 'Poverty . . . produces so much inability to resist evil, both natural and moral, that it is by all virtuous means to be avoided' (*Boswell's Life*, IV, 152). One is confident of the taste of Reynolds' patrons; less so of their having avoided poverty by virtuous means. As for the 'voluptuous' poor, the More sisters instructed them – with great dedication – that nobility was to be attained through pious submission to their fate.

Such teaching was more than a fairytale for the edification of the poor and ignorant. As Paul Fussell has shown us exhaustively, it was dogma for the Augustan humanists.[14] Men and women cannot change circumstances, but they can change their attitudes to them. Thus the notion of free choice is internalized: one may choose the mode of one's *thinking* and *feeling*. But the notion of freedom of choice must be insisted on and preserved in some form, for without it, humanism assumes, man is less than human. It is, however, removed from the realms of history and daily circumstance. If the moral life is internalized, there is little need to affect the external conditions of life. For those who are barely able to live with a particular society's externalities, there might be another way of looking at the matter: if social conditions prevent them from externalizing their capacity of free choice – that is, their humanity – those conditions must be transformed. Marx, for one, assumed that it would take a series of revolutionary transformations for man to leave the realm of necessity and enter the realm of freedom.

But then political economy had taught the eighteenth century that the conditions of society were the conditions of nature. Adam Smith embedded his empirical work in the notion of fate, and referred to the economic process as 'natural liberty'.[15] 'Natural liberty' – it is one more version of the Stoic creed masking as social science. It points to the helplessness of the intelligentsia in the face of the overwhelming changes of the eighteenth century. A humanist, by attaching himself to the cultural interests of those with power and wealth, can pretend to detach himself from the realm of social necessity, live in the past, give body to the symbols of Horatian civilization, and create a culture which for him is timeless and classless. There is, however, a cost. Ordinarily it is paid for by denying freedom of choice to the vast majority of people.

Discipline was (and is) the labourer's version of Stoicism. In eighteenth-century England it was the degrading discipline of the free market and industrialism. The degradation can, however, be argued away if the labourer understands that he or she is being dignified by the working of a secret providence which operates beyond the interference of human beings. Burke wrote some notorious passages on the subject; more interesting is a document like Andrew Ure's *Philosophy of Manufactures*, which sees the factory system as 'the great minister of civilization to the terraqueous globe', diffusing 'the life-blood of science and religion to myriads . . . still lying "in the region and shadow of death"'.[16] Such ideas served to complement the immediate sources of discipline. They transformed discipline into an instrument of fate and civilization.

However, the immiseration of those who had known better days also provided the impulse for angry, often violent, opposition. The riots around the slogan of 'Wilkes and Liberty' were part of a continuous struggle against the ideology of fate. The Hammonds make the point eloquently: 'The existing order, others would argue, was the dispensation of Providence, and it was blasphemy to scrutinise its justice or to try to modify its exactions. The social history of the period is largely the revolt of the working classes against this body of prejudice or superstition or reason, whichever people like to term it.'[17] The anger was directed at 'all the pleasing illusions', as Burke called them, '. . . which harmonized the different shades of life'. Dissolving this lie was a necessary prologue to the quest for a dignified life. The ensuing struggle created the culture of working people in England; it solidified them into a class with a consciousness of its own being and social location. The dignity of working people lay in their refusal, as a class, to submit to their abject condition as if it were a law of nature.

Thesis VIII. Education. Our understanding of eighteenth-century education is coloured by the *philosophes'* educational program: they saw education as the primary instrument of liberation and of spiritual transformation. The notion seems to stand in opposition to the aristocratic educational assumptions of the humanists. Yet even Diderot advocated a tracking system; education's task is not to create equality, but an aristocracy of the educated. Hume, Kant, and Diderot, as Peter Gay points out, all thought the poor to be imbecile, irrational, superstitious, and beyond education.

Locke, not surprisingly, created the model for Augustan theories of education: Latin and other ornaments of civilization for gentlemen; for the poor, 'working schools' where woollen manufacture and religion will be the subjects of instruction. Both Tudor and Augustan humanists believed in education as a source of virtue and civilization. Clearly, what is civilized for one class, may not be virtuous for the other.

Thesis IX. Esthetics. 'A man of a polite imagination', Addison wrote, 'is let into a great many pleasures that the vulgar are not capable of receiving. He can converse with a picture, and find an agreeable companion in a statue.'[18] Or more bluntly, Lord Kames: 'Those who depend for food on bodily labor, are totally void of taste, of such taste at least as can be of use in the fine arts. This consideration bars the greater part of mankind; and of the remaining part, many by a corrupted taste are unqualified for voting.'[19] There is more than snobbery involved. Indeed, Lord Kames's logic and sense of reality are close to impeccable. The connoisseurship developing during the eighteenth century was one reflex of the accumulation of wealth; and connoisseurship became the measure of one's capacity to be involved with the arts. Reynolds, as usual, defines the issue for his age: 'There are, at this time, a greater number of excellent artists than were ever known before at one period in this nation; there is a general desire among our Nobility to be distinguished as lovers and judges of the Arts; there is a greater superfluity of wealth among the people to reward the professors; and above all, we are patronised by a Monarch who, knowing the value of science and of elegance, thinks every art worthy of his notice, that tends to soften and humanise the mind.'[20]

Art had become an amusement – occasionally a solemn leisure activity – for the well-to-do. This separation of the individual arts from everyday social functions led to the birth of esthetics as an area of philosophic investigation. Esthetics: the study of beauty as a quality transcending any specific art: a quality independent of worldly activity. Esthetics was another of the eighteenth century's inventions. Indeed, the modern system of the fine arts – painting, sculpture, architecture, music, and literature as related activities and defined as fine art – did not become fixed until the Enlightenment. Kant burdened esthetics with philosophic legitimacy, and set the terms for nearly all future discussion. 'Everyone', he wrote, 'must concede that judgement about beauty in which the slightest interest interferes is highly partisan and not a pure judgement of taste.'[21] These words are *descriptive* of the leisured and cultivated act of connoisseurship. Kant's stress on judgement (the function of the connoisseur) removes art from the realm of everyday life. Again, he is merely being *descriptive* of the activity of a social class. The very category of Art had become one more instrument for making class distinctions.

Thesis X. Enlightenment. Augustan humanism created the masterpieces of eighteenth-century English literature; it also created an intellectual backwater. The important events in the realm of formal thought – the challenge to and elaboration of traditional ideas – were happening on the continent and in Scotland.

Many of the Augustans attacked the *philosophes* with extraordinary vehemence. Why? After all, there was much to unite the contending groups: the veneration of classical antiquity; the cultivation of the art of elegant living; the cherishing of hierarchy; an intellectual debt to Stoicism. Gibbon, without stretching a point too much, played the dual role of Humanist and *philosophe.*

Despite such common properties, the humanists saw the *philosophes* as a threat to civil society. Yet Kant's tag for the Enlightenment was 'dare to know', not dare to act or dare to struggle. He saw philosophy as an autonomous and civilized activity. The attitude is reflected in Diderot's description of Holbach's salon: 'Conversations sometimes playful,' he wrote to Sophie Volland, 'sometimes serious; a little gambling, a little strolling, in groups or alone; much reading, meditation, silence, solitude, and rest.'[22] The separation between intellect and ordinary life, between speech and action, had earlier been justified by Montesquieu as a protection for free speech. But acceptance of this principle implies that speech is impotent – unless one gets someone like Frederick the Great to pay serious attention. Rousseau saw through this. His reward for insisting that critical method and action be unified was persecution by the *philosophes*. Being civilized, they assumed that no idea, however, is worth fighting over. But here civility indicates the absence of a political program to give body to one's ideas. The *philosophes* were an intellectual vanguard without a political party.

Yet the revolution of 1789 did take place. And it seems to have made use of the *philosophes*' ideas and language. The historian of consciousness should ask how these ideas were absorbed, how the vocabulary was learned, and how both were applied by those sectors of the population which made the revolution. Quoting appropriate phrases from the *Declaration of the Rights of Man* explains very little.

Alas, we have a history of ideas (thought, religion, philosophy) and a history of politics (diplomacy, economics, war); a history of internalities and a history of externalities. 'L'histoire des empires', Gibbon wrote, 'est celle de la misère des hommes. L'histoire des sciences est celle de leur grandeur et de leur bonheur.'[23] But the history of Augustan humanism – indeed, the humanists' very consciousness of themselves as Augustans – teaches us that empire is, in fact, closely related to the pomp of civilization: Augustus and Virgil fulfill each other. Humanism may have been fighting a rearguard action, but it was one tributary feeding the stream of consciousness from which flowed the 'science' of political economy.

The heart of revolution is the reconstruction of civil society and of culture. The *philosophes* were no more revolutionary than the humanists: both groups wanted to legitimize aspects of the traditional culture; and both wanted to maintain civil society in one of its received forms. As for the enactment of this program, there were differences. These were of importance. The cultural commitment of the Augustans was to an ideal aristocracy which was barely, if at all, represented in reality. The *philosophes*, on the other hand, were alive to the potential of the bourgeoisie – its strengths as a social and cultural lever – and created a liberal image for it. Being propagandists for an aristocratic notion of civilization, the humanists were incapable of developing a cultural program based on the realities of bourgeois life. That failure may explain a good deal about England at the end of the eighteenth and the beginning of the nineteenth centuries. It may provide one possible explanation for both the savagery toward labourers of the English bourgeoisie, and the latter's failure to develop a significant revolutionary intelligentsia.

Thesis XI. Thomas Gray. Dr. Johnson thought his sequestration at Cambridge to be unnatural; Paul Fussell has read him out of the humanist movement; few read his English poems voluntarily; fewer have the knowledge to read those in Latin. Yet his example is significant.

He spends most of his life at Cambridge – a place for whose intellectual life he has contempt – because there is nothing else to do. Where is the studious son of a shopkeeper to go? His commonplace books are filled with the raw material of scholarship; he writes detailed descriptions of plants and animals in pocketbooks; he keeps calendars of the seasons, weather, crops. To what end? As Professor of Modern History he outlines lectures, but never delivers them. When the British Museum opens, he spends some time there, and celebrates his return to Cambridge with a 'Hymn to Ignorance'. The 'Elegy', as William Empson has told us, reveals that Gray understands that the possibility of participating in the work of civilization might depend on one's social class: for the poor there are no careers open to talent. But, like his humanist contemporaries, he takes this condition to be a law of nature; one can do little more than to accept one's fate with the wisdom of philosophy.

But his important poems are far from typical. They are sensitive to the fact that the Augustans' perception of what was central in England's culture – the content they gave to the notion of general nature – was unreal. 'The Bard' suggests an image of the poet desperate to be part of the life of a whole people; it is an image which can become real only in an egalitarian and classless society. Gray could not look forward to – indeed, could not fathom – such a society. However, he at least knew how to look back.

Thesis XII. Our Humanism. I want to repeat neither myself, nor others. Enough has been written about the present institutional role of the humanistic tradition to inform those who want to understand. The theorists of counter-insurgency, of Vietnamese 'forced draft urbanization' (that is, devastating the countryside with bombs, and making the peasants come to the city where they can reap the benefits of modernization and civilized life – a new form of enclosure), of the atomic balance of terror – all take pride in being the guardians of Western Civilization. For centuries the major European empires immiserated the colonies; we continue to do so – in the name of Western Civilization.

I shall end with the painful sentiments expressed by Jan Myrdal upon his return from a five-year sojourn in Asia:

> We who are a part of the tradition – the Europeans – and who carry on the tradition we have betrayed with awareness, insight and consciousness, we have carefully analyzed all the wars before they were declared. But we did not stop them. (And many amongst us became the propagandists of the wars as soon as they were declared.) We describe how the poor are plundered by the rich. We live among the rich. Live on the plunder and pander ideas to the rich. ... Now we once more can analyze the world situation and describe the wars and explain why the many are poor and hungry. But we do no more.
>
> We are not the bearers of consciousness. We are the whores of reason.[24]

Perhaps too grandiloquent to describe us, Jan. Not the whores of reason: merely its humanist bureaucrats.

Massachusetts Institute of Technology

Notes

1. Karl Marx, *The Eighteenth Brumaire of Louis Bonaparte* (New York, 1963), p. 15.
2. E. P. Thompson, *The Making of the English Working Class* (London, 1964), p. 9.
3. A. R. Humphreys, *The Augustan World* (London, 1954).
4. Thomas Babington Macaulay, Speech on Parliamentary Reform, 5 July 1831, *Miscellanies*, in *Complete Writings* (Cambridge 1901), i, 22.
5. J. L. Hammond and Barbara Hammond, *The Town Labourer, 1760-1832* (New York, 1967), p. 59.

6. Quoted in *The Town Labourer, 1760-1832*, pp. 177-78.

7. *The Augustan World*, p. 22.

8. Adam Smith, *The Wealth of Nations*, ed. Edwin Cannan, 2 vols. (London, 1961), I, 477.

9. Quoted in *The Augustan World*, p. 87.

10. P. O. Kristeller, *Renaissance Thought: the Classic, Scholastic, and Humanistic Strains* (New York, 1961), p. 139.

11. Quoted in *The Renaissance Philosophy of Man*, ed. Cassirer, Kristeller, and Randall (Chicago, 1948), p. 238.

12. P. O. Kristeller, *Renaissance Thought II: Papers on Humanism and the Arts* (New York, 1965), p. 30.

13. Sir Joshua Reynolds, 'Discourse IX', *Discourses*, ed. Robert R. Wark (San Marino, 1959), p. 171.

14. Paul Fussell, *The Rhetorical World of Augustan Humanism* (Oxford, 1965).

15. *The Wealth of Nations*, II, 208.

16. Andrew Ure, *Philosophy of Manufactures*, 3rd ed. (London, 1861), pp. 18-19.

17. *The Town Labourer, 1760-1832*, p. 97.

18. *The Spectator*, no. 411.

19. Lord Kames, *Elements of Criticism*, 9th ed., 3 vols. (Edinburgh, 1814), II, 446-47.

20. 'Discourse I', *Discourses*, p. 14.

21. Immanuel Kant, *Critique of Judgement*, Book I, 'Analytic of the Beautiful'.

22. Quoted in Peter Gay, *The Enlightenment: An Interpretation* (New York, 1966), p. 177.

23. 'Essai sur l'étude de la litterature', in *Miscellaneous Works*, 2 vols. (1796), II, 449.

24. Jan Myrdal, *Confessions of a Disloyal European* (New York, 1968) pp. 200-1.

DONALD DAVIE | *Afterword*

Rather despondently I had expected the Ottawa conference to resolve itself for much of the time into a ceremonial laying of more or less florid wreaths on the honoured graveslab. A solemn deference, I thought, would be the order of the day. But not at all! We found ourselves taking sides for and against Gray. And yet that's not right either, for Professor Hagstrum's exceptionally deft and delicate tracing of the temper of Gray's sexual consciousness won general assent, I think, and ensured from the first compassionate sympathy for Thomas Gray the man. No, we took sides for and against the view of poetry, more specifically of the proper language for poetry, which is implied by Gray's Odes in particular. This, it turned out, was a living issue, as much in relation to the poetry of 1971 as to that of 200 years ago. Across two centuries the dead poet provoked and challenged us, to side with him or against him. Mr. Lonsdale's erudite and entertaining paper mapped for us a field of controversy, much trampled in Gray's lifetime and through several decades after his death; and this, it turned out, was a field over which we too had to advance and wheel and manoeuvre, though fortunately we managed it with less heat and better manners than the Swan of Lichfield.

On this still live issue I do not have to declare my interest because Professor Greene declared it for me, challenging me to say whether I had changed my mind since *Purity of Diction in English Verse*. I hadn't; though I squirm a little to hear that young man from twenty years ago pontificating with such assurance. However, I still agree with him, cocky as he is, about the relative merits of Johnson's use of language and Gray's. It is just as well that I do; for it would have needed all my temerity to announce a change of heart to Professor Greene, addressing us as 'unreconstructed Johnsonian', determined quite properly to make it clear how little of Gray's poetry can meet Johnsonian standards. Professor Greene more than any one else should get the credit for infusing polemic into our sessions, and polemic not about interpretation or information but about *value*.

In the context thus created, certain papers took on a polemical edge or thrust which their authors could not have foreseen or intended. It gave sharp point for instance to an observation thrown out by Professor Macdonald (in a paper which must have entailed more research than any other presented, unless it were Mr. Lonsdale's), to the effect that Johnson's estimate, because it seemed to many 'provocatively adverse and partial', helped to establish Gray's fame, by ensuring thirty years or more of critical attention and partisanship after the poet's death. Professor Johnston's paper on 'Our Daring Bard' was a rather different case. I thought it was clear that he esteemed Gray's poetry more highly than Professor Greene did, and he scored one shrewd hit when he rebuked Johnson for following Algarotti in supposing 'The Bard' an imitation of Horace. But of course audacity is not *per se* a poetic virtue, nor did Professor Johnston contend that it was; and indeed verbal audacity of as he thought an irresponsible kind is just what Johnson took exception to in Gray. But in any case verbal audacity was only one of the kinds of daring which Professor Johnston uncovered in Gray; and it was certainly valuable to be made to realize how Gray, who took so few risks in his life (as Ian Jack had reminded us with sympathy and challenging comparisons), consistently took so many in his mind and imagination.

On the other hand Professor Mandel's paper, coming after Professor Greene's, could not help but seem a speech for the defence of Gray's practice in his Odes. And a very spirited defence it was. I dare say I reveal my own Johnsonian allegiance when I report that I was not persuaded by it. Indeed there were moments when I wondered if Professor Mandel had persuaded even himself. I had the perhaps unworthy suspicion that he would have been happier elevating Christopher Smart, without having to rescue Gray also, clinging as it were to Smart's coat-tails. In what he claimed for Smart I thought he was entirely convincing, though I wished he had drawn more on the *Hymns and Spiritual Songs*, when Smart was still in his wits, and less on *Rejoice in the Lamb*, when Smart was out of them. But with all respect to Professor Mandel I find I cannot endorse his contention that Gray's 'quenched in dark slumber', his 'sea-encircled coasts' or 'birds of boding cry' exemplify the same concentrated use of language as Smart's 'quick peculiar quince' or his 'blaze and rapture of the sun'.

Professor Mandel's paper was hard to follow when one listened to it, and it is still hard to follow now that we can read it. But this is because he is wrestling with very difficult conceptions, having to do with analogies between the arts and the vision of an art-form in which all or several arts shall be compounded. He persuaded me that thinking along these difficult lines was indeed going on in Gray's time, notably in the mind of Smart. And as Professor Johnston scored a point on 'The Bard', so Professor Mandel firmly controverted Johnson about the first strophe of 'The Progress of Poesy'. I thought he came nearest to turning the flank of Professor Greene's position when he began to speak of how Gray conceived of the Pindaric Ode as a regular poetic 'kind' in which he supposed himself to be writing. For in the theories of poetic *genres* it has nearly always been allowed that the poet may or should depart further from conversational or prosaic usage when practising certain *genres* rather than others. Even Wordsworth, one of the authorities on whom Professor Greene rested his case, seems to make a distinction between kinds when he restricts his rule about diction to 'works of imagination and sentiment, *for of those only have I been treating*' (italics mine). 'The Progress of Poesy' certainly offers itself as a work of imagination; I am not sure that in Wordsworth's usage or in ours it can be described as a work of 'sentiment'. However, now that we have in the notes to Professor Greene's paper his delightfully outrageous remarks on the sonnet as a verse-form, it seems clear that he will not tolerate ' 'tis' or 'ere' or 'I ween' in the sublime ode any more than in other kinds of poem.

For Professor Whalley, the role that Johnson and Wordsworth played in the dispute about diction was 'bludgeonly'. And perhaps it was only politeness that restrained him from applying the same epithet to Professor Greene and myself. Certainly the bludgeon was not Professor Whalley's weapon. And yet he did not use the rapier either. Still less did he summon up any of the more massive engines which he spoke of in a sentence as carefully composed as all his sentences, and as his manner of speaking them: '... when the ballistas, tortoises, and scaling-ladders of modern critical technique are mounted to assault this little handful of verses, the labour seems ill-expended, the booty not profitable ...'. (Professor Whalley was certainly the most quotable of our speakers.) No, he had chosen to arm himself only with the walking-stick of the gentleman-naturalist – an instrument which after all can give a stinging thwack, and is ideal for shearing off the tall heads of dandelions or even, upon occasion, of more poetical flowers. With this in hand, he strolled into, and about in, the estate of Gray's poetry and his scholarship, conducting us charmed and bemused as he pointed out an obscure covert here, a modest prospect there, and the marriage of two lakes at the foot of this or that bosky slope. He swung the sturdy ash-plant with deceptive casualness as he wound into his subject indirectly, then wound about inside it, and came out by as unexpected a route as the one he had gone in by. It was only when he bowed us out of the park-gate that we realized that the walking stick, though wielded with a gentlemanly reluctance, had struck much the same blows as Johnson's bludgeon, and in the same places. Professor Whalley had taken the Johnsonian side after all. He thought of it, however (and quite justly, so it seemed), as Coleridge's side no less – as he had announced in his first sentence, when he presented himself as 'a rough old Coleridgean, with a palate a little coarse for Augustan nuance'. Remembering that sentence, after listening to what was certainly the most urbanely polished performance of the entire Conference, was nothing short of comical. And that effect too was, like all the others, unmistakably calculated!

After so much time had been spent establishing or assuming that Gray and Johnson were at all events as different as chalk from cheese, it was disconcerting, yet perhaps it was salutary, to hear Professor Kampf speaking at such a high level of historical abstraction that from his vantage-point Gray and Johnson were indistinguishable, indeed interchangeable, as instances of 'Augustan humanism'. The astronaut's view of the earth is as true as that of the walker in the city streets; and Professor Kampf's astronaut's view of the eighteenth century seemed to me, in its necessarily schematic and Olympian terms, accurate and illuminating. Thinking of how his case might be challenged, I thought that the Conference should at some point have had its attention turned to the qualities of folk and popular art in the eighteenth century; it might then have appeared that such popular and largely anonymous arts as the mason's and the potter's were at a very high level of accomplishment, testifying (so one might argue) to a rich and finely articulated culture outside the elite. Professor Kampf might, for instance, have had an interesting explanation of why, according to Sola Pinto and Rodway in their work on the street-ballad, the final decline of that popular art-form set it at just the time when, according to Professor Kampf, the exploited classes came to class-consciousness – something which he saw as, for them, distinctly a cultural gain.

No one who listened to Professor Kampf's trenchant and impatient remarks can have failed to remember uneasily a few moments in our earlier sessions at which we had been too comfortable with ourselves and with each other, too securely genteel and unquestioning about what it meant to be 'an eighteenth-century specialist'. That was good for us. Yet the earth from a spacecraft looks strangely uninhabited and uninhabitable. And it was hard to see what Professor Kampf was up to, if it was not to make the eighteenth century uninhabitable for us. He seemed to want us never again to walk in imagination through its city streets, never again to see it on a human scale so that the passers-by we might meet should be as different as Thomas Gray and Samuel Johnson. Our vantage-point, he seemed to say, should be more exalted and presumptuous, perhaps more sublime. Undoubtedly eighteenth-century literature can be presented, can be *taught*, in such a way as to fuel the inflamed resolve of the rancorous revolutionist. Perhaps no one had doubted this; if any had, Professor Kampf showed them quite brilliantly how it should be done. What he cannot have expected us to concede was that any other way of treating it must be trivial or self-indulgent or both.

If one of our ways of taking our bearings on Gray was to measure him up against Johnson, another was to measure him against William Blake. But Professor Jones and Mrs. Tayler, though they both brought out how Blake's illustrations to Gray were in intention and effect polemical, and though it seemed clear that they both thought Blake had the better of the argument, chose not to participate in that argument nor to make it topical. This was surely well-judged on their part. For that polemic could not have been brought down to such a manageable topic as the proper language for poetry, but would have had to be fought out on the far more radical ground of a proper or exemplary attitude to human life, its potencies and its limiting conditions. And that, whatever our or Professor Kampf's students might think, is too tall an order for a learned conference. Instead both speakers, but Mrs. Tayler in particular, with ingratiating tact made us aware of our complacent ignorance about many aspects of eighteenth-century humanist culture, in this instance about the commentary and criticism implicit in great illustrators like Richard Bentley and Blake.

My own contribution to the conference was an evening entertainment, which took the form of readings of some eighteenth-century poems along with others from the present century which seemed to have some vital relationship with those or similar eighteenth-century models. The contemporary poets I read were the Australian A. D. Hope, the Irishman Austin Clarke, the American Ed Dorn, and the north-country Englishman Basil Bunting. When I devised this program, I had it in mind, quite apart from my own amusement, to make the point that eighteenth-century poetry could still be – if not at all directly in its diction or its forms, nevertheless most markedly in the spirit informing those forms – a potent shaping influence on the literature and the life of our own day. But there was no need of such a reminder. I need not have worried – the Conference throughout showed that the poetry of Thomas Gray and his contemporaries is not of merely historical or antiquarian interest; on the contrary it conditions and moulds our sense of who we are now.

Stanford University

Index